# FREUD
## From Youthful Dream
## to Mid-Life Crisis

# FREUD

## From Youthful Dream
## to Mid-Life Crisis

PETER M. NEWTON

THE GUILFORD PRESS
New York London

©1995 The Guilford Press
A Division of Guilford Publications, Inc.
72 Spring Street, New York, NY 10012

Printed in the United States of America

This book is printed on acid-free paper.

Last digit is print number:   9   8   7   6   5   4   3   2   1

**Library of Congress Cataloging-in-Publication Data**

Newton, Peter M.
   Freud: from youthful dream to mid-life crisis / by Peter M.
Newton.
      p.      cm.
   Includes bibliographical references and index.
   ISBN 0-89862-293-X
   1. Freud, Sigmund, 1856–1939.   2. Psychoanalysts—Austria—
Biography.   3. Psychoanalysis—History.   I. Title.
BF109.F74N48   1995
150′.19′52′092—dc20
[B]                                                                                    94-27901
                                     CIP

*For Dorian, Chelsea, and Amelia,*
*and to the memory of my parents*

But these were the dreams of a poet doomed
at last to wake a lexicographer.
—SAMUEL JOHNSON, Preface to the
   *Dictionary of the English Language*


We are all in the gutter, but some
of us are looking at the stars.
—OSCAR WILDE, *Lady Windermere's Fan*

# Acknowledgments

DURING my years as a postdoctoral fellow and Assistant Professor at Yale University, Daniel J. Levinson was my mentor. After a distinguished early career as an academic social psychologist, Levinson, when I met him in 1969, was becoming a biographer, or what one might call a biographical psychologist. Levinson was then in his late 40s and was just beginning his study of adult development. He and his research associates—Edward B. Klein, Charlotte Darrow, Maria Levinson, and Braxton McKee—welcomed me into the faculty seminar built around their research. I was too young to understand much of what they were doing and for the first few years pursued research interests in other directions.

In 1969 I was 26 and had just left graduate school where I had been taught the conventional quantitative research methods of psychology, methods that Levinson was just now leaving behind. I wanted to write, to do research, to use my intellect in some formal and lasting way, to be creative; I could not say exactly what, but I knew I wanted to do something in addition to being a clinician. The problem was that after having completed some half-dozen experimental studies during my undergraduate and graduate years, I had the unmistakable feeling that I hadn't learned much about psychology, though I had learned a fair amount about statistics and experimental design. The empiricism in these studies was "abstracted," the results "thin," as I would later learn C. Wright Mills had said about the same kind of research in sociology. The problems that interested me—personality development, psychodynamics, psychopathology, and the course of lives—had not been illuminated by my studies nor by those I read that were carried out by experimentalists far more competent than I.

The real insight, it seemed to me, came from the great writers of case studies—Freud; Erik Erikson; some of the gifted Sullivanians, such as Frieda Fromm-Reichmann and Harold Searles; the brilliant object relations clinical theorists, such as Melanie Klein, W. R. D. Fairbairn, Donald Winnicott, and Wilfred Bion; and others whose methods relied more on in-depth interviews, such as Kenneth Keniston, Robert J. Lifton, Nevitt Sanford, and Abraham Maslow—and from fiction and biography. But I had never met anyone who did this sort of research; indeed, my graduate education had left me with so narrow a conception of it that I was unsure whether this sort of writing constituted research at all. During one of my attempts to articulate this jumble of ambition and doubt, it occurred to me to ask Levinson if I was required to do research as a condition of my fellowship. His off-handed answer changed my life: "You needn't measure anything," he replied, "but you should have written something by the end of the year."

I did nothing immediately. His simple declaration sank into my preconscious mind, where it must have germinated invisibly for several months because one day toward the end of that academic year I began to write a theoretical essay on the social structural properties of the doctor–patient relationship in psychotherapy. To say that I had decided to undertake a research project makes it sound far too planned. In one sentence (and then of course by further tuition, criticism, research collaboration, and his own example of mid-life intellectual growth) Levinson had cured me of the most limiting of the prejudices I had received in graduate school, namely, the notion that research means measurement, quantification, and statistics. In that same simple utterance he had also placed me under a requirement to do what I most wanted to do: I needn't measure anything, but I *should* do research.

My professional life has been immeasurably enriched by Levinson's freeing me from that "methodological inhibition" (C. Wright Mills's term once again) and replacing it with a transcendent obligation I could embrace with all of the intellectual resources I had and could hope to develop. Without his timely intervention, I believe I would have ended up among the legion of mute clinicians who never write and whose intellectual interests devolve into hobbies or wistful "someday" fantasies of writing a novel; or perhaps I would have become a scientistically mannered researcher in academic psychology, defensively stiffened against the fear that my research generated artifacts suitable only for tenure and promotion. Mentor relationships, at least between men, tend to end badly. Yet between Levinson and myself, a complicated, loving friendship evolved, and it deepened after my days as a protégé had come to an end. Even though it has been many years since Levinson played an active part in my professional life, he retains in my intellectual heavens the brilliance of a bright star.

I was fortunate enough to have had other mentors besides Levinson. During my adolescence James Killian gave me a sustaining ideal to pursue: to become an educated man. The late Nathaniel Wagner at the University of Washington saw promise in an undergraduate piece I wrote about Freud's personality, warmly invited me to get to know him, and helped me gain admission to a highly selective graduate school. At Columbia University the intellect of David Ricks, whose research was scrupulously quantitative, joined psychology, psychoanalysis, and the humanities and gave me a basis for receiving what Levinson would later offer. Ricks personified the wide-ranging life of the mind in a graduate program that otherwise, despite or because of its elitism, tended to become reduced in the experience of its inmates to a grubby contest for survival and release run by devout or intimidated methodologists. After I left Yale and came out West in my 30s, Leonard Michaels at UC Berkeley, one of the best fiction writers of his generation, helped me to clarify my values as a writer and to suffer more discerningly from my imperfect ability to achieve them.

In writing this book I was fortunate to have the help and friendship of two *Kameradinnen*. Beth Steinberg—Dr. Beth Steinberg by the end—was my research assistant. Her duties, performed weekly over several years, ranged from clerical to scholarly, and her diligence in the former was matched by her keen, critical intelligence in the latter. Most importantly, she helped me, amidst a welter of doubts and personal losses, to define my quest and begin. By helping me choose a recreative enterprise, Beth Steinberg, disguised as graduate student research assistant, was the requisite other for this important part of my own mid-life transition and entry into middle age.

My friendship with Dr. Beate Lohser gave me a personal connection to German language and culture. Dr. Lohser, a former Heidelberg University linguist and now a Freud scholar and psychologist practicing and teaching in San Francisco, reviewed all reproductions and translations of German in this book.[1] She also criticized the use of evidence and the making of interpretations about Freud's life and personality in drafts of each chapter. This book is measurably better because of her diligent, penetrating criticism, and countless errors of translation—from misspellings to misunderstandings—have been avoided through her intervention. Other errors no doubt remain to be corrected in subsequent editions, and for these the responsibility remains mine alone.

From 1969 to 1974 Dr. Maurice Marcus, now a training analyst at the San Francisco Psychoanalytic Institute, was my main clinical supervisor at Yale. He has over the years read prepublication drafts of numerous pieces I've written, including, most recently, chapters from this book. He has encouraged me to believe that, however imperfectly,

I am doing something valuable. Scrupulous scholar and effective clinician, Marcus has always represented for me psychoanalysis at its best.
After 25 years I am still in his debt. I am grateful also to Dr. George
Mahl, past President of The Western New England Psychoanalytic Institute and Professor Emeritus at Yale, who, as scholar and clinician,
gave me a lively connection to Freud's thought and practice.

My wife, Dr. Dorian S. Newton, in an utterly characteristic act
of good judgment, helped me see a workable connection when the gap
between what I wanted to write and what my editor, Kitty Moore,
wanted to publish seemed abysmal. Ultimately, Kitty Moore helped
me to understand better the importance of my findings and to make
the evidence for them more explicit. Dr. James Gustafson of the Department of Psychiatry, University of Wisconsin Medical School, generously arranged a visiting scholar's invitation for me in 1989, and it
was there that I made my first formal presentation of this research.
I would also like to thank The Wright Institute, where I work, and
its president, Peter Dybwad, for generous research support of various
kinds, especially the provision of the sabbatical year during which I
was able to begin this project. Ms. Pamela Simi helped at the end, when
help was badly needed.

# Preface

O̲U̲R̲ ability to understand Freud's youth and his entry into middle age, the years during which he formed his dream, his identity, and psychoanalysis itself, has grown radically during the last few years from the publication of his correspondence with Eduard Silberstein and Wilhelm Fliess. The letters to Freud's chum Silberstein cover his adolescent years; the previously available passionate letters from Freud to his fiancée, Martha Bernays, stretch from Freud's mid-20s to age 30. Freud's 30s to his mid-40s are intimately chronicled by his self-revelatory letters to his dear friend Fliess. Although Freud's life after age 45 is beyond the scope of this book, his letters to Carl Jung, Sandor Ferenczi, Karl Abraham, and Ernest Jones show the consequences of his mid-life transition for the ensuing developmental periods.

In order, however, to form this important new information about Freud into a coherent whole, we need to read his letters to Silberstein, Bernays, and Fliess as *developmental records*. Signal events in this record are the formation and bifurcation of his professional dream and his attempts to become a skilled doctor in his mid- to late 20s; his transformative experience with Charcot during his age-30 transition and the end of his conflicted mentor relationship with Josef Breuer; his rejection at age 41 of the seduction theory as the cause of neurosis and the personal crisis this occasioned; his self-analysis and its conclusive role in the discovery of the Oedipus complex; and his dispirited writing of *The Interpretation of Dreams* at 42. Ultimately, as I shall soon describe, we need a theory of lives to make these events in the developmental record meaningful.

Freud was a hungry correspondent. When he had a beloved friend within his epistolary sights, he not only wanted to share his own deepest thoughts and feelings but also insisted on knowing everything his correspondent was thinking. Freud used letters to intimate friends to help him do developmental work, whether on the tasks of adolescence or on those of the mid-life transition. At 17 his task was to leave the childhood past behind him and choose an occupation, and his letters clearly reflect this. At 41 it was to disintoxicate himself of his youthful illusions and reform his deepest personal and professional goals in a way suitable for middle age. Each set of letters reveals marked vicissitudes of spirit, and these mood swings were closely related to the success Freud was having in his own development. When he felt he was making progress, no matter the degree of difficulty, he usually felt buoyant; when he was utterly blocked and unable to proceed, his spirits sank, as in 1897 and 1898 when he could not realize his dream by solving the problem of neurotic etiology.

We have had several good biographies of Freud. Peter Gay's is the most recent and is now the best comprehensive account of Freud's life and work. Gay's scholarship is deep and broad, and his writing is compelling. Despite his outstanding achievement, however, I believe that Gay misunderstands some important aspects of Freud's development as a person and of the evolution of his work. Some of these misunderstandings result from the attempt to do everything in one volume and to integrate, as Gay so masterfully does, the wealth of Freud scholarship that exists in German and English. Others, I believe, stem from his conception of psychological development. Like most psychoanalytically trained scholars and clinicians, Gay writes as though development were largely restricted to childhood. Thus, for example, when Gay reads the Freud–Fliess correspondence, which was written in Freud's 30s and 40s, he reads it primarily for the growth of Freud's thought. Ignoring the possibility that *basic* psychological development and change, comparable in magnitude and even greater in consequence than that which occurs in childhood and adolescence, might be taking place, Gay, in common with other biographers, does not read Freud's letters to Fliess as a record of his ongoing struggles to grow up.

Other misinterpretations originate in Freud's own accounts of his life. Codified in his disciple Ernest Jones's biography, these have been too readily accepted by later biographers. Writers subject to the authority of the psychoanalytic institute, or those who feel singularly indebted to it for their own personal development, seem particularly vulnerable to the romanticization of Freud as scientific hero, an idealization that has tended to cloud observation. We are also familiar with the negative prejudices of writers who, like Jeffrey Masson, are struggling against the authority of the psychoanalytic establishment or who confess themselves to be angry at psychoanalysis in general or, disarmingly, at their own former analysts in particular. Masson's career as a scholar seems now to have been transmogrified into a career as a litigant, leading one to feel both sympathy for him in his mistreatment and impatience with him for his self-indulgence as one used to feel toward the nightclub performer Lenny Bruce. Frederick Crews, a well-known English professor, who one imagines has better things to do with his time, avails himself of popular publications to rail against Freud as though he were still alive and insulting him.

I shall offer here just two examples of commonly accepted errors concerning signal events in Freud's life, these events being his decision to become a practicing physician, not just a research M.D., and his writing of *The Interpretation of Dreams*. Gay understands Freud's decision to become a practitioner to be a consequence of his falling passionately in love with Martha Bernays, whom he later married, and depicts Freud as sweeping Martha away with "masterful impetuosity." My reading of Freud's letters suggests that he was first inhibited and then ambivalent. By Freud's own account, it was Martha who made the opening move, and his letters to her often enough show him content to have her hundreds of miles away in northern Germany while he devoted himself to research in Vienna. I believe that Gay misses Freud's reticence because of his belief that it was Freud's wish to marry Martha and provide well for her that explains his turning from basic science to clinical work in his mid- to late 20s, that only a fervid wish to marry could have forced such a devout scientist into private practice. This was the explanation that Freud proffered in his *Autobiographical Study*. Indeed, Freud liked to say that he had never had much interest in being a doctor, and more than a few psychoanalysts now consider his actual clinical work to have been halfhearted, incompetent, and uninstructive.

I intend to show that becoming a revolutionary healer was a *central aspect of Freud's dream* from 19 on, and that he began his clinical training in earnest at 26 in order to make being a doctor an authentic part of his identity. Characterizing Freud as a scientist forced to support himself in private practice oversimplifies his identity, neglects the complexity of his personal development, and, ironically, underestimates the enormity of his achievement in his early 40s, namely, the creation of a new branch of knowledge in which research and treatment were united. Further, understanding the centrality of the clinical aspect of Freud's dream makes sense of the apparently sudden transformation Freud underwent between 45 and 50 from solitary scientist to revolutionary leader of the psychoanalytic "cause."

Here is the second misunderstanding: *The Interpretation of Dreams,* written between ages 41 and 43, was the first great building

block of psychoanalysis, and it has long been thought to have been
the product of Freud's newly freed creativity. Gay furthers the accepted view that once Freud rid himself of the seduction theory of neurotic etiology at 41, the way was clear for the creative abundance released
by his self-analysis to produce the dream treatise. As the reader will
see, Freud in fact turned to the dream book out of despair and wrote
it for the most part desultorily, amidst the gloom and aimlessness resulting from his failure to solve the really important problem that tantal-
ized and eluded him *both as a scientist and as a clinician*—the cause
of neurosis.

    No writer of biography can claim to be free of transferences toward
his or her subject. However, as an academic clinical psychologist, the
institution of psychoanalysis is largely irrelevant to my career ambitions, even though psychoanalytic knowledge and therapeutic technique
are indispensable to my work. Further, as a middle-aged academic,
some 25 years along in my career, I am freer of the need to flatter or
attack those who are more senior within my own discipline. They are
retired or nearly so, and although I would still like them to admire
me, I am satisfied that some do and am able to do without the others.
Any impatience to overtake them is now mitigated by the recognition
that in several fleeting years I will take their place near the head of
a line that leads to extinction. As for my employers, I have long since
learned that in the academic world, as elsewhere, anything can be used
against you: "Doing a lot of research?—He's neglecting students. Very
involved with students?—He has no deep intellectual commitments.
Balancing the two?—He lacks a coherent professional identity."

    This biography, unlike all but a few others (and none about Freud),
is written with a theory of lives. It is intended for readers who are interested in biography as well as for those, professional and lay, who
are interested in Freud's life in particular. It is not a psychoanalytic
study of Freud's personality. At times, I write in terms of the self and
its parts instead of the ego and its objects. The first usage is phenomenological, the second abstract and theoretical. I see no intrinsic conceptual conflict between the two modes of expression, nor did Freud.[2]
Psychoanalytically oriented readers will look in vain for extended discussions of Freud's narcissism, his Oedipus complex, or his homosexual conflicts, although these matters are discernible and receive some
attention in these pages.

    A person has both a personality and a life. In focusing on Freud's
life, I try to achieve a balanced position from which I can move inward into his personality and outward into his professional world, as
the understanding of a particular choice or event for his development
as a person would seem to require. Childhood receives less emphasis

here, not because I think it is unimportant but because in Freud's case, as in most, the data are so limited. There simply was no record made during Freud's childhood of his thoughts, feelings, dreams, and fantasies. Instead, most of what we know about his experience of those years comes from memories recovered during his mid-life transition and from his autobiography, written when he was an old man. Too often psychological biographers, trapped by the notion that childhood is everything and faced with an insufficiency of evidence, write deductive studies in which the relation between theory and evidence is too one-way and mechanical to be truly satisfying.

Although I try to use it sparingly, the terminology of this developmental theory will be new to some and possibly unwelcome. To write that at 21 Freud was engaged in forming a first adult life structure or that at 28 he was entering an age-30 transition seems to encumber understanding with yet another set of clumsy abstractions. Some readers may find themselves bothered by theoretical terms that have become clichés in the last 20 years. The perfume of *Cosmopolitan* magazine now clings to the concept of the mid-life crisis, as well as to that of developmental transitions more generally. In fact, the term *mid-life crisis* was put into scholarly play by the British Kleinian psychoanalyst Elliott Jaques in 1965 in his study of changes in the works, and in the ways of working, of great artists at mid-life. As American social scientists began investigating the phenomenon in the late 1960s, some journalists who were looking for ideas to simplify living popularized the notion.[3] Clichés feed the appetite for simple answers and constitute a manner of speech now so pervasive that it seems to be the only language most Americans ever master. But good ideas as well as bad ones become clichés. We should not allow the popularization of the concept of mid-life crisis to annoy us into dismissing it, and to fully understand this crisis we need a theory of the life cycle within which to place it. The phenomenon is real, and in Freud's case it is the basis from which the science and practice of psychoanalysis arose.

Among the reasons for the popularity of ideas about adult development is the shift in the age demographics of the developed nations. With women bearing fewer children and medicine finding new ways to keep us alive, the American population is nearing a median age of 35. With more of us living to middle age, there is a greater need for ideas about adult development to help us understand the core problems and possibilities of life after youth. Although our need to better understand this unique epoch in the life cycle is great, we approach books on adult development with mixed feelings of hope and fear. We want to believe that good things remain possible throughout life, but we fear that this may be merely an illusion covering a reality of accumulating losses.

While the population ages, our culture remains heavily youth-centered, perhaps defensively so. We hang on to youth, disparage middle age, and fear becoming old. We mouth bromides such as "You're only as old as you feel," or "Life begins at forty," but our underlying imagery of aging is of decline and decay. In truth, the idea of growth amid decay strikes us as obscene, even dangerous. What, after all, *could* grow after 35 or 40 that wouldn't be ugly or life threatening? We have little by way of cultural wisdom to inform us of the pleasures and virtues of maturity or of new possibilities for vital engagement, and in an uncivil society this is everywhere reflected in a lack of respect for age. Worse, the overvaluation of youth contributes to the frivolousness and superficiality of our culture and cheapens life for people at all ages.

In a culture in which maturity is denigrated and aging feared, the middle-aged woman is simply someone who is no longer sexually attractive. More than one 40-ish female patient has told me that she knew she had become middle-aged when men stopped looking at her when she entered a room. Commonly encountered cultural images of the middle-aged man represent him as psychologically impotent, even castrated. Some are depicted as angry about what has happened to them, others as blandly self-deprecatory. Of the first variety there is the *New Yorker* cartoon of a wife standing in the doorway greeting her scowling, briefcase-toting husband. One imagines that it is the end of the week and that he has completed a grimy trip home on the commuter train from Manhattan. His wife contemplates this dour, tent-shaped specter and says, "Well, let the good times roll." Of the blandly self-deprecatory variety, there is the example of John Poindexter, the former, 50-ish Head of the National Security Council under President Reagan. One morning a colleague found Poindexter eating breakfast at his desk. Returning that night at 7, he found Poindexter having dinner on the other side of his office. Asked why he had changed tables, Poindexter replied, "Variety is the spice of life."

Our cultural imagery of the old person is even more frightening than that of the middle-aged. *She* is a widow living in a retirement ghetto or a nursing home on the life insurance of her deceased husband, or, if she's lucky, she endures as the nomadic and unwelcome guest of her married children. Or she lives in the streets. *He* is utterly useless, possibly even a threat to the innocence of little girls. For both awaits a future of terrifying diagnoses.

For those readers who pick up this book in search of help, or at least illumination, I offer sober encouragement. The good news is that progressive development continues throughout the life cycle. New sources of pleasure and meaning exist, as do genuine opportunities for psychological growth. I can report from my own experience and from my studies of others that life in middle age can be better than life in early adulthood. My research supports Abraham Maslow's finding from his study of the supranormal that "self-actualization" only becomes possible in middle age.[4] Other things being equal (and they never quite are), one is more competent in work, more secure in the world of one's fellows, and less divided within. As I age, life and the self continue to bring wonderful, unimagined surprises, even though (or because) the reality of my own death presses itself upon me more forcefully.

But there is bad news, too. If the developmental tasks and periods of adulthood are given, getting something valuable out of them is not. The kind of biological unfolding that ensures development in childhood and adolescence is largely absent between 17 and 65. Levinson and I have found that no life structure can remain satisfactory for longer than eight or nine years. Repeatedly, contradictions and insufficiencies in one's life (and in the self) must be faced, painful reappraisals undertaken, and risky choices for a new life made. Further, within a new life structure, difficult developmental work will be required in order to exploit opportunities for growth and prevent stagnation.

One cannot accomplish developmental work by running away from times of psychological turmoil, anxiety, and despair. At 41 Freud was forcibly importuned by a new transitional period. He felt, as one often does at such times, that the ground was shifting from beneath his feet, that his very *self* was changing. He could have tried to quell the breaking up of things inside and out and to devote himself to business as usual; instead, he faced these frightening and depressing new movements. Believing they contained psychological riches necessary for his own personal and professional growth, Freud undertook a systematic self-analysis. The result was a mid-life transition of historic creative accomplishment and personal renewal. It is this great, complex story of developmental crisis and triumph that leads us back to Freud's life once again, this time with a theory of lives.

# Contents

# PART ONE

# Getting Ready

# CHAPTER ONE

# A Theory of Lives

In 1895 Sigmund Freud was a 39-year-old neuropathologist who, tormented by neurotic fears of premature death, was urgently trying to create an organic theory of neurosis. Five years later, he had generated many of the ideas that formed the foundation for a new psychological science. Scholars have thought that these profound changes resulted from Freud's intense reaction to the death of his father and from his subsequent self-analysis, but I shall show that they were not simply the result of a critical life event, which might well have occurred at some other time. To the contrary, I believe that Freud's momentous changes during the years from 1895 to 1901 arose from his submitting himself to, and ultimately mastering, developmental forces that were endogenous. These forces were a normal consequence of his aging, though they were made more powerful by the nature of his dream and by the fate of his earlier attempts to achieve it. I shall show that an adult developmental perspective, including the concepts of the dream—that is, visions in which youths invest their most passionate wishes—and the mid-life transition, is required to account for this revolution in Freud's thinking and in his soul. Had Freud been unsuccessful in reforming his early dream, there might be no psychoanalysis and there would not be his instructive example of successful personality growth in middle age.

At 17 Freud's youthful ambitions gathered in a dream of great scientific discovery. At 19 his dream was enriched and complicated by the fantasy of becoming a great healer. As Freud neared 40, he became utterly obsessed with discovering the origins of neurosis. With the seduction theory Freud thought that he had solved the problem of neurotic etiology and that he had in hand at last the important scientific discovery that had eluded him for 20 years. He hoped that this theory would bring him eternal fame, wealth, independence, the freedom to travel, and financial security for his children.[1] Because of the therapeutic significance of the discovery, the seduction theory also provided a way of integrating his identity and realizing both the scientific and clinical aspects of his dream.

The seduction theory was Freud's hypothesis that neurosis results from the sexual molestation of small children, usually by their fathers. In this view, molestation is an environmental *noxa* that constitutes a traumatic blow to the nervous system. This physicalist explanation of neurosis conformed to Freud's scientific training as a neuropathologist. When the theory began to fall apart in the spring of 1897, when he was 41, Freud's hopes for himself and his family were shattered. In the next few years he fought to repair the damage to his psychological integrity and to find a new means for the realization of his dream. During this time he often described his creative work in feminine images of conception, pregnancy, birth, and abortion.

Yet just four years later, by age 45, Freud had proposed the topographic theory of the mind; had achieved insights concerning the primal scene, infantile sexuality, castration anxiety, the Oedipus complex, and sexual perversion; and was ready to create his theory of the libido. *The Interpretation of Dreams* (1899) had been published, as had *The Psychopathology of Everyday Life* (1901). In 1901 he wrote, though did not publish, the case history of Dora (1905), and *Three Essays on the Theory of Sexuality* (1905) gestated peacefully in his imagination. Beyond creating this foundation for psychoanalysis, Freud had marked out for himself a research domain whose exploration would keep him vitally engaged in living throughout the long, second half of his life.

In addition to great scientific advances, Freud's mid-life transition also brought important clinical progress and personal changes. During these years Freud came to rely less on hypnosis and more on psychotherapy by free association and began to understand the importance of the transference relationship between doctor and patient. He learned that through transference the doctor takes on in the patient's imagination the powers of a parent or other person of great emotional significance from childhood. Thus, he came to understand that patients held on to symptoms in order to hold on to him, rather than simply because underlying childhood scenes remained repressed. This insight broadened Freud's understanding of treatment and established his therapeutic competence at a new level. Indeed, I believe that Freud solidified his identity as a clinician only in 1900, at age 44, and that doing so was of deep personal significance to him.

By age 45 Freud had fulfilled his long-held and deeply inhibited wish to visit Rome. He had also overcome his own passivity to wrest from the somnolent Viennese civil administration a long overdue appointment as Professor Extraordinarius. His hypochondriacal obsession with illness and death, which had plagued him during his late 30s, had receded to the background, and he had achieved a far-reaching sublimation of his sexuality into creative work. He had separated from his mentor, Josef Breuer, and his dependent relationship with Wilhelm Fliess was over. He had also brought his professional isolation to an end by forming the Psychological Wednesday Society, a small group of physician pupils who came to his waiting room for weekly discussions of psychoanalytic ideas. This group soon evolved into the Viennese Psychoanalytical Society and became the institutional basis for the new profession of psychoanalysis. Moreover, Freud had succeeded in integrating his identity as a scientist and a clinician. How did he accomplish so much in so short a period of time?

## Prevailing Views of the Origins of Psychoanalysis

The years of crisis and creative transformation in Freud's life around age 40 have been studied by numerous scholars, and their work formed my initial view of the period. Ernest Jones was the first to note that Freud underwent several periods of personality change in the adult years, beginning with one in his late 30s. As noted, most scholars have attributed these changes to Freud's intense reaction to the death of his father in 1896 and to his subsequent self-analysis. Recently, Grinstein found from a study of Freud's dreams that as a result of the self-analysis his oedipal and homosexual conflicts diminished and his capacity for friendship with women increased. However, of all those who have contributed to the enormous body of Freud scholarship, only French psychologist Didier Anzieu has conceived of this time of rapid change as an adult developmental phenomenon. In doing so, he relied for theory upon Jaques's classic essay "Death and the Mid-Life Crisis."

Elliott Jaques, a follower of Melanie Klein and a theorist of great scope and originality in his own right, studied a large group of eminent artists and found that in their late 30s many entered into a midlife crisis whose resolution had great impact on the quantity and quality of their subsequent creative work. Jaques described this change from youth to middle age in the style and pace of work as being from "precipitate" to "sculpted" creativity, and argued that the mid-life crisis involves a reworking of the depressive position. At mid-life, Jaques wrote, individuals confront their own inner destructiveness with a full awareness of mortality. Successful developmental work leads to a sublime and tragic dimension to artistic productions and to an attitude of mourning rather than persecution in regard to one's own death. Failed development results in an impoverishment of creativity or in its cessation.

Jaques's work is highly evocative but incomplete. By focusing on crises rather than on a continuing *sequence of periods,* Jaques's midlife crisis bursts against a dark theoretical firmament. What is happening developmentally in the 20s and 30s that leads up to the midlife crisis? What developmental periods and tasks in the late 40s and in the 50s follow it?

## Gay's Biography of Freud

Gay's account of the years 1896 to 1899, during which Freud abandoned the seduction theory and wrote *The Interpretation of Dreams,* begins with Jacob Freud's death. Gay finds Freud's reaction to the event remarkable both for its extremity and for the speed with which Freud put it to theoretical use. Gay writes, "The death of his father, then, was a profound personal experience from which Freud drew universal implications; it acted like a pebble thrown into a still pond, making successive rings of unsuspected magnitude." He quotes the preface to the second edition of the dream book, which was written when Freud was 52 and in which Freud indicates that the book was part of his self-analysis and his reaction to his father's death.[2]

Feeling uprooted by the loss of his father, Gay's account continues, Freud experienced an increased need to achieve professional security. But a conceptual problem blocked his progress: he had gotten himself enamored of the preposterous idea that all neuroses result from paternal seduction. Finally, in 1897, the idea collapsed under the weight of its own implausibility, though from time to time Freud's belief in it rekindled. On September 21, 1897, a year after Jacob's death, Freud described in detail in a letter to Fliess his reasons for rejecting the theory. In that letter he admitted having gone through a period of perplexity and disorientation, but, as Gay puts it, "his dismay was short-lived."[3] Now, having scuttled the errant theory, Freud faced the future with steady scientific courage. As Gay writes, "The way to his sustained self-analysis, to the recognition of the Oedipus complex and of unconscious fantasies now lay open."[4] The next year, from fall 1897 to fall 1898, was in Gay's view one of rapid progress in research and self-analysis, a year marred only intermittently by "dryness and discouragement."[5] Though Gay offers a full account of the intellectual sources of *The Interpretation of Dreams* and of its structure and argument, he offers no close reading of Freud's nearly two-year-long struggle to write the book. It is as though with seduction out of the way *The Interpretation of Dreams* unfolded with little difficulty.

Gay's book integrates thousands of details about Freud's long life and nearly as many scholarly sources into a compellingly readable and convincing narrative. As a psychoanalytically trained historian, however, Gay accepts a theory of individual development that is more concerned with childhood and adolescence and their enduring residues than with the adult years. Without a theory of adult development, he can only see personal change at mid-life as a reaction to critical life events, such as the death of a parent. His account leaves one wondering if Freud would have remained a neuropathologist if Jacob had died 15 years later. And would his systematic self-analysis have begun only then, at 55? I agree that Jacob's death shook Freud and contributed to the mid-life changes, but I believe that had Jacob lived, Freud would still have suffered a mid-life crisis.

In the beginning, I was strongly swayed by Gay's explanation. Influenced by him and others, it seemed clear to me that Freud went through a period of transition from ages 40 to 45. While a great deal of change occurred within it, I saw no crisis. My theory of development does not equate transitions with crises and therefore does not require them. Freud had begun the period by intensifying his attempts to create a neuronal psychology, but, I thought, underlying changes in his own personality were leading him to care more about psychological explanations. In September 1897 Freud abandoned his explanation of neurosis, felt elated, and began his self-analysis systematically in October. He vowed to write the dream book in November, began it in February 1898, abandoned the seduction theory for good in January 1899, and finished the dream book in a blaze of glory over the next nine months, or so it seemed.

Freud's giving up of the seduction theory looked to me like a natural step in replacing old preoccupations with newer ones. The new, persistent vision was dream interpretation, and finally Freud could no longer resist its exploration; neuronal psychology and seduction (and his biologist friend Fliess) were set aside as the forces of mid-life individuation turned Freud into a psychoanalyst. A dramatic and fruitful transitional period, yes; a mid-life crisis, no. I thought that Freud had had developmental work to do and that he had done it very well indeed.

And it is true that there were numerous occasions between the spring of 1897, when doubts about seduction first arose, and January 1899, when he fell in love at last with the dream book, when Freud felt restored and confident. This is one of the reasons why scholars have missed the severity and duration of Freud's turmoil. I was also correct in thinking that *The Interpretation of Dreams* and the growing general emphasis on psychological explanation were the products of underlying developmental changes. However, these changes were far more complicated, and cost Freud far more, than it was possible to learn from the existing biographies, even such competent ones as Gay's.

## Masson's Translation of the Freud–Fliess Correspondence

When I began to study the primary source material for the period, mainly Masson's publication of the unexpurgated correspondence between Freud and Fliess, my conception of what had happened changed radically. Masson's volume consists of 287 of Freud's letters and theoretical drafts, most of which were written between ages 39 and 45.[6] These average over 500 words in length, occur at a frequency of about one every 10 days, and almost invariably contain both theoretical conundra and personal confidences. We also have Schröter's companion edition of these letters in German, which allows us to compare the English translations with the copies made from the originals.

Before Masson's publication, it simply was not possible to know what Freud went through in the years of greatest importance to the development of psychoanalysis. From a close reading of these remarkably personal letters, it is now possible to see that commonly held ideas about Freud are incorrect, including the idea that he was a cold, uninvolved father; that he was once addicted to cocaine; that the original focus of his interest in childhood (his own and others') was on the oedipal rather than the preoedipal years; and that he created his clinical theory deductively rather than empirically. Further, these letters reveal in the most intimate detail a mid-life crisis of historic importance. To understand this crisis, I needed better evidence about the dream to which Freud had devoted his youth.

I shall briefly preview the conception I derived from a study of Freud's correspondence to Silberstein, Martha Bernays, and Fliess of his early dream, his age-30 transition, his relationship with his mentors, his rejection of the seduction theory, his self-analysis, and the writing of *The Interpretation of Dreams*.

## The Dream of Becoming a Revolutionary Healer and a Great Scientist

The recent publication by Walter Boehlich of the complete correspondence between Freud and his friend Eduard Silberstein allows us to see close up the formation of Freud's dream in adolescence and to learn that it was more complicated than we had hitherto understood. These letters make it clear that in addition to the fantasy of becoming a great scientist, at 19 Freud added a second powerful and enduring wishful fantasy—that of becoming a revolutionary healer. Despite his later insistence that he had never wanted to become a doctor and despite the shaping by biographers of narratives to fit this conception of his identity, we can now see that this was a simplification. In this new light, various critical matters—such as his deep identification with Jean Charcot, his obsessive preoccupation with the problem of the etiology of neurosis, and the mid-life crisis that his inability to solve it occasioned—become more understandable.

The revolutionary healer fantasy was a new, basic, and different element in Freud's ambition and in the growing shape of his identity. It had an origin in his mother's frustrated heroism, which formed a polarity in Freud's parental identifications opposite his father's quiet, scholarly nature. Freud would always be divided by his tastes for the private satisfactions of the disciplined scholar (or scientist), in identification with his father, and for the more dramatic and public achievements that fired his mother's imagination. This polarity was activated first during Freud's age-30 transition and later during his mid-life transition, when he tried first to explain neurosis, then to cure it. Scientific achievement remained primary in Freud's value system throughout his life, as he insisted it was, but at times, such as during his 50s when he became the leader of the psychoanalytic movement, the revolutionary healer part of his identity asserted itself strongly. Indeed, Freud's attempts to get Carl Jung to lead the movement and the well-known difficulties between the two men would be better understood if we took into account the competing parts of Freud's dream (the difficulties also stemmed from Jung's age-driven efforts to become his own man).

The recognition that Freud's dream was always split between science and practice and that both were important to his identity allows us to understand how at age 43, during the winter of 1900 and *following* publication of *The Interpretation of Dreams,* Freud could have suffered what he called a "catastrophic collapse" and undergone a "deep inner crisis."[7] This crisis has been completely overlooked by previous investigators and gives new meaning to Freud's famous declaration to Fliess about being a conquistador, a declaration made on February 1, 1900, during the disappointing first few months when no one read his dream book and while he was struggling unsuccessfully to achieve a clinical breakthrough in lieu of the scientific success that he had hoped the book would bring. Freud had been eagerly expecting the recovery of certain kinds of memories from his patient, whom we know of only as Herr E., that would confirm a new hypothesis about the roots of neurosis. But in this expectation, too, he had recently been disappointed; the childhood scenes had not been forthcoming, and he was mired down again in obscurities. It was at this time that he told Fliess, "I am by temperament nothing but a conquistador—an adventurer, if you want it translated—with all the curiosity, daring, and tenacity characteristic of a man of this sort."

Quoted without its surrounding paragraph and taken out of biographical context, this sentence has been uniformly misunderstood to be a defiant boast, a statement of Freud's fearless combativeness, or at least of his indomitable independence. Actually, its tone is depressive, and it was issued from a position of defeat. Having failed as a scientist with the dream book, Freud had turned his hopes toward his other fundamental aim and now felt that he was failing as a revolutionary healer, too. Consider the entire paragraph from his letter to Fliess:

> If we lived in the same city—this would have to be Berlin, though, not Vienna—much would have turned out differently, and I believe I would never have gotten into such straits (or would have gotten out of them quickly). That is why I have so often regretted our separation. Unfortunately this does not change anything. Perhaps hard times are ahead, both for me and for my practice. On the whole, I have noticed that you usually overestimate me greatly. The motivation for this error, though, disarms any reproach. For I am actually not at all a man of science, not an observer, not an experimenter, not a thinker. I am by temperament nothing but a conquistador—an adventurer, if you want it translated—with all the curiosity, daring, and tenacity characteristic of a man of this sort. *Such people are customarily esteemed only if they have been successful, have really discovered something; otherwise they are dropped by the wayside. And that is not altogether unjust. At the present time, however, luck has left me; I no longer discover anything worthwhile.* [Italics added]

Here we see the strength of the heroic healer aspect of Freud's dream and his despair at failing to realize it. In fact, as we shall see in Chapter Ten, the crisis was resolved by a clinical, not a scientific, breakthrough. Thus, it appears that Freud was attempting to simplify matters in his own life and identity by insisting that the dominance of the scientific element in his motivation excluded all others. In reality, the competition between these two versions of the dream, solitary scholar versus revolutionary healer, was never permanently resolved in favor of one over the other, and the two versions competed for Freud's energies throughout his life.

## Freud's Age-30 Transition and Charcot

Biographers, such as Gay, have seen the importance to Freud of his brief period of study with Charcot at the Salpêtrière Hospital in Paris. Gay writes that during that five-month externship in 1885–1886, Freud became a disciple of Charcot's. Gay depicts Charcot as a brilliant and charismatic teacher who was leading the way in the understanding of the neuroses, and as a man who combined, as it was in Freud's nature to do, imagination with a devotion to exact clinical observation. Charcot was a brilliant clinician-theorist, as Freud himself would be.

To understand the transformative impact of Freud's encounter with Charcot, we need to place it within a developmental context, for Charcot was not only the right man for Freud but the right man at the right time. As Freud reached his mid- to late 20s, the life structure he had formed earlier with pure science at its center was no longer satisfactory. The clinical aspect of his dream, and of his identity, had been too long neglected and feeling fraudulent as a doctor, Freud sought postdoctoral clinical training. Thus, when Freud went to Paris at 29, he was entering into a transitional period. The work of the transition was to rearrange the priorities in his life so as to make more room for the neglected aspects of his dream and to expand his identity to give valued place for the parts of the self invested in the clinical aspect. It was within this developmental readiness that Charcot could mean so much to Freud so fast. Freud left Vienna in the fall of 1885 a research M.D.; in the spring of 1886 he returned a clinician. Three years later, Freud named his first son Jean Martin after Charcot. Without Charcot as a requisite other, Freud might never have gotten free of Brücke's dream and might have become instead a failed exile from laboratory science. André Brouillet's painting of Charcot demonstrating a hysterical case before a group of astonished physicians still hangs today from the wall of Freud's consulting room at 19 Berggasse. Freud had sat across from it for over 40 years, contemplating the master hour after hour and drawing sustenance, discipline, and inspiration as he listened to his patients free-associate on the couch to his left.

## Freud's Relationships with Breuer and Fliess

With the years of his youth drawing to a close and his scientific and clinical ambitions unrealized, in his late 30s Freud felt that time was running out. This anxiety was concretized in diagnostically unverifiable and ultimately harmless cardiac symptoms that terrified him. Indeed, he said that his worst fear was that he would die before he could complete his theoretical discoveries. His *Project for a Scientific Psychology*—a theory of neuronal excitation, conveyance, and discharge—was an effort at age 39 to realize his dream along the lines of his early training in neurophysiology. Meanwhile, he was still emotionally and professionally dependent on his mentor, Josef Breuer. Freud wanted very much to become his own man, and his continuing reliance on Breuer was galling evidence of an enduring immaturity.

As Freud sought to extricate himself from Breuer, he became increasingly dependent on Wilhelm Fliess. This transfer of dependence was reflected by the steep increase in his letters, as well as by his telling Fliess at one point that he loved him. Originally, I agreed with Gay and others that this relationship involved a homosexually tinged, positive transference to a man who was functioning in the role of Freud's analyst. And there certainly were aspects of that. Rereading their correspondence, however, I was able to see that Fliess was not mainly an analyst for Freud or a sublimated homosexual lover. Instead, his primary role was a developmental one: He helped Freud shed Breuer at a time when Freud needed to outgrow his reliance on mentors once and for all. Fliess also provided a sustaining narcissistic medium in which Freud could rework his dream from a neurophysiological to a psychological one. Neither man understood the developmental nature of their friendship or recognized that success at its essential task would render it obsolete.

## Rejection of the Seduction Theory and the Writing of *The Interpretation of Dreams*

In his book *The Assault on Truth,* published in 1984 prior to the publication of his edition of Freud's letters to Fliess, Masson argued that Freud gave up the seduction theory for reasons of professional politics. Testing the validity of Masson's thesis was not among my interests as I began this research. Yet I could not escape noticing that Masson's translation of the letters did not seem to support his own argument. Rather than Freud's abandoning his theory for reasons of expedience, careful examination of the letters revealed, as George Mahl had seen before me, a prolonged and complicated sequence of doubt and reaffirmation. Finally, I saw that the seduction theory had come to reside at the heart of Freud's dream and that these vicissitudes of conviction shook Freud badly. Ultimately, I was forced to the uncomfortable conclusion that Masson's idea that Freud gave up the seduction theory because it alienated his professional colleagues was not only off the mark but bizarre. It was difficult to imagine how anyone who had studied these letters even without a theory of lives that would alert one to the psychological importance of the dream and the crucial role it plays in the mid-life transition, could have imagined such a thing. Had Masson published the letters before rather than after the charges he based on them few people would have taken his accusation seriously. Indeed, Freud never gave up the idea that seduction could cause neurosis; it was only that ultimately he found it impossible to believe that molestation could be the cause in every instance.

It also became clear to me that, contrary to prevailing belief, *The Interpretation of Dreams* had not been written during a period of creative abundance. Gay had furthered the accepted view that once Freud rid himself of the seduction theory in 1897, the way was clear for the creative abundance released by his self-analysis to produce *The Interpretation of Dreams*. As the reader will see in Chapter Nine, Freud in fact turned to the dream book out of the despair that resulted from his failure to answer the important question that plagued him both as a scientist and as a clinician—the cause of neurosis. The failure to solve the problem of neurosis cast a long shadow over Freud's attempts to work on the dream book.

## Freud's Self-Analysis

Biographers have understood Freud's self-analysis as a reaction to his father's death. Yet Freud had engaged in self-analysis since adolescence, and he continued to do so for the rest of his life. Moreover, he did not apply himself systematically to his self-analysis until 10 months after the death of his father. Mahl gives the letter to Fliess of August 14, 1897, as the official beginning of this disciplined self-scrutiny.[8] In it, Freud refers to his own analysis *immediately* after writing that he was "tormented by grave doubts about [his] theory of the neuroses."[9] It was doubts about the seduction theory, not his father's death alone, that stimulated the self-analysis. The most active time in this analysis occurred in October 1897 following Freud's initial abandonment of the seduction theory in September. This was a year after Jacob's death. It was then that Freud confirmed the existence of the Oedipus complex in himself as well as in his patients. This rich October of self-analysis may well have been fueled by an anniversary reaction to his father's death, but its primary biographical context appears to have been a regressive free-fall caused by the collapse of the seduction theory and his frantic attempts to find a new basis for proceeding. Freud's inability to solve the problem of neurosis and realize his dream of being a great scientist-clinician, *together* with the loss of his father, had brought back oedipal memories of feeling like an impotent little boy.

## The Overlapping Eras of Early and Middle Adulthood

The notion of a dream and a mid-life transitional period of several years during which the dream is reappraised helps us to understand why the seduction theory could not simply have been dropped. Identifying an environmental trauma to the nervous system as the cause of neurosis was an expression of 20 years of work; it repaid the faith of Freud's earlier mentor, Ernst Brücke, who lived on in his mind as an inspiring, controlling figure—in psychoanalytic terms, a superego introject—and as an organizing feature of his own personal and professional identity. It was in Brücke's laboratory that Freud had found his first intellectual home as a young adult and had "spent the happiest hours of [his] student life, free from all other desires" and clinging rapturously, as he later put it, quoting Faust, at the "breasts of wisdom."[10]

Indeed, at 42 or 43 Freud had a long, frightening dream about Brücke as he struggled to write the dream book.[11] In it Brücke had assigned him the research task of dissecting the lower half of his own body, which he did. Later in the dream Freud found himself attempting a long journey with weary legs while being helped along by a guide who sometimes carried him.

> At last we reached a small wooden house at the end of which was an open window. There the guide set me down and laid two wooden boards, which were standing ready, upon the window-sill, so as to bridge the chasm which had to be crossed over from the window. At that point I really became frightened about my legs, but instead of the expected crossing, I saw two grown-up men lying on wooden benches that were along the walls of the hut, and what seemed to be two children sleeping beside them. It was as though what was going to make the crossing possible was not the boards but the children. I awoke in a mental fright.

In thinking about the dream Freud recalled memories from his early 20s concerning the first research task Brücke assigned him—the dissection of a fish's nervous system. He also recalled Brücke's taking him to task about his scientific laziness. Freud concluded that the dream had expressed his current thought, namely, "How much longer will my legs carry me?"—that is, his fear that he might not live long enough to accomplish his goals.[12] Perhaps the dream also meant that the

Brücke inside was ordering him to get on with real science, yet doing so in his mentor's way disabled him. It was not yet clear to Freud how to use his scientific training in pursuit of his new psychological interests. *Brücke* means "bridge" in German, but Freud may have begun to wonder if the way to the future didn't lay elsewhere, in still slumbering new life.

Freud could not readily shift his allegiance from a neurophysiological to a psychological version of his dream. Neither could his perplexity be merely intellectual nor limited to a few months while he refocused his energy on a new research task. Instead, the two research tasks, neurotic etiology on top and the psychology of wishes, fantasies, and dreams on the bottom, like the era of youth that was ending and of middle age that was beginning, shifted back and forth like grinding geologic plates. A period of years would be required before Freud could transfer his allegiance from a neurophysiological conception of his dream to a psychoanalytic one, years during which he felt sickeningly off balance and regained his footing only to lose it again.

## Age-Linked Developmental Eras and Periods

In placing Freud's mid-life transition in a life cycle developmental perspective, my work follows in the tradition of Erikson's conception of ongoing stages in ego development.[13] Indeed, Erikson's studies of the young Martin Luther and the middle-aged Mahatma Gandhi have lit the way and set an intimidating standard for all of us who would attempt developmental biographies. I am guided as well by psychoanalyst Hans Loewald's observation that there exist not merely in childhood but throughout the life cycle regularly occurring periods of personality change marked by ego regression and reorganization.[14]

My conception of the life cycle relies most directly on Levinson's theory of an age-linked sequence of developmental *eras* and *periods*.[15] The five eras of the life cycle—preadulthood (birth to age 20), early adulthood (20–40), middle adulthood (40–60), late adulthood (60–80), and late late adulthood (after age 80)—are roughly 20 years in length whereas the periods are five to seven years long. Like the seasons, the eras do not constitute a developmental hierarchy. Rather, the shift in the character of living from one to another is qualitative. Spring is not better than summer but different. Even when we are no longer young, we enter each era as novitiates and must learn as best we can about the era's distinct demands, possibilities, and constraints.

Each era begins with an entry period, which is followed by an intra-era transitional period, and ends with a culminating period. The eras do not have discrete beginnings and endings. Rather, again like the seasons, the eras are joined by and overlap within a major cross-era *transitional period*. This overlap of beginnings and endings gives transitional periods their psychological richness and instability. We think of the major transitional periods in the life cycle as follows: the early adult transition (17–22), the mid-life transition (40–45), the late adult transition (60–65), and the late late adult transition (80–85). We find a variation in age at onset and termination of the periods of about two years. Intra-era transitions occur in the years around 30, 50, and 70. During each of the transitional periods, processes of personality individuation appear to be heightened and can lead to increased integration of split-off parts of the self, as well as to anxiety, fragmentation, and psychological illness.

The existence of these age-linked periods remains a poorly understood empirical finding. In fact, the notion of aged-linked periods in the adult years runs counter to both contemporary thinking in the social sciences and to popular belief.[16] One often finds that people are misled in this matter by the conviction that under modern conditions the life span has lengthened. The fallacious reasoning goes like this: *Notions such as the mid-life crisis arise because people now live so long. One (or five) hundred years ago when life expectancy was only half what it is now, a 40-year-old was considered ancient and a mid-life crisis would have to have occurred at 20.* The mistake here is to confuse the length of the life span with the percentage of the population that endures until its end. The latter has changed but not the former. The biblical three score and ten has long been, more or less, the human life span, and all cultures have ordinarily had some people who have attained this. A visit to an old New England grave site is instructive. There one finds numerous tombstones of 18th- and 19th-century men who died in their 60s, 70s, and 80s. There are similar tombstones of women, but in smaller numbers. Often a man has had two wives, and there are numerous tombstones of women who died in their 20s and 30s. There are also many small stones marking the graves of children. The point is obvious: If women survived the childbearing years, and children survived birth and childhood, a substantial percentage lived into old age, as did many of the men. If you pool all these ages together to derive an average life expectancy, the result is very misleading. Evidence from prehistoric skeletal remains supports the same conclusion.[17]

Implicit in the assumption of a lengthening life span is a Darwinian romanticism in which it is imagined that since things get better and better (i.e., evolve) as we move forward in time, they get worse and worse as we move backward. Yet, as the paleodemographers Acsádi and Nemeskéri write,

It need not be assumed that human life of the remote past existed in completely austere and adverse circumstances, and that the length of human life was increasingly curtailed by the "cruel" conditions as we go back in time. Adult men of ancient times had to overcome a number of difficulties, but they were exposed to fewer hazards than those confronting modern man living in advanced socio-economic circumstances. . . . At a primitive stage of social evolution, owing to the everyday struggle for life and to biological selection, only viable, resistant individuals survived, who then were capable of attaining even older ages than is usually assumed.[18]

If we are justified in thinking of a determinate life span consisting of age-linked segments, what determines the nature and timing of the segments? At this point, we can only say that they appear to arise from an interpenetration of *biopsychosocial* factors. Since it is Freud's mid-life transition that interests us here, I shall briefly describe the factors that appear generally to create this period for men.

The *biological* determinants are subtle but nonetheless important. We begin to decline biologically in late adolescence and some signs of this are apparent by 30. Yet at 30 the accumulated decrements are small. By 40, they are unmistakable: A man must get reading glasses or bifocals; his cardiac capacity is diminished, as is his auditory acuity; his sexual drive, under ordinary circumstances, is reduced; he has facial wrinkles, jowls, and a paunch; commonplace details such as phone numbers elude his memory; and his strength, speed, reflexes, and recuperative powers are markedly diminished. Death is no longer abstract nor a tragic possibility but rather a more or less patient companion.

*Psychologically,* by 40 there has been a qualitative change in a man's sensibility. This is what is being suggested when it is said that at 20 anyone with a heart is a socialist whereas at 40 anyone with a mind is a conservative. With the cooling of the biological fires, one is less impulsive and more reflective. After 20 years of experience as an adult, one's respect for the likelihood of unexpected consequences attendant upon actions is deepened, as is one's sense of the fragility of all human enterprises, including life itself. Qualities of mind such as prudence, patience, judiciousness, perspective, foresight, and wisdom now have their time in the life cycle. Many youths are timid, just as some middle-aged men are impulsive, but in middle age the quality of restraint is leavened by actual experience. It has been *earned*. This is not to say, of course, that a middle-aged person has better judgment than a younger one; it is just that he or she is likely to have better judgment than before. There is a middle-aged version of courage; it is not action and the consequences be damned but perseverance amid a smaller armada of deadly illusions.

A universal *social* determinant of the mid-life transition is to be found in the nature of society as a multigenerational form of collective life and in the fact that human life has always been played out within a social system that has included members in every era of the life cycle (except under conditions of climactic, predatorial, or bacterial catastrophe). The presence of all the generations, described by Homer roughly 2,800 years ago in the *Odyssey,* has given individual development within society its fundamental structure for thousands of years.

My reading of anthropology, history, literature, and biography leads me to the conclusion that age grading is a human universal. Essential characteristics of persons are typically correlated with age, and these biopsychosocial characteristics have been more similar than different across time and culture. Simply put, the tribe has always had members who were not fully grown and thought them young, in need of nurture, socialization, and tuition; it has always had people who were biologically mature but still novices psychologically, and thought them youths possessed of the virtues and liabilities of great biological abundance; it has always known a group of people who were in the middle, biologically neither old nor young but both, possessed of a balance of vigor and experience that made them uniquely suitable for leadership; and it has always had old people who were in relatively rapid biologic decline and whose lives were understood to have entered fully under the shadow of death.[19]

In our everyday transactions others tell us more or less subtly how old we are. At 30 a man is likely to be seen, and to experience himself, as an older sibling to younger people who are themselves now adult. By 40 a man is a full generation older, old enough to be the parent of a member of the upcoming generation of adults. Ordinarily, it is the group from 40 to 65 that holds the positions of highest leadership in the military, governmental, educational, and commercial institutions of society. At around 40 a man is considered eligible to join the senior leadership group in his sector of society.

Finally, *the life structure,* conjointly formed by the aforementioned three forces—the biological, psychological, and social—contains the engine of its own development. The life structure is the overall pattern or design of a person's life at a given time. It is an imperfectly integrated whole that tends toward pattern stability between the transitional periods and toward change within them as it evolves over the eras and periods of the life cycle. The structure has central components, rarely in excess of three or four, as well as peripheral components. (In Freud's case, in his early to mid-30s, the central components were husband–father and doctor.) Changes in the life structure may be external and visible, as in changes in social role brought about by occupational shifts or divorce, but the life structure has an important inner aspect as well in the parts of the self that are invested in the social roles and in the meanings that arise from the interaction of self and role. Thus, important changes in the life structure may be invisible or knowable only through intimate acquaintance. (By his late 30s there had been no change in the central roles Freud occupied but the meaning of the occupational role was changing dramatically.)

No life structure is perfectly integrated or allows full expression of all parts of the self. Some level of contradiction and exclusion is bound to occur. With time, the contradictions rub, and the neglected parts of the self push for expression. At 30 a man may feel that since he is still young, modest reform of the life structure will suffice to realize his dream. Between 35 and 40, the acme of creative productivity has been reached and a decline begins in many realms of endeavor, including the sciences.[20] By 40, one's youth is coming to an end and middle age is beginning. Youth can no longer be reformed. Painful contradictions must either be accepted as permanent disabilities or actively confronted, and suppressed aspects of the self must be freed or left to atrophy further, perhaps irremediably; one's youthful dream must be realized, recast, or abandoned.

## The Formation of the Dream in Childhood and Adolescence

In adopting a life cycle developmental perspective, a psychologist tries first to identify the enduring themes of childhood and adolescence and then to see how these are mediated—that is, transmitted in kind (as in the repetition compulsion), revised, or transformed—by later adult developmental periods and tasks. The dream is a precious, enduring vision that mediates between the themes of childhood, such as the oedipal theme, and later development. It contains fantasies of the kind of person one will become, the world in which one will live, and the gratification success will bring. This inspiring and more or less coherent vision of one's adult self in an adult world exists at various levels of consciousness. What makes the dream endlessly motivating is the profound investment of youthful wishes. One imagines that in realizing one's dream one can make one's parents (or caretakers, siblings, teachers, other authorities, or society) proud—or make them pay.

Dream formation is a complex process that is as yet poorly understood. Dreams are shaped in some measure by the individual's inherited and evolving ability and temperament; by family, societal, and historical circumstance; and by maturing personal values. During the novice phase of adulthood, roughly between 17 and 33 (although sometimes earlier and sometimes never), dreams crystallize out as more or less conscious goals through critical experiences with others — often narcissistically overvalued peers and adults — of an epiphanic nature.[21] Once formed, the dream animates the self and provides a deep psychological basis for making the major life choices of early adulthood.

From an external point of view, the sought-for goal may be as banal as a little house with a white picket fence; as mundane as becoming a successful businessman, doctor, or attorney; or as heroic as tracking down the great white whale. Some dreams are unitary, such as dreams of becoming heavyweight champion of the world, uncovering ancient Troy, or becoming a mother. Others are internally divided, sometimes even contradictory, such as dreams of becoming a social scientist and a literate person, or a moralist and a dean. As noted earlier, by the end of his adolescence, Freud had formed a complicated binary dream.

## The Mentor as a Species of Requisite Other

Homer's *Odyssey* is the first story in our literature of the harrowing developmental adventures of early adulthood and of a crisis in the mid-life transition.[22] King Odysseus had been a very young man when he left for the Trojan Wars. During the 20 years he was gone he experienced many adventures in both love and war. In his long absence his house had become a lounge for rude suitors who bullied his son, Telemachus, plundered his larder, and importuned his wife. During the year the gods had set for his return, Odysseus was to vanquish his rivals and secure his kingdom as a mature, middle-aged ruler. But Odysseus could not return; lost and miserable, he was held captive on a far-off island by the nymph Calypso. Telemachus, confused and immobilized by doubt, was too intimidated by the suitors to defend the sanctity of his father's home. Reminding the gods of the king's faithfulness, the goddess Athene convinces them to intervene. Zeus sends a messenger to tell Calypso that Odysseus must be released, and Athene herself then descends from Olympus and appears before Telemachus in the guise of an old family friend named Mentor. Mentor gives the boy courage, helps him make preparations, and accompanies him on a voyage to seek knowledge of his lost father. From the beginning of the tale to its dramatic conclusion, Athene *qua* Mentor guides both men, helping Telemachus with the developmental tasks of entering early adulthood and Odysseus with those of leaving it.

Aside from the particular nature and fate of a mentor–protégé relationship, gaining or failing to secure a mentor is one of the most developmentally consequential events in adulthood. Today the word *mentor* is widely used everywhere, from the business firm to the academy, as though deep, generative involvement could be mass produced. But true mentor relationships are not so common and can no more result from assignment than love can be created by appointing lovers. In reality, few of us are as fortunate as Telemachus or his father. Since there are always many more aspirants with dreams than mentors to guide them, young people must seek out and win a mentor to help them define and pursue their dreams.

Freud's early adulthood was rich in mentors. Between 17 and 45 he had two: Ernst Brücke and Josef Breuer. The mentor is usually a half-generation or more older than the protégé and established in the field in which the protégé hopes to enact his dream. More than a teacher, counselor, or coach, the mentor gives the dream and its aspiring dreamer a blessing, something badly needed by young people and a gift that goes far beyond advice and promotion. A blessing of this sort lasts an entire lifetime, because an idealized representation of the mentor is internalized into the young person's maturing ego ideal. It is through the internalization of mentors that the young get to become something truly different from their parents (although they will learn in time that the differences are not as great as they had imagined). As an internal figure, the mentor sustains the protégé long after the younger person has had to cut himself loose from the mentor in reality.

Yet to the extent that the protégé's dream is infused with the requirement to further the mentor's legacy—and in some appreciable measure this is likely—the blessing is also a curse. The protégé then feels an ambivalent obligation, concatenated of gratitude and resentment, to secure the immortality of the mentor's dream. Thus, the internalized mentor can become a formidable obstacle to personality individuation in the mid-life transition. During his late 30s, as he was trying to become his own man, Freud came to feel this way about Breuer. This also happened between Freud and Jung a decade or so later, when Jung was himself approaching a mid-life transition and needed desperately to separate from Freud and become his own man.[23]

The mentor is a variant of what I term the *requisite other*.[24] *Requisite* here means required by the distinctive developmental work of a particular period. A requisite other is not a man or woman for all seasons but for a particular one. He or she is a person who has the interest and ability to help with developmental work. Common variants, besides the mentor, are the psychotherapist, teacher, and close

friend. A relative or lover can be a requisite other but may be prevented from assuming this role by having too great a stake in the outcome
of developmental dilemmas.

The mentor appears to be a creature of early adulthood. Our
studies suggest that the individual loses the ability to use mentorial
help by about age 45. However, just as developmental periods and
tasks continue beyond the mid-life transition, so too does our need
for requisite others to help us accomplish developmental work.

## Developmental Work

What is meant by the term *developmental work*? It means, first, listening to inner voices of discontent, the "other voices [in] other
rooms."[25] One may have heard them all along but treated them only
as annoying distractions. At some point, if development is to proceed
optimally, they need to be listened to. One must think about what the
voices are saying; remember what one once wanted; and, feeling the
loss, mourn. Then one must try to imagine having one's dream in a
new way and, finally, dare to act. James Baldwin, reviewing *The Arrangement,* Elia Kazan's novel about the mid-life crisis, described his
sense of the fissures that widen between self and dream, and the necessity of doing developmental work on the gaps. Baldwin was himself
in his early 40s.

> Though we would like to live without regrets, and sometimes proud-
> ly insist that we have none, this is not really possible, if only be-
> cause we are mortal. When more time stretches behind than stretches
> before one, some assessments, however reluctantly and incomplete-
> ly, begin to be made. Between what one wishes to become and what
> one *has* become there is a momentous gap, which will now never
> be closed. And this gap seems to operate as one's final margin, one's
> last opportunity, for creation. And between the self as it is and the
> self as one sees it, there is also a distance, even harder to gauge.
> Some of us are compelled, around the middle of our lives, to make
> a study of this baffling geography, less in the hope of conquering
> these distances than in the determination that the distance shall not
> become any greater.[26]

It takes courage to risk an encounter with inner promptings that
may prove incompatible with the life to which one is committed. As
Freud entered his mid-life transition, increasing doubts about the seduction theory, the value of his work more generally, and the person he
thought himself to be came to Freud as an unwelcome surprise. These

doubts arose unbidden and, jeopardizing his dream as they did, produced strange states of mind that made it impossible for him to go on living and working as usual. Taking these thoughts, feelings, and peculiar moods seriously meant Freud had to face his own aroused superego, for a reappraisal of this sort cannot be done bloodlessly. Again and again, Freud accused himself of being stupid, lazy, clinically inept, neurotic (even crazy), and a failure. Yet rather than try to suppress the developmental problem, he *chose* to engage himself in it fully over a period of many months.

During these months Freud grappled with his particular version of fundamental mid-life questions: What does my work amount to? Why can't I find the origin of neurosis? How am I using my scientific talent and training? Why won't my biological ideas keep up with my psychological ones? What would Brücke think about my work? What does Breuer think? Who am I and what do I really care about? Shouldn't I go back to anatomy, which is so satisfying, and where I know what I'm doing? Is there enough time left, and do I have sufficient energy and intelligence to make fundamental discoveries? What will happen to my children and my family, if I fail? Should we emigrate to Australia? What should I *do*? Trying to decide what to do meant more than tabulating a list of pros and cons. Developmental work on these questions took various forms—from dreaming, remembering, and fantasizing; through anxious worrying, preoccupation, brooding, and stewing; to systematic self-analysis.

The developmental work of transitional periods is often difficult, but we do not equate transitions with crises. A crisis can occur during any period of the life cycle. *The Oxford English Dictionary* tells us that in its Greek origins the word *crisis* meant "decide." A crisis occurs when the individual can see no way of proceeding on the developmental work that confronts him, as was the case with Freud in 1897, when he was 41.

## Mid-Life Individuation

I had read the Freud–Fliess correspondence several times before I noticed how frequently Freud used pregnancy and germination imagery in accounts of his own creativity during his early 40s. It was not something I was looking for nor something that interested me greatly on theoretical grounds. I had completed a psychobiographical study of Samuel Johnson without needing the notion of a masculine–feminine polarity, and I was content to do so again with Freud. When finally I did notice the imagery of pregnancy and germination, I then examined the years prior to Freud's mid-life transition to see if this had been a customary mode of expression for him. It had not. There was only one occasion in the more than 60 letters prior to age 39 when Freud expressed himself in this way.[27] I have examined each instance of this imagery in the German, and in each instance but two the feminine imagery emanates directly from the definitional meaning of the words.[28] Freud's frequent and sometimes dramatic references to pregnancy and to the further maturing of his ideas postpartum certainly call into question the stereotype of Freud as the prototypical Victorian man.

I have noticed this phenomenon in other men at mid-life as well. The notion of mid-life individuation may shed some light on this curious phenomenon. In Levinson's theory, personality individuation is a central task of the mid-life transition, and I have found that processes of personality change are heightened during transitional periods generally. Clearly, personality individuation involves questions of identity. In Freud's case, which I believe is typical, a fully adult identity could not be achieved prior to successful conclusion of the mid-life transition, at about age 45. Indeed, the work of authentic identity is a lifelong project.

As both Jung and Levinson have argued, mid-life individuation involves the integration of psychic polarities, central among which are the masculine and feminine aspects. If a man's personality is not simply to close up from the dwindling of the biological fires, perhaps he needs to make room within for the internal feminine to animate him. This would be especially true to the extent that biologically propelled sexual relations with women are diminishing. Developing his relationship to the feminine as an internal figure may hold out for the man the possibility of continued creative inspiration and growth.

The feminine imagery that emerged during Freud's mid-life transition coincided with a change in his manner of doing creative work. Freud adopted a passive, receptive stance, *awaiting* thrusts or pushes from his unconscious. He no longer tried simply to subdue intellectual problems by brute force of the scientific will that Brücke had instilled in him. As an example, consider the letter Freud wrote Fliess on May 16, 1897, 10 days after his 41st birthday. Amidst gathering doubts about the seduction theory, Freud told Fliess, "No matter where I start, I always am right back with the neuroses and with the [psychic] apparatus." He then added:

> It certainly is neither personal nor objective indifference if I cannot get my pen to write anything else. It ferments and bubbles in me, it only awaits a new thrust. I cannot make up my mind about writing the preliminary outline of the total work [on the theory of neurosis] you desire; I believe what prevents me is an obscure expectation that shortly something essential will turn up.

In his dream about old Brücke described earlier, Freud was assisted in the dissection of his own pelvis and legs by an acquaintance, Louise N. This woman had provided the day residue for the dream by asking Freud to recommend something for her to read; he had suggested the novel *She,* by Rider Haggard. "A strange book," he had told her, "but full of hidden meaning . . . the eternal feminine, the immortality of our emotions." In interpreting his dream Freud also recalled that there is a guide in the novel *She* and that the guide is a woman.[29]

## The Imagery of Masculine and Feminine

In my use of them the terms *masculine* and *feminine* are free of intrinsic gender linkages. Their meanings derive from a social process of *gender splitting,* a process in which a culture distributes (unequally) between the sexes aspects of human personality.[30] The degree of splitting varies from culture to culture and from one period in the history of a given culture to another. Within a given culture individuals internalize gender iconography, a process that compels them to develop qualities attributed to their own sex and, in some measure, to suppress qualities of the other. It then becomes the person's burden to keep the other sex's characteristics undeveloped within; ironically, one of the individuation tasks of transitional periods is to better integrate these characteristics into the personality.

Despite efforts within Western societies to reduce the splitting, being masculine continues generally to mean being dominating (cold-bloodedly), rational, protective, aggressive, whereas being feminine means being submissive, emotional, nurturing, receptive. These underlying cultural prescriptions do not necessarily obtain behaviorally on an individual level. A given man may be more submissive than a given woman and a particular woman may be more aggressive and heartless than a particular man, but the underlying images of what we are supposed to be like change very slowly — at a rate much slower than the speed of political rhetoric.

## Validity and Usefulness
## of the Age-Linked Eras and Periods

Numerous doctoral dissertations applying Levinson's theory of age-linked eras and periods have been completed over the past decade and have shed new light on women's development. The findings of several of these studies are reviewed in my article with Priscilla Roberts. The doctoral studies have ranged in method from the intensive biographical interviewing of small samples to archival studies of single individuals, such as Zelda Fitzgerald, Melanie Klein, and the poet Hilda Doolittle. Now in press is Levinson's study of 45 women, entitled *The Seasons of a Woman's Life,* which illustrates how well the conception of age-linked eras and periods works in studying women's lives. Nonetheless, the idea of age-linked periods during the adult years is not widely accepted. I certainly do not believe that its validity has been established, nor is it my purpose to attempt to do so through the examination of a single life.

Psychologists, teachers, and educated people generally have grown accustomed to thinking of the era of preadulthood as consisting in discrete yet partially overlapping age-linked periods, such as the oral, anal, genital, latency, puberty, and adolescence. Research, theory making, and clinical work have been enriched by this also unproven developmental model. Psychoanalytic theorists and investigators continue to produce interesting and valuable work on the formation of personality in earliest childhood. This work elaborates, modifies, and strengthens the foundation of the theoretical mansion that Freud began. But before the family can move in, the ground and upper floors where they will live have to be built. No amount of work on the foundation will make the house even minimally adequate. We must complete the theory of psychological development for the adult years, the remaining three quarters of life, for which childhood and adolescence are only preparatory and about which so much understanding is needed and so little is known. *To do this, we must seriously entertain the idea that age-linked developmental periods continue.* It is the notion of an age-linked sequence of developmental periods, beginning with Freud and Abraham's psychosexual stages, that has made useful argument possible about development in childhood. There are important differences between the Freud–Abraham conception and, say, that of Melanie Klein. But to investigate these differences becomes pointless without the elemental agreement among all theorists that the oral phase of development begins at birth and lasts until about age two. Here, it is the implicit age linkage that creates sufficient order to make contrasting views illuminating. As Wollheim has recently written, Freudian explanation "contextualizes" desire, conflict, and action in terms of childhood developmental stages.[31] Levinson and I seek to extend this contextualization to include developmental stages beyond childhood and adolescence.

Without the notion of underlying age linkages, no sequencing of developmental periods is possible, and we are lost amidst a welter of critical life events occurring at greatly varying points in the life cycle for different individuals. At this level, no order can be found, nor do

Levinson and I believe any exists beyond the most crudely probabilistic (e.g., that in the developed countries the death of one's parents is likely to precede the death of one's siblings). We believe that our theory of the age linkages provides a good balance between order and flexibility. For example, we say that the mid-life transition usually begins at 40 and ends at 45. Empirically, we note an age variance of about two years for the onset and termination of this and other periods. Thus, in any individual case, the mid-life transition might begin as early as 38 or as late as 42.

Some essential framing in of the upper floors has already been done. Following the pioneering work of Jung, Jaques, and Erikson, Levinson in particular has elaborated a floor plan for early adulthood and the transition to middle age. His theory organizes our thinking about middle adulthood and old age and "contextualizes" findings from the many studies in academic social science on critical life events, stress and coping, occupational and family careers, and the like. Levinson and other theorists have made it possible to approach the individual as a person located at a particular point in the life cycle, a life cycle that has a generational substructure, and to see him or her as engaged in developmental concerns that arise from that substructure and are held in common with others located in the same period. The ways in which the person negotiates the periods, the intrapsychic conflicts that complicate the developmental work and the capacities that facilitate it, and the meanings these have for the individual are distinct and, in their overall configuration, unique. But we can conceive of the developmental problems the person grapples with as universal and timeless.

In this view, great men and women grapple with the same age-generated tasks as the rest of us but by ability, ambition, and historical circumstance are better able to exploit them. The transitional periods in particular are pregnant with possibilities for new beginnings. Freud chose to make full use of them. He might instead have chosen to stay with the work of his 30s, as, for example, Samuel Johnson did in writing the dictionary of the English language (in "beating the path of the alphabet," as he put it), thus suppressing the developmental forces and avoiding the work of the period. Had he done so, Freud might have had a successful but historically insignificant career as a psychotherapist and neuropsychiatrist and learned to live with the failure to realize his dream. Or, like Johnson, he might have found himself unable to continue his work at 48 and severely depressed and utterly immobilized by 50. In time, other psychiatrists would have generated psychodynamic insights, since the data were everywhere and existing explanations and therapeutic procedures were so inadequate. The insights issued from so many ambitious minds would have employed different concepts, language, and imagery and could not have formed a coherent whole. Academic psychology, which has had no great founding genius, is a case in point; it remains a formless aggregate of unintegrated areas of study united only by a devotion to measurement. It seems unlikely that one person would have achieved the great, evolving, and (imperfectly) synthetic theoretical work that Freud wrought during the second half of his life, nor would Freud have achieved it had he not first succeeded in his own development and provided so inspiring a target for emulation and attack.

# CHAPTER TWO

# The Stuff of Dreams

## CULTURAL AND FAMILIAL THREADS

I cannot offer here anything beyond a suggestion of the overall *Zeit-geist* and historical circumstance in which Freud grew up. But I do want to emphasize one central part of the *Zeitgeist,* namely, the idea of progress, because it is important to an understanding of Freud's early dream and to his identifications with his scientific mentors. We stand today on the opposite side from the young Freud of a great dividing line in man's faith in reason, a line drawn by the First World War. It was then that the presumed unity of science and progress was rent asunder, as the advanced technology of warfare created human devastation on an undreamed-of scale.

If the First World War taught us that science and progress are not intrinsically united, the Second World War raised the specter that they may be inimical. No psychoanalyst today, beyond the minuscule number of the demonic and demented, believes that his or her theorizing will bring about a general betterment of the human condition. Social scientists and clinicians hope their work will be of use to students and patients and that people in general will find it illuminating. They hope to contribute something to the general store of knowledge, but they aim for little beyond that. By contrast, when Freud sought to understand neurosis, he was doing *science,* and doing so in the belief that neurosis could be cured not just now and then in some happy coincidence of nature, luck, and interpretation but in general. There are still medical researchers who pursue their work with Freud's zeal, but they, unlike Freud, cannot allow their thoughts to dwell on history, nor do they look out on a cultural landscape in which science and human betterment seem everywhere joined.

On May 25, 1895, shortly after his 39th birthday, Freud, who had been devoting every free moment to research, apologized to Fliess for having neglected their correspondence.

> [A] man like me cannot live without a hobbyhorse, without a consuming passion, without—in Schiller's words—a tyrant. I have found one. In its service I know no limits. It is psychology, which has always been my distant, beckoning goal, and which now, since I have come upon the problem of neuroses, has drawn so much nearer. I am tormented by two aims: to examine what shape the theory of mental functioning takes if one introduces quantitative considerations, a sort of economics of nerve forces; and, second, to peel off from psychopathology a gain for normal psychology.[1]

The idea of an "economics of nerve forces" arose from a positivist conception of psychology in which only physical forces needed to be taken into account. This conception of science was the one he had learned as a young medical student from his teachers, especially from Ernst Brücke. Brücke and his teacher, Hermann Helmholtz, had led a revolution against the romantic vitalist notions about human physiology that were still in currency in the mid-19th century. By the 1870s, they had succeeded. Thus, in 1876 when Freud joined Brücke's physiology laboratory as a 20-year-old medical student, he entered under the tutelage of a man whose ideas had carried the day and who radiated faith in scientific rationalism. Brücke believed devoutly that the application of quantitative materialism to the study of the nervous system would lead to discoveries of the greatest significance for human well-being.

Brücke's scientific faith, like positivism generally, was infused with the ideology of progress.[2] The idea of progress offered a conception of history in which mankind was seen as advancing indefinitely toward a state of future happiness and in which this advance was seen as inevitable, given the nature of both the individual and society. By the mid-1800s, it was becoming the dominant, organizing idea of European civilization. This belief was a source of optimism especially in the rising middle class. Its ethical corollary—the commandment to serve posterity—was the transcendent ideal toward which great efforts were directed and rationalized. One engaged in revolution, wrote constitutions, modernized cities, built businesses, and engaged in scientific research not for present gain, or for present gain alone, but for the happiness and well-being of future generations.

Though by 1850 the idea of progress was familiar to Europeans, it was not everywhere accepted. While historians had succeeded in casting doubt on the authorial integrity of the New Testament and geologists were discrediting the Old Testament account of genesis, it was not until the publication of Darwin's *Origin of Species* in 1859 that a scientific demonstration appeared that seemed to establish decisively the validity of the idea. And it is testimony to the fact that the idea of progress was becoming the intellectual common denominator of the time that Darwin's theory of natural selection did not generally give rise to gloomy thoughts about the future. People might have wondered what sorts of men and societies a changing environment would come to favor, but by and large they did not.[3] In the last half of the 19th century the idea of progress was so pervasive an assumption and the optimism that men invested and drew from it so buoyant that a happy reading of evolution prevailed.

Not just the intellectual but also the political climate of Freud's youth seemed to support the inevitability of progress. Prior to 1848 the Austrian Empire had been politically and economically backward compared with Western Europe.[4] It was a patchwork quilt of races and religions presided over by Europe's last remaining emperor, the amiable idiot Franz Ferdinand. Only Russia was more reactionary. The revolutions of 1848 in Vienna and elsewhere, though not successful in and of themselves, hastened an end to absolute monarchy. In Vienna the revolution was led by students from the university and by members of the liberal middle class. While small in number, Jews, including Freud's maternal uncle, were prominent among the student revolutionaries.[5] Ultimately, the revolution produced its own bloody excesses and was stamped out by the army. Important gains were temporarily lost. The constitution of 1848 was revoked in 1851, and some restrictions were reimposed in 1853. Yet the revolution succeeded in bringing about the replacement of the monarch by Franz Joseph, his more competent nephew, and in 1867 the creation of a constitutional monarchy in which the equality of all citizens and freedom of religion were guaranteed.

By the 1860s the liberal party was firmly in control of parliament. It represented the middle class, whose political and civil rights had now been made constitutional and were guaranteed by the emperor. These rights were formally extended to Austrian Jews in 1867, and restrictions on their travel and marriage were abolished. Thus, a kind of alliance existed in the post-1848 Austro-Hungarian Empire between the liberals and the monarchy. It lasted until the end of the century and undergirded the optimism and sense of progress of the newly rising middle class.

As Frederic Morton so evocatively describes, once liberated, the talented and ambitious from within the borders of the empire and from its far-flung provinces were drawn to the capital as though in anticipation of the realization of their dreams. The population of Vienna increased by a factor of 5 between 1848 and 1914, the city's Jewish population by a factor of 10 or more.[6] In 1869, when Freud was 13, there were some 40,000 Jews in Vienna; in 1900, when Freud was 44, there were 113,500; and by the end of the First World War, when Freud was 62, there were roughly 200,000.[7] The Freud family, including three-year-old Sigmund, came in 1859. Other luminaries-to-be among this migration to the new liberal Vienna were Theodor Herzl, future leader of Zionism; Gustav Mahler, who would become a revolutionary composer; Arthur Schnitzler, destined to be *the* playwright of the fin de siècle; Gustav Klimt, the revolutionary art nouveau painter-to-be; Viktor Adler, future socialist leader; and, in 1887, Wilhelm Fliess, who had come for a period of postgraduate study and a historic meeting with a young lecturer in neurology named Freud. In 1907, a young Hitler came too, possessed by an unrealistic dream of becoming a great painter.

## Freud's Parents, Amalia and Jacob

If Freud's goal of discovering the truth about the nature of the mind and its aberrations was grounded in the idea of progress and scientific positivism, his commitment to this grand enterprise was also initially shaped by the unfulfilled dreams of his parents, Jacob and Amalia. We do not know much about their dreams, but some inferences are possible based partly on new evidence brought to light by Krüll.[8]

Jacob Freud was born on December 18, 1815, in Tysmenitz, a small town in the eastern province of Galicia, now in the Ukraine. Tysmenitz, like Galicia more generally, was an early center for liberal Jewish thought. The town was a market for trade, and this made it permeable to the Enlightenment thinking that was sweeping across Europe. Jewish orthodoxy was also strong in Tysmenitz, and the community was divided by family-rending arguments between progressive and conservative coreligionists.[9] While still in Tysmenitz, Jacob married his first wife, Sally Kanner, at age 16 or 17. The couple had two sons, Emanuel and Philipp, and two other children, who died in childhood. Next to nothing is known about Sally. Beginning in the late 1830s, Jacob began accompanying his merchant grandfather, Abraham Siskind Hoffmann, on his westward business trips home to Moravia. The pair traveled between Galicia and Freiberg (now Příbor in the Czech Republic) trading wool, fabrics, suet, honey, anise, hides, salt, and other raw products. For this occupation they were required to register as *Wanderjuden,* Galician wandering Jews.[10]

The authorities in Moravia were in some ways more liberal than in Galicia, insisting, for example, that Jewish children assimilate by attending German-language public schools rather than Jewish religious ones. Contradictorily, the Austrian authorities in Moravia also insisted on restriction. Jews were allowed to live only in designated areas, such as special inns or spirit houses, and were prohibited from renting private quarters. In order to prevent Galician Jews from settling in Moravia, official "tolerances" were granted only for stays of six months. This meant that Jacob had to continually petition to have his residence permit extended in order to get his business done.

It was on these trips to Moravia that Jacob had his first direct contact with the new life possible for Jews. It was also on these 350-mile trips that the young man had his first relief from the watchful overseers of Jewish shtetl morality in Tysmenitz, where powerful taboos existed against any sexual expression other than that aimed at procreation within marriage. Even masturbation was expressly forbidden. Krüll speculates that on these occasions Jacob engaged in some sort of sexual transgression and that a burden of guilt was part of the legacy he passed on to Sigmund.[11]

The revolution of 1848 and the rights it secured for Jews finally made it possible for Jacob to secure permanent residence in Freiberg. Krüll writes, "The year 1848 must have been the turning point for Jacob Freud and for many Austrian Jews. It was probably then that he took the great step from the narrow life of the Orthodox Jews to that of the emancipated bourgeois and that he began to cut what ties still bound him to his old world."[12] It seems likely that these ties were never cut completely and that both orthodox and assimilationist tendencies coexisted in Jacob.[13]

When Jacob's first wife, Sally, died in 1852, he may have married a woman named Rebekka, about whom even less is known than about Sally. She is presumed to have died shortly after their marriage, for in 1855 Jacob, now a resident of Freiberg, married Amalia Nathansohn. Amalia had been born in Brody in eastern Galicia on August 18, 1835, she had moved to Vienna as a child, living there until she met and married Jacob. At the time of their marriage (July 29, 1855) Jacob was 40 and Amalia 20. The sons from his first marriage, Philipp and Emanuel, were roughly the age of Jacob's new wife.

It is not difficult to imagine why Jacob remarried. He was 40 and, bereft of at least one wife, was beginning life in a new town. But why did this pretty young woman marry Jacob? What were her dreams and how could a future with Jacob fulfill them? He was a full generation older, had grown children of his own, and had proposed to cart her off to a large rented room above a blacksmith's shop near the market square of a provincial village.[14] Surely Amalia had or could imagine better possibilities. Perhaps the marriage was arranged, though the advantage this would have brought her family is unclear. Or perhaps she thought Jacob's circumstances grander than they were. There is some evidence that she was disappointed when she first saw her new home in Freiberg.[15]

The cultural elite among European Jewry was German. As one moved west from eastern Europe toward the German-speaking lands, one ascended the social ladder.[16] Yet Amalia was already living in Vienna by the time Jacob moved to Freiberg, and his origins in Galicia were hardly less provincial than hers.[17] Jacob liked to maintain that his people had been longtime settlers of the German Rhineland around Cologne before being driven east by anti-Semitic attacks, and perhaps Amalia found some charm in Jacob's depicting his odyssey from Tysmenitz to Freiberg (and soon to Vienna) as a *return* to German Austria. It is possible that Jacob promised his young bride a quick return to Vienna should life in the provinces not suit her, for return quickly they did.

We know little about Amalia as a young, or even middle-aged, woman. We know that her family was not much better off financially than Jacob.[18] Her grandson Martin Freud, who sounds rather critical of her, described Amalia in her later years as "a tornado," "indomitable," and "highly intelligent," and as impatient, uncouth, and vain.[19] He recounted Amalia's violent refusal at 90 to consider a new hat that she thought aged her. At 95, two weeks before her death, she complained that a poor reproduction of a photograph in the newspaper made her look 100, a remark that may suggest ironic perspective as well as vanity.[20] Amalia was, Martin wrote, "emotional and untamed, full of life and vitality" and "a typical Polish Jewess, with all the shortcomings that that implies."[21] "These Galician Jews," Martin opined, "had little grace and no manners. . . . They were highly emotional and easily carried away by their feelings."[22]

Amalia does seem to have had a keen appreciation for heroic deeds, a trait Martin also attributed to her ethnic origins. According to him, it was the men of Amalia's branch of Jewry alone who fought the Nazis in the Polish ghetto: "Whenever you hear of Jews showing violence or belligerence, instead of that meekness and what seems poor-spirited acceptance of a hard fate sometimes associated with Jewish peoples, you may safely suspect the presence of men and women of Amalia's race."[23] As an old lady, Amalia proudly recounted for Martin's benefit the leading role taken by Jewish students, including two of her own brothers, at the University of Vienna in the revolution of 1848.[24] Sigmund, too, must have heard these stories when he was growing up.

If dreams of conquest slumbered in Amalia's young mind, marriage to Jacob soon provided her with a possible means for their realization. Nine months and one week after their wedding, Sigismund Schlomo, the conquistador, was born.[25] In a year and a half, the family expanded further with the birth of little Julius. Six months later Julius contracted enteritis and died. Then, in the midst of her grief, Amalia found she was pregnant again, with Anna.

Exactly a month before Julius died, Amalia's youngest brother, Julius, the child's eponym, had died of tuberculosis.[26] The combination of the two losses must have been a terrible blow. There is a photograph of Amalia five years later, in 1864, with her sixth-born, baby Dolfi, on her lap. Her daughter Rosa and eight-year-old Sigmund stand at her side. When this photograph was taken, Dolfi was about the same age as Julius when he died. The young mother's face looks drawn and depressed. In fact, they all look depressed.

In the year before Sigmund's birth, Jacob's records show the beginning of a radical decline in the volume of wool he was able to trade.[27] A railroad had bypassed the town and diminished its value as a market center. In addition, the new machine manufacture of textiles was rendering Jacob's handmade products uncompetitive.[28] Entering middle age, amidst the pressures and pleasures of his young second family, Jacob was forced in 1859 to leave Freiberg in search of employment.[29] The family first tried Leipzig, and after a brief unsuccessful stay they went on to Vienna. At 24, after a separation of four years, Amalia was coming home. With her was Sigmund, three; Anna, one; and another baby, Rosa, growing inside. The Freud family established temporary quarters in Leopoldstadt, the site of the old Jewish ghetto in Vienna. Several moves within the city followed.

Jacob Freud never recouped financially. At mid-life he was a failed merchant. Martin wrote that his grandfather "had much charm, but not much luck in his business affairs in Vienna. . . . [He] became gradually helpless and ineffective in his efforts to bring up his family really well."[30] Instead, Jacob metamorphosed into a successful autodidact, released now by ill fortune to pursue in middle age what many Jews thought was the true calling, the study of the sacred Hebrew writings.[31] Freud recalled his father as far from crushed and as having a merry heart to go with his unrealistic schemes. Describing his father, then 69, to his fiancée in a letter written when he was 27, Freud wrote: "Yesterday I met Father in the street, still full of projects, still hoping. I took it upon myself to write to Emanuel and Philipp urging them to help Father out of his present predicament."[32] Like the hapless Mr. Micawber in Dickens's *David Copperfield,* Jacob lived in the confident expectation that something would soon turn up. Nothing ever did.

Freud's niece, Judith Bernays Heller, who as a child lived with
Jacob and Amalia, confirmed the contrast in their temperaments. She
described Jacob as easygoing and bookish, Amalia as volatile and
vain.[33] Freud's younger brother, Alexander, Jacob's other surviving
son from Amalia, seems to have inherited his father's eupeptic disposition.[34] Sigmund, on the other hand, appears to have inherited his
mother's. He wrote his fiancée, Martha, about his characterological
defiance, and his readiness to die fighting for a worthy cause.[35] Certainly as an adult Freud was a passionate person and easily angered,
although he typically allowed himself only a defiant glare for expression. His self-control was great, but it was control in the Nietzschean
sense of self-overcoming. Freud gained his understanding of the instincts and the problem of their sublimation from direct experience:
He could strike and strike hard, but he chose not to.[36] Meeting Freud
as an old man, Virginia Woolf described him as a half-extinct volcano.

Amalia is said to have had a marked preference for her sons.[37]
Both parents, according to Martin, recognizing early that their firstborn was gifted, firmly believed he would one day be famous.[38] According to Anna, Amalia felt that her son would become famous with
a degree of conviction that exceeded the expectable lunacies of parental narcissism. Young Sigmund evidently agreed: When the four-year-
old soiled one of his mother's chairs, he told her not to worry. "When
I grow up I shall be a great man and then I'll buy you another
chair."[39] Martin's description of family gatherings at Grandmother
Amalia's apartment conveys her excitement about her eldest:

> These were on Christmas Day and New Year's Eve, for Amalia ig-
> nored Jewish feasts. The meals showed opulence; we were usually
> offered roast goose, candied fruits, cakes and punch—the last-named
> being in a weakened form for us children. When I was young, my
> Uncle Alexander was still unmarried, and he took charge of the en-
> tertainment side of the gatherings. He was the heart and soul of
> the parties. He arranged games so that they were played in order,
> and poems, written for each occasion, were recited and given full
> applause.
>
> But always, as the evening went on, an atmosphere of grow-
> ing crisis was felt by all as Amalia became unsettled and anxious.
> There are people who, when they are unsettled and disturbed, will
> hide these feelings because they do not want to affect the peace of
> those around them; but Amalia was not one of these. My father al-
> ways came to these gatherings—I know of no occasion when he dis-
> appointed her—but his working day was a long one and he always
> came much later than any one else. Amalia knew this, but perhaps
> it was a reality she could never accept. Soon she would be seen run-

ning anxiously to the door and out to the landing to stare down the staircase. Was he coming? Where was he? Was it not getting very late? This running in and out might go on for an hour, but it was known that any attempt to stop her would produce an outburst of anger which it was better to avoid by taking as little notice as possible. And my father always came at very much his usual time, but never at a moment when Amalia was waiting for him on the landing.[40]

It seems reasonable to imagine that Amalia, constrained by the severely reduced circumstances of life with Jacob and their large family, was frustrated in the expression of her own heroic strivings and that she passed these strivings on to her "golden son" Sigismund.[41] These fantasies may have been not merely heroic but defiantly so. Achieving wealth or fame would not have sufficed; her firstborn son would have to wrest victory from a prejudiced opposition and become a conquering hero, like the Semite Hannibal, Freud's boyhood idol who made mighty Rome quake. As Freud later wrote of mothers and sons, a mother "can transfer to her son the ambition which she had been obliged to suppress in herself, and she can expect from him the satisfaction of all that has been left over in her of her masculinity complex."[42]

Satisfaction was the word, for at her son's 70th birthday celebration, Amalia introduced herself to one of his students with the simple announcement "I am the mother."[43] Toward the end of her life, she had a dream of her son's funeral in which his casket was attended by the heads of state of the major European nations.[44] She would not be far wrong.

# CHAPTER THREE

# Dream Weaving
## (Birth to Age 17)

Freud liked to remember the early years of his childhood as idyllic. In so doing, he may have been recalling the original bliss of his first 18 months with Amalia, a lost bliss that he ever after associated with his birthplace. On the occasion of his 75th birthday, he wrote the mayor of Freiberg thanking him for a commemorative ceremony in his honor: "Deep within me, although overlaid, there continues to live the happy child from Freiberg, the first-born son of a youthful mother, the boy who received from this air, from this soil, the first indelible impressions."[1] Indeed, I suspect that leaving Freiberg at the age of three was, among few others, a watershed event in Freud's life, one that left him psychologically ever after an exile. Among its professional consequences would be Freud's later scientific and clinical obsession with origins; one of the more personal manifestations would be his implacable hatred for Vienna.

If the Freiberg of Freud's birth, on May 6, 1856, had seemed like paradise, it did not last long. Freud had scarcely had a look around before his little brother, Julius, was born. Among the memories Freud recovered during his mid-life transition was how he had greeted his "one-year younger brother . . . with bad wishes and real childhood jealousy" and how Julius's death had left him with "the germ" of self-reproach.[2] One also imagines that Amalia's emotional availability to her son must have diminished for some months following the deaths of her brother and infant Julius in April 1858. It does appear that for the next nine months, until Anna's birth in December, his nursemaid became more important to Sigmund. Perhaps with the nursemaid he

38

could safely displace part of his love for his mother, since as a substitute she could not wound him so cruelly as Amalia had with Julius and was now doing again with a new pregnancy.

Unfortunately, Sigmund soon suffered the further misfortune of losing his nursemaid. While Amalia was confined giving birth to Anna, his adult half brother Philipp caught the nursemaid stealing and had her arrested. Freud recounted the memory to Fliess at 41, as he was trying to reconstruct his childhood for self-analysis:

> My mother was nowhere to be found; I was crying in despair. My brother Philipp . . . unlocked a wardrobe . . . for me, and when I did not find my mother inside it either, I cried even more until, slender and beautiful, she came in through the door. What can this mean? Why did my brother unlock the wardrobe for me? . . . When I missed my mother, I was afraid she had vanished from me, just as the old woman had a short time before. So I must have heard that the old woman had been locked up and therefore must have believed that my mother had been locked up too.[3]

The disruption in Freud's relationship with his mother brought about by the birth of Julius and Anna would recur five more times in the next eight years and, as Freud later said, pose for him the urgent problem of solving the mystery of his mother's "slender and beautiful" body and its fecundity.[4] Still later, Freud universalized the problem and wrote that the first stimulus to all research is the birth of a sibling, with the first research task being to discover where babies come from so as to prevent reoccurrences.[5] In this distressing perplexity lay a precursor of Freud's dream of great scientific discovery.

## A Screen Memory

Writing in his essay "Screen Memories" at 43, Freud adopted the curious expedient of describing scenes from his own childhood and adolescence as though they were being remembered by one of his patients and recounted in psychotherapy. The "patient" has since been discovered to be fictional.[6] The lengthiest of these memories is from very early childhood and concerns playing in a field of grass and picking yellow dandelions with his cousin John and his niece, Pauline. The two boys stole the girl's flowers and made her cry, but she was consoled by a peasant woman who gave her a delicious slice of freshly baked bread; abandoning their flowers, the boys got some bread, too. Ever after, Freud remembered the unnatural intensity of the yellow of the flowers and the spectacular flavor of the black bread.

Here is Freud *qua* patient remembering the loss of his birthplace:

> When I was about three, the branch of industry in which my father
> was concerned met with a catastrophe. He lost all his means and
> we were forced to leave the place and move to a large town. Long
> and difficult years followed, of which, as it seems to me, nothing
> was worth remembering. I never felt really comfortable in the town.
> I believe now that I was never free from a longing for the beautiful
> woods near our home, in which . . . I used to run off from my
> father, almost before I had learnt to walk.[7]

At 41, Freud wrote Fliess that his "libido toward *matrem* was
awakened . . . on the occasion of a journey with her from Leipzig to
Vienna, during which [they] must have spent the night together and
there must have been an opportunity of seeing her *nudam*." Freud was
three and a half when the family traveled from Leipzig to Vienna in
search of a living after the collapse of Jacob's business in Moravia.
The trip took place in the winter of 1859–1860. Freud's sister Rosa
was born in March of 1860, so the naked mother that Freud saw was
visibly pregnant. And the three-and-a-half-year-old little boy was old
enough to have begun having sexual feelings about her.[8]

## Exiled in Vienna

Now, as Freud's fictive patient described, the screen grew dark for the
next three or four years, years during which his Oedipus complex would
first have germinated and then become dormant. In contrast to the
vivid sensory, especially visual, memories of his first three years, Freud's
memories at age four or five were subdued and discontinuous. Perhaps
Sigmund had already seen and heard too much in the family apartment in Freiberg before he developed his powers of repression. Un-
psychoanalytically, Freud told his colleague Ernest Jones that he did
not remember his first several years in Vienna because they "were hard
times and not worth remembering."[9] Certainly, the part of Leopoldstadt the Freud family dwelt in was dismal, and it was rendered more
so by the contrast to Freiberg.[10] The crowding in the Jewish quarter
was terrific, with individuals subletting portions of their own single-
room dwellings to whole families. This sort of crowding favored the
spread of infectious diseases of all kinds, with tuberculosis claiming
the most deaths. Jacob settled his family first at 114 Weissgärberstrasse;
then four years later at Pillersdorfgasse; and then in 1869 or 1870,
when Freud was 14, at 1 Pfeffergasse. In 1872 they moved again, and
then did so a final time to Kaiser Josefstrasse two years later, when
Freud was 19.[11]

Already bad, the Freud's financial situation worsened in Vienna. There is no record there of Jacob's having resumed any sort of regular business. Rather, the family appears to have gotten along on handouts from Amalia's parents, from Jacob's brother Josef, and perhaps also from fees Jacob could charge for helping merchants make contacts among his business acquaintances in Moravia and Galicia. By 1775, when Freud had entered the university, the family was doing better, helped along by gifts from Amalia's brother Simon and perhaps also through the largess of Philipp and Emanuel.[12] The half brothers had decamped for England when the rest of the family left Freiberg and had made successes of themselves in the woolen textile industry in Manchester.[13]

## Salvation by Thought

When Jacob left Freiberg in 1859, he carried with him an illustrated Bible with both Hebrew and German texts. It was the Bible of the *Haskalah,* the enlightened assimilationist Jews.[14] Jacob gave it to Sigmund on his son's 35th birthday with the following inscription:

> My dear Son,
>     It was in the seventh year of your age that the spirit of God began to move you to learning. I would say the spirit of God speaketh to you: "Read in My book; there will be opened to thee sources of knowledge and of the intellect." It is the Book of Books; it is the well that wise men have digged and from which lawgivers have drawn the waters of their knowledge.[15]

Like that of most children at around age seven, Sigmund's cognitive development had advanced to the point where his thinking was in the main realistic, or governed, as he would later put it, by the reality principle rather than the pleasure principle. This new ability, together with his extraordinary intelligence (and his father's example and guidance), provided him with the means for solving the problem of what to do with his worries about babies and his preoccupation with his mother's body. He would turn these into intellectual curiosity and use it to pull away from the lost continent of his early childhood. Jacob was ready and able to supervise Sigmund's new devotion to learning, and he did so until his son entered the Gymnasium.[16] By the age of eight, Sigmund was reading and collecting books avidly. By nine, he was ready to enter school a year early.

Freud recalled a memory from age seven or eight of urinating in his parents' bedroom in their presence, a memory that may reflect comingled oedipal defiance and identification with his father. Jacob got angry and declared that Sigmund would come to nothing. This attack wounded him and seemed to deepen his resolve to earn his father's love. Indeed, years later Jacob's dismissal still haunted his dreams, and he often found himself listing accomplishments to combat it. In *The Interpretation of Dreams* Freud presented this childhood memory as an association to one of his own dreams, the second part of which involved helping a blind old man use a portable urinal. A further association involved the fact that Freud was the first to discover the anesthetic properties of cocaine, a discovery that proved particularly useful in operations on the eye, an operation Jacob had in 1885 and at which Freud assisted as a physician. The dream seemed to say, "You see I *have* amounted to something and have made reparation for hurting you too."[17]

## A Question of Fraudulence

In 1866, when Sigmund was nine, a strange and poorly understood event occurred. Josef, Jacob's brother, was convicted of passing counterfeit money. The counterfeit bills originated in England and may have been part of a scheme to get money to Polish nationalists who were fighting for independence. It is possible that Sigmund's half brothers, Philipp and Emanuel, were involved and that their departure for Manchester at the time of Jacob's move to Vienna was to avoid detection. We know about the incident mainly from another dream that Freud reproduced and analyzed in his *The Interpretation of Dreams*. In his book he recounted that his father's hair had turned gray from grief within days of his brother's arrest. The grief may have been adulterated with anxiety, since there is some evidence that Jacob and his older sons were implicated in Josef Freud's schemes. Or it may be that they were not directly involved but that Josef was helping to support Jacob with forged bank notes.[18] As noted, there is no record of Jacob's doing any work to support the family in Vienna.

If Jacob was a suitable model for boyish bookishness, he was also sufficiently unheroic for the pubescent Freud to de-idealize him. When Freud was 10 or 12, Jacob told him the now well-known story of an anti-Semite's knocking his hat into the mud in Freiberg:

"And what did you do?" I asked. "I went into the roadway and picked up my cap," was [Jacob's] quiet reply. This struck me as unheroic conduct on the part of the big, strong man who was holding the little boy by the hand. I contrasted this situation with another which fitted my feelings better: The scene in which Hannibal's father, Hamilcar Barca, made his boy swear before the household altar to take vengeance on the Romans. Ever since that time Hannibal had had a place in my phantasies.[19]

Freud did not know that the liberal tolerance that prevailed in the Austria of his youth was a fragile novelty and that assertiveness in Jews was more acceptable then than in his father's day. Besides, approaching adolescence he needed to knock his father down a peg or two. We know that after a visit to England at 19 Freud had fantasies of how much better it would have been if he had been his half brother Emanuel's son rather than Jacob's.[20] He may have had thoughts of this sort earlier in his adolescence as well.

Yet however Micawberesque and eupeptic Jacob might have been, he was still a Jewish father with millennia of paternal authority on his side and of an age to command considerable respect. There was little danger that Sigmund would carry his disillusionment with Jacob to extremes. A contemporary of young Freud's named Rosenthal told of arguing with his own father in the street when Jacob came along. "What," Jacob exclaimed, "are you contradicting your father? My Sigmund's little toe is cleverer than my head, but he would never dare to contradict me!"[21] I believe that Jacob remained in Freud's imagination a worthy but not overpowering antagonist for his oedipal rivalry.

As for himself, Freud was always ready for a fight. Although it was a time of official tolerance toward Jews, he sensed anti-Semitic feeling among some of the boys at the Gymnasium. It was in this context that his identification with Hannibal and other warlike Semitic heroes—not to mention Amalia—strengthened.

## A Chum

At the Leopoldstädter Gymnasium Freud came under the influence of an older boy, Heinrich Braun, who led him into a period of rebelliousness and lowered academic achievement in the second half of his sophomore year.[22] Ultimately, however, despite this delinquent detour, Freud excelled at the Gymnasium. He graduated summa cum laude after passing written examinations in German, Latin, Greek, and mathematics and oral examinations in a variety of subjects. At the Gymnasium he made a best friend, as important an event for his emotional growth and well-being as his academic success was for his intellect. Without Eduard Silberstein or someone like him Freud might well have developed an obsessive–compulsive neurosis given his intensifying book-ishness and the oedipal conflicts it defended him against. The relation-ship with Silberstein also provided a creatively regressive outlet for oedipal anxieties about his adolescent de-idealization of his father and its displacement in antiauthority attitudes generally. The two boys creat-ed a private society, the Spanish Academy, with themselves as its only members. They named themselves after Cervantes's dogs, Cipion and Berganza, and insulted friends, teachers, and parents in letters to each other in rudimentary Spanish, which they preserved in secret archives. Whatever the calumnies expressed and mischief engaged in, in this make-believe world they were, after all, only Quixotes—or playful puppies—not genuine rebels subject to a rebel's fate.

## A First Love and Another Disappointment

Whe Freud was 11, a fortune teller predicted that he would become a cabinet minister. This was very much the sort of future—success in a dramatic, public way—Amalia seems to have had in mind for her boy and one newly possible for a Jew in the Vienna of the Liberal Party. Freud even had a card made up: *Sigismund Freud: Student der Rechte.*[23] Indeed, both he and Silberstein were set on careers in law. In this, Freud was following the example of Heinrich Braun. Before long, however, Freud would abandon law, deviate from his mother's wishes, and separate his future from that of his friends.

During the summer of 1871 Freud and Silberstein traveled to Freiberg for a holiday. On this trip Freud stayed with the large and prosperous Fluss family, whom the Freuds had known since their Freiberg days.[24] There he became infatuated with one of their daugh-ters, Gisela.[25] Gisela was about 12, the same age as Freud's beauti-ful and favorite younger sister, Rosa. Gisela already had many admirers and seems not to have noticed Freud. Freud later told her brother Emil, who had been promoting the liaison, that during this visit he and his friend Silberstein had "represented only a minute fraction of a large group whose pearl was 'Ichthyosaura.' "[26] Freud nicknamed Gisela "Ichthyosaura" after an extinct river dweller. *Fluss* means "river" in German, and the *Ichthyosaura* was the subject of a popular poem of the day.[27] Apparently, the Fluss family visited Vienna the following spring and summer, for Freud wrote Silberstein in March 1872 of be-ing disappointed at having seen Emil but not his sister and in July of not having seen Gisela for two weeks.[28] Indeed, Boehlich surmises that it was this first trip to Freiberg and Freud's infatuation that led to the formation of the Spanish Academy and the necessity of a secret code for all written communications concerning girls.

The next summer Freud made a second visit to Freiberg, this time alone. He was 16. Freud had his fictional patient recall that visit too in the paper on screen memories:

> [When I returned to Freiberg] I could compare the comfort reigning there with our own style of living at home in the town. . . . I must admit that there was something else that excited me powerfully. I was seventeen, and in the family where I was staying there was a daughter of fifteen, with whom I immediately fell in love. It was my first calf-love and sufficiently intense, but I kept it completely secret.

The girl soon went back to school, and Freud's imaginary patient moped about the fields wishing he and his family had never left Freiberg:

> If only the smash had not occurred! If only I had stopped at home and grown up in the country and grown as strong as the young men in the house, the brothers of my love! . . . I can remember quite well for what a long time afterwards I was affected by the yellow colour of the dress she was wearing when we first met, whenever I saw the same colour anywhere else.[29]

Freud wrote Silberstein on August 17 of his infatuation with Gisela, admitting that he had begun a diary that he would show him later.[30] Yet Freud's timidity was such that he remained unable to speak to the girl; for her part, Gisela still showed little preference for what must have seemed to her to be an oddly intense, mute young man. On September 4, 1872, Freud told Silberstein that he had found Gisela's "beauty . . . wild, I might say Thracian: the aquiline nose, the long black hair, and the firm lips come from the mother, the dark complexion and the sometimes indifferent expression from the father."[31] Freud told his friend that his feelings for the young girl were so unsettling that he hoped her imminent departure would restore his equanimity. The reality of her departure proved different. Still in Freiberg, Freud wrote the following to Silberstein on September 4:

> On Wednesday . . . she departed, not without playing me a trick that annoyed me for some time. I said good-bye sadly and walked to Hochwald, my little paradise, where I spent a most pleasant hour. I have soothed all my turbulent thoughts and only flinch slightly when her mother mentions Gisela's name at table. The affection appeared like a beautiful spring day, and only the nonsensical Hamlet in me, my diffidence, stood in the way of my finding it a refreshing pleasure to converse with the half-naive, half-cultured young lady.
> One day I shall explain to you the difference between my affec-

tion and another passion at some length; for the moment let me just add that I did not suffer any conflict between ideal and reality, and that I am incapable of making fun of Gisela. So please avoid all allusions to her in the presence of Rosanes or others. His wit is like a distorting mirror; he must ridicule everything in order to render it ridiculous; he has no feeling for frankness or purity. . . . He could never feel passionate . . . and if he ever discovered our hearts' affections his first reaction would be to laugh and his second to be astonished.[32]

After Gisela's departure from Freiberg, Freud followed her to neighboring Roznau, 12 miles south of Freiberg at the foot of Mt. Radhost, only to find, like a knight returned from the Holy Land whose love had entered a nunnery (as he put it), that she had already left. Despite his irritation, he could not rid his mind of Gisela's image.[33] He began a novel about the search, *The Journey to Roznau,* and perhaps in an attempt to exorcise the entire affair, a second novel about Gisela as well.[34]

Freud was also smitten with Gisela's mother, Frau Fluss, whom he praised to his friend, trying to maintain that his love for the girl was only an extension of his admiration for her mother. In reading Freud's account to Silberstein, it is at times hard to tell when he is describing the mother and when the daughter. It seems true enough that in the verdant fecundities of Freiberg's meadows, Freud was emotionally back within the maternal paradise of his earliest days. But in the end, his attempt to pass off Gisela as merely a stand-in for her mother seems defensive and unconvincing. In reality, Gisela would turn out to be the only romance this passionate young man would have until he met Martha at age 25.[35]

## Hurt, Angry, and Disoriented

Back home in Vienna there ensued an eight-month period of painful self-doubt. Freud wrote Gisela's brother, Emil, of an inner "Tower of Babel" and of a merciless dissection of feelings that revealed the absence of inner certainty of either purpose or worth.[36] But he did not tell Emil that his state of mind had to do with Gisela. The correspondence with Gisela's brother seems to have constituted a compromise between Freud's need to express his feelings to someone close to her and his wish to hide his disappointment from the Flusses. In this scheme, he may have been trying to use Gisela's brother as a conduit, though whether Emil ever conveyed the desired impressions to his sister is unknown.

In the first of these letters to Emil, which he composed on returning to Vienna on September 18, 1872, Freud wrote of being depressed and dissociated. He had "lost almost all recollection of past events," felt "dazed," and had become passive and mute. Without mentioning Gisela, he filled pages with an account of an enchanting 12-year-old girl ("with the face of an angel") whom he had seen on the train to Vienna. He did not mention Gisela (abbreviated "Ich.") until the very end of the letter, as though he were sidestepping what distressed him until it could no longer be avoided. "I have faithfully told you my story," he wrote. "I shall spare you a description of my impression of Vienna. I felt disgusted. Farewell, and let me know whatever is of interest to a Freibergian and a friend of your family. Should you in your next letter," he concluded, "ask for the story about Ich. which I have not yet told you, I shall not refuse."[37]

Obligingly, Emil inquired. Now Freud could insult Gisela gratuitously without revealing his hurt and disappointment. In his next letter he insisted that his thoughts were only of his future profession. By contrast, Gisela and everything else that belonged to the past paled into insignificance. He told Emil that he was unwilling to cast himself in the role of lover, "least of all now when I have more serious things to think of."

> To satisfy your wish to reveal the [pre-Freiberg] events, as promised, is not easy. It makes me feel like a scientist who is asked about the past of our planet. This whole period is as remote to me as can be, however much it once seemed part of me. I have thrown myself heart and soul into the future. That at one time I found myself in one place, took refreshments at another—how soon do these things fade from memory if all one's concentration is on the goal alone!

The idea that he had been seriously affected by Gisela was absurd.

> But if you want me to entertain you with reports about Ichthyosaura, let me tell you that there was more irony, yes, mockery, than seriousness in this whole flirtation. You were never present at a meeting of the "Spanish Academy" (the name of our two-member society). But had you heard how the poor creature was torn to shreds, you would have had a different picture of "our" relationship to her. Any detailed description would have to be prefaced by Goethe's line: "A fairy-tale . . . it was once upon a time."[38]

## Out of a Personal Disappointment
## Emerges a New Future

In the next letter to Emil some five months later, on February 7, 1873, Freud, declaring himself "filled with envy," belittled an affectionate gesture shown to Emil by his girlfriend, Ottilie. Freud did so by dismissing as meaningless a similar act of preferment that Gisela had shown Silberstein on their first visit to Freiberg.[39] A subsequent letter on March 17 makes clear that Freud was putting the disappointment with Gisela to reactive uses. He began by granting Emil his triumph in love, then moved directly to the displacement of his own hopes into work:

> I shall no longer try to dispute your happiness. If, as you say so triumphantly, I was envious, there is now no longer any cause for it [because Emil and Ottilie were separated]. . . .
>
> As for me, I can report what is perhaps the most important bit of news in my miserable life. If this [life] will ever be of any value, it will be thanks to this event. But the matter is as yet undecided; I should not like to present something half-baked as fact and then have to take it back later. I therefore say no more about it at this stage and will give you more detailed news some other time. Do not make too much of what I am alluding to, but equally, do not think of it as mere toying with an idea. That way you will come closest to the truth.[40]

Still not yet certain himself, and perhaps attempting to intrigue the Flusses, Freud promised to be more specific later. In the next letter he wrote, "When I lift the veil of secrecy, will you not be disappointed? . . . I have decided to be a Natural Scientist. . . . I shall gain insight into the age-old dossiers of Nature, perhaps even eavesdrop on her eternal processes, and share my findings with anyone who wants to learn."[41]

Looking back from the standpoint of full maturity, Freud had his imaginary patient pass the Gisela episode off as "calf-love" and as a screen memory, yet he also wrote that his few screen memories stood for the true turning points in his life.[42] Eissler asserts that this is one of only two instances in which Freud considers that a memory of an *earlier* event is used as a screen for a later memory. Ordinarily, in Freud's theory later events serve as screens for earlier ones. The other instance also came from his own life, and it concerned his nursemaid, whom, as we've seen, he also lost traumatically. He withheld "Screen Memories" from publication until he expunged from *The Interpretation of Dreams* a reference that would have made it plain that he, not a patient, was the true source of the memory.[43] And if it had been only calf-love, the calf had a long memory. Some 35 years later, the Rat Man, Freud's famous patient, mentioned the name of Gisela Fluss during an analytic hour, and Freud, writing a note to himself about this session, marked three exclamations point after her name.[44]

## Subduing Nature

At 17, it was time for Freud to put aside Hamlet-like doubts; assemble a workable, if provisional, identity; and choose a direction for all his inherited ability, conflicted passions, and evolving intellectual preferences. This choice would need to connect the larval elements of his dream with the hopes and wishes of his parents yet point a direction into the future that would seem free of the emotional dangers of the past. Freud's future was beckoning, and if he was to rise to the heavens, he would need all of the sublimation he could gather. In March 1873, six months after his visit with Gisela and under the shadow of the approaching *Matura* examinations at the Gymnasium, Freud heard Professor Carl Brühl read a paean on nature attributed to Goethe at the Zootomic Institute.[45] The lecture was on comparative anatomy, and the fact that the man who read it was a charismatic teacher and a renowned professor can only have added to the evocative power of the experience.[46] Here was not only what to study but the sort of man one could become by studying it.

In this essay, nature is rhapsodized ad nauseum in maternally erotic and mysterious tones.[47] It begins, "Nature! We are surrounded by her, embraced by her—impossible to release ourselves from her and impossible to enter more deeply into her." It continues:

> She creates ever new forms; what exists has never existed before; what has existed returns not again—everything is new and yet always old.
>
> We live in her midst, and yet we are strangers to her. She speaks constantly with us, but betrays not her secret to us. We are continually at work upon her, yet have no power over her.

And it goes on and on in this manner.

Within a year Freud was characterizing Brühl as "bilious," "nihilistic" and his lectures as "stale" and "ineffectual." Yet looking back at 67, Freud recalled that

> neither at that time, nor indeed in my later life, did I feel any particular predilection for the career of a doctor. I was moved, rather, by a sort of curiosity, which was, however, directed more towards human concerns than towards natural objects; nor had I grasped the importance of observation as one of the best means of gratifying it. My deep engrossment in the Bible story (almost as soon as I had learnt the art of reading) had, as I recognized much later, an enduring effect upon the direction of my interest. Under the powerful influence of a school friendship with a boy [Heinrich Braun]

rather my senior who grew up to be a well-known politician, I developed a wish to study law like him and to engage in social activities. At the same time, the theories of Darwin, which were then of topical interest, strongly attracted me, for they held out hopes of an extraordinary advance in our understanding of the world; and it was hearing Goethe's beautiful essay on Nature read aloud at a popular lecture by Professor Carl Brühl just before I left school that decided me to become a medical student.[48]

Perhaps it was less mortifying to recall that an inspirational lecture had changed the direction of his career than to attribute the change to adolescent heartbreak.[49] In reality, both seem important. The young Freud succeeded in using the disappointment with Gisela to strengthen his sublimatory powers, and these rose up to meet the Brül lecture in full flight. Added to his earlier disappointments in love with his mother in childhood, the disappointment in this adolescent romance had created, as he later put it, an "overpowering need" to subdue nature by intellectual means.[50] Thus, the Gisela episode decisively joined his infantile preoccupation with the feminine to the intellectual methods for mastering disappointments that his father had begun teaching him in earnest at age seven. In March 1873 Freud described his new interest to Emil Fluss as one that would be no *"leere Tändelei* [empty flirtation]."[51] He would renounce his interest in law and become a *Naturforscher,* a researcher into nature.

At 17 a dream was taking explicit, conscious shape in Freud's imagination: He would make basic scientific discoveries about nature and become famous and financially secure as a result. Yet it may have been the case that in his unconscious mind Nature was associated with Amalia's body and derivatively the bodies of his sisters and, ultimately, all women. Achieving the dream would then constitute a possessive knowing, a conquering control of these women, and a triumphant defeat of his father and little brother. If so, the unconscious substratum of Freud's dream would have shackled his ambitions with guilt concerning the usurpation of his father's rightful role and the destruction of yet another little brother.[52]

We can only speculate about the oedipal roots and defensive functions of Freud's dream. What we can see more clearly is that the scientific aspect of Freud's adolescent dream would soon be joined by a different fantasy of greatness. In his 20s Freud would dedicate himself first to one version and then the other until, during his age-30 transition, the problem of their integration into a coherent, authentic identity would rival the importance of either.

# PART TWO

# Setting Sail

## CHAPTER FOUR

# The Journey from Adolescence to the Adult World
## (Ages 17–22)
### A SECOND ELEMENT ADDED TO THE DREAM

W<small>E</small> can now follow the vicissitudes of Freud's development—his resilient vitality and the powerful pull of the future as well as the depressive bitterness and regressive intoxications of the past—by studying his letters to Eduard Silberstein. Silberstein was the only person to whom, however fretfully, he entrusted both the secrets of his wounded heart and his dreams of a transcendent future. As we shall see, Freud's dream of the future was about to expand to include a surprising new element.

We have 76 letters from Freud to Silberstein written over a 10-year period beginning when Freud was 15.[1] These letters average over 800 words each. Silberstein's letters to Freud were lost or destroyed. There is a large gap in the epistolary record between September 4, 1872, when Freud wrote the long letter about Gisela and her Thracian beauty after she had left him in Freiberg to wander sadly about the Hochwald, and July 10, 1873, when Freud announced to Silberstein the successful completion of his *Matura* examinations. It is possible that the letters from these months of suffering were among those in the Spanish Academy archives that Freud later destroyed. Fortunately, as we have seen, Freud's letters to Gisela's brother, Emil, are available to fill part of the gap.

Silberstein's family lived in Braila, Rumania, but he attended the

Leopoldstädter Gymnasium apparently because it offered greater educational advantages and he had relatives in Vienna with whom he could stay. During the most active period of the correspondence, from the summer of 1873 through the summer of 1875, when Freud was between the ages of 17 and 19, Silberstein was back in Braila, studying at the university in Leipzig, or vacationing in Roznau, near Freiberg. In the fall of 1875 Silberstein left Leipzig to complete his legal studies at Vienna University, which he did in 1879.[2] For his part, Freud, usually in Vienna, spent a leisurely holiday with his half brothers and their families in Manchester, England, during the summer of 1875 and was away on two research visits to Trieste in the spring and fall of 1876.[3]

    This intimate relationship sustained by letter across a substantial distance was a forerunner of Freud's later friendship with Wilhelm Fliess in Berlin. Like the correspondence with Fliess, the frequency of letters increased dramatically as Freud entered a transitional period, peaked within it, and then declined rapidly as the period came to a close. Even though the correspondence spanned a 10-year period, 70 percent of Freud's letters were written between ages 17 and 21. They double in frequency from ages 16 to 17 and double again from 17 to 18; they remain at a high level of frequency until 20 and then begin a steep decline. In these letters to Silberstein we can see Freud working to form an identity as a scientist, in part as a defensive attempt to lift himself above the thorny mundanities of love.

    The letters following Freud's matriculation at Vienna University, while often boyishly funny, are remarkable for their mixture of morbid secrecy about matters of the heart and precocious wisdom concerning other aspects of life. Like Freud, Silberstein appears to have been going through intermittent and painful periods of doubt about himself and his future. Although Silberstein was several months younger, he seems to have been the more extroverted of the two. His interests lay in public affairs, politics, and the law, as well as in actual relations with girls. His letters, especially after he arrived in Leipzig, tell of dancing, flirtations, kissing, and, or so it seemed to Freud, the ready likelihood of yet more dangerous excesses. The more perfervid of Silberstein's accounts from the ballrooms of Leipzig made it impossible for Freud to study and sent him, steamy and Hyde-like, to prowl the streets of Vienna.[4] Confronted with accounts of this sort, Freud gathered himself up in the full authority of his greater age and in all the high-mindedness of the pure scientist summoned Silberstein to an awareness of his responsibilities. A "thinking man," he reminded Silberstein on one such occasion, might relax his morals because he was "his own legislator, confessor, and absolver."[5] But the objects of Silberstein's intrigues—the "principles," as they were called in the Spanish Academy—were, as Freud imagined them, lacking in these internal controls and thus too vulnerable; with equal projective ease, Freud at other times imagined that the girls, in concert with their mothers, were scheming and duplicitous.

Freud was able to respond to Silberstein's less crimson reports with some warmth and good humor and tried to temper his envious censoriousness with an understanding that Silberstein needed these affairs to combat his intermittent depressions. "Your account of the ballroom events," Freud wrote his friend, "reads like a veritable idyll, albeit a modern French, not a classical one. . . . All in all, I have abstracted a prescription for my small psychological medicine chest from it. If you wish to be in an idyllic mood, then don tails and white kid gloves. The sun will seem warmer and, though the trees are bare, the buds will burst open and you will feel like a great big happy child."[6] Try as he might, Freud could not keep a drop of venom from adulterating his sympathy.

Most importantly, we learn from these letters that, contrary to his own and others' later simplifications of his identity and career ideals, in late adolescence Freud added a second major component to his dream of great scientific discovery—the wish to become a famous doctor through bold and effective innovations in treatment. Although it would lie dormant for several years, this new piece of his dream would later assert itself, complicating and enriching Freud's development over the next 20 years and beyond. Recurrently, it would pose for him the personal and professional problem whose elusive solution would constitute the ultimate triumph of his maturity, namely, how to integrate in one identity, one career, and one life the ordinarily disparate pursuits of research and practice, scientist and leader, as he would later put it, "of a great movement in the interpretation and treatment of nervous diseases."[7]

## Waiting to Begin

In July 1873 Freud passed his *Matura* examination with distinction and received a special commendation for the literary quality of his writing. Among other tasks, he had been asked to translate a passage from Sophocles's *Oedipus Rex*. Having studied the play, Freud was ready to win a first victory from Sophocles's unhappy tale, while laying the groundwork for a much greater one later on. The worries about the *Matura* behind him, Freud waited restively to enter the university. His spirits, dragged down since the previous September by the Gisela affair, had rebounded, but the struggle to free himself completely from her was complicated by the developmental task that now confronted him of leaving the world of his family.

Freud's future lay in the part of the adult world where science and medicine were practiced, and it was toward that beckoning, intimidating, liberating new continent that Freud expectantly looked. Yet the past remained close by and his vulnerability to it great. For Gisela was not merely a pretty girl with whom Freud had fallen in love. As he wrote in his paper on screen memories, Gisela reminded him of his childhood home in Freiberg and aroused a longing, which would never leave him, for the beautiful meadows, woods, and mountains of his birthplace, all of which had been forfeited by his father's business failure, a failure that was then made perpetual by the long and difficult years in the Leopoldstadt ghetto that had followed it.

Apparently, Gisela stimulated in Freud the illusion that he could both live out and master his past at the same time. Gisela was the daughter of a well-to-do family that had risen greatly in the world since the Freuds' move from Freiberg, a family whose comfort compared painfully with his own, and Freud's desire to win her constituted a wish to take the best part of the past into the future. Moreover, Gisela was not connected only to Freud's childhood; the two families remained intertwined through the continuing friendships and visits among the adolescent girls. Through the connection to Freud's sisters, Gisela may also have personified a future inexhaustibly sweetened from within by a disguised incestuous center. "If only .[the economic crash] had not occurred!" he wrote in his paper on screen memories. "If only I had stopped at home and grown up in the country and grown as strong as the young men in the house, the brothers of my love! And then if only I had followed my father's profession and if I had finally married her — for I should have known her intimately all those years!"[8] Repeatedly when lonely, the past (and the defeated attempt at a future made up of the past), embodied in memories of Gisela, rose up to claim him. When it did, Freud required great efforts of sublimation and suppression to right himself and to continue forward in pursuit of his future. In this critical developmental effort, Eduard Silberstein was Freud's requisite other.

The period between the *Matura* examination in July and matriculation at the University of Vienna in October proved purgatorial. The *Matura,* now passed, had provided a worthy orienting object for fear and hope and a source of meaning. Yet the university, also a focus of hopes, fears, and dreams, still lay off in the distance. The prospect of a trip to England to visit his half brothers in Manchester appeared and disappeared disappointingly. In addition, for reasons unknown,

Freud's father forbade him to go to Roznau where the Flusses; his brother, Alexander; Rosa and his other sisters; and Silberstein were gathered. Amalia was also in Roznau, at the health resort she frequented. We are not certain of the nature of her illness; Krüll speculates that she may have contracted tuberculosis during the early years in the Leopoldstadt ghetto. August was also the first anniversary of the Gisela enchantment and loss, and Freud was stuck in hot, wearying Vienna with too much idle time to avoid remembering. Long letters and literary parables to Silberstein, together with magical herbs, gathered by Silberstein and sent to Freud from the groves of Freibergia, were the anodyne.

Freud wrote his friend on July 16, 1873, that his sense of well-being had a "large hole, that [could not] be patched, and [that grew] bigger by the day." He was "often tempted to look for a remedy—but then—." At this point in the letter, Freud's thoughts turned abruptly from love to science. He told Silberstein that he had decided to spend his upcoming first year at university studying the humanities, "which have nothing to do with my later field but will not be unprofitable for all that. . . . So, If anyone [?] asks me, or you on my behalf, what I intend to be, refrain from giving a definite answer, and simply say: a scientist, a professor, or something like that."[9] Perhaps Freud hoped that Gisela—or her mother or at least her sister (who might then be counted on to tell Gisela)—would ask about him and be intrigued! Freud ended his letter by enjoining Silberstein to keep it confidential.

Freud had been insistent throughout his correspondence with Silberstein that letters describing his feelings about Gisela not be read by others—especially not by their boorish friend Ignaz Rosanes, whom Freud feared would ridicule him. Freud had taken to expressing his feelings in allegories to further protect himself against discovery. In the week following his writing of the aforementioned letter, Freud wrote a long biblical allegory containing highly personal, even mortifying, sentiments about Gisela and sent it to Silberstein. His friend had asked for a book, and Freud had included it as well as some money together with the letter containing the allegory. "I am wretched and annoyed," his letter of July 24 began,

> at the news in your letter that you have received neither book nor letter from me. . . . I am rather more worried, I confess, about the letter—the fifty kreuzer in two twenties and a ten-piece coin may have been noticeable and attracted the attention of the post office staff [who knew Freud and the Flusses]. . . . Since neither of the two has arrived they must, in the opinion of the post office here, and in my own as well, be *waiting in Roznau*. So please apply to

Halumiczek, whose genius is probably responsible for the delay, and to [the] postmaster, who is, after all, an amiable fellow, and ask them for what I sent you.[10]

Freud wanted Silberstein to pursue the matter zealously. "For in all honesty," Freud confided, "if it is not found the loss would be great. . . . Write to me *by return mail* to tell me the results of your efforts; until the matter is cleared up you will receive no *decent and sensible* letter from me. The form and content of this letter can be excused only on the grounds of haste and vexation."[11] This letter also went awry, leading Freud to wonder whether there was someone in the post office with a special interest in their correspondence. His letter of July 30 sent up another lament for the lost biblical piece. The good spirits that had enabled him to write about Gisela in "so sensitive . . . and so gay" a manner had been lost, and he felt depressed.[12]

Silberstein tried to console Freud, but Freud brushed him aside. "It is in vain that you try to console me upon the loss of my biblical study; I have not suffered a similar loss for years." In this letter of August 2, 1873, Freud filled in the gap left by the errant letters, doing so haphazardly since he had other concerns. The first involved the confidentiality of his letters: "You complain about my unclear script, adding that you yourself have become used to it. To whom else do you show my letters?" Freud next criticized his friend for his newfound interest in philosophy. Silberstein had evidently become a votary of a philosopher in Roznau and conveyed to Freud that he had turned to philosophy out of despair and in search of a saving direction.[13] Freud objected to the impracticality of the subject. Freud himself had taken up swimming to pass the time. He reported that he had been to see several plays but lacked companionship since Rosanes had been holding himself aloof from him. "Revolutions," Freud wrote, "are occurring in him, too, but of a liquid sort, not fiery as with us."

This said, Freud's thoughts in this avowedly free-associative letter turned to Gisela. "Incidentally, it is one year since my trip to Freiberg. If you have the time, do consult the diary daily for what happened to me a year ago. I did a great deal of living in those six weeks. But that you know, for I have told you a good many things over and over again." It irked Freud that his friend could be so miserable near the longed-for mountains around Roznau and Freiberg when he was consigned to the aridities of summertime Vienna. "Get up into the mountains by yourself," he urged Silberstein, "and let books and society rot. Get into the mountains, I say, and eat strawberries." Freud had been on a very second-rate outing of his own in the hills surrounding Vienna, and it had turned his thoughts painfully to the superiorities of Freiberg's meadows. "A few days ago, when I myself picked straw-berries and raspberries on the Sofienalpe near Dornbach, I was over-come with nostalgia. Since you went away, I have been up in the mountains four times; but my heart's in the highlands, down here I find not one step is worth the trouble."[14]

Reminiscing about Freiberg led Freud to think of his lost letter. "Why couldn't ten of my other scribblings have been lost, and the one incomparable [letter] be saved!" Silberstein had suggested that he write another. "Don't speak to me of substitutes," Freud protested. "If the sun should explode one day and we should dwell in darkness, what substitute could you find for it? If the sea dried up and the heavenly sources, what substitute for water would you prescribe? So don't speak to me of substitutes; it is irretrievably lost and will never return." Freud had not only lost Gisela he had now lost his most successful attempt to master the loss by writing about it. This attempt at mastery, worse than defeated, had been obliterated. The loss of his letter, together with the absence of those he loved most—Amalia, Gisela, Rosa, and Silberstein—seems to have left Freud feeling empty, for in his extremity he now turned to symbolic substitutes:

> I have a small favor to ask, which may well seem peculiar to you. In the first field of the meadowland opposite the house in which my mother stayed last year, and before that as well, there is a tree that looks like a cypress or an arbor vitae and whose twigs and small needles have a marvelously spicy and acrid taste. As you know, I am quite an expert on the grasses of the field and the herbs of the woods and have tasted all sorts of greenery, but nothing ever pleased me more than the twigs of that tree. So please be good enough to seek it out . . . taste it and enclose a sample in your next letter, or if possible send me a small packetful, for which service I shall remain obliged to you until ten years after the Resurrection.[15]

By mid-August 1873 Freud was busying himself with learning French and studying philosophy, despite his doubts about the useful-ness of the latter. But he was not yet too busy to think of Gisela. "I believe," he wrote Silberstein, "that my mother will soon be leaving Roznau and I would like to know when your family will be doing like-wise. The 'Rivers' [Flusses] with the small brooks and the rest will ar-rive in Vienna in early September."[16] Again, his thoughts moved directly from Gisela to incorporation: "I have eaten the cypress sam-ples you sent me with gratitude," his letter continued. "They come from two species, but the difference between them is so small that you have to be a seasoned eater of leaves and branches like myself to detect it." It was as though he were still referring to his mother and Gisela, as he had been in the paragraph before. "If it is not too much too ask," his letter went on, "I would beg you to try the taste of a few of these cypresses . . . and to choose for me those with the most particularly bitter taste."

Freud next offered Silberstein an ironic counsel of patience concerning a child about whom his friend was fantasizing as a prospective wife. Silberstein should not be defeated, Freud wrote, if the mother insists that he wait until her daughter comes of age before they marry. He should remain attentive to the "orphan child," whom Freud presumed was now in Roznau. "If it should scream a great deal and have a good, strong voice, it will turn into a wholesome girl worthy of your attentions. Don't be put off by all the screaming, because in a few years' time you will be calling her voice a silvery one, and the owner of the silvery bell a little angel." Gisela had been 11 when Freud became infatuated with her, 12 when he fell in love. She was only 13 now, while he was the proud possessor of a *Matura* diploma, earned with distinction, and was embarking on his university career. Yet shamefully, he still loved her.

Freud closed his letter of August 16, 1873, with a parable entitled "Highway of the Heavenly Host" and consisting of a conversation between a cooling star and one that had burned out. It appears to have been an effort similar to the lost biblical allegory, though Freud considered it distinctly inferior.[17] What does one do, this parable seems to ask, when one's passion is gone? The answer given in the parable is "devote yourself to your duties." What is to be achieved by such scrupulousness? "To be destroyed by dreams anyway." This was a credo—disciplined work in the face of a malevolent fate—that the young Freud was now forging, a credo from which he as a mature man would never stray long or far. Freud ended the letter by proclaiming himself to be in an "extremely bad mood."

By August 20, Freud declared that his interest in young ladies was over. He had decided that all girls were boring, even if one conversed with them in French, in the study of which he continued to occupy himself. He had hoped Silberstein might send a photograph—of himself or of Gisela?—but no longer. "I used to feel your letters before opening them, and guess whether there might be something thicker inside than a sheet of paper, a photograph perhaps, but I have given up this so-called hope, and also—I trust you to believe me, for otherwise I would tell you nothing—the attachment that bound me to Gisela."[18] No one had taken her place, and he was content to leave that role in his life uncast. The void would be filled with work. "I have grown tired of and been led astray by this overlong game."

He could not, however, keep from concluding his letter with a playful inquiry about the females in another family he had met near Freiberg the year before. "I believe," he concluded incongruously, "that we should let no opportunity go by to discover whatever we can about those mysterious beings." However he might try to ignore them, females remained the most interesting creatures on earth. Yet the letter the following week makes no reference, direct or allegorical, to Gisela. It is the last one we have from 1873.

## Under Way

Little is known about Freud's first year at the university other than that, by his own account, he was made to feel an outsider by the anti-Semitism of some of his classmates.[19] We know that he entered the medical department, which served students who wished either to become physicians or to work toward the Ph.D. degree in biology. Students were allowed to range widely in their studies, free of the constraints of early and repeated examination, and we know that Freud did so, as he had earlier told Emil Fluss he would do. There is a brief note to Silberstein in January 1874 written from a dissection hall.[20] We do not encounter the first full letter until the next summer, when Freud was 18. From it, and those that follow, we can see that Freud had made great, if incomplete, progress in getting over Gisela. In the main, his spirits were buoyant and his engagement in his studies vital. He was enjoying being a student and conjuring fantasies of his future. This letter of August 13, 1874, is long and witty, written in "the youthful vigor and strength of purpose that becomes a finished Gymnasium scholar and future citizen of Academe." He described himself happily as "one of those human beings who can be found most of the day between two pieces of furniture, one formed vertically, the armchair, and one extending horizontally, the table." From this position, he was "compelled . . . to engage in two activities: reading and writing."[21]

These high spirits and good humor continued through the next letter, of August 22, 1874. Silberstein was about to embark on his university career and had sought Freud's advice about universities. Freud argued against "dreary Leipzig" and for Heidelberg or Switzerland. He hoped his friend would return to Vienna but restrained himself from urging it lest Silberstein be made timid in the face of a possible adventure abroad.[22] In September Freud continued in the role of Silberstein's advisor. Silberstein was still considering Leipzig for his law studies. Uncertain whether his family's resources could support a full student life abroad, Silberstein broached the possibility of giving private lessons in some unspecified subject, perhaps music or French.

Freud thought the idea penny-wise, pound-foolish, and the turning of scrupulosity into an irrational vice. "I cannot understand the feverish haste with which you want to escape your youth," Freud exclaimed. "Use your time for your own good; youth is but the close season in which destiny allows us to gain strength so that we can amuse her by our resistance if she later decides to hunt us down."[23]

By late October 1874 university had begun, and Freud was the less diligent correspondent. He hoped to make up for the neglect with a full account of events and mutual friends. Vienna University had elected a new rector for the law school—Wilhelm Wahlberg—and he had begun his tenure with a rousing address in which academic bureaucracy and requirements were denounced, individual attention to students urged, and academic freedom demanded. This, together with the students' hooting at the retiring conservative rector, delighted Freud. He described to Silberstein the academic paths chosen by several of their friends from the Gymnasium and enclosed a copy of his schedule. He was taking two courses in philosophy—one on metaphysics, one on Mill's utilitarianism—together with courses in zoology, physiology, anatomy, and dissection. He would have been taking yet another course had he not become responsible for supervising the education of his sister Rosa. He had visited a Fluss in Vienna, but which one and for what purpose, he did not say. Presumably, it was Emil.

## The Academic Drudges

By November 1874 the allure of new intellectual acquisitions had been eclipsed by the gloom of academic chores that had settled in around Freud, appallingly so around Silberstein, who had chosen to spend his first year in Leipzig. Freud wrote his friend: "A kind of tremor is passing through the world; the mortally ill hasten to die, the sickly redouble their coughing and those still in good health surround themselves with bad conductors of heat and exhale clouds of fog from their lungs." They both needed to take more walks and attend to the needs of their bodies, especially Silberstein, whose scrupulosity had overtaken him to the point where he was attending lectures six hours a day. "For a lawyer, you have adopted a schedule so rare that it ought to be pickled in alcohol and exhibited in a museum," Freud chastised. And the subjects—public finance, economics, statistics, and the like! "Have you ever heard," Freud demanded to know, "that we only live once? Even a professor of statistics must have been young in his day and could not possibly have undertaken as a freshman, the maternal eggshell of the Gymnasium still stuck to his back, the arid stuff you pursue."

Contemplating the tedium of Silberstein's studies brightened Freud's mood, since bad as it was for Freud—who now proclaimed himself a "godless medical man and empiricist"—he still got to read Feuerbach and study philosophy. He had little news to offer about mutual friends in some of whom, like the insensitive Rosanes, the spirit continued to slumber. An exception: Josef Herzig had secretly become affianced to a charming girl who towered over him. Freud felt certain that Silberstein, like himself, preferred "to be still looking for [his] future bride than to have her around every day and hour."[24]

During the next two months Freud's correspondence diminished, and in early December 1874 he explained his epistolary tardiness. He had recently written Silberstein a letter but had forgotten to send it promptly, instead carrying "it around in [his] pocket for three days, like a marsupial harboring its young on its body after birth." It would be wrong for Silberstein to hold him responsible for this error, he wrote, because as a poor medical student he had no will of his own. "Rather, [he was] a drop of liquid pumped by complicated pressure devices from one lecture theater to the next, from one suburb to the next, and forced, by the laws of mechanics, to traverse his path with minimum friction and in the shortest possible time."[25]

## Student of the Sciences

By the Christmas holidays Freud had settled happily back into harness as a student of the sciences. He had an open account at the bookseller's and was adding monthly to his "beloved small library." But Silberstein was still feeling melancholy and missed Freud the more on account of the holidays. He complained that correspondence could not take the place of conversation. Though not depressed, Freud too felt that his friend's absence had created a void. By his own reckoning, he had many more enemies than friends. Josef Paneth was perhaps closest to him in aspiration and interests. "But Paneth, though otherwise amiable enough, is so intoxicated by his own perfection that it would hardly enter his head to seek his complement in a friend. When you return, therefore, you will find that nothing in my attitude toward you has changed."[26] Freud ended his letter of December 11, 1874, with a postscript. "Don't let your social democrats prejudice you against the Chancellor. Bismarck is a devil of a fellow and a decent man." This is one of the few political opinions Freud expressed in these letters.[27] Earlier in this same letter he had recommended that Silberstein follow his example and not join a fraternity, thus avoiding "that supercilious breed who booze and gossip and brood over political drivel instead of pursuing their studies."[28]

The two boys had been arguing—Freud in the affirmative—about whether the statutes of the Spanish Academy allowed birthday presents to be given. In late December Freud wrote, "Your birthday has passed without my having a chance to allow even a token of my friendly interest to flutter across to Leipzig."[29] Freud also regretted not having his company at holiday celebrations. It had been their custom to spend Christmas and New Year's together, with Silberstein helping Freud out with the family social obligations. "Today," Freud lamented, "my courage is failing me because I am on my own and am expected this evening, with my own resources, to entertain the youthful company that has gathered for my sister's [Anna's 16th] birthday." Gisela Fluss and her sister would be among Anna's guests.[30] His postscript about the evening noted Gisela's presence but offered no comment about it.

## New Year's Eve with Gisela

Silberstein wrote Freud about his fantasy of how the New Year's party had gone. Evidently, the account featured a chivalrous Freud in possession of an alluring temptress. Freud protested this construction of events but insisted that the evening had gone well enough. "About New Year's Eve," he wrote, " . . . a postscript for your peace of mind: authoritative sources have remarked, and told my family, that I was merrier than normal." He might not yet be a gay blade like Silberstein, Freud wrote, but then Silberstein was not quite yet Homer, since he had failed to describe "the color of the eyes and the hair in [his] description of a person destined to play the heroine." Silberstein himself had flirted and danced with a "principle" but had failed in his account to supply needed details.[31]

Merrier than normal may have meant that Freud had defended himself with manic denial. Indeed, the New Year's Eve reunion with Gisela does seem to have reissued a bitter excrescence from the nearly healed wound. Silberstein had often asked Freud to urge his sisters Anna and Rosa to write to him. On January 24, Freud told his friend that his ballroom graces would endear him to his sisters as they were now set on taking dancing lessons themselves:

> As a dancer, you will be very popular with my sisters, because: it is "proposed," "it is generally said," etc., that they, too, are to learn the noble art, needless to say not without the Flusses, for what can possibly take place nowadays without the Flusses![32] They are the example my lady sisters are endeavoring to emulate now: so if they take dancing lessons, it will be in the company of G. and S. [Sidonia]

Fluss, and when you come here you will have the pleasure, which cannot be expressed in words, or only feebly and inadequately, of "touching" Gisela, something which I have less motive and occasion to do.[33]

Freud's thoughts then turned directly from Gisela to his career. He had decided to spend the next winter in Berlin, even though it meant a prolongation of the separation from Silberstein, attending the lectures of the leaders of the positivist revolution in science: Du Bois-Reymond, Helmholtz, and Virchow. "I am," he wrote, "as happy as a sandboy at the thought and could not bear the idea of giving up the project."[34]

## Dedication to Science Redoubled

In a letter written later on in January 1875 Freud, now halfway through his second year at the university, gave Silberstein a detailed, enthusiastic account of his program of studies and his way of working. Ordinarily, he studied from 10 in the evening until 2 in the morning, although he got carried away sometimes and worked far longer, ruining his ability to concentrate for the next couple of days. He liked starting new academic projects at the beginnings of weeks, months, and years, a preference he considered odd but indulged anyway. He had set for himself the task of completing a mastery of the basic principles of anatomy, physiology, biology, zoology, Darwinian evolution, chemistry, geology, botany, astronomy, mathematics, and physics in two years. In addition to mastering the basic principles of these disciplines, he had identified several topics he wanted to explore in depth. So occupied, he had little time for literature, devoting the odd free moment to Lessing, Goethe, and Cervantes.[35]

At times, this regimen proved a bit much even for Freud, and he found himself longing for love. He was, as he told Silberstein on February 21, 1875, in "a time of transition." The old "principles" had been forsworn, yet he had found no new ones. Meanwhile, Silberstein had gotten himself two. "Two principles," Freud gasped. And the only question was, Which was the sweeter? They had written of two "principles" in the old days of the Spanish Academy, Freud reminded his friend, but then it was one each and never had matters "of taste discrimination" arisen. He was genuinely concerned that his friend might go too far. "Won't you pack your bags . . . and come and spend the next semester in cosy, virtuous old Vienna?"[36]

Silberstein's racy letter had found Freud in a state of ennui. Instead of studying, he had been "growing excessively nervous, languid, and bored, with the feeling that [his] limbs had been glued together and were now coming apart again, and experiencing all the painful and shaming sensations of a tomcat." He had "been roaming instead through the streets of Vienna studying the masses." Amalia's illness had gotten worse, and Freud was worried about her. In his letter to Silberstein of February 27, 1875, Freud described his mother as suffering from a "protracted illness admitting of no quick improvement: infiltration of the lungs; she is bedridden and weak, and will be going to Roznau at the beginning of May."

Nonetheless, his bad mood passed quickly enough, and Freud was able to return to his academic labors. Most recently he was indulging himself in a rereading of the Spanish Academy archives, which he had gotten from Silberstein's brother. It is from his account of reading through these archives that we learn that Freud had attempted the two novels about the Gisela affair. The second of these novels now pleased Freud greatly, including, as it apparently did, the meting out of punishment to Gisela. "I need only remind you," he wrote Silberstein, "of the letters between D. Berganza and D. Cipion, of D. Kürschner's willfulness, of D. Möler's grief in love, of his lover's plaint, composed by you, of the scenes in the house of Ichthyosaura, of her bitter monologue, of her biblical lamentation for Roznau, of her relationship to Achilles, Hector, and Briseis and similar foolishness, and finally of Amor and Cazadora."[37]

Silberstein's next letter deepened Freud's concern about his friend's conduct. He had apparently succeeded in flattering a 16-year-old girl into an infatuation that her parents were very much against and that Silberstein, without much genuine feeling for the girl, was about to exploit. Sounding like the protective older brother of adolescent sisters, Freud wrote a long letter appealing to his friend's better self.[38] "It is very wrong of you, and causes grave harm to yourself and deep sorrow to me, to encourage the imprudent affection of a sixteen-year old girl and—the inevitable outcome—to take advantage of it," he wrote. The costs, Freud reminded Silberstein, would be much greater for the girl.

Not only was Silberstein dangerously at fault in the present circumstance, but Freud felt it necessary to extend his "sermonizing" to his friend's conduct with girls generally. He charged Silberstein with misusing his talent for flattery in order to feed his own vanity, meanwhile accustoming girls to treatment they would find little enough of as adults. "How often have I not complained of the miserable education of girls, deploring their ineptitude for life's serious tasks. What is a poor woman to make of the exertions demanded of her as a wife and mother," Freud asked, "when she thinks back on the flatteries with which she was treated and spoiled as a girl?"

Pleased to find that Silberstein had not been alienated by the sermon, in his next letter Freud redoubled it. Silberstein had evidently decided that the girl's mother was actually trying, by feigning disapproval, to lure him into an attempt to capture her daughter, and he had sworn off the affair. Freud leveled the charge of vanity at his friend again, and this time offered a deflating interpretation. The mother, Freud insisted, had simply been encouraging the girl to practice coquettish wiles, which could be set to better purpose later. Silberstein had been, Freud insisted, merely "a dressmaker's dummy masculini generis." Then, having straightened Silberstein up with a left, Freud flattened him with a right. "If there is anything to console your injured self-esteem for this discovery, it can only be the realization that she has been playing no nobler part in your eyes. You were plainly rehearsing the role of the tragic lover that you intend to enact one day."[39]

## Brentano and a Path Not Taken

Freud's letter of March 7, 1875, also carried the important news of having made a personal connection with a professor at the university. He and his friend Paneth had been attending Brentano's lectures in philosophy, and the two students had dared to write him about some objections they had to his arguments. Brentano responded kindly and invited them to his home for private discussion. This led to a second letter from Freud and Paneth and, in turn, a second invitation from Brentano to visit.

Franz Brentano was a new and controversial addition to the University of Vienna faculty. Formerly a Catholic priest, he had denounced the doctrine of papal infallibility and left his academic post at Würzburg. Brentano had recently (in 1873) published his book *Psychology from an Empirical Standpoint*. He was 37, freshly blossoming into his own man, and in search of protégés. Freud found him both brilliant and personally admirable, so much so that under his "fruitful influence" he abruptly decided on a change in degree program.[40] He would seek not only the M.D. degree but also, simultaneously, a combined Ph.D. in philosophy and zoology. With Brentano's help and encouragement, Freud decided to apply for admission to the philosophy department. Rather than go to Berlin the next winter, as he and Silberstein had been fantasizing doing together, he decided he would stay in Vienna and prepare for his oral exam for the Ph.D.

Brentano's initial appeal to Freud may have been like Carl Brühl's. He, too, was a charismatic teacher who managed to combine the mistiness of the *Geist* with the solid terra firma of empirical science. But as with Brühl, Freud's initial attraction would turn to contempt. Nonetheless, Brentano was also the first psychologist Freud had ever met. Brentano was already thinking seriously about several constituent elements of what would later be Freud's psychological discoveries.[41] These ideas concerned the ubiquitous nature of intentionality, the association of ideas, and the conditions governing their strength and recall, the motivational primacy of the instincts of love and hate, and the psychological development of the infant from normal psychic autism to relatedness. Certainly, Brentano's method of "inner perception" and his insistence on the lawful nature of the psychological processes studied in this way impressed Freud at the time and would later become absolutely fundamental tenets when Freud turned *his* hand to psychology.

Most important to Freud, this philosopher, in contrast to those who espoused the dominant tradition of German idealism, was a staunch empiricist. Brentano told Freud and Paneth that he considered Kantian idealism dangerous for young minds, called Kant's follower Hegel a swindler, and encouraged them to read Auguste Comte, the father of positivism, instead.[42] Encouraged by Paneth's complaints, Brentano criticized the unscientific state of philosophy at Vienna. Brentano, Freud wrote Silberstein, then "declared himself unreservedly a follower of the empiricist school which applies the method of science to philosophy and to psychology in particular (in fact, this is the main advantage of his philosophy, which alone renders it tolerable for me), and mentioned a few remarkable psychological observations."[43]

Freud especially admired Brentano's ability to be rational about highly emotional questions. "His great distinction is that he abhors all glib phrases, all emotionality, and all intolerance of other views. He demonstrates the existence of God with as little bias and as much precision as another might argue the advantage of the wave over the emission theory."[44] But not even Brentano could ever succeed in stimulating a religious impulse in Freud. "Needless to say," Freud wrote his friend, "I am only a theist by necessity, and am honest enough to confess my helplessness in the face of his argument; however, I have no intention of surrendering so quickly or completely."[45] Freud intended to study Brentano's philosophy more carefully before making up his mind about God. Freud could not refute the philosopher's theistic argument, but he did come to see that Brentano's God was little more than a "logical principle" that had no role in the affairs of men.[46]

Freud was still entertaining the fantasy of the double doctorate and on April 11, 1875, proudly announced that he would soon, in the next semester, appear in the new guise of philosopher and zoologist. He was enjoying for the first time the "academic happiness . . . which . . . derives from the realization that one is close to the source from which science springs at its purest and from which one will be taking a good long drink."[47] Silberstein, too, Freud was glad to note, was wrestling with important questions rather than simply chasing after girls. "You are searching for truth in life with the same urgency as I try to seek [it] in science. The big question you must be asking yourself daily is, Third or Fourth Estate? Republican or Social Democrat—for me it is theist or materialist, causality or skepticism."[48]

Happy as he was in his studies, there was "a dark side" to it all, and that was religion.[49] In April Freud confessed to Silberstein that he found himself in the awkward position of being uncertain about the existence of God. The "dark side" for Freud was that if one followed Brentano's argument without being able to object decisively, it seemed that science itself required the existence of God as a hypothesis. "The principle of the conservation of energy," he wrote, "of the interaction of natural forces, which we consider as the best fruits of scientific research, seem to involve the end no less than the beginning of the world."[50] Ultimately, Freud's allegiance would be to skepticism. As he put it 50 years later in *The Future of an Illusion*, one needn't be able to disprove the existence of God; to the contrary, he wrote, "Ignorance is ignorance; no right to believe anything can be derived from it."[51]

Silberstein had complained that Freud had no interest in social problems, which were his primary interest, particularly the platform of the Social Democrats. Freud insisted that this was not the case, although, like Brentano, he did object to their rejection of religion on a priori grounds.

> For let them [the Social Democrats] not be deceived, the existence of God cannot be settled by union debates, parliamentary speeches, or speculation, but only by logical and psychological studies, for which not everyone has a taste, no more so than for astronomical computations. Hence it is just as wrong to think everyone is competent to pronounce on the existence of God as on the existence of Neptune.[52]

William McGrath has pointed out the significance of Freud's connection to Brentano but missed his decisive turning away from Brentano and philosophy, a rejection that was of great consequence developmentally.[53] Already by March 15, 1875, some distance had set in between the two men. On that date Freud told Silberstein at length about his and Paneth's conversations with Brentano. The philosopher had told the students that the minister of education had charged him with the task of training future lecturers in philosophy, which Freud had already decided he was unlikely to become. While he still found Brentano brilliant, and his theistic arguments irrefutable, Freud felt too great a degree of expedience in Brentano's encouragement. "He came here," Freud told Silberstein, "to found a school and to gain disciples, and hence proffers his friendship and time to all who need it."[54] He had been well pleased to be invited to the professor's home but noted that Brentano had extended the same invitation to "thousands of others."[55]

At a time when Freud was still struggling to tame the longings of his soul, to embed himself in the world of demonstrable realities, and to center an identity in science, philosophy — even one as empiricist as Brentano's — though tempting, was still too much in the ether. Freud could not refute Brentano's theism, but he did not like it. In particular, while maintaining a belief in evolution, Brentano so criticized Darwin's explanation of it as to temporarily shatter Freud's belief in Darwin's theory. Brentano's Catholicism may also have been an obstacle for Freud, although Freud's first mentor, Brücke, still three years in the future, was not Jewish either.

Siegfried Bernfeld has suggested that Brentano was not sufficiently senior to fully evoke an admiring transference from the younger man, since Freud's father was not one but two generations older. This explanation is contradicted by Freud's later mentorial attachment to Josef Breuer, who was yet closer in age to Freud than Brentano was. The intellectual differences, the developmental demands of Freud's identity formation, his sense of not being individually chosen — these seem to constitute the main reasons why the flirtation between Freud and Brentano did not progress to a full mentor relationship.

McGrath's depiction of Freud as setting forth from age 19 on with a conscious vision of Brentanoist psychological studies is not supported by a developmental reading of his letters to Silberstein, yet something of this sort might have happened.[56] And the fact that it did not is of great moment, for the tempting but rejected paths of youth tend to beckon later, especially — and this would be the case for Freud — during the transition from youth to middle age. Had the two succeeded in forming a mentor–protégé relationship, Freud might well have gotten the Ph.D. degree and become a real professor rather than the Professor Extraordinarius he ended up becoming (*Extraordinarius* does not mean stellar but irregular, or adjunct). When Freud became famous and had followers, they called him Professor because they knew what he wanted most, but the reality is that Freud never became a salaried faculty member with regular teaching responsibilities. Those of us who have know what a tragedy that was.

Of more intimate matters he had little to report in this long letter of April 11, 1875. Gisela Fluss had been to Italy and had been enchanting his sisters with tales of her travels. Meanwhile, Silberstein's relationship to his "principle" had advanced to kissing, and Freud was moved to offer a caveat:

> The equanimity with which you mention the first kiss you exchanged with your principle strikes me as an evil omen in two respects, first that you accept kisses so easily and second that you take kisses so lightly. It is my duty to draw your attention to a calculation by the famous statistician Malthus, who proved that kisses tend to multiply in proportions that increase with such unusual speed that, soon after the beginning of the series, the facial area no longer suffices and [they] are then forced to migrate.[57]

Freud then turned his thoughts to his studies and a plan for the summer semester that would outdo previous exertions. He described to Silberstein a schedule of lectures in the sciences from Monday through Saturday that totaled over 50 hours a week. Having constructed this academic monstrosity, Freud stood back to contemplate its abstinent intellectuality with satisfaction. "As you can see, I am not short of courses, almost all of them stimulating, and if I manage to do everything as I have set it out, the semester will be a model of how to spend one's time."[58] Evenings, he noted with libertine anticipation, had been left free for reading in philosophy and natural history.

## Manchester, England, and a New Element to the Dream

Freud turned 19 that May 1875 amidst preparation for an important examination in zoology, which was to be followed in July by the long-promised trip to visit his half brothers in England. In mid-July Freud left Vienna by train for Hamburg, stopping on the way in Leipzig to visit Silberstein. At midnight on July 20, Freud set sail from Hamburg to Grimsby, England, where he planned to travel immediately to Manchester. From Manchester Freud wrote Silberstein that he was having such a wonderful time on "that blessed island," relaxing with his beautiful nieces in the home of his generous older half brother Emanuel, that he would have no time to write.[59]

Back home in Vienna after his seven week holiday, Freud wrote his friend on September 9, 1875, about a psychological event of great significance that occurred in Manchester. He began by describing meeting his charming niece, Pauline. Like Freud, she too had been born in Freiberg in 1856 and had left there in 1859. Later, during his self-analysis, Freud would remember her as the object of his earliest love. In addition to Pauline, he found many other things to like, even prefer, about England, so much so that he could imagine one day immigrating. One such virtue was the English respect for practical accomplishments. Indeed, Freud had returned yet more skeptical of the airy abstractions of philosophy and more enthralled by the great English empirical scientists, such as Darwin. Under the spell of the island, the clarity of its thinkers, the warmth of Emanuel's home, and the charm of its women, he had chosen a second basic thread to his dream. "Let me confess to you," he wrote Silberstein,

> *I now have more than one ideal, a practical one having been added to the theoretical one of earlier years.* Had I been asked last year what was my dearest wish, I would have replied: a laboratory and free time, or a ship on the ocean with all the instruments a scientist needs; *now I waver about whether I should not rather say: a large hospital and plenty of money in order to reduce or wipe out some of the ills that afflict our body.* That is to say, if I wished to influence a large number of people instead of a small number of readers or fellow scientists, England would be just the place for that purpose. A respected man, supported by the press and the rich, could do wonders in alleviating physical ills, *if only he were enough of an explorer to strike out on new therapeutic paths.* All these are still vague ideas, and I must stop here.[60] [Italics added]

The fact that his mother's chronic illness had recently worsened must have contributed to his wish to help the afflicted. Freud's sister Anna remembered this change in her brother's goals. "It was in England," she wrote, "that Sigmund resolved to study medicine on his return to Vienna, and so informed my father. Not satisfied with his decision, father stated his objections, claiming that Sigmund was much too soft-hearted for the task. But Sigmund's mind was made up, though at first he planned to do only research. 'I want to help people who suffer,' was his reply."[61] At 26 Freud would tell his fiancée that the trip to England "had a decisive influence on [his] whole life" and that he thought they might establish his practice there.[62]

## A Revolutionary Healer

This letter of September 9, 1875, to Silberstein is very important for an understanding of Freud's identity formation, for his later development, and, indeed, for the peculiar Janus-like science–practice character of psychoanalysis itself. Prior to Boehlich's publication of the complete correspondence to Silberstein, it had not been available. *We need to be clear that this letter is not merely one among others in which he proposed to Silberstein or anyone else a variety of alternative goals.* As we saw in his letter to Emil Fluss in which he announced his intention to become a natural scientist, Freud made such pronouncements with a strong, even dramatic, sense of their (and his) importance. He does so only twice — once to Emil and once to Silberstein.

Up until now, biographers have been content to accept Freud's insistence that he never wanted to be a doctor, that he became one only out of necessity, and that he never had a calling for it. To the contrary, if it is read developmentally, this letter, written during the crucible years of the formation of Freud's dream and of his identity, allows us to see that the matter had become more complicated. In Manchester Freud added a different sort of element to the foundation of his dream, joining the decision made two years earlier to become a natural scientist. Though he did nothing with it until his mid-20s, the clinician fantasy would recurrently surface. As we shall see, he would try first to become a scientist, then to become a clinician, and during his age-30 and mid-life transitions to integrate the two.[63]

The sojourn with his favorite brother, Emanuel, a wool merchant who, though not wealthy, was well respected, seems to have activated the showier, more dramatic part of Freud's ambitiousness. The presence too of the "beautiful" and "charming" Pauline, perhaps reminding Freud of Gisela, may have added fuel to the new fantasy of greatness.[64] Silberstein evidently thought so and in his reply to Freud's September 9, 1875, letter wrote something to the effect that Freud was experiencing "*Erinnerungsschwelgerei[e]n* [wallowing in nostalgia]" and this is McGrath's interpretation as well.[65] Freud wrote back rejecting Silberstein's interpretation and turned directly from girls and love to an account of lectures and studies.

As in Freiberg, where Gisela's family owned a dye works and lived a very comfortable life, Freud had found in Manchester a world of desirable women and successful, competent men who contrasted sharply with his impecunious Bible scholar father and himself, the diffident *Yeshiva-Bokker*-turned-scientist son. Although Freud dismissed Silberstein's suggestion that his memories of England were "mixed up with matters of love," years later, during his self-analysis, he came to see that Silberstein had been right.[66]

Whatever the similarities in the love and career fantasies that grew out of the Freiberg and Manchester visits, there was an essential difference. At 19 Freud was a young person of some accomplishment and possessed of a firmer identity. He held the *Matura* diploma, earned with distinction. He had been taken seriously as a budding intellectual—even recruited—by Professor Brentano. He was successfully launched on a rigorous program of scientific studies. In Manchester he had been able to speak fluently in English and in German, whereas in Freiberg he had been painfully reticent. Pauline had not been rude to him, nor had she made him the brunt of insensitive jokes. Thus unlike the aftermath of the Freiberg fiasco, Freud returned to Vienna eager to pursue his program of scientific study and build a foundation necessary for either science or practice. Indeed, he was now sufficiently secure in his goals and self-esteem to *enjoy* a pleasurable fantasy of returning to England the next year or—who knew?—years later to become a rich and famous healer.[67]

## Gisela Again

As it happened, Freud's equanimity was soon struck a gratuitously hurtful blow. Within days of his return he heard that Gisela had married. On October 2, 1875, he wrote Silberstein a poem dripping with contempt for the new couple, which he mailed in a spirit of "sadness and jest."[68] Feigning to praise Gisela ("Sing me, oh Muse, the praises of Ichthyosaura communis, / Once great in the Lias and other [geologic] Formations"), he went on to describe her as fat and dim-witted and the couple as grubby materialists who would "live out their allotted span, / Like the insects and worms that inhabit the earth."[69]

In the recently discovered draft notes for the poem that accompanied the letter, Freud wrote of a "wretched, abominable despair" into which the news about Gisela had plunged him.[70] Freud told of rage and pain so unbearable as to make several means of suicide preferable. It seems plain that at points he was consciously exaggerating, but the pain was nevertheless real. Freud attached an addendum to the poem. It bespeaks a break with the past, with memory, and with childish heartbreak:

> Herewith this Formation [the geological stratum to which Ichthyosaurus belonged] comes to an end. I now bury the magic wand that aided her education, and may a new age begin without forces working in secret, that has no need of poetry and fantasy! Let no one seek a principle save in the present, not in the alluvium or diluvium, nowhere save among the children of man, not in the gruesome primeval past when wild creatures could consume the oxygen of the atmosphere unpunished by man.[71]

The news of Gisela's marriage turned out to be false. In fact, she did not marry for another six years.[72] By then Freud was engaged and was able to confess the existence of his first love to his fiancée, Martha, inviting her to have a laugh at his lack of taste.[73]

Developmentally, this was the last straw. Freud had gained some distance, piece of mind, and concrete achievement by suppressing his love for Gisela and his desire for "principles," but the mare's nest of Gisela's betrothal had shown him that he was still too vulnerable. As a consequence, he set aside his fantasies about the clinical path to the Paulines and Giselas of his world, and gave himself over determinedly to science—*once*, he vowed, *and for all.*

## The Zoological Station in Trieste

Again there is a gap in the correspondence, as there had been following the first Gisela disappointment, the missing letters perhaps having been destroyed by Freud. The next letters from Freud to Silberstein come from the spring of 1876, when Freud was turning 20. During the interim Freud had succeeded in setting the clinical aspect of his dream aside, had redoubled his commitment to science, and had begun working under the supervision of Carl Claus, chief of the Institute for Comparative Anatomy at Vienna. Like Brentano, Claus had recently been recruited to Vienna to upgrade the university's department of zoology. Claus had selected a small group of outstanding students, including Freud, to work on important scientific problems at his newly established zoological station in Trieste.

The Polish scientist Syrski had announced the discovery of a lobe in the eel that he considered to be its hidden testicles, thus solving a mystery that had long baffled scientists and had led them to the assumption that the eel is hermaphroditic. Hermaphroditism in animals was Claus's own particular research area. Claus gave Freud the task of checking on Syrski's findings, which he painstakingly did, obtaining consistent but inconclusive findings in the affirmative. According to Freud's drawings, the reproductive organs of male and female eels look grossly similar. Although the female's ova could be seen on gross examination, microscopic examination was necessary to reveal the presence of spermatozoa in testes.[74] Claus sponsored the publication of Freud's "Observations on the Form and Finer Structure of the Lobed Organs of the Eel, Described as Testes" in the April 1877 issue of the *Bulletin of the Academy of Sciences.*[75]

Freud's effort to banish fantasy and confine his ambitions to science was largely successful, for his letters to Silberstein from Trieste have a relaxed good humor about them, even though the theme of the "principles" returns. The longer letters are richly novelistic in their description of places, incidents, and characters. The first of these, written on April 5, 1876, was accompanied by delightfully comic drawings of Freud's room, local people and animals, Trieste Bay, and the various sea creatures delivered each day to be carved up by him and his fellow votaries of "the beast-killing science."

On his first day in Trieste, Freud had seen nothing but "Italian goddesses" and was filled with anxiety. The anxiety quickly turned into excitement, and he set about on his second day with high hopes of seeing others only to find that the beauties had mysteriously decamped. Then he decided that the women failed to meet standards of German beauty. Some of these Trieste woman wore a lock of hair luridly over one eye, he told Silberstein, a curiosity that moved Freud to include an illustrative drawing among those of his fishes. Characteristically, his thoughts then turned to work.

Each day fishermen brought their catch to the zoologists so that they could select their specimens. Freud chose sharks, eels, rays, and others whose anatomies he studied with particular regard to their reproductive organs. "I have been tormenting myself and the eels," Freud wrote, "in a vain effort to rediscover [Syrski's] male eels, but all the eels I cut open are of the gentler sex." Freud included a drawing of a "gentler" eel, which truly seems, at least to an observer armed with the knowledge of her gender, to be feminine in a quiet, unostentatious way.

## A Visit to the "Jewish" Village of Muggia

Freud had been too happily engaged to write much, but two weeks later the weather turned wet and gloomy. Fish did not stir, fishing boats stayed in their berths, and the only employment for zoologists was cursing about the weather.

> The fishes and other beasts, too, simply do not go out in bad weather. The sharks and rays stay in their cubbyholes at the bottom of the sea, perhaps talking politics or cursing the facchini [porters] and the perils of the straits, the less highly organized bony fish drink coffee at home or play cards, while all the maritime rabble, whose sole purpose is normally to be devoured or caught, all the pelagic matter that sports itself on the waves of the Adriatic, exerts its every hydrostatic skill to sink out of sight so as to survive until a better day.[76]

During the inclement weather, when work was impossible, Freud and a fellow zoologist took an excursion to the nearby medieval fishing village of Muggia. Freud was deeply impressed by the visit and described the village to Silberstein in detail.[77] He was struck by an inscription in Latin on the town hall commemorating the mayor's expulsion of the Jews in 1532, which he mistranslated as celebrating the forced *internment* of the Jews in Muggia.

But what impressed Freud most about Muggia were "three massive signboards with beautifully flowing letters and the full names" to advertise the services of midwives. What seemed a superfluity of midwives—how, he wondered, could such a small village need so many?—proved otherwise when he began to encounter children and pregnant women everywhere. And they were as noteworthy for their beauty as for their number. "It was . . . interesting and gratifying," he told Silberstein, "to find that the girls and children in the ancient ruins were assai belle [pretty enough], half of them rustic beauties, and that even the women were pleasing to behold, whereas the corresponding class of population in Trieste, which ought by rights to be beautiful, is brutta, brutta [ugly]."[78] These Muggian women were "mostly blonde, oddly enough, which accords with neither Italian nor Jewish descent; the locals are not Slavs either."[79] Following his misunderstanding of the inscription on the town hall, Freud seems to have imagined that the local population was largely Jewish, the progeny of generations of inbreeding.

Freud wrote vividly of the local characters whom he met at the village inns. There was an impoverished drunk whom a pregnant landlady harangued and the children taunted; there were, among the patrons, "three pullets, a dim-witted dog, and a magnificent white cat with yellow-brown spots and stripes"; an "ancient woman" who had come in to beg, followed by two entertainers; and "a small boy with a concertina and a woman carrying a guitar in a coarse sack. . . . The poor woman, presumably his mother, had such pale features and sunken eyes, and so pointed a nose, looked so wretched and scraped away at her instrument so desperately, coughing all the while," Freud told Silberstein, "that we were inclined to believe theirs was genuine misery." He and his friend gave them money and left the inn but got caught in a deluge that forced them to take shelter in a second inn. Here they found another pregnant landlady with "two golden-haired children." Here too was a noisy drunk, who made political speeches, saluted the other patrons as Garibaldi, and got himself into repeated altercations with the landlady. Returning to their boat in the Muggia harbor, Freud found that

the local beauties were out promenading on the molo, inspecting and laughing at the strangers. A beautiful woman with a lovely boy

who had been visiting his uncle in Muggia and had been given a
present of a chick, yellow all over, tied up in a fazzoletto [hand-
kerchief] and squawking pitifully whenever it was squeezed, kept
us company during our crossing. I gave the boy a few shells I had
picked up on the seashore, and parted from him with a kiss as be-
fits a zio [uncle], an office which has been bestowed on me again
in the last few days in Manchester [earlier that month a son had
been born to Freud's half brother Philipp].[80]

Back home in Vienna over the summer, sweltering in the August
heat, Freud good-naturedly missed Silberstein, who was in Roznau,
as were Freud's mother and sisters.[81] In September Freud returned to
Trieste for a second research externship of a month's duration. Unfortunately, we have no letters from that visit or, for that matter, from
the next year, except for a letter counseling Silberstein on his younger
sister's education. The next full letter was written August 15, 1877,
when Freud was 21; this letter tells us little developmentally other than
that his spirits remained good.
    It appears that as the transition from adolescence to first adult-
hood came to a close, Freud's need for intimacy with Silberstein
diminished.[82] Even in the longer letters there is the kind of newsiness
that leaves the self undisclosed. The next letter, on September 7, 1877,
is of this sort. After professing little fresh knowledge of the doings of
mutual friends, Freud noted tellingly: "This is an example of how old
attachments can evaporate."[83] "I invite you," he wrote Silberstein, "to
conjure up a nice winter evening when together we shall burn the archives [of the Spanish Academy] in a solemn auto-da-fé. Out of bore-
dom, I am keeping a diary once again, but, like my present
circumstances, it is rather bleak and uninteresting."[84] A time of developmental quiet was setting in.

> Nothing much else [than waiting for reliable news about the Russo-
> Turkish war] is happening either. It rains for a few days so that
> people can acquire colds, then the weather turns fine for no good
> reason, and then it rains again until in the end the misery of winter
> will be upon us. Today all the world is preparing for the High Holi-
> day; I am told we are to have a leap year. There is much cooking
> and baking going on at home and the only result will be that I shall
> have a worse night's sleep than usual. I remember with pleasure
> that the whole spectacle passed me by last year in Trieste.[85]

Freud considered that "gorging oneself on such a scale" could be justified only if one is among many guests, in which case the food is celebra-
tory. Otherwise, it is merely an assault on the digestive system. "We

young people who have half left our own families and have not yet found a new one are in fact singularly unsuited to the enjoyment of holidays." It rankled that despite his readiness to begin the business of being an adult, he still had to live at home.

Psychologically, his bag was packed to overflowing. Rather than a simple unitary dream, Freud was entering the adult world with a complicated one. The scholar-scientist part was a gift from his father, the revolutionary clinician part a legacy from his mother, and all of it was conditioned by his cultural position as an exiled provincial Jew in Catholic Vienna and by his location in a century in which the Jews were enfranchised and science and medicine were becoming triumphant.

# CHAPTER FIVE

# Entering the Adult World
## (Ages 22–28)

$A$FTER his introduction to zoological research in Trieste, Freud moved on to study physiology. At 20 he secured a position as a research student in Ernst Brücke's physiology laboratory at the University of Vienna. Poorly housed, Brücke's ramshackle laboratory was nonetheless a center of intellectual discovery and excitement within the medical school. Brücke was 60 when Freud became his student, and, like Brentano in philosophy and Claus in zoology, he too had been recruited from Germany to bring the modern empirical outlook to Vienna. Brücke was Prussian Protestant, a leading member of the Helmholtzian positivist revolution in science and medicine, and a man for whom the work of science was infused with religious zeal and principle.

With his colleague Du Bois-Reymond, Brücke had "pledged a solemn oath" to eschew all nonmaterial explanations of physiology and "in those cases which cannot . . . be explained by these forces . . . to find the specific way or form of their action" through mathematical methods "or to assume new forces equal in dignity to the chemical–physical forces inherent in matter, reducible to the force of attraction and repulsion."[1] His Berlin colleagues, savoring the good fortune of remaining in the *Hauptstadt* of German science, enjoyed referring to Brücke as "our Ambassador to the Far East." Indeed, with his High German dialect and strict personal and scientific scruples he stood in marked contrast to the easygoing duplicities of Vienna, its Low German speech, and general self-indulgence.

Brücke was an evolutionary biologist for whom Darwin was the principal inspiration. His research ranged among zoology, histology, and biochemistry, and he had explored problems with important psychological aspects, such as speech, perception, audition, language, and art. Brücke's conception of medicine was elaborated in his *Lectures on Physiology,* published in 1876, the year Freud began studying with him. In the next few years Brücke published articles in chemistry, public health, physics, art, clinical medicine, neurophysiology, and the liberal arts education of physicians.[2]

Freud soon came to identify with Brücke, making this inspiring, intimidating exemplar of scientific commitment a permanent part of his inner psychic world. Based on his senior's example, Freud's early research in physiology concerned the principles and results of evolution. Thus, when Freud studied the nervous system of the *Petromyzon,* a primitive form of fish, he was joining in the endeavor not only to learn more about how it functioned but also to further establish the connections between primitive and advanced species such as man himself.

## A Mentor for Freud's Dream of Science

All medical students were expected to take Brücke's courses on physiology and human anatomy and to spend one term in his laboratory.[3] During the academic years 1875–1876 and 1876–1877, Freud took six courses, despite the fact that Brücke was a dreaded member of an examination team. Five of these courses were taught by Brücke's assistants, Ernst von Fleischl-Marxow and Sigmund von Exner.[4] If a student muffed Brücke's first question, the professor refused to participate further, withdrawing instead into an adamantine and disapproving silence. Jones reports as typical an anecdote in which a student wrote the phrase "Superficial observation reveals" and got the paper back from Brücke with the words crossed out and the angry prohibition "One is not to observe superficially!"[5]

Freud, too, ran afoul of the old man in an awful event that was still doing him good 20 years later. It was a signal moment in Freud's professional socialization as a scientist and formed a screen memory of adulthood (by which I mean a memory from the adult past pregnant with significances gathered from a number of similar, though less dramatic, occurrences).

> I had been a demonstrator at the Physiological Institute and was due to start work early in the morning. It came to Brücke's ears that I sometimes reached the students' laboratory late. One morning he turned up punctually at the hour of opening and awaited

my arrival. His words were brief and to the point. But it was not they that mattered. What overwhelmed me were the terrible blue eyes with which he looked at me and by which I was reduced to nothing. . . . No one who can remember the great man's eyes, which retained their striking beauty even in his old age, and who has ever seen him in anger, will find it difficult to picture the young sinner's emotions.[6]

Despite Brücke's severity, some young men succeeded in winning his approval, and to them he offered himself as a mentor in the true sense of the word, offering interest, counsel, and protection well beyond the helpfulness of a well-intentioned professor. This he would do for Freud some few years later when Freud applied to the faculty for a travel grant and Brücke beat back the opposition on his behalf.[7] He was also above the preening middle-aged vanities so offensive to the young, including the sort of careerism that leads professors to press-gang students into their own research programs. Brücke preferred instead that his students follow their own inclinations, although he was ready to supply one if needed.[8]

Far from alienating Freud by intimidation, as Gay writes, the aging scientist impregnated his young protégé with "the ideal of professional self-discipline in action."[9] Freud later said that Brücke was the greatest authority who had ever worked on him and wrote in his autobiography that after having tried various departments in the university, he found a home in Brücke's laboratory, complete with men he could take as his "models: the great Brücke himself, and his assistants Sigmund von Exner and Ernst von Fleischl-Marxow." Freud considered the latter "a brilliant man" and felt privileged to be on terms of friendship with him.[10]

## Brücke over Claus

As a fledgling adult of 20, Freud needed something to believe in, and he found it in science personified by Brücke.[11] Yet one might wonder why Freud embraced Brücke as a scientific mentor instead of Claus. Claus was certainly as great a scientist and had strongly encouraged Freud's aspirations. Writers have speculated about Brücke's greater transference suitability, noting his similarity in age to Jacob Freud; that is, Brücke was two generations older than Sigmund whereas Claus was senior by only one. But, as mentioned earlier, Josef Breuer, who would be Freud's next and final mentor, was only 14 years older, a fact that casts doubt on this theory. The reasons for Brücke's greater influence appear twofold. The first has to do with Freud's preference for naturalistic observation over experimentation, the second with the presence in Brücke's laboratory of Fleischl-Marxow and Exner, two gifted young men who provided a psychological bridge between the young Freud and the old professor.

Jones was the first to suggest that the explanation resides in the fit between subject matter and Freud's temperament. Claus's field, zoology, required dissecting animals. Freud apparently hated messiness and was considered squeamish by his family.[12] Jones wrote that not only was Freud incapable of cruelty but he had a strong aversion even to interfering with people. The Kleinian psychoanalyst Joan Riviere commented too that Freud had little interest in directly influencing other people.[13] Jones thought that this resulted from a markedly passive side to Freud's nature and theorized that this was the basis for his predilection for observation, such as the study of histology by microscope, rather than the study of physiology by experimentation. And it is relevant in this regard that the summer before joining Brücke, Freud had tried a summer of research in Salomon Stricker's experimental pathology laboratory. He had received a warm welcome and had set eagerly to work doing experiments on salivary secretion in dogs.[14] Yet Freud apparently failed as an experimentalist.[15]

In his autobiography Freud wrote that a decisive turn in his development as a scientist occurred when he realized that for him observation was the requisite tool. And it certainly seems true that Freud liked to watch. But his attitude seems to have been not so much passive, as Jones suggested, as poised; as is, for example, one's attitude when one studies something with intense interest, such as the free associations of an analysand, or the posture of a lion (and this is the kind of simile Freud would later use to describe his psychoanalytic stance) watching a nearing gazelle or, we might add, an oedipal little boy in the presence of a nude and pregnant mother.

If part of the attachment to Brücke was Freud's predilection for observation, the other was the appeal of Fleischl-Marxow and Exner.[16] Having an admired senior and glamorous younger intermediaries, especially Fleischl-Marxow, constituted an unusually nutritive mentorial soil from which to grow an identity as a scientist. For if Brücke represented an end point of development, his younger assistants—only a half-generation older than Freud and still young in an absolute sense—demonstrated a midpoint of development that was within closer reach. With sufficient age to put them largely beyond the rivalry felt by a sibling and secure in their own accomplishments, these men in their 30s delighted in Freud's progress.[17] Fleischl-Marxow, especially, seems almost from the start to have felt a warm preference for Freud, and his attitude, apparently accepted by Brücke, provided a rich provender from which the narcissism of the hungry and gifted young man fed heartily. When Brücke asked Fleischl-Marxow what he should examine Freud on, Fleischl-Marxow had replied that Freud would probably know everything.[18]

Fleischl-Marxow showed Freud how one could be a dedicated scientist *and* a young man. This was critical to the development of the 21-year-old's identity. To be too much like Brücke would have meant identity foreclosure and a premature suppression of youthfulness, or, more colloquially, precocious old-farthood, a fetid persona for which we have seen in his censorious letters to Silberstein that Freud had some predilection. Fleischl-Marxow, despite a painful chronic illness, retained an irreverent wit and sparkled in conversation. Women found him charming.[19] Freud liked to quote Fleischl-Marxow's tendency to first marvel at the beauty of a scientific hypothesis before concerning himself with its validity — "If you further take into consideration that the matter is even true . . . " — a nice antidote to Brücke's scientific puritanism.[20] Freud found in Fleischl-Marxow a constellation of intellectual and physical virtues nearly Greek in its perfection.[21]

Nonetheless, while Freud loved and admired Fleischl-Marxow, a distance dictated by 10 years' disparity in age remained between them. And Fleischl-Marxow was, after all, one of Freud's teachers and would be his examiner for the first *Rigorosum* examination for the M.D. degree.[22] The distance between the two may have increased as Fleischl-Marxow's interest in others became eclipsed by the increasing pain in his hand.[23] There was also the fact, which became more significant as Freud's research accomplishments grew, that Fleischl-Marxow (and Exner) stood in the way of Freud's promotion within the laboratory.

Some may feel that to characterize such favoritism as mentorial is to dignify it. Isn't this simply the old boy–young boy network at work? In reality, what was going on here was far more complicated than mere favoritism; there are deep developmental processes involved, and they are reciprocal. For just as younger people need mentors to grow up, older people need protégés to help them grow old well. Seeing their work living on in upcoming generations of adults helps older people feel that their lives have been, and continue to be, worthwhile. When older men are treated well enough by the tribe (here, the medical school), their generativity flows naturally — provided, of course, that their capacities for generativity were not stunted by inadequate mentoring when they themselves were young. When the circumstances of older men (social, familial, or organizational) are too depriving or exigent, they tend to avoid — or, in the most extreme cases, to envy, hate, and even seek to ruin—the younger ones. Thus, under good-enough circumstances, older men *need* to be mentors to avoid stagnation.[24]

By virtue of his persistence, intellectual gifts, and talent for accepting mentorial help gracefully rather than with patricidally symptomatic acts, Freud succeeded in attracting the attention, then the affection, of these older men. Their approval and interest not only reassured Freud but spurred him on to greater efforts, for he then had to warrant their good opinion of him, even though it made it easier for him to succeed. Since Freud had already proven himself to them, the elders tended to overlook some of the blemishes in his performance, as Brücke did when he examined Freud's laboratory knowledge and skills; their attitude toward him was no longer, in the main, definitively evaluative.[25] This change in attitude is essential to the formation of a real mentor relationship, which rarely occurs when evaluation is in the foreground, even though, usefully, this aspect never disappears entirely—especially in the protégé's imagination. Thus, Fleischl-Marxow and Brücke's belief in Freud made it possible for him to develop into the scientist he as yet only dreamed of becoming and placed him under a debt of gratitude to do so.

## Brücke Gives Freud a Direction

Perhaps encouraging the line of research Freud had already begun in zoology under Claus, Brücke suggested in 1876 that Freud investigate the unresolved problem of the very large cells that had been discovered in the spinal cord of the *Petromyzon*. Freud accepted the assignment and solved the problem quickly. He showed that the roots of some posterior cells of the nervous system began in these large cells. Brücke thought the finding sufficiently interesting to ask Freud to prepare it for publication, which the younger man did, and Brücke submitted the paper to the Academy of Science on January 4, 1877.[26] Although Freud had written the article on the gonads of the eel earlier, this paper on the *Petromyzon* was his first article to appear in print; the eel paper was published later that year. During the next year Freud was full of scientific enthusiasm, writing to Silberstein for the first time of being possessed by a "scientific demon."[27]

Beginning under Claus's and more so under Brücke's supervision, Freud published five scientific papers between 1876 and 1882.[28] There were two on the neuroanatomy of the *Petromyzon,* one on the gonads of the eel, one describing a new chemical preparation for the microscopic study of nerve tissue, and one on the nerve cells of the crayfish. The pace and quality of these publications set Freud in line for promotion to Brücke's assistant, a position similar to an assistant professorship in an American university. However, Brücke had only two assistantships, and these were already filled.

Freud's relationship to these early publications shows an interesting developmental progression. His first two, appearing while he was still in his early 20s, were offered to the world by his teachers, and Freud himself minimized their value.[29] After publishing these articles and with a third in galleys, he joked, perhaps nervously, of an analogy between publishing articles and murdering kings. Future publications, he wrote his old Gymnasium friend Knöpfmacher, kept "appearing in [his] prescient mind, which [was] startled by them like Macbeth by the ghosts of the English kings: 'What! Will the line stretch out to the crack of doom?' "[30] The third publication, again on the *Petromyzon*, was also filed by his teacher, Brücke, but this time Freud's attitude toward it was unapologetic. The next year, at 23, he was delighted to find his work on the spinal ganglia referred to in a publication by another scientist and to see himself described in that paper as "the aforementioned research scientist."[31] His fourth publication was one page long and described a small but successful modification of an existing technique for preparing nerve tissue. Finally, Freud submitted his fifth study, on the nerve cells of the crayfish, to the Academy of Sciences himself on December 15, 1881, when he was 25. In this paper he conceived of the nerve cell and its fiber as one anatomical entity and in so doing anticipated the momentous creation of the neuron theory, which lay 10 years in the future. Brücke considered this a very important study, and Freud was not shy about it either.[32] Freud presented the results of his researches in neuroanatomy in a lecture to the psychiatric society in 1882 or 1883.[33]

At 27 Freud published his discovery of a radically new preparation for the histological study of nervous system tissue. Not only did he undertake to publish the discovery on his own this time, but he was quick to publish a brief account of his new technique in order to ensure priority. Simultaneously, he published an account of his method in the English journal *Brain*.[34] The three clinical papers in neuropathology Freud then published between 28 and 30 were written with obvious enthusiasm.[35]

## The M.D. Degree

In the spring of 1880 Freud began to prepare for his M.D. examinations. These were held between June 9, 1880, and March 30, 1881.[36]

Fleischl presided over the first examination, which was in botany, biology, and chemistry, bestowing upon Freud—who was never certain why—the grade of "Excellent."[37] On July 22 Freud had his second theoretical examination, this time in pharmacology. The day before, he told his friend Carl Koller of his failure to prepare for it. As it happened, the examiners did criticize his inaccurate use of some theoretical terms and urged greater diligence, but they did not fail him. Under God's protective hand, Freud later wrote Koller, he had won an unearned victory and felt undeservedly proud and happy.[38] The important point in terms of Freud's identity is the feeling of fraudulence as a physician.

On the 24th Freud received official notification of the results of the examination and wrote Koller again. He had received outstanding grades in pathological anatomy, general pathology, and gastroenterology. In pharmacology his answers to all questions had been adequate, even though he knew that his halting responses evidenced poor preparation.[39] That same day he also wrote Silberstein about his success and told his friend that he was about to celebrate by taking a brief trip to the mountains with his "two roses," one being a cousin and the other his younger sister.[40] Two letters of little consequence follow. With the announcement of this good news to his best friend, the youthful correspondence with Silberstein had come to an end, though intermittent visits continued. Freud received his M.D. degree on March 30, 1881, while still just 24.[41] The Fluss family was among his well-wishers at the graduation, although whether Gisela herself was there, we do not know.[42]

One year later Freud met Martha Bernays while she was visiting his sisters. As he had once done with Gisela, Freud fell precipitously in love. Two months later, on June 17, 1882, they were engaged, a betrothal that would take more than four years to consummate. The day after their engagement Martha left with her mother to spend the summer far to the north in Wandsbek, outside Hamburg, Germany. Although she returned in the fall, the couple was separated for most of the next four years, with Martha living with her mother in Wandsbek and Freud living in Vienna.

According to Jones, Freud wrote more than 900 letters to Martha and visited her in Wandsbek a half-dozen times.[43] Thus, the published letters from their correspondence constitute only a fraction of the total. Nonetheless, Freud strips himself bare in these letters. As a lover he is at turns possessive, tender, forlorn, desperate, as filled with fury and threats as the God of the old Testament, and penitent. Freud's feelings were so violent that Gay likens them to the possessive rages of a firstborn confronted with a sibling.[44] Indeed, for anyone who has ever sought happiness in love and thought he has found it, these letters are painful to read, for we know the fate of this youthful illusion in general and in Freud's case, too.

As a middle-aged man of 52 who had by then been married for some 20 years, Freud wrote about sexual fulfillment in marriage in his article " 'Civilized' Sexual Morality."[45] Because of the risk of pregnancy and the obstructions of prevention, he argued,

> satisfying sexual intercourse in marriage takes place only for a few years. . . . After these three, four or five years, the marriage becomes a failure in so far as it has promised the satisfaction of sexual needs. . . . Fear of the consequences of sexual intercourse first brings the married couple's physical affection to an end; and then, as a remoter result, it usually puts a stop as well to the mental sympathy between them, which should have been the successor to their original passionate love. The spiritual disillusionment and bodily deprivation to which most marriages are thus doomed puts both partners back in the state they were in before their marriage, except for being the poorer by the loss of an illusion, and they must once more have recourse to their fortitude in mastering and deflecting their sexual instinct. . . . Thus the married state, which is held out as a consolation to the sexual instinct of the civilized person in his youth, proves to be inadequate even to the demands of the actual period of life covered by it. There is no question of its being able to compensate for the deprivation which precedes it.

Was Freud describing the rule to which his own marriage was the happy exception? From his letters to Fliess, we shall see that this is as unlikely as is the possibility that he was writing only about his personal situation. Freud did not exempt himself from his theorizing about the human condition in other instances; there is no reason to imagine he was doing so here.

## A Principle at Last

We are rather dependent on Ernest Jones for some of our knowledge of the early relationship between Sigmund and Martha. Jones knew them both and besides his personal reminiscences presumably had access to unpublished letters and diaries. Among these personal documents was the *Geheime Chronik,* or secret diary, kept by the couple. Jones paints Sigmund and Martha's engagement in Dickensian hues and his cannot be taken as an objective account.

Gay is more factual. He has Jones's account as well as access to unpublished letters. He too pictures Freud as a determined lover; he writes that when Freud met Martha, he knew right away what he wanted and that his "masterful impetuosity carried her with him."[46] Yet Freud's own account of their first meeting suggests that Martha took the initiative. Indeed, particularly during the first year, but in some measure throughout, Freud seemed ambivalent, not simply about the short, unprepossessing, and determined 20-year-old he had promised to marry but about the life structure to which he was committing himself.

If it does not appear that Freud seized the initiative, it is nonetheless true that his feelings toward Martha, denied all but the most proper outlet, were tumultuous. The courtship was Jane Austenesque, consisting in small gestures infused with significance. He sent her roses and likened her to a fairy princess; she sent him a cake; he sent her a copy of *David Copperfield*. A dinner guest at the Freuds', Martha's place was designated by a name card; he took possession of the card, she pressed his hand under the table.[47] A small act certainly, one hardly able now to capture the erotic interest of any but the most repressed and imaginative. Yet after 10 years of fantasies about Gisela and 10 postpubertal years of living at close quarters with Amalia; after living with Rosa, roughly Martha's age,[48] and with Dolfi, Mitzi, Paula, and, yes, Anna too; after months of reading Silberstein's letters from Leipzig, which drove him out into the night through streets perfumed with prostitutes and aglitter with actresses, chanteuses, and shop girls; after years of being the envious, disapproving witness to the erotic exploits of other middle-class Jewish boys; after seaside excursions among the exotic Southern women of Trieste and Muggia, after years of abstinence, sublimation, and denial — after all the stimulation and deprivation, now, finally, this actual, available female person had sat next to him and, under the table, *nearly touched it!* Words stuck in his throat. On the 15th of June, just before their engagement and her departure to Wandsbek, Freud wrote on stationery engraved with his father's name:

> In the few minutes we shall have together I shall not find the leisure and perhaps the courage to talk over everything with you. . . . It was so wonderful today in your home, near to you, but I could not bring myself to use in my own interests the few moments Eli [Martha's brother] left us alone; it would have seemed to me to be a violation of the hospitality so warmly accorded, and I would not do anything base when near you. . . .
>
> It won't come. I cannot say here to Martha what I still have to say. I lack the confidence to finish the sentence, the line that the girl's glance and gesture forbids or allows. I will only allow myself

to say one thing: the last time that we see each other I should like
to address the loved one, the adored one, as "Du." . . .
How much I venture in writing that![49]

The passage from the formal *Sie* to the intimate *Du* is a momentous
one in German (then and often enough even now), but masterful impetuosity this was not. Ardent and heartfelt, fed by deep sources of
passion and ambivalence, yes; but impetuous, no.

A few days later Freud wrote his love: "Martha is mine, the sweet
girl of whom everyone speaks with admiration, who despite all my
resistance captivated my heart at our first meeting, the girl I feared
to court and who came toward me with high-minded confidence. . . .
When you return . . . I shall have conquered the shyness and awkward-
ness which have hitherto inhibited me in your presence."[50]

As Freud's account of her initiative suggests, Martha seems to have
been a much stronger personality than has been commonly thought.[51]
Despite being five years younger and, at 20, barely adult, in relation
to Freud she behaved with a sturdy sense of her own worth. As the
middle child of three, she was not prominently placed in the sibling
order, but she was her brother Eli's favorite and she was the oldest
sister. Eli's being only a year older had perhaps given her an indelible
experience of authority relations between males and females in which
the tilt in authority is only modest; the boy she had fought with and
loved all of her life had not been far above her. Though she does not
look good in photographs (neither did her young fiancé), as Freud himself told her at the time, she must have been more attractive in person, when her features were animated by her personality.[52] Men were
certainly drawn to her: her devoted brother; her former teacher Fritz
Wahle, who was inconsolable about her engagement; her cousin, the
middle-aged Hamburg businessman Max Mayer, who had asked for
her hand before she met Freud, as had her father's friend Hugo
Kadisch.[53]

Martha also had the security that comes from class and culture.
In both respects, her position was elevated well above Freud's own,
and this superiority may have held part of her allure for him. She was
North German and came from a religiously orthodox and cultured
home. Her uncles were language scholars. Her father, who had died
of a heart attack in 1879, had been a merchant appointed as secretary
to a Viennese economist. Her paternal grandfather had been the chief
rabbi of Hamburg and had fought the reform movement in Judaism
let loose by the revolutions of 1848. It is said that even as a mature
woman Martha continued to speak *Hochdeutsch* to Viennese trades-

people, who found it nearly incomprehensible. Martha's mother, Emmeline Bernays (née Philipp), was also a highly educated woman, whose parents had come from Scandinavia. Emmeline was as religiously conservative as her husband had been.

One may wonder what Martha saw in an impoverished young physician. Today a fledgling doctor has status and is likely to make a good living, but this was in no sense assured in Freud's time. Further, Freud was, as he himself said, reticent with all but close male friends and family. His demeanor and social behavior could be graceless, even tortured. He was not well dressed nor particularly well groomed. He possessed little of the sort of charm that could excite a young woman's heart, and brilliant as he obviously was, it was the musty brilliance of laboratory science, largely devoid of communicable drama. Perhaps it was the recent death of her father and her wish to reduce her mother's financial burdens that led Martha to seek a mate in earnest. And perhaps she was inclined toward Freud in particular because she sensed the smoldering heroic passions gathered within the awkward youth's breast. These poured forth upon sincere invitation, and if they were not always well directed, they *were* exciting. I imagine she sensed that if it were at all possible, Freud would become someone in the world, and she knew that with proper feminine guidance Freud would keep his word to her.

During the early days of their engagement Martha so firmly told Freud to stop giving her expensive presents that he objected to her being categorical and to her attempts to exercise her customary authority as "eldest daughter and superior sister."[54] Later on in the engagement, in a mood of reappraisal, Freud wrote:

> Do you remember how you often used to tell me that I had a talent for repeatedly provoking your resistance? How we were always fighting, and you would never give in to me. . . . And you admitted that I had no influence over you. I found you so fully matured and every corner in you occupied, and you were hard and reserved and I had no power over you. This resistance of yours only made you the more precious to me, but at the same time I was very unhappy, and when at the corner of the *Alser Strasse* we said goodbye for thirteen months, my hopes were very low, and I walked away like a soldier who knows he is defending a lost position. And whereas our being together threatened to estrange us, during the separation I received signs that I might be victorious after all . . . [and I noticed during reunions] that the stiffness and reserve which you yourself so often deplored would vanish the moment we were together.[55]

One year after their engagement, in June 1883, Emmeline Bernays moved her family back to Hamburg—perhaps, as Freud's letter suggests, not a minute too soon. The first year the couple spent together in Vienna had nearly done them in. For the remaining three years of their engagement, other than for short visits, Martha and Sigmund were separated. These years when neither could get their hands on the other allowed them both to mature and, in Freud's case if not in Martha's, to tame the tempest of ambivalence.

Freud's ambivalence manifested itself in repeated ultimata, each of which carried the possibility of a final break, and in the recurrent notes of satisfaction with the status quo—that is, Freud working productively in Vienna, his beloved safely tucked away 325 miles to the northwest—that crept into his correspondence. According to Jones, Freud had even tried to get Martha to agree to a one-year probationary engagement, a suggestion she quite rightly rejected as nonsense.[56] Apparently at one point Martha accused him of *letting* her leave Vienna so that he could be alone with his beloved research.[57] One is reminded of Freud's earlier remark to Silberstein that looking for the right woman was preferable to having one around and under foot. This was Freud's version of the Augustine prayer "Make me chaste, Lord, but not yet!" The temptation that Freud was yielding to was not sex but solitude and work. Marriage was the blessed state to which he aspired but "not yet," Freud insisted, while blaming Emmeline and company for the separation, "not yet!"

Freud's ambivalence was also revealed in the perfervid idolatry of his love letters to Martha. As he would later teach us, every mental attitude has its opposite in the unconscious, and none more strongly than those that violently dominate our conscious minds. Indeed, some writers have delighted themselves and their readers by making Freud look absurdly Victorian and paternalistic, quoting the many occasions in his love letters to Martha in which he extols her virtues as a dear, sweet, silent, acquiescent, and intellectually vapid perfect little darling. Writers who enjoy this sort of ridicule seem unaware that people a hundred years from now may find our gender ideals and our ways of expressing love equally comic. They also overlook the fact that, on occasion, Freud could be as deflating as the most prosaic egalitarian. Moreover, there is a contrary yet equally strong thread running through these letters, and this thread has received little notice. It issues from Freud's genuine appreciation of Martha's qualities as a person and expresses his wish that Martha be his equal and that disagreements between them be openly faced. That this wish had its opposite in Freud's inclination to subordinate her does not make it insincere.

Freud voiced this wish in one of his first letters to Martha: "If

I may repeat [*sic*] a request today, please don't be taciturn or reticent with me, rather share with me any minor or even major discontent which we can straighten out and bear together as honest friends and good pals."[58] True enough, Freud wanted a wife who would devote herself to creating "a small world of happiness" for him and their family, but he also wanted an equal, a *Kameraden,* not just a sweet little girl.[59] Freud was offering Martha, herself in the initial stage in the formation of her identity as an adult, a developmental opportunity, if only she would take it. "We must face all [the disagreements and disappointments] as equals," he wrote Martha on September 25, 1882.

> Would I shed a tear if you remonstrated with me? We have taken upon ourselves a difficult task and in carrying it out we must support and correct one another. Words of love alone cannot do this; living together does not mean hiding unpleasant things from one another or glossing over them. . . . You will understand me when I say that even for a beloved girl there is still one further step up: to that of friend, and that it would be a ghastly loss for us both if I were compelled to decide to love you as a dear girl, yet not as an equal, someone from whom I would have to hide my thoughts and opinions— in short, the truth.[60]

"You must be able to take some criticism and return it if you feel like doing so," he urged Martha, after one such disagreement.[61] Toward the end of their engagement, complaining about Martha's attempt to avoid a disagreement with him through artifice, Freud wrote, "One of these subterfuges kept annoying me for almost two years, and I would rather think of you with false teeth in your mouth than one dishonest word."[62] Within days of their wedding Freud wrote Martha that he had "taken [her] to [him]self in every respect, as sweetheart, as wife, as comrade, as working companion."[63]

Freud's wish for genuine intimacy with Martha sprang in part from his love of the truth. In a cynical age, jaded in part by Freudian insights inherited without his personal integrity to go with them, such an assertion may seem risible. To say that Freud loved truth is not to say that he was always truthful nor that he was always correct about what he perceived to be true. Rather, it is to say that among the values that people can come to hold dear, truthfulness was for Freud central. If this is overpraising Freud, we may note that devotion to the truth can become tyrannical, as can less lofty pursuits. One form Freud's love of truth took was his insatiable appetite for the contents of the mind, which was already apparent in his adolescence in his demands on Silberstein for full epistolary disclosure and in his complaints when his friend failed to be fully forthcoming with the minutia of his mental life and experience. This appetite would later be formulated in the requirement of free association, *die Analytische Grundregel,* in satisfaction of which psychoanalytic patients strive to give voice to all their thoughts without editing or censoring.

It seems likely, too, that Freud's insistence on honesty was fed by his suspiciousness, which with some intimates could render even the mundane duplicities of everyday life unacceptable. After all, among his earliest memories was the one of being tricked by his half brother Philipp when he had been looking desperately for his mother, and he may have felt that Amalia, too, had tricked him with an implied promise of exclusive devotion. He certainly felt that way about Gisela's departure from Freiberg after he had fallen in love with her. Now Freud suspected that Martha was harboring allegiances to her family, which he had demanded she renounce as a condition of their betrothal. When Martha tried to argue that he needn't know everything about the small matters that concerned her, Freud insisted, "This is just what I demand of you, and I do it myself. You have also often promised me to do it and I have always been so happy when I have been able to think of you with absolute trust."[64]

Yet Freud was not blind to this mania and at times recognized his own tendency to brood excessively about harmless quotidian intrigues.[65] Freud, as we know, had good projective reasons for thinking Martha secretive—he loved secret allegiances himself. We recall the Spanish Academy with Silberstein and the morbid fantasies of discovery that had followed Freud's confidences about Gisela in their correspondence. We also know the secret rings that lay in Freud's distant future, rings that he and his middle-aged acolytes—all old enough to know better—would wear to signify their membership in the hidden inner circle of psychoanalysis.

Furthermore, in the beginning Freud felt that his engagement to Martha had to be kept a secret from both families and most of their friends, presumably because Freud's poverty would have made impossible the parental permission both he and Martha were bound by custom and fidelity to secure. Although Freud may have exaggerated the necessity for concealment, the attempt to keep the engagement secret made even correspondence difficult. Couriers and accomplices had to be recruited, entrusted, and, if found errant, harshly corrected. Martha chose their mutual friend Fritz Wahle to address the envelopes Freud would send to her. Freud found a colleague in Brücke's laboratory to serve as the addressee to whom Martha would send her letters.

In the event, Freud's boyhood experience in the Spanish Academy proved no match for the intelligence experts who now surrounded him and into whose area of special expertise he had blundered. Rosa immediately sensed the new direction of her brother's feelings, and after that, so did Mitzi, Dolfi, and Paula. Even Anna, long relegated to the French Foreign Legion of her brother's affections, got the news.[66] It could not be long then, and it wasn't, before both families knew of the engagement.

## Fritz Wahle

Martha's choice of Fritz Wahle as secret agent proved a mistake, although one that rendered her irresistible. While Martha insisted that her former teacher's interest in her was merely friendly and their continuing intimacies mentorial, Freud began to suspect otherwise. For one thing, Fritz did not seem to understand that his position as Martha's confidant must end. For another, Martha seemed a little vague about this necessity herself. As his suspicions grew, Freud turned to Ignaz Schönberg for the facts. Schönberg had become engaged to marry Martha's younger sister Minna, and he knew Wahle well. Freud demanded that Schönberg disclose what he knew of the relationship between Martha and Fritz. Schönberg obliged and told Freud that indeed Martha had accepted a kiss from Wahle and had done so after Freud and Martha had become intimate; worse, Martha had done so on the very day when she and Sigmund had first walked together alone. When Freud next demanded that Schönberg divulge everything, Schönberg recalled an additional, suspicious detail: At the moment Wahle learned of Martha's engagement, he had burst into tears; afterwards he took to complaining about the dimming of Martha's interest.[67]

These disclosures drove a wedge between Freud and Wahle, and Schönberg, wishing to reunite them, arranged a meeting to straighten things out. All three men met in a café, where Wahle took the occasion to become hysterical. He threatened to shoot Freud and himself if Freud failed to make Martha happy. Evidently, Freud laughed, trying to rise above the histrionics. Wahle blustered that if he asked Martha to do so, she would drop Freud in an instant. Freud dismissed this too, and Wahle, maddened, immediately penned a letter directing Martha to break off the engagement. Freud demanded to see the letter. Wahle surrendered it, and Freud read words like "beloved" and "undying love." Freud bellowed and ripped the letter to shreds; Wahle ran out into the street. Outside, the two friends dissolved into tears and embraced. But by the next day Freud had become adamantine— Wahle must go, and if he did not, dire though unspecified consequences awaited him.[68]

Yet Martha continued to insist, not only that her relationship with her former teacher was an innocent one but that it continue as well. She had been close to Fritz, Martha argued; why should she have to give up her friends in order to marry Freud? And after all, she pointed out, Wahle had been a friend of Freud's as well as hers, and Fritz was engaged to marry Martha's own cousin. Yet in the end Martha had to accept the obvious: Fritz Wahle was in love with her and the friendship had to end.

Freud's reaction to the Fritz Wahle business may appear pathological to people who have never fallen in love, or never deeply, and it certainly was extreme. But in addition to Freud's wounded narcissism, we also need to keep in mind that what was at stake for Freud was not only a person, Martha, but a *life* he was desperately trying to build and, episodically, avoid. Having been successful in his initial attempts to create an occupation, Freud felt that marriage to Martha represented the missing piece of the life structure that would set the stage for and ultimately enshrine the realization of his dream.

Freud had other reasons to react so strongly. Now that he was fully committed for the first time, the loss of Martha would have been a grievous blow. Freud had closed out his adolescence and begun his adult years as a hurt young man; losing Martha might have meant living the rest of his life as a truly damaged person unable fully to trust and love a woman again. About that first summer of their engagement, Freud later wrote Martha: "When the memory of your letter to Fritz and our day on the Kahlenberg comes back to me I lose all control of myself, and had I the power to destroy the whole world, ourselves included, to let it start all over again—even at the risk that it might not create Martha and myself—I would do so without hesitation."[69] Three years later he said that the Wahle episode had been so painful that it was "unforgettable."[70]


## Eli and Emmeline

It did not take long for Freud's combative possessiveness to focus upon the two leaders of the Bernays family, Emmeline and Eli. On August 14, 1882, two months into their engagement, Freud issued Martha a warning. "From now on," he advised, "you are but a guest in your family."[71] Criticizing Martha for compromising with her mother's insistence that letters not be written on the Sabbath, he told her, "Eli little knows what a heathen I am going to make of you." In his first reference to Emmeline, Freud added, "She is fascinating, but alien, and will always remain so to me. I seek for similarities with you, but find hardly any. Her very warm-heartedness has an air of condescension, and she exacts admiration. I can foresee more than one opportunity of making myself disagreeable to her and I don't intend to avoid them."[72]

As Jones quipped, Freud insisted on driving all the men from Martha's life, including her mother.[73] Freud thought that Emmeline had taken over too much of the authority left by the death of her husband and that she was abusing it by insisting on taking the family back to Hamburg, where she felt happier being surrounded by relatives and old friends. Emmeline persisted in her determination to return even though both of her daughters were engaged to marry men who lived in Vienna, and despite the fact that finding a suitable fiancé for Minna, less prepossessing than Martha, had been a signal victory (after the death of her fiancé in 1886, it would prove unrepeatable). While the Bernays family had more money than the Freuds, they did not have enough to render the maintenance of Minna's engagement insignificant. Freud saw this and criticized the mother for her refusal to sacrifice her own satisfaction to the requirements of her daughters' futures. For her part, Martha admired her mother's indomitability and largely accepted her dominion over herself. By contrast, Minna was critical of her mother and sided with Freud, beginning a close and enduring friendship.

Freud had liked Eli prior to his engagement to Martha, and in the three years since her father's death Martha had become more dependent on her doting brother. But now differences arose. Freud's younger brother, Alexander, had begun serving what seems to have been an informal and unpaid *Lehre* with Eli in finance. Although it was customary for apprenticeships of this sort to be unpaid, Freud declared this to be mistreatment and forced a confrontation. Emmeline took Eli's side; Freud demanded that Martha take his side — or else. Martha did but objected to his "sharpness" with her family.[74] A temporary reconciliation occurred in January 1883, when Eli became engaged to Freud's sister Anna. Socially and economically, this engagement was entirely to Anna's advantage, and Eli's generosity in the matter softened Freud's feelings toward him. In fact, Martha and Sigmund took the happy occasion to disclose the secret of their own engagement to Emmeline. Unfortunately, neither Martha's engagement nor Minna's to Schönberg affected Emmeline's intention to move the family back to Hamburg the following summer. Eli, who worked in Vienna and thus would not be separated from Anna, supported the decision, reopening the breach with Freud.[75]

## Becoming a Competent Young Physician

Freud had become engaged to Martha shortly after his 26th birthday. At around this time the dormant clinical aspect of Freud's dream re-asserted itself. For the first time, the achievement of clinical competence became important to him, not simply so that he could support himself and Martha in private practice but so that he could express a deep fantasy and pursue an authentic identity. During the next three years, between ages 26 and 29, Freud became a physician, not simply a researcher who had passed his examination for the M.D. degree. Placing his emphasis on becoming a physician did not mean that Freud abandoned the scientific part of his dream. Rather, for a time he reversed the priority between his scientific aspirations and his fantasy of becoming a great healer.[76] Along the way, Freud suffered a wrenching near miss at realizing his clinical dream in the discovery of the anesthetic properties of cocaine.

By his mid-20s Freud was looked upon so highly as a young scientist that he was the presumptive heir to the first assistantship that fell open in Brücke's laboratory. It was then that he began publicly to stand by his research achievements and make a claim for their value. However, at 26 Freud tried his hand at experimental work in chemistry and met with a "humiliating" lack of success. So bad was the failure that he later called the year 1882 the "gloomiest and least successful" of his professional life.[77] Perhaps it was time for a change, and perhaps the scientific failure represented not true incompetence but a withdrawal of the spirit from science in preparation for a reinvestment of it in clinical work.

In his *Autobiographical Study* Freud gave his own version of the change from science to medicine. He recalled that although his father had told him to pursue his interests freely at the university, he nevertheless found that "the various branches of medicine proper, apart from psychiatry, had no attraction for [him]."

> The turning-point came in 1882, when my teacher [Brücke], for whom I felt the highest possible esteem, corrected my father's generous improvidence by strongly advising me, in view of my bad financial position, to abandon my theoretical career. I followed his advice, left the physiological laboratory and entered the General Hospital as an *Aspirant* [clinical assistant]. I was soon afterwards promoted to being a *Sekundararzt* [junior or house physician], and worked in various departments of the hospital, among others for more than six months under Meynert, *by whose work and personality I had been greatly struck while I was still a student.*[78] [Italics added]

In the myth of the heroic scientist, which he promoted and others have furthered, Freud was driven from science and propelled toward practice by his indigence and by his desire to marry and start a family. Gay subsumes Freud's clinical training under the section on his betrothal to Martha and devotes but one paragraph to it.[79] Yet Freud acknowledged in the foregoing quotation that he had earlier been highly impressed by Meynert, a brilliant cerebral anatomist, and had had from the onset of his medical studies an interest in psychiatry. We know that since his trip to Manchester at 19 he had had a strong secondary fantasy of becoming a great healer. Indeed, Jones sensed that Freud's protestations about his lack of affinity for practice arose from inhibition and that he regarded clinical work as a "Forbidden Land," suggesting the presence of conflicted desire.[80] And although it is true that late in life Freud opined that he was not a great therapist, he was never overheard to say that he wasn't a damned good one. As shall become clear, the excitement that Freud felt about becoming clinically competent makes it unlikely that it was simply poverty that drove him from science to practice.

In July 1882, three months after meeting Martha and a month after their engagement, Freud started work at Vienna General Hospital.[81] During the next year he became an assistant chief in Meynert's psychiatry section, was given a room in the hospital, and was finally able to move out of his parents' home.[82] McGrath has pointed out that here again a redirection of career appears to have been occasioned by a romantic event: With Gisela, it was from law to science; with Freud's niece Pauline in Manchester, it was from science to practice; and with Martha, it was again from science to practice. It certainly seems that a woman's admiration tended to turn Freud's ambitions toward the affairs of the world and that a woman's disregard tended to turn him inward.

Viewed developmentally, however, these events are more complicated. Rather than one event or relationship appearing to cause a shift in occupational direction, *both* infatuation *and* occupational choice appear to have been attempts to create a life structure in which his identity could be built in an authentic and valued way. Becoming a husband and a doctor was Freud's way of leaving his childhood family and creating a domestic and occupational basis for life in the world as an independent, if still novice, person in pursuit of his dreams. The occupational possibilities of the world in which Freud as a middle-class man sought to establish himself, a world in which men made money, married, had families, and exercised authority concerning other peoples lives, were the fields of law, business, medicine, the military, or government. How his scientific aspirations could be integrated within the life structure of marriage, family, and private practice remained as yet obscure.

In a letter of October 5, 1882, Freud described to Martha in vivid, lengthy detail an interview with Professor Hermann Nothnagel, director of the Second Medical Clinic, during which he applied for a teaching assistantship at Vienna General Hospital.[83] Since no opening was likely in the near future in his physiology laboratory, Brücke had advised Freud to seek opportunities elsewhere. Freud presented a letter of introduction from Meynert recommending him on account of his "valuable histological work." He also brought with him his reprints, which Nothnagel asked to see. As Nothnagel looked these over, Freud explained that he had begun in zoology and had changed to physiology and then to histology. Nothnagel received Freud's application with gracious interest, but the assistantship had already been filled. In the meantime, Nothnagel advised, Freud should continue with his scientific research until a new opening arose. Freud objected that he could not afford to do that, explaining that he had to prepare himself to set up a practice as quickly as possible, perhaps in England where he had relatives (and we note, where he had imagined he might become a rich and famous clinical innovator).[84] He told Nothnagel that he could no longer devote himself to producing scientific publications, where upon Nothnagel replied that there was no necessary conflict between research and practice, that medicine could and should be practiced scientifically, and that one could write scientific articles about clinical findings. Freud insisted again that he needed to acquire clinical skills, and Nothnagel assured him that becoming more clinical in his work and writing would not prejudice any future application.[85]

Freud told Martha that he had not been discouraged by the interview. Rather, he felt his prospects for a future opening were good. "For the time being . . . , I shall go on working as though there is no hope. What I am going to tackle next I am not quite sure. I am considering dermatology, not a very appetizing field, but for general practice very important and interesting in itself." It was not merely love but the complex richness of Freud's dream, and the excitement of creating new life structure in which the larval but heroic clinical aspect of it could be lived out, that made even dermatology seem interesting. Indeed, the entire encounter with Nothnagel is told with the enthusiasm of a young man entering a new and exciting world.

The following August (1883) Freud wrote Martha for the first time of his patients. Anyone who has undergone clinical training knows what having one's own patients means to the growth of a young adult's identity. Having his own patients meant that Freud was *responsible* for the fate of their treatment. He was now considered to be a person who *knew*, a person who must know (or must quickly learn), what he was doing. As such, he was becoming *mature enough to face*, if not accept, the most fervent wishes and abysmal fears from the patient himself and those who loved him. And he was becoming a person whom doctors considered *capable* of caring for patients and whom other doctors would admire and envy for his success and criticize and condemn for his failures. All of this added up to a tremendous growth in Freud's sense of self-worth and manhood, as well as to a staggering sense of responsibility that his self would have to expand to incorporate if he was to carry it well.

Only the month before, in July 1883, Freud's senior clinician friend, Josef Breuer, whom he had met in Brücke's laboratory, had told him a harrowing personal epic of a failed treatment. Breuer had begun referring patients to Freud for private treatment, and Freud was relying on him for clinical consultation. Freud had visited the Breuers on a hot summer evening and had been invited to refresh himself with a cool bath; afterward, the two men had dined comfortably in shirtsleeves. Freud wrote Martha, "A lengthy medical conversation on moral insanity and nervous diseases and strange case histories [took place] — your friend Bertha Pappenheim also cropped up — and then we became rather personal and very intimate and he told me a number of things about his wife and children and asked me to repeat what he had said only 'after you are married to Martha.' " Freud assured Breuer that his fiancée already had his full confidence.[86]

Bertha Pappenheim would become the famous Anna O. of Breuer and Freud's *Studies on Hysteria,* published in 1895. The previous summer, Miss Pappenheim's treatment had blown up in Breuer's face just when he thought he was bringing it to a successful conclusion. Now Breuer confided to Freud the intriguing, horrifying tale of a strangely intimate new way of being a doctor and its attendant personal dangers. Over the course of a year and a half Breuer had tried heroically to alleviate the young woman's bewildering array of pseudoneurological symptoms through hypnosis and suggestion. At the same time, powerful erotic transferences and countertransferences had developed between them, which the physician did not understand and had no technical means to master. Left to gather strength unnoticed, these transferences had intensified in both doctor and patient, but especially so in Miss Pappenheim who ultimately became so overwhelmed by her fantasies that, according to Jones's account, she believed herself to be pregnant with Breuer's baby.[87] Breuer had been horrified by this inexplicable appearance of insanity just when he thought the patient had been cured, and he committed Miss Pappenheim to a sanitarium.[88] We shall have more to say about this dramatic clinical case later.

Two weeks after hearing Breuer's clinical travail the 27-year-old Freud wrote Martha, "I came to my patient today completely at a loss how to find the necessary sympathy and attentiveness for him; I felt so limp and apathetic. But this feeling vanished when he began to complain and I to realize that I have a function and an influence here. I don't think I have ever attended him with greater care, nor made such an impression on him; work really is a blessing."[89] In September he wrote Martha that Breuer was away and that he missed him for both personal and professional reasons.[90] Meanwhile, he was so busy with his responsibilities on the wards that life had the quality of delirium. On October 9, 1883, Freud told Martha,

> I function in the wards as a *Sekundararzt,* busy learning, writing, and occasionally acting as surgeon. . . . Cases, theories, diagnostics, formulas have moved into brain accommodations most of which have been standing empty, the whole of medicine is becoming familiar and fluid to me, here bacteria live, sometimes turning green, sometimes blue, there come the remedies for cholera, all of which make good reading but are probably useless. Loudest of all is the cry: tuberculosis! Is it contagious? Is it acquired? Where does it come from? Is Master Koch of Berlin right in saying that he has discovered the bacillus responsible for it?[91]

By the winter of 1883–1884, not only was Freud treating paying patients in the clinic and publishing clinical papers but he was also tutoring private pupils and lecturing to professional societies. He had been asked to lecture to the Physiological and Psychiatric Clubs, and Meynert had invited him to give a lecture to the Medical Society as well. Freud described his new and fragile competence as clinical lecturer to Martha:

> I really do wish you had been present to hear my lecture today, Marty. I haven't had such a triumph for a long time. Just imagine your timid lover, confronted by the severe Meynert and an assembly of psychiatrists and several colleagues, trying to draw attention to one of his earlier works, the very one which had been overlooked by Prof. Kufer.[92] Imagine him beginning with allusions, unable to control his voice, then drawing on the blackboard, in the middle of it all managing to make a joke at which the audience bursts out laughing! The moments in which he is afraid of getting stuck, each time fortunately concealed, become fewer, he slides into the waters of discussion where he sails about for a full hour, then Meynert with some words of praise expresses the assembly's vote of thanks, follows this up with a few appreciative observations, then dissolves the meeting and shakes him by the hand.[93]

On the basis of this talk Freud published a paper on the structure of the nervous system in the 1884 *Yearbook for Psychiatry*.[94] Further, his new method for the preparation of brain slides was translated into Russian, the third language in which he was now being published.

Freud's hospital duties and clinic practice had grown to such an extent that they were interfering with research.[95] In January 1884 Freud began work in the Department of Nervous Diseases of Vienna General Hospital under Franz Scholz. Despite miserable conditions on the ward, Freud stuck with it. In January 1884 Freud also completed his first clinical paper on the localization of cerebral hemorrhage in a case of scurvy, a paper he had written in 10 days.[96] He was also enjoying cheering letters from Martha in Hamburg. "A moment ago," he wrote, "my beloved treasure, I put the finishing touches to my first clinical publication. There it lies now, eighteen pages long, and it will spread itself in two to three issues."[97]

Indeed, Freud was taking so much satisfaction in his work, and in his epistolary love affair with Martha, that he was content to imagine a prolongation of the status quo. He told his fiancée of a wife who had waited 15 years for her husband and suggested that Martha might have to do the same. For himself, he wrote, he had already accepted the possibility that she would be 30 when they married (Martha was then 23). "Everything is so sweet of you and about you," he rhapsodized. "Do you think you can continue to love me if things go on like this for years: I buried in work and struggling for elusive success, and you lonely and far away?"[98]

Excited by his achievements and new status, Freud, in a letter to Martha on February 7, 1884, described a reunion with Silberstein as though his old friend were a figure from the prehistoric past. "Silberstein was here again today," he wrote, " . . . as devoted to me as ever. We became friends at a time when one doesn't look upon friendship as a sport or an asset, but when one needs a friend with whom to share things." He recalled that they had spent all of their time together and had created the imaginary world of the Spanish Academy, which they alone had inhabited and in whose language they had corresponded, cavorting like puppies. Silberstein's intellectual appetites, Freud informed Martha, had since become middle-brow and his imagination romantic. "Then you appeared on the scene and everything that came with you; a new friend, new struggles, new aims." For a time, Freud had continued to offer Silberstein advice about his love life: "The drifting apart which had gradually developed between us became apparent again when I advised him from Wandsbek against marrying a stupid rich girl whom he had been sent to have a look at." Then the friends, Freud explained, "lost contact with each other."[99] Now Silberstein had resurfaced in Vienna, was readying himself to marry the benighted heiress, and had become a banker. "Today he is about to gather together again his old boon companions in Hernals, but I am on duty, and in any case my thoughts are not in the past, but elsewhere."[100]

Freud's research was flourishing, and the prospect of fame—or at least of the *Dozentur*—had brightened. The position of *Privatdozent*, similar to a lectureship in an American university, carried no salary nor regular faculty duties, but it did allow one to teach and charge tuition and was a sine qua non first step up the ladder of the medical aristocracy.[101] In late May 1884 Freud had another conversation with Nothnagel about his future. Evidently, Nothnagel had noticed how pleased Freud was feeling with his life and how little he was doing to make marriage possible. He invited the young man to accompany him to a meeting of his medical club and offered Freud some advice along the way. Freud wrote about their séance to Martha on May 29, 1884, a couple of weeks after turning 28. Nothnagel told Freud to go to the Austrian provinces or further abroad to make money. Then, perhaps after Breuer retired, Freud could come back to Vienna and establish a practice. But now Freud was armed with fresh accomplishments and not so willing to leave. He told Nothnagel that he was still considering immigrating but wanted first to see if he could make it in Vienna, that he would give himself a year to secure a position as *Dozent* and get his lectures going. Nothnagel warned Freud that it would be difficult to attract students and admitted that in his first attempt, he himself had only attracted four. He recommended that if Freud insisted on trying to set up practice in Vienna, he should practice the new electrotherapy in order to attract referrals from general practitioners, on whom the development of a neurology practice would depend. The general practitioners would not be impressed with Freud's scientific papers on the nervous system, Nothnagel cautioned. He knew what they would think: "What's the good of Freud's knowledge of brain anatomy? That won't help him to treat a radialis paralysis!"[102] He urged Freud to publish more clinical papers and to lecture to the medical societies.

Freud admitted to Martha feeling an "irresistible temptation to devote [his] life without remuneration or recognition to the solving of [scientific] problems unconnected with our personal situation, [and that this] could postpone or even destroy [their] chances of sharing life." He noted that it had been three years since he became a doctor.[103] In June 1884 Scholz left Freud in charge of the department.[104] "I have never felt better," he wrote Martha, concluding, "I am very much respected in the department."[105] Junior doctors and nurses were

placed under Freud's authority, for he now functioned as Superinten-
dent. "Ruling," he complained with satisfaction, "is so difficult," adding proudly, "In these weeks I have really become a doctor."[106] By
August he was giving a "very successful" treatment for buzzing in the
ear. He sent Martha his picture, depicting "a dispossessed man of importance"; Scholz had returned. By January 1885 Freud was experimenting with injections for facial neuralgia and feeling excited by
his apparent success.[107]

Research and doctoring were going so well that Freud was feeling full of himself. By August 3, 1884, he could write:

> Work, nothing but work; I myself am surprised at the amount of
> work I can get through. But I know what's driving me; the heart
> is well again, the giant strong again, gigantically strong. Are you
> laughing at me for calling myself a giant? Sometimes I have such
> a sense of power I feel there must be something I could still do to
> bring us together sooner. How I will love you then, laugh at you
> and scold you, and you won't say a word, because you are a silent
> darling.[108]

## A Missed Opportunity to Realize the Clinical Dream

Shortly before his conversation with Nothnagel and within days of his
28th birthday, Freud had decided to attempt a "therapeutic experiment."[109] He had been reading about the use of cocaine to enhance
the strength and stamina of soldiers and had decided to send away
for some. He planned to test it in cases of heart disease and "nervous
exhaustion." The nervously exhausted whom Freud evidently had in
mind were himself and his friend Fleischl-Marxow. Freud's neurasthenia
was mild, chronic, and recurrent, and his drug use would now be considered experimental or recreational. Fleischl-Marxow had become addicted to morphine to combat the awful postoperative suffering from
surgery to remove neuromas in his hand and now was having to undergo in addition the effects of morphine withdrawal.[110] Not knowing that cocaine was potentially addictive and finding no craving for
the drug in himself, Freud imagined that it would provide Fleischl-
Marxow with a harmless pain-killing substitute for the morphine.

Freud's enthusiasm for cocaine initially knew no bounds. This was
his first chance to achieve a clinical breakthrough of the revolutionary sort that he had imagined in Manchester, England, when he was
19. He called it a "magic drug" and was using it with dramatic success on himself and others. Within a few months he published two
more clinical papers in the medical journals, one on the therapeutic

uses of the drug.[111] His first scientific paper on the subject was a curious combination of science and insistent advocacy, with Freud declaring that cocaine was useful in treating depression and morphine addiction and suggesting that it might also have value as a local anesthetic.

But rather than pursue the hypothesis experimentally, Freud abandoned it in favor of a visit to Wandsbek and Martha. Before departing, he suggested to his ophthalmologist friend Koller that cocaine might be useful in eye surgery, and Koller successfully followed up on Freud's suggestion. Soon Koller became famous for having made an important clinical discovery. Freud was forced to settle for the satisfaction of assisting Koller that April in a successful operation on Jacob Freud, who had developed glaucoma.

Initially, Freud's reaction to Koller's discovery was congratulatory. According to Jones, Freud thought that Koller's finding was of only secondary importance and that he himself would demonstrate the most important uses of cocaine. It took some time for the bitter truth to sink in, namely, that he had, through his "laziness"—his Brückean word for the failure—neglected to establish priority concerning the drug's primary clinical application.[112] When at last the truth sank in, Freud felt bad on two counts: first, because in his haste to visit Martha he had not followed through sufficiently (*One must not observe superficially!*) in his research and, second, because his friend Fleischl-Marxow had become addicted to the drug. Gay writes that this failed opportunity left Freud filled with rage and resentment, which lay dormant for many years. As Gay notes, Freud's dreams in his 40s contained numerous references to this missed opportunity, and the Irma dream (which we will turn to later), the foundation dream of psychoanalysis, is replete with it.

Furthermore, in his effort both to follow Nothnagel's advice and to realize his own clinical ambitions, Freud had blundered into his first controversy with his medical colleagues. Freud did get credit from some quarters for having hypothesized the drug's anesthetic value, but he was vilified by others for having offered a new and dangerous temptation to those desperate for relief of pain as well as to unsuspecting pleasure seekers. Freud's conscience was too sensitive and his ambition too great for this first public criticism not to have stung him and left an indelible mark. Three years later he still felt it necessary to respond in print to the charge that he had recklessly sponsored a new addiction, and Jones believed that this first public argument with some members of the medical community set the stage for later ones concerning male hysteria.[113] It was not until much later, when he had led his own revolution in clinical work, that Freud was able to give a dispassionate, if clipped, account in his *Autobiographical Study* of Koller's right to the discovery. There he refers to cocaine as a side but "deep" interest and jokingly blames and forgives his fiancée for preventing him from securing early fame.[114]

Jones surmised that cocaine held a conflicted significance for Freud derived from its enlivening effects against Freud's own recurrent depressions. Though the drug certainly had that pleasant effect on Freud, its personal significance had less to do with passing euphorias than with the exciting, frightening prospect of an early realization of his clinical dream. Being able actually to help patients with the drug carried the excitement of growing clinical competence; indeed, he had achieved a remarkable success with it in the treatment of gastric pain. "In short," he wrote Martha, "it is only now that I feel I am a doctor, since I have helped one patient and hope to help more."[115] Clinical fame, however, went beyond helping a patient or two and may have made Freud anxious about whether he really had sufficient clinical ability to make claims for himself beyond an initial, fragile proficiency.

Certainly, Freud's hope of helping Fleischl-Marxow had turned into a horrible mockery. Fleischl-Marxow became dependent on huge doses of cocaine, which still only controlled the pain in his hand imperfectly. Yet even though Freud was confronted with an immediate clinical failure, the failure stirred inchoate visions of a future clinical success. More than once, Fleischl-Marxow demanded that Freud spend the night by his side as he lay submerged in a warm bath, slipping in and out of consciousness and ranting deliriously from misery and intoxication. Freud's account to Martha of these meetings shows that they had an unmistakable free-associative quality. Freud wondered if he would ever again see "anything so agitating or exciting as these nights. . . . [Fleischl-Marxow's] talk, his explanations of all possible obscure things, his judgments on the persons in our circle, his manifold activity interrupted by states of the completest exhaustion relieved by morphia and cocaine: all that makes an *ensemble* that cannot be described."[116]

Here was an analogue of the psychoanalytic treatment of the future. In it would be joined Freud's insatiable appetite for the uncensored contents of the mind, his intensely engaged yet spectatorial interest, and his readiness to embrace suffering even when he could not relieve it. This is an odd quality in a physician. Most doctors want to get rid of suffering by curative treatment; if this isn't possible, or doesn't work, they become avoidant. In the private argot of American medicine, patients who do not respond to treatment and continue to intrude their suffering upon physicians are called "crocks." Uncommonly, Freud managed to find even incurable suffering interesting and to be sympathetic to the sufferer.

However, it was not a time for appraisal but for doing, and, as
Gay writes, Freud's regret lay largely dormant. Business was picking
up, and the year he told Nothnagel he would give himself to get established in Vienna was proving good. By the summer of 1884 Freud
had succeeded in gaining some paying pupils in brain anatomy. By
November his lecture course had six students, all English, and he was
feeling rich.[117] By January he had 11,[118] despite his lacking explicit
authority from the medical school to offer a course.

## Working at Science, Too

As Freud worked to acquire practical skills and write clinical papers,
he did not neglect the scientific part of his dream entirely. After leaving Brücke's lab for Meynert and Vienna General Hospital, Freud continued to do research in the histology of the nervous system. In fact,
in his autobiography Freud makes no mention of his new clinical skills
or clinical papers but describes as seamless the continuation of his
research interests in basic science:

> In a certain sense I nevertheless remained faithful to the line of work
> upon which I had originally started. The subject which Brücke had
> proposed for my investigations had been the spinal cord of one of
> the lowest of the fishes (Ammocoetes Petromyzon); and I now passed
> on to the human central nervous system. . . . The fact that I be-
> gan by choosing the medulla oblongata as the one and only subject
> of my work was another sign of the continuity of my de-
> velopment.[119]

He had been pursuing a new chemical method for preparing brain
slides, a method that would reveal more clearly than existing preparations the relations of the nerve fibers and cells under microscopic
examination. On October 23, 1883, he told Martha that he had found
"a new gold method" that seemed the best yet. "Yesterday in my joy
I went to see Breuer as late as 9:30. . . . 'Let's go for a walk,' he said.
We went arm in arm toward the Karl Theater and when I broke my
news and talked of it for a long time and finally asked his forgiveness
for holding forth on a subject which might not interest him, he was
good enough to say: 'Few things interest me more.' "

At 27 Freud summed up the achievements of this first period of
his adult life:

> Apart from its practical importance, this discovery has an emotional
> significance for me as well. I have succeeded in doing something

I have been trying to do over and over again for many years. When I survey the time since I first began to tackle this problem, I realize that my life has progressed. I have longed so often for a sweet girl who might be everything to me, and now I have her. The same men whom I have admired from afar as inaccessible, I now meet on equal terms and they show me their friendship. I have remained in good health and done nothing dishonorable; even though I have remained poor, those things which mean something to me have become available, and I feel safe from the worst fate, that of loneliness. Thus if I work I may hope to acquire some of the things that are still missing and to have my Marty, now so far away and lonely as her letter shows, close by me, have her all to myself, and in her tender embrace look forward to the further development of our life.[120]

On the back of the envelope enclosing this letter Freud had written in English "HOPE AND JOY."

Two months later, in January 1884, Freud was thinking of neurology as *his* area. "It infuriates me," he wrote his fiancée, "to see how everyone is making straight for the unexploited legacy of nervous diseases."[121] "In one field of science," he declared to Martha in April, "I am independent enough to make contributions without any further contacts or assistance, by which I mean my knowledge of the nervous system."[122]


## Another Audience with Nothnagel

On January 16, 1885, Freud, then 28, appeared before Nothnagel as petitioner for a third time, now in an attempt to secure his support for an application for the *Dozentur*. "Today," he wrote Martha, "I had my wild beard trimmed and went to see Nothnagel, handed in my card: '[Dr. Sigmund Freud] takes the liberty of asking if and when the Herr Hofrat can be seen on an important personal matter.' " Freud sat down in a waiting room that teemed with patients who began to grumble at the prospect of the young doctor being allowed in first. "At last came [their] disappointment," Freud wrote, "for I was admitted ahead of them all to the man who had so often played a decisive part in my life." Did the professor have time to consider a request? Freud inquired. Nothnagel said that he did if it were brief. Freud asked if he would support his application for the *Dozentur*. " 'What are your papers on, Doctor? Coca——,' " Freud wrote to Martha, quoting Nothnagel. When Freud produced his reprints, Nothnagel had fingered them, saying, "You seem to have eight or nine. . . . Oh, by all means send in your application. When I think of the kind of people who get the

*Dozentur* . . . ! There won't be the slightest objection." But Freud had gathered himself in expectation of greater obstacles and could not keep from rushing forward. "But I have several more things to be published, two of them in the immediate future," he said. Nothnagel waved him off: "You won't need them; these are more than enough."

The meeting was archetypal. Here is the young man who had turned himself inside out trying to meet the requirements the older man had seemed to set for him, and there with the appearance and authority of a Teutonic god is the middle-aged man who (out of caprice, incompetence, Valhallian preoccupation with weightier matters, a good digestion?) is telling the young Jewish chap standing before him, hopes in hand, that his costly and strenuous efforts have far exceeded what was necessary.

"But there isn't much about neuropathology among them," Freud insisted, wondering if he still was too weak in the clinical domain. But the *Herr Professor Doktor* Nothnagel was in an approving vein; besides, he was busy. "That doesn't matter. Who knows anything about neuropathology unless he has studied anatomy and physiology? You do want the *Dozentur* for neuropathology, don't you?" Nothnagel assured Freud that he, Meynert, and Bamberger had the authority to push the appointment through the department in the unlikely event of opposition.

Disorganized by the easy victory, Freud could not keep from giving further expression to his sense of clinical fraudulence. "It's a question of legalizing an unauthorized lecture course I'm giving. Actually, I'm only lecturing to some English people in their language, but there's quite a run on it." But even this did not avail against the prevailing good will, and Freud left the office in a thick haze of Nothnagelian beneficence.[123]

## The Decade of Freud's 20s Comes to a Close

Freud in his 20s had made a highly successful debut as a novice adult. At the beginning of that decade he had secured a position as an apprentice scientist in Brücke's laboratory and had acquired Brücke as a mentor for the scientific part of his dream. He published his first scientific papers in physiology and successfully fulfilled his military obligation at age 23 by caring for army patients hospitalized in Vienna.[124]

During his mid-20s Freud settled upon the nervous system as his area of specialization within biology. He published scientific papers in neurology and histology, passed his examinations in medicine, and earned his M.D. degree. He met his future wife, Martha, fell in love, and became engaged to marry. Despite the many opportunities for failure provided by the long engagement and separation and despite the inevitable ambivalence of an inexperienced young man making a commitment that would extend further into the future than he could truly imagine, Freud succeeded in sustaining his warrant to Martha. In so doing, he stepped manfully forward to suffer what George Bernard Shaw called the second of life's two great tragedies — getting what one wants.

In his late 20s Freud began what we would now call a clinical residency and took his first steps toward realizing the fantasy he had neglected while he was single-mindedly pursuing science — that of becoming a healer. He published clinical papers, lectured in the hospital, had paying pupils and patients, and felt proud of an expanding reputation as a competent young physician. Contrary to his own later assertions, being a doctor became by his late 20s (and would remain) an important, if secondary, part of his identity.[125] At 27 Freud joined the psychiatrist Theodor Meynert in his Cerebral Anatomy Laboratory and made the decision to be a neurologist, but he still did not have a mentor for his clinical aspirations. Nonetheless, in the space of only a few years and through great effort, ability, and the help of older men, Freud made remarkable progress in building an entry life structure for early adulthood.

But as Freud's 29th birthday neared, the stable period of building a life structure, which had begun in his early 20s, began to come to an end. On March 10, 1885, Freud wrote Martha, "Today, you know, marks a clear dividing line in my life; all the old things have been finished, and I am in a completely new situation. But it has been a good time." He had just applied for the clinical position of *Sekundararzt*. The promotion would be a step up the career ladder he had been steadily pursuing since entering the hospital at 26 and would enrich the life structure he had built for himself. But the therapeutic repertoires of the greatest neuropathologists, including Meynert, were too limited to hold further appeal for Freud. All they could do was make diagnoses, and these could only be confirmed by autopsy. The developmental possibilities of the clinical aspect of his life structure now seemed to Freud exhausted, and it was time for a change. He wrote Martha that it seemed likely he would get the appointment, yet, surprisingly, he found he no longer wanted it.

> At the moment I have little desire to become once more part of the hospital establishment. What I want, as you know, is to go to Paris [to study with Charcot] via Wandsbek, have enough leisure to fin-

ish my work on the brain, and then the independence to find out
what chances there are for us here. . . . . If I renounce the journey
and continue with the hospital routine, I would soon lose my patience. It's true, of course, I haven't got the traveling grant yet; lots
of people would say it is sheer folly to turn down a job I applied
for a month ago. But a human being's demon is the best part of
him, it is himself. One shouldn't embark on anything unless one
feels wholehearted about it. . . . .

It is four years today since I got my doctor's degree, and I
celebrated the occasion by doing nothing and paying a call on Breuer
at noon.[126]

One month later, on April 28, 1885, Freud took a further step toward
breaking free of the past. "This has been a bad, barren month," he
wrote Martha. "How glad I am it is soon coming to an end! I do nothing all day; sometimes I browse in Russian history, and now and again
I torture the two rabbits which nibble away at turnips in the little room
and make a mess of the floor." He was carrying out a deed that would
befuddle his future biographers. "I have destroyed," he announced,
"all my notes of the past fourteen years, as well as letters, scientific
excerpts, and the manuscripts of my papers." Presumably, this included
all of the Giseliana still in his possession. "As for letters, only those
from the family have been spared." Martha's, he hastened to assure
her, had never been in jeopardy.

In keeping with the reappraisal now claiming his time, Freud did
not simply destroy the archives, he reviewed them.

In doing so all old friendships and relationships presented themselves once again and then silently received the *coup de grâce* . . . all
my thoughts and feelings about the world in general and about myself in particular have been found unworthy of further existence. . . .
That stuff [had settled] round me like sand drifts round the Sphinx;
soon nothing but my nostrils would have been visible above the
paper; I couldn't have matured or died without worrying about who
would get hold of those old papers. Everything, moreover, that lies
beyond the great turning point in my life, beyond our love and my
choice of profession, died long ago and must not be deprived of
a worthy funeral.[127]

Freud looked forward, he told Martha, to watching his future biographers fail in their attempts to understand "The Development of
the Hero."[128]

# The Age-30 Transition
## (Ages 28–33)
### FROM STUDENT TO PHYSICIAN
### AND PATERFAMILIAS

FREUD continued his work on the nervous system under Meynert's guidance at Vienna General Hospital by studying the medulla oblongata in human brains. The nerve tracts in the medulla are exceedingly difficult to follow, and Freud soon came to feel that the conventional approach of examining multiple cross sections to chart the tracts was futile. Aided by his new gold chloride method for preparing slides, Freud opted for a developmental approach. He chose to study the simpler brains of fetuses on the assumption that the structures found there would endure as the brain matured and that the principles of their organization would continue to hold true.[1] Meynert not only supported this research but offered to turn over his position as lecturer to Freud.

Despite the apparent generosity of Meynert's offer, Freud declined. The task seemed too large, and Freud found something crabbed in the man that fatally adulterated his generativity. Although he considered Meynert a preeminent neuroanatomist, Freud found it impossible to get along with him. He complained to Martha that Meynert did not listen and never seemed to understand what he was saying.[2] In saying no to Meynert, Freud rejected a mentorial successor to the line of neuroscientists that began with Claus and Brücke, a successor who was well placed to further his career as a neuroanatomist in Vienna. Instead, the priority of his concerns shifting from scientific to clinical,

Freud moved closer to Breuer, a man who had earlier established himself as a scientist and who was now one of the most respected practitioners in Vienna. At the same time, Freud nourished the fantasy of a brief but intensive training experience in hypnosis with Charcot.

In his *Autobiographical Study* Freud indulged his preference for describing the unfolding of his identity as a scientist as *the* story line of his development. Since then, the argument among his biographers has been mainly about the constituent elements in Freud's scientific development and their respective priority.[3] Though in his autobiography Freud alluded to a misalliance with Meynert, he presented the change from cerebral anatomy to clinical work and his trip to Paris as one required by "pecuniary considerations." He had to make a living as a doctor, he argued, and the best opportunity that presented itself given the particularities of his own training—he knew a lot about neurology and not much about anything else—was based on the shortage of specialists in nervous diseases. When Freud looked about for a master who had committed himself fully to this field, he saw that "in the distance shone the great name of Charcot."[4]

In fact, as we have seen, this was not merely a matter of expedience and practicality. Freud's dream contained both scientific and clinical elements, and he had built a foundation for each in his professional identity, even though the clinical part remained relatively undeveloped. Now, surprisingly, after all the hard work of his 20s, both aspects of Freud's dream and of his professional identity were in flux. Charcot held out not only a luminous example of clinical brilliance in the field of the neuroses but also the possibility of integrating the parts. The chance to study with him animated Freud's heroic healer fantasy without overpowering his scientific dream, since Charcot was a renowned scientist as well as a charismatic clinician. It was this hybrid identity, with creative tension between the parts yet with sufficient integration overall to permit authentic identity and a measure of inner peace, that Freud seemed to need. But the parts could not be integrated as long as the clinical function remained so weak. He had devoted the past couple of years to clinical training and had achieved a rudimentary version of clinical competence by his mid- to late 20s, but it remained very limited compared with his scientific training and accomplishments. Now it was time not only to strengthen the weaker part but to confront the problem of integrating both. In this critical piece of developmental work Charcot became not Freud's mentor, for their association was too brief, but his requisite other.

By age 27 Freud had already acquired a reputation in Vienna as a cerebral anatomist with an unusual ability to localize brain lesions. But he himself knew that his ability to apply his scientific knowledge to clinical cases was unreliable. The contrast between his growing reputation for diagnostic wizardry and his own inner estimation made him feel like an impostor. Commenting in his autobiography on this sense of fraudulence, he related an adult screen memory of being humiliated by a group of clinical students: Lecturing to a small assembly of physicians, Freud presented a case of chronic headache, which he diagnosed as cerebral meningitis. The students immediately saw that the patient was neurotic and showed Freud that he had misdiagnosed the case. "They all quite rightly rose in revolt and deserted me," he wrote in his autobiography, "and my premature activities as a teacher came to an end."[5] At this moment—or in the moments gathered together in this vivid and mortifying screen memory—Freud realized that he was not yet a competent physician and that he was certainly not ready to teach other doctors about diagnosis. Although he had begun his quest as a clinician, his pretensions were still too far ahead of the reality. He knew that if he was not to be a poseur—and for a poor Jew from the provinces with grand, defiant ambitions to be exposed as one would have been shattering—it was essential that he get more clinical training.

As is often the case in development, contradictory casting about preceded and was part of the not fully conscious process of making a real choice. As is also often the case when the parts of the dream permit integration, the things gathered in the casting about prove serviceable to the choice ultimately made. The position of *Privatdozent* in neuropathology, which Freud had applied for in January 1885, represented a first step up the *academic* research ladder. With Brücke leading the support, strongly assisted by Nothnagel and Meynert, Freud won the recommendation of the medical school faculty in July 1885 and the confirmation of the Ministry for Public Instruction in September.[6] The position of senior *Sekundararzt,* which Freud applied for on March 10, was a step up the *clinical* ladder in the hospital. But, two weeks later and in the face of brightening prospects for the clinical appointment, Freud applied for a travel grant to go abroad for a period of study with Charcot. As we have seen, he had suddenly decided that he did not want to become part of the hospital neuropathology establishment.[7] His hope was to visit Martha in Wandsbek on the way to Paris, and in anticipation of the grant Freud borrowed money to pay for the Wandsbek portion of the trip.

Now for the first time, Freud wrote of actually *dreaming* about his future. He had turned 29 on May 6. Soon he was having lifelike dreams about receiving the travel grant.[8] By June 19 Freud told Martha that he was dreaming about the grant every night. As it happened, the very next day he received news that the grant was his. Since he had already borrowed sufficient money to visit Martha, it was not the reunion with his sweetheart that hung in the balance. "Oh, how wonderful it will be!" he wrote Martha on hearing the good news.

> I am coming with money and staying a long time and bringing something beautiful for you and then go on to Paris and become *a great scholar* and then come back to Vienna with a huge, enormous halo, and then we will soon get married, and I will *cure all the incurable nervous cases* and through you I shall be healthy and I will go on kissing you till you are strong and gay and happy.[9] [Italics added]

Here Freud wishfully attempts to integrate the scholar (scientist) and revolutionary healer fantasies through the device of a run-on sentence.

On the same day, June 20, 1885, Freud learned that his *Dozentur* had been overwhelmingly approved by the faculty. Only a ceremonial lecture remained to be given before the senior faculty, and they had assigned Freud a topic in brain anatomy. The following week Freud wrote Martha, "Strange to think that I shall be standing in Brücke's auditorium where I did my first work and with an enthusiasm I have never known since, and where I had hoped to stand at least as an assistant beside the old man. Could this be an omen suggesting that I may after all return here for scientific work and teaching?"[10] If the clinician part of Freud's dream and identity was about to receive greater attention, the scientific aspiration remained primary.

## Charcot: The Napoleon of the Neuroses

Charcot was 60 in 1885, and he had just recently taken on the directorship of a new clinic for nervous cases at the Salpêtrière Hospital. In the transition from middle to old age and having shifted his research focus from organic illness to neurosis, Charcot may very well have been in a period of accelerated developmental change himself. Such animation could have been a source of what Freud saw as his "charisma," and this coincidence of developmental change in the two men would have been part of the magic of their encounter. For Freud, the primary source of the magic was his own developmental hunger for a clinical mentor, one committed, unlike Breuer, to the neuroses.

Hysteria was, as Freud later wrote, the most "enigmatic" of nervous diseases, and Charcot's placing it at the center of his clinical and research interests greatly expanded medical interest in the illness.

> This [disease] had just then fallen into thorough discredit; and this discredit extended not only to the patients but to the physicians who concerned themselves with the neurosis. It was held that in hysteria

> anything was possible, and no credence was given to a hysteric about anything. The first thing that Charcot's work did was to restore its dignity to the topic. . . . [He] had thrown the whole weight of his authority on the side of the genuineness and objectivity of hysterical phenomena. . . . Once the blind fear of being made a fool of by the unfortunate patient had been given up—a fear which till then had stood in the way of a serious study of the neurosis—the question could arise as to what method of approach would lead most quickly to a solution of the problem.[11]

Charcot had taken a major step in explaining hysteria when he succeeded in artificially reproducing under hypnosis paralyses that were identical to those that followed traumatic injury to the central nervous system. Clearly, ideas alone could cause paralyses.[12]

Freud arrived in Paris in mid-October after a long and happy reunion of some six weeks with Martha at the Bernays home outside Hamburg.[13] Not surprisingly, he arrived feeling uprooted and bereft. Among his happy anticipatory fantasies had been the hope of mastering French. But now this hope was sagging under the reality that he had no one to talk to. "Every day," he wrote Martha, "I seem to get worse at uttering these wretched sounds."[14] He had already given up entirely the fantasy of achieving a decent accent; the only question that remained was whether he would ever be able to construct a sentence properly. Unlike the first day he had spent as a research extern in Trieste at 19, Freud could not even find a pretty face to admire. Indeed, he found the general run of French people covertly hostile, dishonest, even volatile.

After a few days of desultory wandering about, on the 19th of October Freud screwed up his courage and presented himself at the Salpêtrière. There he asked for Charcot's assistant, the *chef de clinique,* Dr. Pierre Marie, only to find him gone.[15] Charcot was in the hospital, but Freud had not intended to approach the great man directly and had not brought his letter of introduction. So, he wrote Martha, he had had to conclude that "this step upon which so much depend[ed]" would have to wait.

On the 20th, Freud tried a second time, and on this occasion the introduction went just as Freud wanted. He joined a group of foreign doctors observing Dr. Marie examining patients in the outpatient clinic and presented his card. When Charcot arrived to take over the demonstrations, Marie handed him Freud's card. After concluding the clinical demonstrations, during which Freud had been struck by Charcot's eager curiosity and diagnostic brilliance—"so unlike what we are accustomed to from our great men with their veneer of distinguished superficiality," he wrote Martha—Charcot invited Freud forward to present his letter of introduction from the Viennese neurologist Benedikt.

He recognized Benedikt's handwriting, stepped aside to read it, said
"Charmé de vous voir," and invited me to accompany him. He advised me to make my working arrangements with the Chef de
Clinique, and without any further ado I was accepted. He then
proceeded to show me everything in the laboratory and the lecture
hall, passed through several wards and explained a great many
things to me. In short, although fewer formalities were exchanged
than I had expected, I soon felt very much at ease, and I realized
that in the most inconspicuous fashion he was showing me a great
deal of consideration. I asked his permission to show him some of
my [cerebral anatomical] slides, which I did briefly today.[16]

This introduction left Freud "full of hope."[17] Soon he was "completely happy to be back at work," dividing his time between attending clinical lectures and demonstrations, practicing his diagnostic and
hypnotherapeutic skills with patients, and continuing his research in
child cerebral anatomy. Although he initially found some of the other
doctors cliquish, within a month or so Freud had won a position of
respect among this larger group of doctors and had found among the
pleasures of Paris those that moved him — the Egyptian and Assyrian
antiques in the Louvre and the grand architecture and mysterious inner space of Notre Dame Cathedral.[18] Freud's alienation was also
considerably abetted by the hospitality shown him by the Ricchettis,
an older couple who welcomed him into their home. Ricchetti was one
of the foreign physicians who had come from Italy to study with Charcot. Despite being professionally established and wealthy, Ricchetti,
like so many of the physicians who had come to the Salpêtrière, apparently viewed Charcot as a demigod.

After just a month with Charcot, Freud felt a tranformation taking place.

I am really very comfortably installed now and I think I am changing a great deal. I will tell you in detail what is affecting me. Charcot, who is one of the greatest of physicians and a man whose
common sense borders on genius, is simply wrecking all my aims
and opinions.[19] I sometimes come out of his lectures as from out
of Notre Dame, with an entirely new idea about perfection. But
he exhausts me; when I come away from him I no longer have any
desire to work at my own silly things; it is three whole days since
I have done any work and I have no feelings of guilt. My brain is
sated as after an evening in the theater. *Whether the seed will ever
bear any fruit, I don't know; but what I do know is that no other
human being has ever affected me in the same way.*[20] [Italics
added]

To be welcomed by a great teacher who could catapult him to a new level of clinical competence and who conformed so closely to his most cherished imagining constituted a profound "new beginning."[21] Freud later wrote that "each of [Charcot's] lectures was a little work of art in construction and composition; it was perfect in form and made such an impression that for the rest of the day one could not get the sound of what he had said out of one's ears or the thought of what he had demonstrated out of one's mind."[22] Charcot also conducted impromptu intake diagnoses in the outpatient clinic, where, observed by his students, he made the full range of his thinking visible, including bewilderment and error, thus alluringly narrowing the gap between master and apprentice.

Being shown about the Salpêtrière by Charcot, a "museum of clinical facts," as Freud later called it, was to be escorted through the capacious hospital by one of the world's foremost clinical curators.[23] Listening to Charcot lecture, watching him examine patients, touring the wards with him, and overhearing his offhand clinical observations made Freud feel callow, back in the beginning stages of a clinical career rather than advanced along the path of scientific discovery that he had been successfully traveling since the age of 20. Thus, the inspiriting identification with Charcot, as all such identifications do, came at a cost. Getting clearer about the actual limitations of his knowledge and expertise both inspired Freud and left him feeling inadequate. The exhaustion of the previous life structure built around science was also apparent.

> When I get home I feel completely resigned and say to myself: the great problems are for men between fifty and seventy; for young people like us there is Life itself. My ambition would be satisfied by a long life spent learning to understand something of the world, and my plans for the future are that we get married, love each other and work with the object of enjoying life together instead of exerting every ounce of my energy trying to pass the post first, like a race horse—in other words, trying to build myself a home that would involve such effort and privation that I couldn't expect to be granted more than two or three years of mental health.[24]

It was Charcot as physician whose influence Freud was finding transformative and, at moments, enervating. Because of the new importance to Freud of clinical work, his research on children's brains, which he was continuing in Charcot's Pathological Laboratory at the Salpêtrière, was losing its appeal.[25] Freud ended the letter to Martha by describing a symptomatic act: in an attempt to save a small amount of money on one of Charcot's books, he had ended up becoming a subscriber to Charcot's *Archives* at a far higher cost.[26]

At some point in his first few weeks at the Salpêtrière, Freud, trying to distinguish himself decisively from the crowd that encircled Charcot, volunteered to translate his *Lectures on the Diseases of the Nervous System* into German.[27] On December 12, 1885, Charcot agreed. It was this gift from the young Freud to his senior that gave him a special place in Charcot's world.[28] Freud was so pleased by the honor, by the prospect of a strengthened connection to Charcot, and by the boost it would give his reputation and practice in Vienna that he decided to extend his stay in Paris. He was as excited as he had been on the day he had received his travel grant. He felt like "shouting and jumping for joy," both for this great good news and for the prospect of a Christmas visit to Martha in Wandsbek.[29] Freud also presented Charcot with a prospectus for an article on hysterical paralyses. The essential and new idea that Freud was working on was that hysterical pseudoneurological symptoms defy scientific anatomy and conform instead to popular lay notions about how the body works. Charcot was not convinced but encouraged Freud to develop his hypothesis nonetheless, offering to publish it in his *Archives de Neurologie.*

On January 17 Freud went to Charcot's home to pick up some sheets of his lectures for translation, and the two men met in Charcot's study for an hour. Freud told Martha that Charcot's study was as large as the entire apartment they hoped to have together and was "worthy of the magic castle in which he lives."[30] It consisted of two sections, one being devoted to science and the other to comfortable sitting. One section contained a large library. Tables were layered with books and journals while manuscripts and reference works lay bestrewn across Charcot's writing desk. There were Indian and Chinese antiques on display, and the walls were covered with paintings. A window overlooked the garden. It was, the dazzled young physician wrote his fiancée, "a museum."[31] Although on a grander scale, it was similar to the one Freud would later create for himself in Vienna at 19 Berggasse.

## Taking Stock

The Ricchettis were about to return to Italy, and to mark the event Charcot invited them to dinner. Ricchetti was taken aback and declined, but he bowed to Charcot's insistence that he and his wife come for dessert on January 19. Charcot suggested that Freud join them. In addition to the opportunity to get closer to Charcot, the invitation also constituted a debut in high society for the self-proclaimed "German provincial." The Charcots entertained guests drawn from an international elite, and Freud and Ricchetti, worried about fitting in, spent the afternoon fretting about their dress. It was one of Ricchetti's scruples not to live off his wife's wealth, and so the doctor, restricted to the proceeds from his own practice, went about shabbily attired. On this special occasion, however, his wife insisted that he go to the tailor and buy new trousers and a hat. Ricchetti did as his wife told him and received from his tailor the further advice that tails were unnecessary — the new pants and hat would be sufficient. In the event, he was the only guest who was not in full evening dress.

Freud was cannier. He wore his new tailcoat, in addition to a new shirt and white gloves. He also had his hair coiffed and his beard trimmed "in the French style." He wrote Martha that he "looked very fine and made a favorable impression on myself." Ready at last, Freud took some cocaine for extra confidence and mounted a carriage with the trembling and underdressed Ricchetti.

> We were the first after-dinner guests and as we had to wait for the others to come from the dining room, we spent the time admiring the wonderful salons. But then they came and we were under fire: M. and Madame Charcot; Mlle Charcot; M. Léon Charcot; a young M. Daudet, an unattractive youth, son of Alphonse Daudet; Prof. Brouardel, doctor of forensic medicine, a manly, intelligent head; M. Strauss, an assistant of Pasteur and well known for his work on cholera; Prof. Lepine of Lyons, one of France's most distinguished clinicians, a small, sickly man; M. Giles [sic] de la Tourette, former assistant to Charcot, now to Brouardel, a true Provençal; a Prof. Brock, *membre de l'Institut,* mathematician and astronomer who at once started talking German and turned out to be a Norwegian; then came Charcot's brother, a gentleman who looked like Prof. Vulpian but wasn't, and several others whose names I never learned; also an Italian painter, Tofano.[32]

In this company Freud proffered his imitation of an urbane and sophisticated doctor without, as he was delighted to write Martha, even the "slightest mishap."[33] He "drank beer, smoked like a chimney, and felt very much at ease." He succeeded in conversing freely in French and had even managed a drollery. The evening was such a success that Freud indulged a fantasy of courting Mademoiselle Charcot, who bore a surprising likeness to her father. So happy was Freud to have one Charcot, he considered acquiring another. He further indulged himself by confessing the fantasy of winning this two-for-one prize to Martha, but added that such an attempt on his part could only end up a farce.

## The Truth Is for Us Alone

Freud was the only foreigner left among the physicians in the hospital after the Christmas holidays, and he succeeded in winning greater favor with Charcot when he quoted the director's own writings in connection with a patient Charcot and his assistants were examining. Charcot then turned to one of his assistants and told him that he should consult with Freud about a diagnostically puzzling case. "After we had decided to postpone the final observation till 4 P.M., the assistant invited me (!!) to lunch with him and the other hospital doctors in the Salles des Internes—as their guest, of course. And all this in response to one nod from the Master!" This evidence of Charcot's confidence in Freud's clinical acumen notwithstanding, the sense of inferiority that Charcot's brilliance inspired continued to assail him. "How hard this little victory has been for me," he complained to Martha, "and how easy [it was] for Ricchetti!" Freud complained that he lacked a winning way with others and had to fight for every ounce of esteem. He believed there was something alienating about his looks.[34]

Martha wrote back to tell him that his worries about his appearance were unwarranted, although there *were* certain difficulties in his character. Freud was in a mood to consider these. He was getting ready for a second *soirée* at the Charcots' and had sustained himself with another magic pellet of cocaine. Made talkative by the drug, he sat down to return Martha's letter and compiled his own list of personal debilities: "poverty, long struggle for success, little favor among men, oversensitiveness, nervousness, and worries."[35] In fact, he had been feeling "out of sorts" all day, "neurasthenic," as he put it.

> I believe people see something alien in me and the real reason for this is that in my youth I was never young and now that I am entering the age of maturity I cannot mature properly. There was a time when I was all ambition and eager to learn, when day after day I felt aggrieved that nature had not, in one of her benevolent moods, stamped my face with that mark of genius which now and again she bestows on men. Now for a long time I have known that I am not a genius and cannot understand how I ever could have wanted to be one. I am not even very gifted; my whole capacity for work probably springs from my character and from the absence of outstanding intellectual weaknesses.

With Charcot, Freud at 29 felt poised between past and future. Charcot marked the clinical horizon. Could he get there? In answering this question Freud needed to assess his past in the way a general reviews his troops before a great battle. What was his real strength? What could his prospects realistically be?

But I know that this combination is very conducive to slow success, and that given favorable conditions I could achieve more than Nothnagel, to whom I consider myself superior, and might possibly reach the level of Charcot. By which I don't mean to say that I will get as far as that, for these favorable conditions no longer come my way, and I don't possess the genius, the power, to bring them about. Oh, how I run on! I really wanted to say something quite different.

In discussing his character problems Martha had pointed out his reserve, even abruptness, with strangers. In reply Freud recounted his combativeness during adolescence. "One would hardly guess it from looking at me," he wrote, "and yet even at school I was always the bold oppositionist, always on hand when an extreme had to be defended and usually ready to atone for it. As I moved up into the favored position of head boy, where I remained for years and was generally trusted, people no longer had any reason to complain about me." Freud then recalled an encounter from when he was 26 and newly engaged:

> You know what Breuer told me one evening? I was so moved by what he said that in return I disclosed to him the secret of our engagement. He told me he had discovered that hidden under the surface of timidity there lay in me an extremely daring and fearless human being. I had always thought so, but never dared tell anyone.[36]

At this point in his letter to Martha, Freud confided a precious aspect of his dream, one derived, I think, from his mother's unrealized heroic passions. "I have often felt as though I had inherited all the defiance and all the passions with which our ancestors defended their Temple and could gladly sacrifice my life for one great moment in history." He had never found an outlet for these passions, and the question of whether he ever would was becoming more pressing. "And at the same time," he continued, "I always felt so helpless and incapable of expressing these ardent passions even by a word or a poem. So I have always restrained myself, and it is this, I think, which people must see in me."

What place did these heroic passions have in the laboratory, inventing new chemical preparations for displaying brain tissue or stooped over a microscope peering at cross sections of children's brains? But to be a great doctor like Charcot, a man who could with a single word cause to appear and disappear the most terrible neurological ailments and who did this before the wondering eyes of physicians drawn from every corner of Europe and beyond!

Here I am, making silly confessions to you, my sweet darling, and
really without any reason whatever unless it is the cocaine that
makes me talk so much. But now I must go out to supper and then
dress myself up and do some more writing. Tomorrow I will report
to you quite truthfully on how the evening at Charcot's turned out.
You of course must tell everyone that I had a wonderful time, and
I shall write the same to Vienna. The truth is for us alone.[37]

## Momentarily Deflated

At midnight Freud returned from the Charcots' and resumed his letter. The evening had not been a success. The out-of-sortsness, or out-
of-selfness, that Freud had been feeling all day before going to the Charcots' had stayed with him. There had been too many guests who were
strangers to one another and who remained so. Mademoiselle Charcot had not been interested in him. He had tried to engage Madame
Charcot in conversation, but she directed him to her husband, who
was in another room. "The old man wasn't very agile, sat most of the
time in his chair and seemed very tired. Of course he didn't fail to offer
me some refreshment," wrote Freud, "which was the only thing I got
from him." The transference had gone flat, and without that facilitat-
ing magical connection, even Freud's French had been "worse than
usual. No one paid any attention to me," he told Martha, "or could
pay attention to me, which was quite all right and I was prepared for
it."[38] At this pivotal point in Freud's development, Charcot constituted the bridge to the future Freud hoped to gain and to which he felt
unequal, a future of which he felt at times unworthy. If Charcot had
nothing for him, then for the moment Freud felt that he was nothing
and would come to nothing, as his father had once angrily prophesied.

At the end of the evening Freud had gotten into a disagreeable
political argument with another physician, Gilles de la Tourette, "during
which he of course predicted the most ferocious war with Germany."
Freud had promptly explained, "I am a Jew, adhering neither to Germany or Austria." But this dodge did not sit well with Freud; it seemed
inauthentic, especially after the protestations of heroism he had made
to Martha earlier in the evening, and false just at a time when he was
trying to use Charcot in forging a more complex and, in his own eyes,
admirable identity as a clinician scientist and cosmopolitan intellectual. How disagreeable then to have one of Charcot's native sons try
to push him back across the border. To make matters worse, Freud
was, in reality, German *and* Jewish, the son of Goethe, Schiller, and
Brücke as well as Hannibal, Masséna, and Breuer. "Such conversations," he now told Martha, "are always very embarrassing to me, for

I feel stirring within me something German which I long ago decided to suppress."[39]

By the 10th of February, the gloom had passed and Freud's spirits lifted once again. He had spent the previous evening with the Charcots, and it had been the most successful evening yet, indeed, the most delightful of any he had spent in Paris. He sent his place card from the Charcots' dinner table to Martha with instructions to keep it for their archive. "What a magic city this Paris is!" Freud began his account to his fiancée.[40] He had been part of a small dinner group of some 10 or 12 and had felt relaxed and competent. Mademoiselle Charcot, next to whom he had been seated, had at least been amiable, if still reserved. In addition to Charcot's family, there had been an assistant from the hospital and, more notably, his wife, who had sat silent as a statue in a "somewhat denuded state for which, considering her beauty," Freud felt, "one could hardly blame her." Freud had gotten to speak with Charcot alone and told him about the progress of the translation and about his formulation of a case Charcot had referred to him. The old man was impressed and told Freud that Paris had obviously been good for him, that he had been "*engraissé*" by the experience, that is, spiritually and intellectually enriched.

After dinner the party was joined by numerous other guests, including the great Daudet and his wife. The evening had so successfully united people that Freud left with his former antagonist, Gilles de la Tourette. "The following day I couldn't help thinking what an ass I am to be leaving Paris now that spring is coming, Notre Dame looking so beautiful in the sunlight, and I have only to say one word to Charcot and I can do whatever I like with the patients. But I feel neither courageous nor reckless enough to stay any longer."[41]

Freud had played at a high-stakes table; wagered his most precious hopes for the future and pretensions about himself, including his very self-esteem; and won. Now he wanted to go home while he still had his winnings in hand. On the way out he was given the door prize. There had been an arrogant colleague, "a hydrotherapist" from Vienna who had joined the Charcot circle of foreign doctors. This man had been condescending to Freud until Charcot made it clear that his acquaintance with Freud was all that recommended him. Further, a famous ophthalmologist from New York, a Dr. Knapp, had arrived, and he knew and respected Freud's research on cocaine. In Knapp's presence the Viennese hydrotherapist turned to Freud and asked him if it was true that he had written about cocaine. Knapp intervened: "Of course he has, it was he who started it all."[42] Freud was pleased to report to Martha that after this encounter his countryman's behavior toward him improved markedly.

## The Battle of Vienna

Somewhere around the beginning of March 1886, Freud left Paris, pausing for a short reunion with Martha in Wandsbek. Then he went on to Berlin to study pediatric neuropathology at Adolf Baginsky's clinic in the Kaiser Friedrich Hospital. From Berlin he wrote Rosa that he was not expecting much from his stay and was instead feeling ready to return to Vienna and determine once and for all if he could make a living there.[43] As it turned out, Freud found that he liked working with children and imagined that if he could only study a little longer in Berlin, he could very happily devote his practice to them. But he felt impelled to return home and face his future while the inspiration received from Charcot remained strong.

> I am afraid [a longer stay] is out of the question; the days of my reckless daring have evaporated. Vienna weighs upon me and perhaps more than is right. I am afraid I am sinning nowadays against my otherwise loyally adhered to principle of not tormenting myself with new situations until I am in the midst of them. But I will conquer my present mood, and then I won't worry about anything till I see with my own eyes the detestable tower of St. Stephen's.[44]

He was spending his mornings at Baginsky's clinic finishing the translation of Charcot's lectures. "I have never enjoyed work so much," he wrote Martha on March 19, 1886. "I have been left with such a friendly, edifying memory of Charcot, in its way not unlike the one I had after the ten days with you. I feel I have experienced something precious that cannot be taken away from me. I feel increasingly self-confident, more urbane, more adroit in dealing with colleagues. . . . Just now I feel so ready to be very happy."[45]

In solidifying his self-confidence as a clinician, the experience with Charcot also firmed up his sense of being an adult man. On March 19, 1886, Freud wrote Martha from Berlin:

> I dare say greater revolutions have taken place in the world than that a man who has nothing now, later acquires a few thousand gulden. I have very little fear of the future. In any case, and this comes first among the achievements of this year of travel: I am coming to fetch you like an overdue bill of exchange on June 15, 1887—if this hasn't been possible before. Are you absolutely determined to be ready by then, my little girl?[46]

In late April Freud was back in Vienna and ran an advertisement in the newspaper that he was holding consulting hours at Rathausstrasse No. 7.[47] Vienna seemed unmoved by this news, and on his 30th birthday Freud wrote Martha that he was ready to immigrate, if only they could be together and the long purgatory of their engagement finally brought to a happy end.

> I am now so old, as you know, and yet on the eve of the fourth anniversary of our engagement we still don't know when the married state which we have so often visualized will become a reality. But although still as far as ever from the goal, we are less far from the certainty. In a few weeks the money—which I still haven't touched—will have come to an end, and then we shall see if I can go on living in Vienna. I would like to think that the next birthday will be just as you describe it, that you will be waking me up with a kiss and I won't be waiting for a letter from you. I really no longer care where this will be, whether here or in America, Australia or anywhere else. But I don't want to be much longer without you. I can put up with any amount of worry and hard work, but no longer alone. And between ourselves, I have very little hope of being able to make my way in Vienna.[48]

Despite the paucity of patients, Freud had nonetheless remained animated intellectually and had returned to the laboratory full of new ideas about anatomy as well as about therapy. Within a week Freud's waiting room, too, suddenly filled to overflowing, though few of the patients Breuer was referring could pay much and the others were physicians entitled to professional courtesy. Freud was working on a case of sciatica, and there was an American physician with an obscure nervous condition and a complicated relationship with a beautiful wife, whom Freud was also treating. The woman, Freud told his fiancée, had been in his office twice and on both occasions his picture of Martha had fallen to the floor. This seemed "weird" to Freud, who never liked such portents.

On his return to Vienna Freud had tried to get Breuer to tell him more about the case of Anna O.[49] Freud was now studying mental cases with a sharpened sense of purpose, as his practice and the life he hoped to build on it increasingly depended on his ability to treat them. He sensed that Breuer's exploration of Anna O.'s ailment offered a closer approach to a true explanation and an effective treatment of hysteria. What struck Freud as the critical element in Breuer's method was getting the patient to remember the experience that had occasioned the symptom in the first place. It appeared to Freud that when the original suppressed mental act was relived under hypnosis with its accompanying emotional charge, the symptom would disappear. Yet, as Freud later put it, "a veil of obscurity" rested over the final stage of Anna O.'s treatment, which Breuer refused to raise even for Freud.[50]

Why not? In 1932 Freud wrote Stefan Zweig that "on the evening of the day when all her symptoms had been disposed of, he [Breuer] was summoned to the patient again, found her confused and writhing in abdominal cramps. Asked what was wrong with her, she replied: 'Now Dr. B's child is coming!' At this moment [Breuer] held in his hand the key that would have opened the 'doors to the Mothers [the secrets of nature],' but he let it drop. With all his great intellectual gifts there was nothing Faustian in his nature."[51] While Breuer's biographer, Hirschmüller, has raised questions about Freud's interpretation of Breuer's reticence (to be discussed later), he does agree that the depth of Breuer's emotional involvement in the case was extraordinary; that the treatment did not end in the patient's cure, as Breuer would represent in the *Studies on Hysteria,* but in her hospitalization; and that Breuer never treated hysterical patients psychotherapeutically again.[52]

As we shall see, Freud's emphasis on the therapeutic, not just the explanatory, importance of *origins* would ever after (as it had from earliest childhood) dominate his investigations of neurosis. Not only would a preoccupation with this subject lead Freud mistakenly to the seduction theory, but it remains a hallmark preoccupation of psychoanalysis today.[53] The only methods of treating mental cases available to Freud besides hypnosis were electrical stimulation to painful or debilitated areas of the body and the referral of patients to sanatoriums. Hypnosis, or hypnotic-like states, and the memories and feelings it made available seemed the way toward the future, and Freud wrote Martha that he had lectured successfully on hypnosis to the Physiology Club and would soon do so again to the Psychiatric Club. He was also scheduled to describe his studies in Paris to the Medical Association. "The battle of Vienna," he told Martha, was "in full swing."[54]

With business improving, the couple had begun to think that marriage would soon be possible. Then, unexpectedly, Freud was called up for an extra four weeks of military duty in mid-August 1886 and sent to Moravia. This interruption of Freud's fragile practice threatened to table once again the couple's plans to marry. Besides involving a loss of income, even a short stay in the military required preparatory expenses of its own. Yet Freud was adamant that this final obstacle not be allowed to disrupt their plans, and his insistence rekindled the hostilities with Emmeline Bernays that seemed to have been permanently quelled during his visits with the family in Wandsbek. Now Frau Bernays sent Freud a humiliating directive that the wedding be postponed. The tone and content of the letter make more understandable Freud's earlier hostility toward Emmeline.

The letter began "Dear Sigi" and moved quickly to characterize his desire to marry in the face of reduced financial circumstances as "an abysmally irresponsible piece of *recklessness. Another* word would be more fitting," Emmeline added, "but I will not use it. I shall *not* give my consent to such an idea." Insultingly, Emmeline reminded Freud that "when a man without means or prospect gets engaged to a poor girl he tacitly shoulders a heavy burden for years to come, but he cannot make anyone else responsible for it." Instead, Frau Bernays advised, Freud should begin his practice anew after returning from maneuvers, and if it went well he and Martha could marry at the end of the year. Emmeline Bernays went on to describe as "pathological" Freud's "ill-humor and despondency" at the prospect of further postponement. "Become once more a sensible *man,*" she concluded. "At the moment you are like a spoilt *child* who can't get his own way and cries, in the belief that in that way he can get everything."[55]

We have no record of Freud's response, but before Freud left for Moravia Martha's relatives rescued the couple by giving them money to furnish a flat. Friends and relatives on both sides provided additional gifts in the form of loans, whose repayment was optional. In Vienna Freud found a flat suitable for their apartment and his consulting rooms on Maria Theresienstrasse in the new Kaiserliches Stiftungshaus, or, as it was called, the House of Atonement, recently built on the site of the Ringtheater, which had burned down with much loss of life in 1881. In Martha's absence, Rosa provided her brother with expert feminine counsel concerning decor. Everything was in a state of readiness before Freud's departure for military duties; and the wedding took place within days of his return, on September 13, 1886, in Wandsbek, Germany. As if Frau Bernays's attack hadn't been maddening enough, Freud now learned that the civil ceremony in Germany did not set aside the Austrian legal requirement of a religious one. The couple would have to wed again. They compromised on a minimal ceremony on September 14 in Frau Bernays's house with little ritual and only a few friends and relatives. The couple honeymooned for two weeks, first in Lübeck and then on the Baltic at Travemünde in Holstein.

Freud's hostility toward Emmeline must have been reawakened by the recent contretemps, and it may have been this that led him to aggressively reassert his authority by forbidding Martha to light the Sabbath lights on the first Friday night after her wedding, as required by her religion.[56] These initial difficulties notwithstanding, Jones describes the Freud marriage as possessing an unimpaired domestic harmony and opines that few marriages could have been more successful.[57] According to Jones, in the early period of the marriage Freud even discussed his cases with Martha and stopped doing so only when it became clear that Martha lacked the intellectual wherewithal to follow his thinking. Perhaps, but other explanations are possible. Martha soon had other people making claims on her attention, for six children enlivened the first 10 years of the Freuds' marriage. It may have been this, rather than intellectual limitation, that dimmed the glint of interest in her eye. Moreover, after a time any spousal enthusiasm is likely to become tiresome.

## An Unfriendly Reunion

On the couple's return to Vienna, Freud found that his practice, which with Breuer's help and Charcot's aura had been so promising prior to its interruption, had gone sour just as Emmeline had warned. Nonetheless, Freud felt optimistic.[58] In the lengthy and newsy letter to his old friend Koller in which he wrote about this and other matters, he made no reference to his upcoming presentation to the College of Professors in the Faculty of Medicine.[59] This lecture was required as a condition of his travel fellowship, and two days after writing to Koller, on October 15, 1886, Freud gave it.

The title Freud chose for his presentation was "On Male Hysteria," managing with terse economy to challenge both conventional medical wisdom and his former professor's in particular. For after all, everyone knew that the very word *hysteria* derived from the Greek word for womb and Meynert, who would certainly be in the audience, was on record as believing that hysteria was an organic condition for which treatment by hypnosis was absurd.[60] Clearly, Freud was in a combative mood; he had been to Paris, studied with the great Charcot, and won his favor. He now knew more about hysteria and its treatment than anyone else in Vienna except Breuer — and Breuer, who would also be at Freud's lecture, was no longer willing to treat such cases psychotherapeutically.[61] Now, Freud was ready to tell his Viennese seniors that they did not know what they were doing, and tell them he did.

Not surprisingly, the doctors did not like it. These middle-aged men had generously paid for Freud's trip, and here the promising young man they had sent off to Paris had returned an insolent ingrate. The group tolerated the lecture restively, until Meynert finally challenged Freud to present a case of a purely functional hysteria and one occurring, as Freud insisted it could, in a man. Freud accepted the challenge, but when in the days after the meeting he went in search of such patients in the hospital, he found the ward chiefs uncooperative. He was forced to turn to physician friends in the community to help him find a suitable case. Six weeks later Freud answered Meynert's challenge by presenting a hysterical man to a second meeting of the society.[62]

This time the reception to Freud's paper and to his in situ demonstration of his patient was warmer. Nonetheless, he felt rejected. He wrote in his *Autobiographical Study:*

> [My] impression that the high authorities had rejected my innovations remained unshaken; and, with my hysteria in men and my production of hysterical paralyses by suggestion, I found myself forced into the Opposition. As I was soon afterwards excluded from the laboratory of cerebral anatomy [by Meynert] and for terms on end had nowhere to deliver my lectures, I withdrew from academic life and ceased to attend the learned societies.

"It is a whole generation," Freud wrote at 68, "since I have visited the Society of Medicine."[63]

These presentations, pregnant as they were with the young man's wish to please and defy, to be loved and to wound, were a great marker event in Freud's life and helped to form an adult screen memory that long sustained him. Freud had achieved the first break with his profession and the isolation that he needed for creative work. At 30 he was no longer a boy; he was a doctor in private practice and a husband, and he expected soon to be the head of his own family. From late adolescence on he had needed a lot of help from older men, and he had received it. He was grateful, but the gratitude itself was becoming an encumbrance. It was time to strike out on his own and to turn to defiant use the hostility engendered by his own rebelliousness. To say this is not to say that Freud liked isolation and hostility but only that being opposed unleashed the sort of combative heroic fantasies that fueled his creative drive and quelled the anxiety arising from his own continuing, if diminished, vulnerability.

This attack may have been a courting gift to Breuer, who Freud hoped would become a more forthcoming mentor. It is possible that, unbeknownst to either man, Freud was acting out for Breuer by pulling the beards of the academic medical establishment on behalf of his bland and accommodating older colleague. Although Breuer was physician to several of the medical school faculty, the school had not been as forthcoming with honorific academic titles as Breuer would have liked. One can imagine the confusion of pride, horror, and satisfaction that Breuer, the establishment family physician, would have felt as he watched his impecunious protégé begin his career as private practitioner by alienating himself from his medical colleagues. After all, Breuer also knew that Meynert's views on hysteria were nonsense and must have considered his colleague's dogmatic ignorance obscene.

Freud's assault on his former professors did not help business. During his first month back in practice, income, when he really needed it, fell far short of expenses. By the beginning of the new year (1887) Freud told his friend Koller that his practice was going poorly, that he was receiving no help from the senior physicians, "*die hohen Herren*" (prominent gentlemen) as he called them, dripping with sarcasm; and that he would have to make it on his own.[64] That month Martha became pregnant. On October 16, 1887, Martha gave birth to a girl, whom they named Mathilde after Frau Breuer. Freud was 31 and was now learning about the roller coaster life of the private practitioner to which he had coupled his family's fortunes. During the course of Martha's pregnancy his practice had been up and had then fallen off again. On the day of Mathilde's birth his waiting room filled, as though by their suffering the neurotics had come to celebrate Freud's paternity. Likewise, a lecture course he had been offering on cerebral anatomy, previously undersubscribed, now added paying customers.[65]

Freud's love for Martha was deepened by their daughter's birth. The labor had been prolonged, but Martha had held up well. Finally, the baby had to be delivered by forceps. He wrote Emmeline Bernays:

> Martha was all for it, wasn't in the least frightened, and at every free moment joked with her two helpers and her fellow sufferer — that was me — and I am actually so tired I feel as though I had gone through it all myself. . . . I have now lived with her for thirteen months and I have never ceased to congratulate myself on having been so bold as to propose to her before I really knew her; ever since then I have treasured the priceless possession I acquired in her, but I have never seen her so magnificent in her simplicity and goodness as on this critical occasion, which after all doesn't permit any pretenses.[66]

Now there was another girl with whom he was in love. "How can one write so much about a creature only five hours old?" he wondered in his letter to Emmeline. "The fact is I already love her very much." Freud thought that his daughter resembled him and had inherited his exigent appetite and propensity for indigestion. Little Mathilde was the first child born in the rebuilt House of Atonement, and the Emperor himself saw fit to commemorate the glad event with a letter of congratulations to the parents. Frau Breuer, Mathilde's namesake, and her husband made themselves solicitous, admiring, and frequent visitors.

## A Promising New Acquaintance

A month after Mathilde's birth Breuer introduced Freud to a visitor from Berlin, Wilhelm Fliess. Freud was immediately attracted to Fliess, but his relationship to him remained only occasional until his mid-30s. From then on, I shall be quoting often from Masson's edition of Freud's letters to Fliess. These quotes are identified either by note or by date in the adjacent text. His first letter to Fliess, in November 1887, shows Freud engaged in electrical treatments, writing three papers simultaneously, and delighting in his thriving daughter. That December Freud wrote Fliess to thank him for a Christmas present and to proclaim his good luck at having won him as a friend.[67] In this letter Freud told Fliess that he had recently "thrown" himself into doing hypnotic treatments and had achieved numerous small successes. He also announced his intention to translate a book on suggestion by the French hypnotist Hippolyte Bernheim. Although moody, he was working on two publications of his own as well, one on brain anatomy and the other on hysteria. Although he was experimenting with hypnosis, Freud's next letter to Fliess, on February 4, 1888, shows him relying on electro- and hydrotherapies with renewed confidence. He mentions having finished a first draft of a piece on hysteria, titled "Hysterical Paralysis," while he neglected his research on brain anatomy.

Here is a good snapshot of Freud and his life from May 28, 1888: He had just turned 32 and was starting to enjoy the results of the transitional period he had been in since age 29, a period that was now approaching an end. A quieter period was dawning. "I have at this moment a lady in hypnosis lying in front of me," he wrote Fliess, "and therefore can go on writing in peace."

> We are living rather happily in steadily growing modesty. When our little Mathilde laughs, we imagine that hearing her laugh is the most beautiful thing that could happen to us, and in other respects we are not ambitious and not very industrious. My practice increased somewhat during the winter and spring, is now decreasing again, and barely keeps us alive. Time and leisure for work have been spent on several articles for Villaret, portions of the translation of Bernheim's *Suggestion,* and similar things, not worthy of note. Wait! The first draft of "Hysterical Paralysis" also is finished; uncertain when the second will be. In short, one manages; and life is generally known to be very difficult and very complicated and, as we say in Vienna, there are many roads to the Central cemetery. . . . The time for the hypnosis is up.[68]

"Hysterical Paralysis" was the article Freud had discussed with Charcot in Paris two years earlier. But Freud's priority in his early 30s was on his practice and his steadily expanding family, and he did not get around to publishing this article until 1893, when he was 37.[69] Meanwhile, Freud continued to publish and write minor articles on brain anatomy.

In the summer of 1889, when he was 33, Freud made a trip to France to consult with Bernheim in Nancy and to attend a congress on hypnosis in Paris. Freud made the trip in the hope that Bernheim could help him both to improve his hypnotic skills generally and to treat a specially problematic case in particular. Indeed, this problematic patient had become so special that he took her with him. Freud and his first long-term psychotherapy case had found one another.

## Freud's First Psychotherapy Patient

As we have noted, of the therapeutic means at Freud's disposal hypnosis seemed the most promising. Yet Freud was far from routinely successful in his attempts to induce hypnosis, nor could he readily deepen the hypnotic trance to levels he believed necessary to achieve full therapeutic results. This was Freud's dilemma when he learned that Bernheim was evolving a technique in Nancy that put greater emphasis on suggestion for its therapeutic results. Thus, the prospect arose of making a major step forward in strengthening his therapeutic technique. The Swiss psychiatrist Auguste Forel, with whom Freud had been in contact, evidently thought this possible and provided Freud with an introduction to Bernheim.[70]

The patient who accompanied Freud to Nancy was Baroness Anna von Lieben (née Todesco), who would become the Cäcilie M. of the *Studies on Hysteria*.[71] It appears that Freud had begun treating von Lieben for facial neuralgia as early as 1887, when he was 31.[72] He had been called in countless times in this extraordinary case to interrupt acute hysterical attacks by hypnosis.[73] His success in doing so had been as dramatic as it was short-lived; within a day or so another crisis would follow, and he would be called back to von Lieben's bedside. Freud attributed this unsatisfactory result to his inability to induce a trance of sufficient depth to cause somnambulism and amnesia.

Breuer may well have referred the baroness to Freud, and if he did not, he would certainly have been in a position as the Todescos' family physician to endorse the recommendation. In either case, Freud consulted closely with Breuer over von Lieben's progress.[74] It was from this patient that Freud learned that hysteria could coexist with marked intellectual gifts, which in von Lieben's case included writing, painting, and chess. This contradicted Charcot's view that hysteria represented a condition of intellectual inadequacy or degeneration. Indeed, Freud considered von Lieben a gifted writer. This case was of such importance to Freud's growth as a clinician that we shall go into it in some detail. It shows how young Freud was when he began doing psychotherapy, and how long it took him to become good at it—at least 10 years.

Anna Todesco was born in 1847 and raised amidst palatial wealth. Her mother presided over a salon frequented by, among luminaries from the arts, such as Brahms, Liszt, and Johann Strauss, her uncle Theodor Gomperz, Theodor Meynert, Josef Breuer, Fleischl-Marxow, Exner, and Franz Brentano (who married Anna Todesco's husband's younger sister). Anna had a long history of nervous illness that commenced, or perhaps only became unmistakable, in adolescence. At 23 she married Leopold von Lieben, a rich Jewish banker. She bore five children, three within the first four years of her marriage. Initially, the marriage seemed to suit her, and relatives commented on the improvement in her health. She thrived during the first pregnancy but then became depressed afterward and in between the others, during which times her marriage and maternal responsibilities—nominal as these were—seemed onerous to her. Over time she developed insomnia and became obese, episodically resorting to strict diets of champagne and caviar to lose weight.

When Freud met her, the 40-year-old von Lieben had begun to immerse herself in a reappraisal of her life, a review so self-condemnatory that it left her feeling wretched about herself and her future.[75] This reappraisal was accompanied by severe facial neuralgias, sharp pain between the eyes, and foot pain so severe as to make walking impossible. The baroness also had marked bouts of anxiety, dysphoria, anger, hallucinations, incontinent speechifying, and mental absence. As a neurologist, Freud was initially summoned in response to the severe attacks of facial neuralgia. Only gradually, and apparently with misgiving, did he evolve a psychological approach consisting of hypnosis, catharsis, and suggestion. By the end of 1888, or roughly a year of treatment, this approach may have come to follow (as had Breuer's treatment of Anna O. seven years earlier) a daily, sometimes twice daily, regimen. Her family noted this development with misgiving and referred to Freud, because of his strange treatments, as *der Zauberer*, the Magician.

If at age 40 the baroness was entering her own mid-life transition, psychoanalysis would have profited, if only germinally, from an intimate acquaintance with such travails. Some of her poetry certainly speaks directly of a terribly painful review of youthful memories.[76] Indeed, the effect on Freud of this introduction to the mid-life transition may have been cumulative, since at the same time he began the treatment of Frau Emmy von N., whom he described in the *Studies on Hysteria* as "a lady of about forty years of age, whose symptoms and personality interested me so greatly that I devoted a large part of my time to her and determined to do all I could for her recovery."[77]

Thus, it is possible that Freud began his career as a psychother-apist deeply involved in the treatment of two patients who were tell-ing him variants of the same story concerning the years of childish wishes, youthful dreams, and dawning disillusion. Perhaps these women were in a retrospective attitude, needing to remember and assess, as the initial part of the developmental work necessary to create a life worth living in middle age. If so, it would have been Freud's genius and error, not knowing why their interest in the past was so strong, to think that the emphasis on remembering meant that the problem lay simply in the past rather than in the present and the future as well. Of course, it did in part, but the past was only the prologue and first act in these women's stories; it was not the stories themselves. For a young man, and one with a brand new life structure — marriage, fam-ily, and private practice — the preview of the future provided by these 40-year-old women may have been too frightening to face fully, yet too compellingly awful to ignore.

Freud referred to von Lieben as his main client and in a letter to Fliess 10 years later, as his *Lehrmeisterin* (his "master teacher"), using the same word many years later to describe her in a letter to one of her relatives in 1938.[78] The study of von Lieben's case led directly to the writing of the preliminary communication on hysteria with Breuer in 1893, Freud's first major publication on neurosis, when he was 37.[79] In the *Studies on Hysteria* Freud wrote that "personal consider-ation" prevented him from making von Lieben's case the centerpiece that, by virtue of its severity, duration, and the intimacy of his knowledge, it deserved to be. In fact, he knew her far better than the other cases he contributed to the volume. This "personal considera-tion" may have concerned her social prominence in Vienna and the impossibility of keeping her identity a secret if too many details of her case were given. Nonetheless, *Studies on Hysteria* is sprinkled with vignettes drawn from his work with the baroness.

During the first year of treatment Freud sent von Lieben to Char-cot, who may have seen her before that since he wrote Freud that she had *improved* under Freud's care and urged him to stay with a psy-chological approach.[80] No doubt Freud was encouraged by Charcot's findings, yet as a young and ambitious physician he could not be satis-fied by the amelioration of symptoms and transient improvement. He had to feel that if only his hypnotic technique were better, he could achieve a cure, and at this point in his life everything seemed to de-pend on it.

In 1889, as noted, Freud took von Lieben with him to Nancy to see Bernheim. However, it turned out that Bernheim could not put von Lieben into a deep trance either, and he confessed to Freud that this had been typical of his experience with private patients. Bernheim told Freud that he had generally achieved his best results with clinic patients. Evidently, as Freud would later come to appreciate, hypnosis relies on the covert workings of transference, and transference is at its most devout when the inequality between patient and physician makes the latter seem godlike. Although Bernheim had not been able to cure von Lieben, watching him work reinforced Freud's growing belief that unconscious ideas and feelings could produce neurotic illness,[81] for Bernheim showed Freud that patients only seemed to forget what they had remembered under hypnosis and that with the physician's insistence they could be induced to remember while awake. Freud made no immediate use of this insight, but it did not take him long to conclude that patients know everything necessary about the genesis of their illness and that the physician has "simply" to persuade them to render up their secrets.

Anna von Lieben's treatment ended after six years, although it is not known why; Freud made reference to having "lost" her in a letter to Fliess on November 27, 1893.[82] From subsequent accounts by friends and physicians it appears that she was helped by Freud but far from cured. Von Lieben would then have been about 46, or near the end of a mid-life transition, and perhaps for that reason, whatever the status of her psychopathology, she may have felt that she had gotten from her treatment all that she could use. It is not uncommon for patients to enter psychotherapy in the early part of a developmental period and leave near its end. With her developmental transition past and the force of its propulsion spent to whatever effect, von Lieben may have felt it was time to do something else. What the something else might have been, we do not know. She died of a heart attack seven years later at the age of 53. A volume of von Lieben's poetry took up permanent residence in Freud's library.

After two weeks with Bernheim Freud left to attend the congress in Paris (where von Lieben went, we do not know). There he saw firsthand that the French were having success in getting patients to abreact etiologically traumatic events under hypnosis. Peter Swales quite rightly points out, as did Henri Ellenberger, that a psychotherapy based on the recovery of traumatic experiences and their abreaction was, by the mid- to late 1880s, waiting for someone to make it part of science by embedding it within a rational and comprehensive conception of the mind. In Vienna the neurologist Benedikt, who attended the Paris congress and who had provided Freud with a letter of recommendation to Charcot, had also been evolving a treatment for hysteria that centered on the ferreting out of "pathogenic secrets."[83] Moreover, Brentano had touched on these matters in his book in 1874. Janet also attended the Paris congress, and Freud acknowledged in his *Autobio-graphical Study* that it had been pressure from Pierre Janet's research in 1893 that helped him convince Breuer to publish their preliminary communication on hysteria.[84] If *he* was to become the revolutionary healer of hysteria, Freud would have to move fast.

## A Deepened Dependence upon His Mentor

On his return to Vienna in 1889 Freud began to rely more and more on Breuer's hypnotic–cathartic method.[85] He employed it for the first time that year with Frau Emmy von N.[86] Although Freud's use of the techniques of hypnosis, catharsis, suggestion, exhortation, hand pressure, and free association overlapped at least until 1904, he may also have been employing the modern method of free association from the very beginning. It is possible that it was Freud's disappointing experiences with hypnosis, coupled with his having learned more from Bernheim about the power of suggestion, that led him to experiment with free association. The American psychiatrist Brill, who had been in correspondence with Freud, wrote in 1921 that Freud first used free association with Baroness von Lieben, presumably after the first months when other methods failed. By contrast, Freud tells us that it was not until five years later, in 1892, that he, unable to deeply hypnotize the Miss Lucy R. of the *Studies on Hysteria,* abandoned hypnosis and carried out the treatment with the patient in a more or less ordinary state of mind. In this state, the patient was told to lie back, close her eyes, and concentrate uncritically on the thoughts and images that arose.[87] Freud called this his "concentration" technique.

> I decided to start from the assumption that my patients knew everything that was of any pathogenic significance and that it was only a question of obliging them to communicate it. Thus when I reached a point at which, after asking a patient some question such as: "How long have you had this symptom?" or: "What was its origin?", I was met with the answer: "I really don't know," I proceeded as follows. I placed my hand on the patient's forehead or took her head between my hands and said: "You will think of it under the pressure of my hand. At the moment at which I relax my pressure you will see something in front of you or something will come into your head. Catch hold of it. It will be what we are looking for. — Well, what have you seen or what has occurred to you?"[88]

With his hopes for hypnosis dimmed, Freud had only Breuer for guidance.[89] In a letter on May 3, 1889, Freud, about to turn 33, addressed Breuer as "Dearest Friend and best loved of men!" and reminded Breuer to use the familiar *du* consistently when addressing him. Not entirely consciously, Freud was trying to define a new quest—the psychological treatment of hysteria—and Breuer was the only person who could help him do it. Yet this was the very battlefield from which Breuer had been driven by Anna O. and to which he vowed never to return.[90] At the same time, the deeply troubling nature of the experience with Anna O. put Breuer in need of abreaction himself, and it had been this, together with Freud's evocatively receptive interest, that had repeatedly led Breuer to confide to Freud vivid, if incomplete, accounts of the case.

At age 33 Freud was coming to the end not only of the transitional period of the last few years, but of his entire novitiate as an adult, begun at 17. Now he was entering a stable period, lonely, fallow, settled down, and relatively untroubled. He had made good beginnings on both the scientific and clinical aspects of his dream, and he had had a numinous experience with Charcot as an exemplar of their integration. He still longed for greater help from a scientist-clinician mentor, certainly for more consistent help than Breuer could provide, but because the underlying life structure of work and family that he had put into place during his age-30 transition was solid, he could feel needy without feeling desperate. In reality, no mentor existed who fully united the science and treatment of hysteria. Neither Charcot nor Bernheim could treat it successfully, and Breuer's failed efforts had led him to abandon further attempts.

There would be no other mentor in Freud's life after Breuer. As long as his clinical understanding and skill were increasing, Freud could accept this; there was still plenty of time to complete his quest. In a few years, the feeling of adequate time would disappear, and he would urgently seek help in realizing his dream. The series of requisite others that had begun with Eduard Silberstein at age 16 would then issue a strange new edition.

# CHAPTER SEVEN

# Settling Down and
# Becoming His Own Man
## (Ages 33–40)

FOLLOWING the dramatic changes in life structure made during his age-30 transition, Freud's mid-30s were a relatively quiet time. He used it primarily to enrich the new structure with further investments in both family and private practice. At age 35 Freud moved his family into their permanent home at 19 Berggasse, where both residence and professional offices were established. All of the Freuds' six children were born during Sigmund's 30s, with Jean Martin, Oliver, and Ernst arriving during the middle years of that decade. Freud persisted in his treatment of Baroness von Lieben, who during the summer of 1890, when Freud was 34, underwent some sort of emotional crisis. This exigency led Freud to cancel a visit with Fliess because he could not, he joked to his friend, afford to have his "most important patient" get well in his absence. He added that family obligations interfered, too, a "combination of minor reasons which comes about so easily in the case of a practicing physician and father of a family."[1]

Freud was getting more involved with Fliess, enjoyed his intellectual stimulation and encouragement in his work on the neuroses, and regretted having to cancel their reunion. He felt "isolated, scientifically dulled, lazy, and resigned" yet "otherwise quite content, happy if you will."[2] Freud's mentorial relationship with Breuer continued, even though it remained less than fully satisfactory. "For many years now," he told Fliess, "I have been without a teacher."[3] His life structure was good enough that for several years he continued to feel all right.

However, as Freud entered his late 30s he began to feel that the time to realize his dream was running out. And in his growing anxiety, he sought to narrow his dream and strengthen the recently neglected scientific part by emphasizing once again basic neuropsychological research. Under the shadow of his 39th birthday, Freud began a tremendously ambitious attempt to draft a neuropsychological theory of the mind, the *Project for a Scientific Psychology*.[4] With a determination that exceeded even his former predilection for research work, Freud drove himself for some eight months to complete the *Project*. Yet the attempt to simplify his identity and his dream did not work. He was unable to solve the several theoretical conundra that attended the *Project*, and he could not suppress the clinical aspect of his dream, which continued to grow as his daily clinical experience deepened his insight about psychotherapy and neurosis.

In his impatience Freud became sharply dissatisfied with Breuer and at times even construed him as an obstacle to his ambitions, divining beneath Breuer's apparent generosity a darker reality of neurotic ambivalence. Whatever the state of Breuer's less conscious feelings, there is little question that Freud's wishes toward Breuer were in conflict. On the one hand, Freud wanted to establish his position in medical science and psychiatric practice on his own, shedding all vestiges of dependence on his elders. On the other hand, he wanted Breuer to help him and to do so now, decisively, before his youth was gone and he was forced to stand denuded before the world, a middle-aged failure. In either state of mind, it was maddening to Freud to be so old and still in need of so much help. To blame himself was to become depressed. To blame Breuer and his other professional colleagues was to enter into a protective cocoon of illusion and live in a state of paranoid defiance. To render himself up to either state of mind for very long would ensure defeat. For if anyone was to take Freud's grandest claims about himself seriously, a great deal of extremely difficult work had yet to be done.[5]

His late 30s were the years when Freud strove most strenuously to become his own man. This phase can be identified with reasonable certainty. It began when he was 37 and peaked at 39.[6] Freud lost his two most important teachers at 37; Ernst Brücke died in 1893, as did Jean Charcot, for whom Freud wrote a moving obituary.[7] The departure of these teachers both cleared the field and increased Freud's own inner need to be self-reliant. At age 37 Freud's productivity as a scientific writer, reflecting his increased attempts to establish his seniority, underwent a sharp increase from its previous modest levels. The next year, at 38, his scientific productivity climbed to the level of what would be its lifetime median of 82 *Standard Edition* pages per year; then at

39, it soared to a level four times higher than that. Over the remaining 40-odd years of writing, this latter mark would be exceeded only twice.[8]

We are also aided in determining the onset of the phase by an increase in the frequency of Freud's correspondence with Fliess. Reflecting the intensification of Freud's developmental efforts, the volume of letters now rose steeply. Begun at age 31, the letters issued forth at a stable low level until age 36, when they more than tripled in frequency to 10; doubled to 20 at age 37; and continued to rise more gradually to a peak of 46 letters at age 43, the year Freud finished *The Interpretation of Dreams*. The letters from Freud then declined precipitously until age 46 and come to an end altogether at 48. The frequency of the letters not only increased dramatically at around age 37, their content clearly documents an acceleration of Freud's efforts to achieve the scientific aspect of his dream.

The pattern of visits between the two men followed the rise and fall of their correspondence. Between their first meeting in 1887 and their estrangement in 1904, they met about 20 times.[9] Of the 17 visits we can be certain occurred, 3 took place prior to 1894, when Freud was 38. The remaining 14 "congresses," as they grandly called them, took place between then and when Freud was 44.

The transformation of Freud's friendship with Fliess into an intense dependence has been an embarrassment to psychoanalysis. Fliess was an ear, nose, and throat specialist with peculiar ideas about human anatomy and physiology. He believed that the nose controlled the sexual organs and that there was an underlying biological periodicity that governed practically all of human life. How could Freud have become so involved with such a crackpot? Recognizing the enormity of the scientific task the 39-year-old Freud was undertaking helps put this dependency, as well as Freud's difficulties in giving up Breuer, in perspective. With no tools at hand other than clinical observation and thought, Freud had now set forth to establish his scientific reputation once and for all by building a complete theory of the human mind and its aberrations, one that would interconnect organic and psychological mechanisms. Today, nearly a century later, we do not seem to be much nearer this goal than Freud was.[10]

In these letters to his new confidant Freud described his theoretical ideas as fetal, mourned disconfirmed hypotheses as stillborn, and celebrated his conceptual triumphs as glorious births. Was Freud caught up in an aim-inhibited homosexual romance? Freud himself, looking back on the relationship from the vantage point of his mid-50s, thought there had been a homosexual element in it, and on an unconscious level there probably was. Yet there is no evidence that Freud had conscious sexual wishes, fears, or fantasies about Fliess. One can insist on the essential homosexual nature of the Freud–Fliess relationship on the theoretical grounds that all affiliative instincts are basically sexual, but doing so does not account for the timing of the dramatic increase, and equally dramatic decline, of their involvement, timing that corresponds with the expected onset and termination of the mid-life transition. The two men had been friends since Freud was 31, and they corresponded throughout his 30s. But with only a single exception, feminine imagery does not appear in Freud's letters until the end of that decade. Nor can the imagery be attributed to an increase in homosexual longing occasioned by the illness and death of Freud's father, since the imagery began to appear in earnest prior to the summer and fall of 1896, when Jacob became ill. In our conception of development, the masculine–feminine polarity is an underlying one, and work on it is an intrinsic part of mid-life.

From an adult developmental standpoint, the marked and continuing increase in the production of letters that began when Freud was 36 reflected the fact that Fliess was becoming the requisite other for Freud's attempts to become his own man and begin his mid-life transition. Fliess offered the opportunity for a temporary dependence while Freud effected the transition from youth to middle age and from protégé to leader of his profession. Freud could luxuriate in his dependency on Fliess because, after all, Fliess was no Breuer. While brilliantly imaginative and professionally successful, Fliess was still scientifically larval, even defective. Fliess's theoretical ambitions—to create an exact biology based upon mathematical conjurings with presumed 28-day female and 23-day male periods existent in *both* sexes— were, as Freud came increasingly to recognize, unrealizable.[11]

Thus dependence on Fliess was safe. Freud had no fear that he would be held in thrall forever, as he had been with Charcot and wished to be with the more formidable, capacious, and beneficent Breuer. In addition, Fliess possessed the signal virtue of knowing nothing about psychology. As he pressed ahead on his theory of neurosis, Freud could rely on Fliess as a sounding board without encountering informed opposition to his ideas. Nonetheless, Fliess was a biologist and for that reason the natural heir to Freud's positive (and positivist) projections as the most recent in the long line of scientific heroes of Freud's youth.

In addition, only a year and a half apart in age, Freud and Fliess shared a common vantage point and, presumably, similar adult developmental problems. Each headed young and growing families; each cherished as-yet-unrealized dreams of scientific greatness *and* clinical brilliance. Together they could revel in adolescent conquistador fantasies as each tried to establish priority in his respective sector of the medical world. They encouraged in each other a bent toward the-sky-is-the-limit theoretical speculation. Both were obsessed with sexuality and reproduction, and in this way Fliess was connected to the germ of Freud's dream in childhood. To Freud, Fliess's sexual cycle number-juggling seemed to promise so perfect a prediction of female fecundity as to offer complete contraceptive control of it; he appeared to be gaining, as Freud wrote him when Fliess correctly predicted the date of his son's birth, "the key to restraining the power of the female sex."[12] Fliess also gave Freud the idea of universal bisexuality. Fliess's idea that bisexuality was a biological given helped Freud begin to value his own femininity, those neglected psychic qualities he would soon need in order to recast his dream during the mid-life transition.[13]

By the completion of *The Interpretation of Dreams* at age 43, Freud's letters to Fliess began to decline steeply in frequency and both men acknowledged an increasing distance. After age 46 Freud would never again press upon older men the sorts of conflictual dependent demands he pressed upon Breuer in his late 30s. His need for mentors would be over, though he would never outgrow — as, indeed, none of us do — the need for requisite others to help him with subsequent developmental work.[14]

In 1895, when Freud was 39, he did not know consciously that he needed to get rid of Breuer nor that he was using Fliess to do so. The shedding of Breuer was a serpentine and lengthy process that continued into Freud's early 40s. By age 45 Freud had forgiven Breuer for being a disappointing mentor, but by then the two men were permanently estranged. In the meantime, having succeeded in unifying his dream, Freud had begun to sluff off Fliess as well. Sometimes the value of a friend can be measured, Erik Erikson wrote of Freud's relationship with Fliess, by the enormity of the problem one leaves behind with him.

## A Preliminary and Then a Final Collaboration with Breuer

Just before his 35th birthday Freud wrote Fliess a cheerful note in which he announced the birth of his son Oliver (named after Cromwell), already three months old, and his book on aphasia, in which he delighted — nervously — in having been impudent toward Meynert.[15] That year Freud also published a study with Oscar Rie, his friend and fellow physician, on cerebral palsies in children. Having recently discovered the existence and effects of cerebral lesions, neurologists were trying to connect more and more specific behaviors to more and more presumed lesions. In his book on aphasia Freud criticized the existing Wernicke–Lichtheim theory which attempted to account for variations in aphasias on the basis of such presumed subcortical lesions. Freud insisted that this approach was too mechanical. The variation could be better accounted for by developmental differences in the language learning history of the individual patient and anatomically by taking a systemic view in which cerebral damage was seen as having radiating effects.

In making a systemic argument Freud embraced the theory of mental dissolution proposed by the English neuropsychologist John Hughlings Jackson, a theory that stressed the regression from later cerebral organizations to earlier ones. More important, Freud's emphasis on development, trauma, and regression clearly prefigured essential psychoanalytic notions of the future. However, if Freud's book on aphasia was, in its dynamic and developmental emphasis, the first "Freudian" book, it was still preparatory. After 15 years of research in neurology and 10 years of treating patients, Freud was now ready to point out errors in the conceptions of his seniors, but he was not yet ready to leave neurology. This was a work of culmination, not of new beginnings.

Though many of Freud's criticisms have been proved correct and some of his own ideas were prescient, his book on aphasia did very poorly and did not find a permanent, even minor, place in neurology. Freud dedicated it to Josef Breuer, who accepted the gift clumsily. Breuer's reaction, Freud told Minna Bernays, had been odd: "He hardly thanked me for it, was very embarrassed, made only derogatory comments on it, couldn't recollect any of its good points, and in the end tried to soften the blow by saying that it was very well written. I believe his thoughts were miles away." Freud feared that his attempt to narrow a growing breach between himself and his mentor had only made matters worse.[16]

Despite these disappointments, Freud soon turned his attention to a more ambitious project. He wrote Fliess in June 1892 that Breuer had "declared his willingness to publish jointly [their] detailed theory of abreaction, and [their] other joint witticisms on hysteria."[17] This project would become their *Studies on Hysteria,* with Breuer as senior author. The witticism joke declared by denial the book's importance to Freud, for the reality was that he had written relatively little during his 30s and had yet to publish a major work in psychiatry.[18] At 36 he had published "A Case of Successful Treatment by Hypnotism," which, like the book on aphasia, also contained some protopsychoanalytic ideas, but the level of psychological insight was low.[19]

The "joint witticisms" joke may also have expressed Freud's im-

patience with his mentor's reluctance and contempt for his own continuing dependence on him.[20] It had not been easy to secure Breuer's
agreement to collaborate on the *Studies on Hysteria*. The fact that it
would have to include as their most dramatic clinical exhibit the case
of Anna O. must have played some role in Breuer's reluctance. According to Jones, it was only after Freud told Breuer that a patient
had once importuned *him* with an embrace—and offered the idea of
transference to account for it—that Breuer's scientific curiosity was
restored and his wish to better understand his own experience rekindled.[21] Nonetheless, Breuer would not be able to keep from falsely
declaring in the *Studies* that Anna O. had been cured by the end of
her treatment.

Breuer and Freud's first step was to write an article entitled "The
Psychical Mechanism of Hysterical Phenomena: Preliminary Communication" and based largely on Freud's treatment of Baroness Anna
von Lieben, or "Frau Cäcilie M.," as they called her in print.[22] The
essay was published in 1893 and constituted the creative apogee of
the Freud–Breuer relationship. In July 1892 Freud wrote Fliess that
though he and Breuer were working separately on different sections
of the "Preliminary Communication," they were "still in complete agreement."[23] Indeed, the essay reads seamlessly, as though written by
authors who were not only in confident possession of their materials
but of their personal and professional relationship as well. There were
difficulties, but these could still be joked about.[24] The advance in psychological understanding over "The Successful Treatment by Hypnotism" paper was extraordinary. Here appeared for the first time ideas
of the childhood etiology of hysteria, of the symbolic expression of
trauma in symptoms, and of the role of repressed memory as the active pathogenic element, expressed in their dictum "*Hysterics suffer
mainly from reminiscences.*" Now the road grew more difficult as Freud
and Breuer sought to combine their energies on the fuller statement
required for the *Studies on Hysteria* and as Freud approached an age
when the mentor–protégé relationship with Breuer needed to come to
an end.

Whatever the other sources of difficulty in writing the book, intellectual differences were now arising between the two men. Breuer
felt that Freud was starting to emphasize the role played by sexuality
in neurosis. While Breuer agreed that sexuality was important in neurosis, he did not want it overemphasized. There were other disagreements as well. In seeking to understand psychopathology Freud used
neurophysiological constructs not merely for illustrative purposes but
as explanations, and at this point in his development he was more of
a positivist than Breuer. By contrast, in some small but ineluctable meas-

ure Breuer remained a vitalist. He believed that mental life could never finally be understood without resort to considerations of the organism's purposes and that a gap between psychological and neurological explanations was irreducible. Additionally, in the specific matter of hysteria Breuer preferred his explanation that the roots of neurosis lay in "hypnoid states," that is, states of mind in which the individual is unable to discharge the tension produced by noxious stimuli. Freud, to the contrary, increasingly insisted on defense as the essential factor.[25]

Freud supplied four of the five clinical cases for the book, together with the chapter on therapy. The really important scientific theoretical chapter was done by Breuer. Thus the book continued the subordination of its second author. However, within a few months after beginning to collaborate with Breuer on the *Studies on Hysteria,* Freud deployed his main forces elsewhere by privately writing his own theory of the neuroses which included the seduction hypothesis.[26] By the time *Studies on Hysteria* appeared in print, Freud was so involved in his own work that he did not mention its publication to Fliess.[27] Freud's first publication of *his* theoretical work on neurosis would not appear until 1896[28] — and then he would declare that Breuer's hypnoid state was a mare's nest.

## The Riddle of the Neuroses Pursues Freud Heavenward

In the summer of 1893, Freud, then 37, was on vacation in Reichenau, where he wrote a letter to Fliess canceling an upcoming congress. Freud had been mountain climbing with his friend Oscar Rie, and while relaxing in an alpine hut, he had been surprised by Martha, who had followed him into his own sacred world of hiking. Freud's letter describing the event to Fliess provides some insight into the marriage between the still-youthful Freuds, including Sigmund's sympathy for Martha's situation as a harried mother and the persistence of Martha's wish to have an intimate, exclusive relationship with her husband. She was 32.

> Suddenly someone entered the room, completely flushed from the heat of the day, whom initially I stared at as at an apparition and then had to recognize as my wife. . . . She had followed me, had borne up well under the strain, and was enchanted by the view and the place. She expressed the wish to spend several days with me up here, where the accommodations are excellent, and I felt obliged to afford her this pleasure.

It had been years since Martha had been able to get free of the children.

> For the past six years, since child followed child, there has been little room for change and relaxation in her life. I do not believe I can deny her this wish. You can imagine what is behind it; gratitude, a feeling of coming back to life again of the woman who for the time being does not have to expect a child for a year because we are now living in abstinence; and you know the reasons for this as well.

He too, Freud had to confess, wanted the vacation prolonged. He had been unable to stop obsessing about "medical ideas" and hoped that more vacation would help to clear his head. "For the rest," he wrote, *"the etiology of the neuroses pursues me everywhere,* as the Marlborough song follows the traveling Englishman. Recently I was consulted by the daughter of the innkeeper on the Rax; it was a nice case for me."[29]

The innkeeper's daughter was Katharina, one of the cases that Freud would contribute to the *Studies on Hysteria.* While Freud was vacationing at the inn, Katharina had sought his advice about a troubling nervous condition. In response to Freud's questions, she confided memories of having been molested by her uncle.[30] "At the end of these two sets of memories she came to a stop. She was like someone transformed. The sulky, unhappy face had grown lively, her eyes were bright, she was lightened and exalted. Meanwhile the understanding of her case had become clear to me."[31] Freud was so inflated, he thought he had understood the young woman after only a brief conversation.

In September 1893 Freud's vacation was over, and he was back at work in Vienna. He wrote to Fliess complaining that his practice was down. Breuer was not "paving the way" to the extent that Freud had expected, and Freud was coming to consider him "an obstacle to [his] professional progress in Vienna. He dominates the very circles on which I had counted."[32] On October 18 Freud wrote Fliess about a mortifying misunderstanding with Breuer over money:[33] Breuer had made loans to Freud during his student days. Freud had been grateful, but now the unpaid debt constituted a humiliation. Breuer graciously informed the still financially marginal Freud that repayment was unnecessary. This benevolence would recur in the next few years and would anger Freud, for Breuer's generosity aggravated the younger man's developmental conflicts. Freud *had* to pay the money back, and he didn't fully *want* to pay it back; he wanted to become his own man even as he wished to remain the beloved, promising, and dependent youth.

## Soaring toward the Heavens and Falling to the Earth

The October 18 letter complaining about the disagreement with Breuer contained Freud's first reference to his belief that he was suffering from a dangerous heart condition. Freud later told Fliess that the symptoms had made their appearance in 1889. Now for the first time they claimed his attention, and Freud's expansive moods began to alternate with states of thanatopic dread.[34] In December 1893 Freud wrote Fliess that he was "literally loaded with news about the neuroses and neuropsychoses, but [that it was] still rather chaotic." "The neuroses and neuropsychoses" referred to his own private theorizing about neurosis, which over the next several months would be shared only with Fliess. Indeed, the letters to Fliess during this time rarely contain references to the *Studies on Hysteria*. Increasingly, Freud's work on the book with Breuer was being done on the side while he devoted his main energies to his own theoretical work. In January 1894 Freud sent Fliess a copy of a manuscript on "the theory of neuroses."[35] By February the *Studies on Hysteria* was half finished, and it appears that peace was restored in the relation between Freud and Breuer.

By April 19, 1894, as Freud approached his 38th birthday, his heart condition had reached a level of "severe cardiac misery." There had been "the most violent arrhythmia, constant tension, pressure, burning in the heart region; shooting pains down my left arm; some dyspnea, all of it essentially in attacks extending continuously over two-thirds of the day . . . and with it a feeling of depression which took the form of visions of death and departure in place of the usual frenzy of activity." Freud's uncertainty about whether his symptoms were organic or hypochondriacal now became so intolerable that he felt forced to consult Breuer for diagnostic advice, disagreeably enacting his continuing dependence.

Freud experienced the cardiac symptoms as a threat to his dream. "It was painful to realize," his April 19 letter continued, "that in the event of a chronic illness, I could not count on doing scientific work, since I was so completely unable to work. . . . The 'present state of the theory of the neuroses' broke off in mid-sentence; everything is as in the castle of Sleeping Beauty when catalepsy suddenly overtook it." Yet by the time he wrote to Fliess about the episode he was full of himself, looking "forward with confidence again to a long life and undiminished pleasure in resuming the battle." Within a week he was promising "a sketch of an analysis in which one can see down to the roots of the neurosis."[36]

On May 6, 1894, the day of his 38th birthday, Freud was

depressed again and unable to finish a theoretical draft on the "Introduction to the Neuroses." "My mood and ability to work," he wrote Fliess, "are really at a low ebb." His discouragement over his blocked progress was such that he yearned to return to laboratory science. "During the summer," Freud concluded, "I should like to go back to anatomy for a while; that is, after all, the only gratifying thing."

Two weeks later Freud told Fliess that his Viennese colleagues "look upon me as pretty much of a monomaniac, while I have the distinct feeling that I have touched upon one of the great secrets of nature." During the preceding few months of terrifying cardiac symptoms, depressing thoughts of being unable to prove his thesis about the sexual etiology of neurosis had been most depressing, exceeded only by concerns about his wife and children.[37]

Freud demanded that Fliess tell him what to do about his heart condition, and Fliess told him to stop smoking. Freud complied, after a fashion. "I have not smoked for seven weeks," he wrote, "since the day of your prohibition. At first I felt, as expected, outrageously bad. Cardiac symptoms accompanied by mild depression, as well as the horrible misery of abstinence. . . . [I was left] completely incapable of working, a beaten man." So Freud had returned to smoking. He reported that despite feeling "aged, sluggish, [and] not healthy" he had regained control of his moods.

> What tortures me is the uncertainty about what to make of . . . [my own medical] story. It would embarrass me to suggest a hypochondriacal evaluation. . . . I am very dissatisfied with the treatment I am receiving here. Breuer is full of apparent contradictions. When I say that I am feeling better, the answer is, You don't know *how* glad I am to hear this. This would lead me to conclude that my condition is serious. When I ask another time what it actually is, I get the answer, Nothing; in any event something that is already over. Moreover, he shows no concern for me at all, does not see me for two weeks at a stretch; I do not know whether this is policy, genuine indifference, or fully justified.[38]

"I would," Freud concluded, "be endlessly obliged to you, though, if you were to give me a definite explanation, since I secretly believe that you know precisely what it is, and that you have been so absolute and strict in your prohibition of smoking—the justification for which is after all relative—only because of its educational and soothing effect." He added, "Scientific contact with Breuer has stopped, I have to rely solely upon myself, which is why progress is so slow."[39]

Freud's work on the neuroses continued to be his primary preoccupation, but he was encountering difficulties; meanwhile, the *Studies* on *Hysteria* had to be completed. The work with Breuer, Freud wrote, now contained five case histories and "an essay by him, from which I wholly disassociate myself, on the theories of hysteria . . . and one by me on therapy, which I have not yet begun." He longed for the summer and the prospect of "a few days [with Fliess] without undue interruptions." In August he would go to Reichenau again; "on September 1 I want to go with my wife to Abbazia [Opatija] for eight to ten days, something she very much desires and richly deserves. Most of the time life appears so uncertain to me that I am inclined not to postpone long-held wishes any longer."[10] Freud felt that he and his wife were "about to become old."[41] Fliess responded by again urging abstinence from cigars. Once more, Freud tried to comply and failed. Freud's cardiac discomforts rose and fell again in July, and by August 7, 1894, he was writing:

> I really look forward to seeing you again. . . .
> It has been a bad year for both of us. It is not impossible, however, that during this period both of us will find recovery from afflictions that have lasted for years. I am not feeling nearly so well as a while back, the last time I wrote you. I can see that you are not feeling well because you show so much patience this time. When I think of the many weeks when I felt uncertain about my life, my need to be with you again increases greatly.

## Manic Unreality and a Dangerous Lapse in Medical Judgment

In late August 1894 Freud visited Fliess in Munich and returned aglow from a renewed and deepened connection with his friend. From Vienna Freud wrote Fliess a letter full of happy prophecies for the future. Fliess responded complaining of migraine headache. Gaily disclaiming any medical knowledge that could help his friend, Freud next sent Fliess a packet of case histories and theoretical sketches from his work on neurosis.

By January 24, 1895, Freud was expressing joy over his own recovery:

> I must hurriedly write to you about something that greatly astonishes me; otherwise I would be truly ungrateful. In the last few days I have felt quite unbelievably well, as though everything had been erased—a feeling which in spite of better times I have not known for ten months. Last time I wrote you [that] a cocainization of the left nostril had helped me to an amazing extent. I now continue

> my report. The next day I kept the nose under cocaine, which one should not really do . . . during this time I discharged what in my experience is a copious amount of thick pus; and since then I have felt wonderful. . . . Arrhythmia is still present, but rarely and not badly.

Apparently, Fliess had come to Vienna the month before and had operated on Freud's nose. Since Fliess believed that nasal reflexes controlled matters at distant bodily sites, he may have thought that nasal surgery could be done to good effect on Freud's cardiovascular system too. Fliess also believed that application of cocaine to particular parts of the inside of the nose was therapeutic.

Other operations beckoned tantalizingly in the future. Fliess was coming to Vienna to perform more surgery, this time not only on Freud's nose but also on that of one of Freud's patients, Emma Eckstein.[42] "Now only one more week separates us from the operation [on Eckstein], or at least from the preparations for it," Freud wrote Fliess on January 24, 1895. "The time has passed quickly, and I gladly avoid putting myself through a self-examination to ascertain what right I have to expect so much from it."[43]

A manic unreality was entering the Freud–Fliess relationship and now created one of the most dreadful episodes in the history of psychoanalysis, the infamous case of Emma Eckstein and the botched operation on her nose that nearly killed her. Extensive accounts of the episode are extant. Our interest is not in what seems by contemporary standards to have been scandalous malpractice but in the state of mind—or, better, state of relationship (with Fliess)—that led Freud to embark on this harebrained venture to begin with. In the letter of January 24 just quoted, Freud continued, "My lack of medical knowledge once again weighs heavily on me. But I keep repeating to myself; so far as I have some insight into the matter, the cure must be achievable by this route. I would not have dared to invent this plan of treatment on my own, but I confidently join you in it."

Emma Eckstein was a 32-year-old woman who was in treatment with Freud for hysterical abdominal symptoms. She was also a friend of the family whom Freud genuinely liked. As he had done with some of his other patients, Freud asked Fliess to conduct an examination to determine if nasal pathology was contributing to the abdominal pain.[44] It seems preposterous to us that Freud, a highly trained neuropathologist, could have seriously entertained the possibility of such a connection. And it does seem to reflect the level of unreality that had now arisen between these two medical conquistadors as Freud strove to become his own man. However, this view must be tempered by the knowledge, based on recent evidence, that the prudent and accomplished Breuer also sent patients, even family members, to Fliess for such surgeries.[45] In Eckstein's case, Fliess reached an affirmative diagnostic conclusion apparently from information Freud sent him by letter, and in February 1895 he came to Vienna and operated. He then returned to Berlin, leaving the patient's postoperative care to Freud.

Eckstein did not do well. On March 4, 1895, Freud wrote Fliess that "Eckstein's condition [was] still unsatisfactory." The patient was suffering from swelling, pain, a fetid smell, copious secretions, and even hemorrhage. It had been necessary to bring in consultants, who recommended new surgery. Four days later, a crisis had been reached.

> I arranged for Gersuny to be called in; he inserted a drainage tube, hoping that things would work out once discharge was reestablished; but otherwise he was rather reserved. Two days later I was awakened in the morning . . . profuse bleeding from the nose and mouth; the fetid odor was very bad. Rosanes cleaned the area surrounding the opening, removed some sticky blood clots, and suddenly pulled at something like a thread, kept on pulling. Before either of us had time to think, at least half a meter of gauze had been removed from the cavity. The next moment came a flood of blood. The patient turned white, her eyes bulged, and she had no pulse. Immediately thereafter, however, he again packed the cavity with fresh iodoform gauze and the hemorrhage stopped. It lasted about half a minute, but this was enough to make the poor creature, whom by then we had lying flat, unrecognizable.

Freud immediately realized that his patient had been suffering from an iatrogenic condition for which he and Fliess were responsible.

> I felt sick. After she had been packed, I fled to the next room, drank a bottle of water, and felt miserable. The brave Frau Doktor then brought me a small glass of cognac and I became myself again. . . . When I returned to the room somewhat shaky, [the patient] greeted me with the condescending remark, "So this is the strong sex."

Freud did not think that it was the blood that had undone him but, rather, an overpowering sense of culpability.

> She was not at all abnormal, rather, a piece of iodoform gauze had gotten torn off as you were removing it and stayed in for fourteen days, preventing healing; at the end it tore off and provoked the bleeding. That this mishap should have happened to you; how you will react to it when you hear about it; what others could make

of it; how wrong I was to urge you to operate in a foreign city where
you could not follow through on the case; how my intention to do
my best for this poor girl was insidiously thwarted and resulted in
endangering her life—all this came over me simultaneously. . . .

Of course, no one is blaming you, nor would I know why they
should.

Who said anything about blame? This last sentence appears to
state Freud's criticism of his friend by negation. Perhaps unconsciously he was coming to understand that Fliess's theories were improbable
and that Freud's own posing as a competent physician, beyond certain strict limits, was fraudulent. Turning a case over to Fliess for surgery, in the face of his own ignorance, exceeded the bounds of good
sense and descended into dangerous adolescent irresponsibility. The
horror of the Eckstein episode may have involved a temporary shattering of Freud's denial about his friend and about their relationship
and the terrible return of his negative identity as a pretentious and very
unevenly educated physician. Perhaps too, hurting a woman damaged
Freud's relationship to his own femininity, a part of his personality
on which his creativity was coming to depend.

## Breuer's Obdurate Friendliness

Meanwhile, Freud's relationship with Breuer was running its ambivalent downhill course. Breuer persisted in being decent and friendly,
at times making it impossible for the younger man to dislike him. Breuer
had gone so far as to give credence to Fliess's nasal reflex theory in
the theoretical chapter he was writing for the *Studies on Hysteria* and
to embrace all of Freud's newly developing ideas on neurotic conver-
sion and defense. Freud wrote Fliess, "When you are absent and I get
the anger out of my system, [Breuer] again rises a great deal in my
estimation."[46] A week later Freud's resentment had rebounded. His
practice was down, and he was worried about Emma Eckstein. "It [had]
been a dreadful period . . . in almost every respect." Freud wrote on
March 15, "Breuer is like King David; when someone is dead, he becomes cheerful." Yet the work with Breuer on the *Studies on Hysteria*
was progressing.

Eckstein's condition varied considerably over the next month, then
darkened once more. After having been declared by the consultants
to be embarked on a recovery, she began to bleed again. Her physicians conducted another examination. No new pathology could be
found, and her nasal cavity was repacked. Again the bleeding recurred

and the nose was repacked. Perplexity reigned. In pursuit of a new explanation Freud's old friend Ignaz Rosanes reexamined the cavity. On April 11, 1895, Freud wrote:

> As soon as the packing was partly removed, there was a new, life-threatening hemorrhage which I witnessed. It did not spurt, it surged. . . . It must have been a large vessel, but which one and from where? Of course, nothing could be seen and it was a relief to have the packing back in again. . . . We do not know what to do . . , I am really very shaken to think that such a mishap could have arisen from an operation that was purported to be harmless.

Apparently, Fliess wrote back urging Freud to tell the physicians not to be panicked by Eckstein's bleeding. He asked as well for a letter clearing him of malpractice. On April 20, 1895, Freud replied:

> I did of course immediately inform Rosanes of your recommendations concerning E. At close range many things look different — for instance, the hemorrhages. I can confirm that in their case there could be no question of biding one's time. There was bleeding as though from the carotid artery; within half a minute she again would have bled to death. Now, however, she is doing better. . . .
>
> The writer of this is still very miserable, but also offended that you deem it necessary to have a testimonial certificate from Gersuny for your rehabilitation. For me you remain the physician, the type of man into whose hands one confidently puts one's life and that of one's family. . . . I wanted to pour forth my tale of woe and perhaps obtain your advice concerning E., not reproach you with anything. That would have been stupid, unjustified, and in clear contradiction to all my feelings.

In this letter Freud, nearing his 39th birthday, told of having finished reading the last of the galley proofs of the *Studies on Hysteria,* which he promised to send Fliess. The book was published soon after.

Fliess's sexual cycle calculations were now advancing to the point where it seemed that conception could be reliably avoided. On May 25, 1895, Freud rejoiced in his friend's apparent scientific breakthrough, although he regretted that it had come too late by a few months to do him any good. Martha was pregnant again. As for Emma Eckstein, she was "finally doing very well." She had resumed her psychotherapy with Freud, and it was proceeding successfully. Though the episode left an indelible mark on Freud, Eckstein recovered, and she remained a friend of the family. Remarkably, she had never blamed either Freud or Fliess for her travail. Instead, she became a psychoanalyst, which may have helped to master the experience.

## Scientific Psychology Becomes the Focus of the Dream

That spring (1895) Freud had directed his research efforts toward creating a theory not simply of neurosis but of the mind in its entirety, a theory that integrated organic and phenomenological aspects, what we now know of as the *Project for a Scientific Psychology*. On April 27, Freud wrote Fliess, "Scientifically, I am in a bad way; namely, caught up in 'The Psychology for Neurologists,' which regularly consumes me totally until, actually overworked, I must break off. *I have never before experienced such a high degree of preoccupation* [Italics added]."[47] Freud did not write Fliess again for another month, and when he did he described in more vivid detail his new obsession. In this letter of May 25, 1895, which I quoted briefly in Chapter Two, he offered apologies for his epistolary tardiness. He had been treating patients 10 to 11 hours a day, and what little free time remained had been consumed by his new scientific preoccupation. The *Studies on Hysteria* had just been published.

> I have regularly been incapable of picking up my pen to write you a little, when in fact I would have had a great deal to say. The main reason, however, was this: a man like me cannot live without a hobbyhorse, without a consuming passion, without—in Schiller's words—a tyrant. I have found one. In its service I know no limits. It is psychology, which has always been my distant, beckoning goal, and which now, since I have come upon the problem of neuroses, has drawn so much nearer.

Freud was sharpening the definition of his dream. He was no longer trying simply to explain neurosis; by "psychology" Freud meant a general theory of the mind. "I am tormented," he wrote, "by two aims: to examine what shape the theory of mental functioning takes if one introduces quantitative considerations, a sort of economics of nerve forces; and second, to peel off from psychopathology a gain for normal psychology." He had come to feel that neurosis could not be understood without an adequate conception of psychology generally. "During the past weeks," he wrote, "I have devoted every free minute to such work; have spent the hours of the night from eleven to two with such fantasizing, interpreting, and guessing, and invariably stopped only when somewhere I came up against an absurdity or when I actually and seriously overworked, so that I had no interest left in my daily medical activities."

Most of the time, these Faustian exertions were nourished by his clinical responsibilities. "I derive," he continued, "vast pleasure from working with neuroses in my practice. Almost everything is confirmed daily, new things are added, and the certainty that I have the core of the matter in my hand does me good." It was at this time that Breuer told Fliess, "Freud's intellect is soaring at its highest. I gaze after him as a hen at a hawk."[48] Apparently, Fliess too was in full flight. "I felt like shouting," Freud wrote, "when I got your news. If you really have solved the problem of conception, just make up your mind immediately which kind of marble is most likely to meet with your approval."[49] The solution to the problem of conception was to learn how to predict the likelihood of its occurrence with such precision that it could easily be prevented. This would be a great general boon to the happiness of humankind. Freud also believed it would have the specific result of preventing neurosis by eliminating the *noxa* that accompanied every existing method of contraception, relying as they all did on some form of abstinence.[50]

Freud even liked Breuer again. "Breuer," he continued in his letter to Fliess, " . . . is not recognizable. One cannot help but like him again without any reservations. He has accepted the whole of your nose [theory] and is promoting an enormous reputation for you in Vienna, just as he has become fully converted to my theory of sexuality. He is indeed an entirely different fellow from the one we were accustomed to." Pleasingly embalmed, Breuer now disappeared from Freud's correspondence for the next six months.[51]

## Freud Conceives

I have written that as Freud's mid-life transition neared, his femininity asserted itself. This occurred both in relation to Fliess and also in relation to his research. Increasingly, he described his research work in germination and gestation imagery and characterized his own relationship to his unconscious creativity in feminine terms.[52]

In his next letter, on June 12, 1895, Freud wrote:

My dear Wilhelm,
       Your kindheartedness is one of the reasons I love you. . . .
       You are right in surmising that I am overflowing with new ideas, theoretical ones as well. My theories on defense have made an important advance of which I shall give you an account in a brief paper next time. Even the psychological construction behaves as if it would come together, which would give me immense pleasure. Naturally I cannot yet say for certain. Reporting on it now would be like sending a six-month fetus of a girl to a ball.

He had resumed smoking and needed the indulgence for his writing. Would Fliess prohibit it again?[53] He did. "My dear," Freud wrote Fliess on June 17, 1895, "I grumble, will again be sorely deprived, but cannot do other than obey you. But I have the hope that after careful reconsideration you will again permit it to me." Yet not even cigar abstinence could leaden his soaring spirits. "I feel so well," he went on, "that there need be no question of hurry [in arranging their congress]. My heart is wholly with the psychology. If I succeed in this, I will be satisfied with everything else." He was still working determinedly on his "Psychology for Neurologists."

Five days later, Freud's salutation was "Hail, cherished Wilhelm!" on the occasion of the announcement of Frau Fliess's pregnancy. Freud proposed early September for their next congress, announcing that his admiration would then feed hungrily on the details of Fliess's great scientific breakthrough. "You would be the strongest of men," he wrote of Fliess's nearing ability to predict conception, "holding in your hands the reins of sexuality, which governs all mankind: you could do anything and prevent anything." In July Freud wrote that he would come to the congress "laden with rudiments and germinating embryos."[54] Now Ida Fliess, Martha Freud, and Sigmund were pregnant. As we do not have Fliess's letters from this time, we cannot know if he symbolized his creative work in this way. But certainly Frau Fliess and Martha were growing, and Sigmund imagined himself full of gestating theories.

Freud's love for Fliess grew with his pregnancy. In his letter of July 24, 1895, he asked, "Daimonie, why don't you write? How are you? Don't you care at all any more about what I am doing? What is happening to the nose, menstruation, labor pains, neuroses, your dear wife, and the budding little one?" Though he did not mention it to Fliess, the night before writing him Freud had had the famous Irma dream. He kept it to himself for several years until publishing it in *The Interpretation of Dreams,* where he noted that it was the first dream he had ever subjected to detailed interpretation. In the Irma dream, a patient whom Freud has treated psychotherapeutically continues to be symptomatic and he fears that he has missed something organic. "I took her to the window and looked down her throat. . . . On the right I found a big white patch; at another place I saw extensive whitish grey scabs upon some remarkable curly structures which were evidently modelled on the turbinal bones of the nose. — I at once called in Dr. M., and he repeated the examination and confirmed it."[55]

The Irma dream is rich in meaning and has been illuminated by various interpretations. Following Max Schur and others, I take Dr. M. mainly to represent Breuer.[56] For our purposes, it is important to note the preoccupation with the connection between the psychological and the organic, a problem that troubled Freud theoretically and in his relationship with Fliess. One also sees the continuing ambivalent subordination to Breuer, whose opinion Freud seeks, resents, and fears. In the dream, Breuer is made to look "quite different from usual; he was very pale, he walked with a limp"[57]; he is also made to utter a prognostic absurdity by predicting that dysentery will set in and cure the patient. Freud's posttraumatic reactions to the Emma Eckstein fiasco are evident, as are his continuing doubts about his competence and, by implication, the authenticity of his identity as a physician.

On August 6, 1895, Freud wrote Fliess:

> Dearest,
>
> Am letting you know that after prolonged mental labor I believe I have penetrated to an understanding of pathological defense, and thereby to many important psychological processes. Clinically, it all fitted together long ago, but the psychological theories I needed were arrived at only very laboriously. . . .
>
> It is not anywhere near ready yet, but I can at least talk about it and with regard to many points avail myself of your superior scientific education. It is bold but beautiful, as you will see. I very much look forward to telling you about it.[58]

In mid-August, Freud's work on the general psychological part of the theory came to a halt. "Shortly after I sounded the alarm," he wrote, "with my communication that called for congratulations, and after I had scaled one of the first peaks, I found myself confronted with new difficulties, but without sufficient breath left for new work. So . . . I threw the whole thing aside. . . . " The work on clinical matters was going better, but, he wrote, "Psychology is really a cross to bear. . . . All I was trying to do was to explain defense, but just try to explain something from the very core of nature! I had to work my way through the problem of quality, sleep, memory — in short, all of psychology."[59] Exhausted, Freud turned his full attention to planning a vacation that would culminate in a visit to Fliess.

Freud and his brother, Alexander, traveled to Berlin during the first two weeks of September 1895, where each anticipated, among other Fliessian enchantments, an operation on his nose. Operations, social visits, and private congresses apparently all went so well that Freud, back home, reluctantly accepted the end of the vacation's "vainglorious happiness." In addition to performing a fine operation on Freud's ethmoid bone, Fliess strongly encouraged him to continue his attempts to create a neuronal theory of psychology.

## The *Project for a Scientific Psychology*

Freud described the trip back to Vienna in tones reminiscent of the earlier train ride home from Gisela and Freiberg during his adolescence.

In his letter to Fliess of September 15, 1895, he wrote that "it helps a parting if one immediately thereafter encounters different circumstances that give one something to do," and went on to lampoon his carriage-mates, or "neighbors." Complaining of draft, one neighbor tried to close the windows only to encounter Freud's militant objection. After battling with Freud over windows and seats, "Mr. Neighbor" got the advantage by catching Freud in a piece of apparent criminality: Freud was looking in his bag for writing materials with which to begin revising his neuronal psychology in light of Fliess's suggestions. It was these notebooks that were posthumously discovered and published as the *Project for a Scientific Psychology*. Groping about in his bag, Freud was aghast to come across what seemed to be undeclared purchases. This "attracted the liveliest attention of Mr. Neighbor. . . . The apprehension rose in me that I could not in good conscience tell the customs official, 'Everything belongs to me,' and it took a while before I could explain [to myself] these findings by the assumption of a hereditary disposition to smuggle."

By a "hereditary disposition," Freud was referring to the time in his childhood when his uncle Josef had been arrested for passing counterfeit notes. This sudden visitation by the sin of Jacob's brother noticeably unsettled Freud and emboldened his smirking carriage-mate to offer advice on how to escape detection by the customs officials. Why Freud should have felt fraudulent on this occasion—perhaps it had something to do with his attempting so ambitious a scientific theory as the *Project*—is not clear, but this reaction is evidence that Freud's identity at the age of 39 was still not fully formed.

## Redoubled Attempts at Science

Back home in Vienna Freud steadfastly bent his invigorated imagination to scientific purposes. On September 23, 1895, he wrote Fliess that he was continuing with the writing work he had begun on the train and that it already amounted to a substantial volume. Earlier problems were now yielding readily, and several new points had fallen into place. He was not sure that these solutions would not prove illusory, but he was sailing ahead of the strong tail wind of Fliess's encouragement.

By October 8, 1895, the clinical theory of hysteria and obsessional neurosis was moving along nicely. He was beginning to suspect that these illnesses resulted from sexual experiences in childhood. But the elucidation of the psychopathology of repression—that is, exactly the point at which general psychology and clinical psychology would meet—continued to vex Freud. The first two of the three notebooks of the *Project,* concerning cerebral neurology and cognition, had posed less difficulty and, at least in elementary form, were done. The last one required continued revision. "I had to work once again with new drafts and in the process became alternately proud and overjoyed and ashamed and miserable—until now, after an excess of mental torment, I apathetically tell myself; it does not yet, perhaps never will, hang together." Freud, "alone with a head in which so much [was] germinating and . . . thrashing around," yearned for Fliess's company.

A week later Freud declared his correspondence "crazy." He had been in a "writing fever" for two weeks, during which time he at first thought he had solved the theoretical problems and then, realizing he had not, abandoned the whole thing. Meanwhile, he had discovered a "great clinical secret," namely, that "hysteria is the consequence of a presexual *sexual shock.* Obsessional neurosis is the consequence of a presexual *sexual pleasure,* which is later transformed into [self-] *reproach.*" Freud explained that by *presexual* he meant "actually before puberty, before the release of sexual substances; the relevant events become effective only as *memories.*"[60]

The next day he was again "all mixed up." He had "conquered" the two neuroses, but the general psychology remained stubbornly obscure.

> I am almost certain that I have solved the riddles of hysteria and obsessional neurosis . . . and I am equally certain that both neuroses are, in general, curable—not just individual symptoms but the neurotic disposition itself. This gives me a kind of faint joy—for having lived some forty years not quite in vain—and yet no genuine satisfaction because the psychological gap in the new knowledge claims my entire interest.[61]

By "psychological gap" Freud was referring to the neuronal psychology that he was trying so hard to complete.

Four days later, he thought that he had broken through both to an understanding of psychology and to an integration of consciousness and neurosis:

> Now listen to this. During an industrious night last week, when I was suffering from that degree of pain which brings about the optimal condition for my mental activities, the barriers suddenly lifted, the veils dropped, and everything became transparent—from the details of the neuroses to the determinants of consciousness. Everything seemed to fall into place, the cogs meshed, I had the impression that the thing now really was a machine that shortly

would function on its own. The three systems of n [neurones]; the
free and bound states of Qn [quantity]; the primary and secondary
processes; the main tendency and the compromise tendency of the
nervous system; the two biological rules of attention and defense;
the characteristics of quality, reality, and thought; the state of the
psychosexual group; the sexual determination of repression; finally, the factors determining consciousness, as a function of
perception—all that was correct and still is today! Naturally, I can
scarcely manage to contain my delight. . . .

Other confirmations concerning the neuroses are pouring in
on me. The thing is really true and genuine.[62]

Eleven days later, on October 31, 1895, Freud described himself
as "dead tired" and "drained."[63] The theoretical contraption he had
built was still standing, but Freud did not "trust the individual parts"
and had tried different ones. Some had had to be abandoned altogether.
Only a paragraph further, the parts seemed correct but the arrangement wrong. Insights from the consulting room still yielded the greatest
clarity. "Fortunately for me, all these theories must flow into the clinical estuary of repression, where I have daily opportunities to be corrected or enlightened." Two days later one of Freud's hysterical male
patients had presented fresh clinical evidence of infantile seduction,
and this had "strengthened [his] confidence in the validity of [his] psychological constructions," allowing him to announce, "Now I am really
enjoying a moment of satisfaction."[64] Yet Freud knew that much remained to be done. In addition to working on the remaining problems
in his theory of neurosis, there was the small book on infantile paralyses
that he had promised to write by the end of the year for a series edited
by Nothnagel. Nothnagel's continuing support was critical to his hopes
for promotion at the university, but he had not even begun the book.

On November 8 he wrote Fliess that he had "rebelled against [his]
tyrant." Attempts to work on *Infantile Paralyses* led him to the realization that his ideas about psychology needed major revision. "I felt
overworked, irritated, confused, and incapable of mastering it all. So
I threw everything away. . . . I hope that in two months' time I shall
be able to clarify the whole thing. The clinical solution of hysteria,
however, still stands; it is appealing and simple." Two days later he
wrote, "I am completely stuck in the infantile paralyses, which do not
interest me at all.[65] Since I have put the [neuronal psychology] aside,
I feel beaten and disenchanted. . . . I now feel a void."[66]

## Breuer Strikes Again

As we have seen, mention of Breuer had nearly disappeared from Freud's
correspondence since the previous May, when Freud had reported to

Fliess that the older man was so improved as to be unrecognizable. Now, just when Freud was feeling low, Breuer committed an act of adulterated generosity: He set his own reservations aside and publicly championed Freud's sexual theories. "Recently at the College of Physicians Breuer gave a big speech in my honor and introduced himself as a *converted* adherent to the sexual etiology. When I thanked him for this in private, he spoiled my pleasure by saying, 'But all the same, I don't believe it.' " Incredulous, Freud asked Fliess, "Do you understand this? I don't."[67]

Three weeks later, on November 29, 1895 — Martha was due any day with Anna — Freud wrote Fliess that he was feeling "amazingly well." His nose was finally behaving thanks to Fliess's skillful interventions during their August congress. His practice was full, providing "the most beautiful things . . . all sorts of new material," which had simply to be stored away, the book on infantile paralyses claiming the energy he had left for scientific work. He was starting to wonder if the *Project* was a product of delirium. "I no longer understand," he wrote, "the state of mind in which I hatched the psychology; cannot conceive how I could have inflicted it on you. . . . To me it appears to have been a kind of madness." In contrast, the clinical conception still stood.

On December 3, the Freuds' last child, Anna, was born. "Today at 3:15," he announced, "she pushed her way into my consulting hour, appears to be a nice complete little female who, thanks to Fleischmann's care, did not do her mother any harm." On New Year's Day, 1896, Freud wrote Fliess brimming with gratitude for his contribution to Freud's many blessings.

> How much I owe you: solace, understanding, stimulation in my loneliness, meaning to my life that I gained through you, and finally even health that no one else could have given back to me. It is primarily through your example that intellectually I gained the strength to trust my judgment, even when I am left alone — though not by you — and, like you, to face with lofty humility all the difficulties that the future may bring. For all that, accept my humble thanks! I know that you do not need me as much as I need you, but I also know that I have a secure place in your affection.

Both men imagined that they were making strides in solving fundamental scientific problems and that contemporaneously they were each drawing nearer to their first, treasured destination. "I see how, via the detour of medical practice, you are reaching your first ideal of understanding human beings as a physiologist, just as I most secretly nourish the hope of arriving, via these same paths, at my initial goal of philosophy. For that is what I wanted originally, when it was not yet at all clear to me to what end I was in the world."[68]

By "philosophy" Freud meant psychology understood at such a fundamental level as to reveal basic underlying truths, the great discoveries achieved by the *Naturforschung* he had dreamed of pursuing at 17. It remained his intention to base his psychology in neurophysiology and to realize the basic science aspect of his dream. Thus, Freud followed the remark about his initial goal with a lengthy essay on his neuronal theory of the psychic apparatus in which he attempted to interconnect his theory with Fliess's theory of the nasal reflex mechanism.

He also enclosed with the New Year's letter an even longer theoretical draft entitled "The Neuroses of Defense," flippantly subtitling it "A Christmas Fairy Tale." This draft described in considerable detail an etiology for several of the neuroses, together with a temporal sequence for their development in childhood. The flippancy shows Freud's efforts to keep science primary and avoid the complications in his own development of unifying the scientific and clinical aspects of his dream. Yet the clinical aspect would not go away, in part because Freud was attempting to do science through pure speculation while in his clinical work he was immersed daily in observable data. "The Christmas Fairy Tale" again offered sexual seduction as the cause of neurosis. This was the first detailed publication of Freud's seduction theory, which he had initially suggested to Fliess in October and whose later abandonment became so controversial, the vicissitudes of his belief in which we shall follow through his mid-life transition.[69] It represented Freud's first, rather mechanical, attempt to integrate science and treatment under the developmental aegis of his mid-life transition.

Other tendrils of the coming developmental period appeared. In his letter of February 6, 1896, Freud explained the five week hiatus in his correspondence as the result of one of his "writing attacks," during which he had sent scientific communiqués flying off in all directions. The most important of these essays concerned the heredity and etiology of the neuroses, which he published in a French neurological journal. In it, Freud used the word *psychoanalysis* for the first time in print.[70] This flurry of scientific productivity required that the lid be closed on his relationship with Breuer. "I simply can no longer get along with Breuer at all; what I had to take in the way of bad treatment and weakness of judgment that is nonetheless ingenious during the past months finally deadened me, internally, to the loss. But, please, do not say a word about it that might find its way back here." A week later he wrote Fliess that "in spite of everything, I find it very painful that [Breuer] has so completely removed himself from my life." Yet despite and because of the end of his mentorial relationship with Breuer, Freud continued to be buoyed by his certainty that both he and Fliess had "got hold of a beautiful piece of objective truth." He reported being "continually occupied with psychology," amending the word for the first time to "metapsychology."[71] By "metapsychology" Freud meant a general psychology of a very basic scientific sort as opposed to a clinical science of the nervous system or the mind.

## Breuer Expresses a Reservation

Breuer had written a letter to Fliess in which he pointed to gaps in Freud's theory of the neuroses and offered some observations of his own. Freud asked Fliess to send it to him. "I was less angry about Breuer's letter," Freud wrote Fliess after reading it, "than I had expected to be."

> Our personal relationship, mended on the surface, casts a deep shadow over my existence here. I can do nothing right for him and have given up trying. . . . I believe he will never forgive that in the *Studies* I dragged him along and involved him in something where he unfailingly knows three candidates for the position of one truth and abhors all generalizations, regarding them as presumptuous. That everything one enjoys in life has to be paid for so dearly is decidedly not an admirable arrangement. Will the two of us experience the same thing with each other?[72]

On March 16, 1896, Freud wrote that despite feeling irresistibly compelled by the problem of the general psychology, he was imagining a "beautiful work" entitled "Psychology and Psychotherapy of the Neuroses of Defense," a work for which, he said, "I am allowing myself years of preparation and into which I shall put my whole soul." On April 2, on the eve of their congress, Freud reported that work on the psychology of the neuroses was going well, and that he would be bringing new thoughts on metapsychology, too. "As a young man I knew no longing other than for philosophical knowledge, and now I am about to fulfill it as I move from medicine to psychology. I became a therapist against my will; I am convinced that, given certain conditions in regard to the person and the case, I can definitely cure hysteria and obsessional neurosis."[73]

Theirs was a deliciously refreshing Easter congress during which Fliess obliged Freud by urging him to remain in isolation from his scientific colleagues. By April, close upon his 40th birthday and still drugged from the Fliessian ambrosia imbibed at their spring congress, Freud was trying once again to work out a neuronal theory of the mind and connect it to Fliess's conjectures. "I have become downright obsessed with the problem of neuronic motion," he wrote Fliess. "Stimulated by your chemical theories, and after the most unbelievable trials, I have likewise arrived at a chemical conception that instills confidence in me. As soon as the story fits together, you shall have it." He had found it easy to follow his friend's advice about isolating himself. Indeed, in this matter he was reminded of a joke about a doctor who advised his patient to give up wine, women, and song and who received this response from the patient: "Very well, I'll stop *singing*." Freud noted that he had "not yet seen Breuer and have given up complaining."[74] A week later metapsychology was banished completely in the exertion to wed his theory to Fliess's biological speculations. "I believe," he wrote, "more and more firmly in the chemical neurone theory; I started with assumptions similar to those you described, but now I am stuck after I ruined my head with it yesterday."[75]

Thus Freud cast about first in the direction of biological science, then in the direction of pure psychology, and then toward the neuroses and their cure for some version of his dream that he could accept and achieve. The attempts he had been making to direct himself uniformly toward a neuronal psychology had not succeeded. He had been able neither to create the new biopsychological theory nor to suppress his own striving toward a new and effective clinical theory. Although Freud had recently given a lecture on dream interpretation to a Jewish reading circle, professionally he remained isolated, and it was not clear how interpreting dreams was going to change that.

# PART THREE

# The Mid-Life Transition

## CHAPTER EIGHT

# Losing the Way
## (Ages 40–41)

### THE INITIAL PHASE
### OF THE MID-LIFE TRANSITION

FREUD'S developmental problem at mid-life was to integrate the disparate aspects of his dream in a way that would be viable in the world and allow the fullest expression of an authentic identity. Achieving a more fully formed version of his dream held out for Freud the promise not only of worldly success but also of deep and abiding inner satisfaction. Failure would raise grave questions about his pretensions. The first step in reforming the dream was to assess his progress to date, and Freud found a culminating event to help him do so. The culminating event would help to get the initial phase of Freud's mid-life transition under way by signifying the success of his professional efforts during the era of early adulthood.

Culminating events come in a myriad of forms, such as election to high office, critical acclaim, promotion, a prestigious award, a salary increase, the granting of tenure, marriage, the birth of a baby — or the failure to achieve any one of these. The possibilities vary as widely as the realms of endeavor and the personal values of the individual. The event is a symbol that derives its importance from the meanings the person attributes to it. The individual may not know the deep purposes for which he or she is using the event. Rather, underlying developmental forces work their way through the person's behavior while the individual struggles to understand what is happening.

The culminating event may be invested with great significance in advance or only afterward, and its actual importance may be trivial, mixed, or fleeting. Because reappraisal is a developmental task of the mid-life transition, the individual typically feels that the event signifies a failure or, at best, a blemished success that calls everything into question. If one is promoted, one has been humiliated in the process; if one makes a scientific discovery, one regrets having given so much credit to colleagues; if the individual wins the Nobel Prize, he or she is depressed by the thought that it was awarded for the wrong reasons; if a person becomes a millionaire, he or she becomes painfully aware of never having been in love; if one finally begins a family, one regrets that this step was not taken earlier, and so on.

The culminating event of Freud's youth occurred on April 21, 1896, just before he turned 40. On that day he presented the seduction theory to the Viennese Society for Psychiatry and Neurology in a meeting chaired by the eminent psychopathologist Richard von Krafft-Ebing. Freud began his lecture by reviewing Breuer's cathartic method, about which his remarks were respectful in both tone and substance. He made it clear that the method he had used to discover the origins of hysteria was merely an extension of Breuer's. But he also forthrightly marked out a position contrary to Breuer's concerning etiology. Breuer's "hypnoid state"—the state of mind in which *any* experience could constitute the traumatic cause of later hysterical symptoms—was rejected on several grounds: There was rarely evidence for the existence of such states; worse, the scenes recalled by the patient were often innocuous or unsuited in content to the actual symptom; and, ultimately, the recall of such scenes rarely led to therapeutic success.

What was needed, Freud argued, was a new idea, and he had it.[1] The analysis of associations must be pursued back *beyond* the initial recovered memory. Doing so, Freud insisted, always yielded memories that were sufficient both in "traumatic force" and determining "suitability" to have created the foundation for the illness in its specific form; further, these memories were always of childhood sexual experiences.[2] "So here for the first time," he announced to his colleagues, "we seem to have discovered an aetiological precondition for hysterical symptoms."[3]

If he had been a bit deferential toward Breuer, Freud's tone in anticipation of his audience's criticisms was now flatly uncompromising. "From previous experience I can foresee that it is precisely against this assertion or against its universal validity that your contradiction, Gentlemen, will be directed. Perhaps it would be better to say, your *inclination* to contradict; for none of you, no doubt, have as yet any investigations at your disposal which, based upon the same procedure, might have yielded a different result." He, by contrast, had analyzed

18 cases, 12 female and 6 male, and had found his hypothesis correct in every one of them.

At the bottom of every case of hysteria, Freud insisted, there existed one or more premature sexual experiences, which could be revealed by sufficiently persistent investigation. Freud declared this "an important revelation, the discovery of a *caput Nili* [source of the Nile] in neuropathology."[4] For the first time it was possible to say why the outbreak of hysterical symptoms did not appear until after puberty: Noxious sexual ideas in adolescence could be repressed and replaced by symptoms when in the unconscious there existed *memories* of sexual events to which the current idea could be associatively connected.

Freud's colleagues were not convinced. A week later Freud wrote Fliess that his lecture on the etiology of hysteria to the psychiatric society had been "given an icy reception by the asses and a strange evaluation by Krafft-Ebing: 'It sounds like a scientific fairy tale.' " Freud was furious. "And this," he exclaimed, "after one has demonstrated to them the solution of a more-than-thousand-year-old problem, a *caput Nili!* They can go to hell."[5] The next month he told Fliess that he was publishing his lecture—under the title "The Aetiology of Hysteria"—"in defiance of [his] colleagues."[6]

Indeed, Krafft-Ebing's derisive dismissal came to characterize for Freud the response of the entire group, even the entire medical community. As Gay knowingly writes, it "was an evening Freud chose never to forget."[7] Indeed, he gave the occasion singular place in his "History of the Psycho-Analytic Movement" written 18 years later. There he identified it as the decisive event that cut him off from his profession. In this later account one can see the disparity between what Freud actually did and his own assessment of it. "I innocently addressed a meeting of the Vienna Society for Psychiatry and Neurology with Krafft-Ebing in the chair . . . expecting that the material losses I had willingly undergone would be made up for by the interest and recognition of my colleagues." Perceiving himself as having been far from provocative, Freud insisted that he had "treated [his] discoveries as ordinary contributions of science and hoped they would be received in the same spirit."

Freud had not been innocent, and he had not treated his discoveries as ordinary. Yet he attributed his colleagues' reaction not to his own combative assertiveness but to resistance against the idea of infantile sexuality.

> But the silence which my communications met with, the void which formed itself about me, the hints that were conveyed to me, gradually made me realize that assertions on the part played by sexuality

in the aetiology of the neuroses cannot count upon meeting with
the same kind of treatment as other communications. I understood
that from now onwards I was one of those who have "disturbed
the sleep of the world" . . . and that I could not reckon upon ob-
jectivity and tolerance. . . . [Yet] I was prepared to accept the fate
that sometimes accompanies such [important] discoveries. I pictured
the future as follows: — I should probably succeed in maintaining
myself by means of the therapeutic success of the new procedure,
but science would ignore me entirely during my lifetime; some decades later, someone else would infallibly come upon the same
things — for which the time was not now ripe — would achieve recognition for them and bring me honour as a forerunner whose failure
had been inevitable.

Freud *had* gained sufficient perspective to realize that his lecture had
been an act of heroism and, by implication, one encased in the simple
charm of youthful illusion. And, tellingly, he recalled that the isolation he imagined it had brought on had been splendid. "Meanwhile,
like Robinson Crusoe, I settled down as comfortably as possible on
my desert island. When I look back to those lonely years, away from
the pressures and confusions of to-day, its seems liked a glorious heroic
age. My 'splendid isolation' was not without its advantages and
charms."[8] In his letter to Fliess on May 4, 1896, two days before his
40th birthday, he reported the consequences of his lecture: "Word [has
been] given out to abandon me, for a void is forming all around me."
He bore it with "equanimity," being now, he said, "as isolated as you
would wish me to be."

In reality, Freud had begun to isolate himself months before.


## The Seduction Theory and Freud's Dream

After publicly announcing the seduction theory on that day in April
of 1896, Freud began to have doubts about it. These doubts became
so strong that he abandoned the theory for the first time a year and
a half later. Masson has argued that Freud abandoned the theory because it created a breach between himself and his colleagues.[9] Yet as
we are seeing, Freud, besotted with heroic fantasies, *sought* isolation
from the professional community and sometimes found it glorious —
both at the time and in retrospect. Moreover, he *needed* it for his own
further development inasmuch as he was trying to free himself from
the influence of his teachers. Feeling that his isolation was forced on
him also enabled him to summon his combativeness for a great developmental leap. In addition, as we will see, Freud had a hard time letting

go of the theory, re-embracing and rejecting it over the course of many months.

We have followed Freud's struggles throughout the close of his 30s to find connections between his own emerging psychological theories and biological ones, between his ideas and Fliess's. The split in his theory between the neuronal aspect of the psychic apparatus and the origins and mechanisms of neurosis troubled him, as did his inability to connect the two. The seduction theory offered a solution to this troubling scientific and personal problem. Childhood sexual seduction was a *physicalist* explanation of the cause of neurosis. "*The symptoms of hysteria . . . ,* " he wrote in "The Aetiology of Hysteria," "*are determined by certain experiences of the patient's which have operated in a traumatic fashion and which are being reproduced in his psychical life in the form of mnemic symbols.*"[10] These "grave sexual injuries" are *reproduced* in the psychical sphere; that is, the experiences are taken from the physical sphere into the psychical one.[11] As a consequence of premature sexual irritation, some undischarged sexual quantum invaded the psyche and damaged it.[12] As Freud put it in his January 1, 1896, letter to Fliess, in which he first elaborated the seduction theory: "Hysteria begins with the overwhelming of the ego. . . . The raising of tension at the primary experience of unpleasure is so great that the ego does not resist it and forms no psychic symptom but is obliged to allow a manifestation of discharge. . . . [The] primary symptom is the *manifestation of fright* accompanied by a *gap* in the psyche."[13]

More importantly, the seduction theory also offered the transformative prospect of unifying Freud's dream and integrating his identity, for the problem of neurotic etiology—unlike the earlier neuronal psychology or, later, the meaning of dreams—was at one and the same time important both scientifically and clinically. The discovery of the origins of neurosis solved, as Freud had asserted to his colleagues, a thousand-year-old scientific problem and, given the nature of his solution, pointed directly to a cure. Repressed memories could be abreacted, and the continuing activity of their destructive force dispelled.

## Becalmed

Freud's withdrawal from his medical colleagues began in the January *preceding* his talk to the Viennese Society for Psychiatry and Neurology and deepened during that winter and spring. On January 1 he wrote Fliess of being "left alone" but of facing difficulties with a "lofty humility." On February 6 he wrote of being the only one applauding his work and of having suffered a "vicious" review of the *Studies on Hysteria* by Strümpell in the *Deutsche Zeitschrift für Nervenheilkunde.* In disagreement with Freud's reading of the review, others have found it positive, and it seems at least temperate.[14] On February 13 Freud wrote that he was lonely yet beyond Strümpell's criticism since both he and Fliess could "do without recognition from strangers." His health, he noted laconically, did not deserve inquiry. "I have rapidly turned gray," he reported, declaring himself, with the exception of an undying interest in psychology, "scarcely human any longer."

On February 23 Freud was "somewhat miserable," perhaps from flu. On March 7, physically well, he was still "miserable" and his life "monotonous, often disagreeable," although he had begun to look forward with excitement to their next congress. He had received an invitation to speak at the 68th meeting of the Society of German Natural Scientists and Physicians[15] in Frankfurt. He greeted this opportunity with the same sense of being importuned with which he regarded his obligation to speak on the etiology of hysteria at the Viennese Society, an obligation to be discharged in April. "One really cannot decline, but it does not suit me in any respect."

On March 16 he wrote that he was "contending with hostility and . . . [living] in such isolation that one might imagine [he] had discovered the greatest truths." On April 2, three weeks before his lecture to the Viennese Society and buoyed by the prospect of an Easter congress, Freud was savoring the prospect of further isolation from his colleagues. "If both of us are still granted a few more years for quiet work, we shall certainly leave behind something that can justify our existence. Knowing this, I feel strong in the face of all daily cares and worries."

On April 16, on his return from a refreshing reunion with Fliess, Freud wrote him, "In accordance with your request, I have started to isolate myself in every respect and find it easy to bear." He noted that he did, however, have a "prior commitment" to lecture to the Viennese Society for Psychiatry and Neurology that coming Tuesday. Otherwise, his isolation would be unblemished. He reported that he had not seen Breuer and had "avoided an unnecessary encounter with him at the home of a patient who at times [was seeing] both of [them]." Since the congress with Fliess, he had not been able to summon "the modicum of misery" necessary for creative work. Note that Freud viewed the Viennese Society presentation as an unwelcome interruption of his solitude, an isolation that he liked to imagine as Fliess's requirement, and that he was also avoiding Breuer. We have already noted Freud's reaction to the reception he would receive at the Viennese Society.

On May 6 Freud turned 40. A few days later, his sister Rosa married Heinrich Graf, an attorney. Freud admired Graf and found the excitement of the wedding "a ray of sunshine in winter."[16] His letter to Fliess of May 30 included extensive theoretical material that extended his theory of the etiology of the neuroses; he attributed the choice of neurosis to the developmental period in which the sexual seduction occurred. Nevertheless, Freud felt that the "[academic] year had exhausted [his] moral strength."

Anticipating the next congress, Freud wrote Fliess on June 4, 1896, that he would have disappointingly little to bring by way of fresh ideas. His spirits were weighed down by the obligation to write his book on infantile paralyses. "These times have brought me, intellectually and morally, to the very point of losing my strength. . . . I really need [a congress], often do not recognize myself — that is how much the experiences with colleagues and patients have taken their toll — which is, after all, really ridiculous. . . . I have not seen Breuer again, except for a moment at the wedding; have no further need of doing so." In his next letter, on June 9, Freud began, "I could now say, our next congress is really superfluous because I have nothing to tell you. . . . I am in a very dull period." This was the last letter Freud wrote before he learned that his father was seriously ill.

## The Death of Freud's Father

In mid-June Freud's 81-year-old father became gravely ill. Four months later, on October 23, 1896, Jacob died. This event has been given critical importance in other explanations of the origins of psychoanalysis. The reasoning, widely accepted, has gone as follows: Freud's strong emotional reaction to his father's death led him to engage systematically in his own self-analysis. This self-analysis led to the discovery of his Oedipus complex and to a recognition of the role of incestuous fantasies in the formation of neurosis generally. Once Freud had grasped the traumatic nature of infantile fantasy, external events, such as infantile seduction, were unnecessary to explain neurosis. The way was then open to the pure psychological theory of *The Interpretation of Dreams* and to all of psychoanalysis. In the preface to the second edition of *The Interpretation of Dreams,* Freud himself linked the book and his self-analysis to Jacob's death.[17]

Yet as we have seen, Freud had been in a period of withdrawal for several months prior to his father's illness. During this time his interest in dreams grew, and he wrote to Fliess of his theory that dreams are wish fulfilling. He took material on dream theory to their congress in April 1896. His growing interest in the psychology of dreams was the product of his inability to generate biological explanations apace with his psychological insights and of his continuing difficulties in solving to his own satisfaction the problem of neurosis. Yet he could not give himself fully to dream theory while the transcendent scientific and clinical problem of neurotic etiology remained unsolved. Dreams did not yet have important clinical significance to Freud.

It is important to see that Freud's withdrawal, isolation, and low spirits had begun prior to Jacob's terminal illness. Doing so helps us keep clear that Freud's mid-life transition — with its emotional turmoil (including his self-analysis), theoretical conundra (including the vicissitudes of his belief in the seduction theory and the danger such uncertainty posed for the integration of his identity as a psychiatrist and for the realization of his dream), and creative triumphs (such as *The Interpretation of Dreams*) — was part of an ongoing sequence of normal development, not the consequence of a major life event that might have happened at some other time.

On June 9, 1896, Freud was working on the idea that repression accounted for the delayed appearance of symptoms following childhood seduction, but he could not get it right. Sometime in mid-June Jacob fell ill. Freud wrote Fliess on June 30 that his father was "in a most shaky state, with heart failure, paralysis of the bladder, and so forth" and that "eagerly waiting for news and traveling to see him were the only things of interest in [the preceding] two weeks." This made the usual planning for their next congress impossible. But Freud had been needing one badly and proposed the possibility of coming on 24 hours' notice, should news of Jacob's health permit. "I feel a pall has been cast over me," he wrote, "and all I can say is that I am looking forward to our congress as to the slaking of hunger and thirst." The intellectually arid period that had begun prior to Jacob's illness had persisted, and Freud was having his first doubts about the seduction theory. How could the symptoms of childhood hysteria remain repressed until adolescence? He was eager for inspiration from Fliess.

> I [would bring to our next congress] nothing but two open ears and one temporal lobe lubricated for reception. . . . With regard to the repression theory, I have run into doubts that could be dispelled by a few words from you, in particular about male and female menstruation in the same individual. Anxiety, chemical factors, and so forth — perhaps with your help I shall find the solid ground on which I can cease to give psychological explanations and begin to find a physiological foundation!

In the only letter extant from July 1986 Freud was still intellectually in "urgent need for the introduction of a fertilizing stream from elsewhere."[18] The feminine imagery appears again here and in the lubricated lobe simile in the passage just quoted. Freud was working halfheartedly to finish *Infantile Paralyses,* and Jacob's precarious state made it impossible to complete plans for the next congress. About his father, Freud wrote:

> The old man's condition . . . does not depress me. I do not begrudge him the well-deserved rest that he himself desires. He was an interesting human being, very happy within himself; he is suffering very little now, and is fading with decency and dignity. I do not wish him a prolonged sickbed, nor do I wish it for my unmarried sister, who is nursing him and suffering in the process.

Freud was on vacation in August. His spirits and creativity had revived, as had Jacob's health, and he eagerly awaited the next congress, which finally took place at the end of the month.[19] Freud emerged from the congress restored, and his buoyancy was still holding up in early October, despite flu, work on *Infantile Paralyses,* professional isolation, and a deterioration of his father's health. A new patient had revived his confidence in his seduction theory. He had taken a friend's wife into treatment and reported, "It [is] sheer joy to see once again how everything fits and tallies in hysteria." He hoped within a year or two to be able to express his theory in formulas understandable to everyone.[20]

On October 23 Jacob died. Freud wrote Fliess:

> Yesterday we buried the old man, who died during the night of October 23. He bore himself bravely to the end, just like the altogether unusual man he had been. At the end he must have had meningeal hemorrhages, soporous attacks with unexplained fever, hyperesthesia, and spasms from which he would then awake free of fever. The last attack was followed by pulmonary edema and quite an easy death. All of it happened in my [Fliessian] critical period, and I am really quite down because of it.[21]

## You Are Requested to Close the Eyes

In his next letter to Fliess, dated November 2, 1896, Freud told him a dream. "I must tell you about a nice dream I had the night after the funeral. I was in a place where I read a sign:

> You are requested
> to close the eyes."

Freud recognized the location as his barbershop, where in reality he had been kept waiting on the day of the funeral. His family had been offended by his tardiness as well as by the inadequacy of the funeral arrangements he had made. Freud interpreted the sentence on the sign as having two meanings: "One should do one's duty to the dead (an apology as though I had not done it and were in need of leniency), and the actual duty itself. The dream thus stems from the inclination to self-reproach that regularly sets in among the survivors."[22] In the same letter he told Fliess, "By one of those dark pathways behind the official consciousness the old man's death has affected me deeply. I valued him highly, understood him very well, and with his peculiar mixture of deep wisdom and fantastic light-heartedness he had a significant effect on my life." Freud felt that inside his "whole past has been reawakened," and he "now felt quite uprooted."

## Intensification of Freud's Attempts to Join His Theory to Fliess's

Doubts about his seduction theory, together with Jacob's death, produced a regressive deepening of Freud's dependence on Fliess, which was manifested in perfervid and quite fantastic attempts to join their theories. On December 4, Freud wrote that he was feeling better and reported, "I am dealing with something that cements your work to mine, places my structure on your base. . . . I am so isolated here that I hear nothing about your book."

Fliess's book was *The Relationship between the Nose and the Female Sexual Organs: Presented from the Point of View of its Biological Significance.*[23] It was not published until the next year, 1897, so either Freud was confused about its publication date or advance copies had been circulated. On December 6 Freud sent Fliess a draft of his most elaborate attempt to relate his work on the role of memory in mediating between infantile sexual trauma and the appearance of neurotic symptoms in adolescence to his old neuronal psychological preoccupations and all of this finally to Fliess's theory of periodicity.[24]

He was trying, he wrote, to place the "superstructure" of his ideas on "its organic foundations." What had to be explained, he reasoned, was how what is pleasurable in one period became unpleasurable or at least compulsive in another. The answer was to "trace the derivation of the different epochs, psychological and sexual. You have taught me to recognize the latter as special multiples of the 28-day female period." There then followed a truly bizarre set of calculations in which Freud, using Fliess's theory, imagined he was able to account for all psychic periods as multiples of 23-day periods (p) if I *include in the calculation* the period of gestation (276 days = 12 p). . . .[25] This would mean that psychic development occurs according to 23[-day] periods, which would summate to multiples of 3, 6, 12, . . . , 24, in which case the duodecimal system would become effective [ellipses in the original]. The unit would in each case be the *period of gestation,* which equals 10 p or 12 p (approximately). The only result would be that psychic development would progress in accordance with multiples of 3, 6, 12 of the same, whereas the period of gestation *equals* 12 p; and sexual development would proceed according to the multiples of 5, 10, 20, whereas this time *equals* 10 p.

This extraordinary piece of pseudoscientific reasoning went on to produce further oddments such as a confirmation of "the intellectual nature of males" and a distinction between neurasthenia and anxiety neurosis based on "the existence of the two 23-day and 28-day substances."

The letter closed with Freud's first reference to collecting statuary. "I have now adorned my room with plaster casts of Florentine statues. It was a source of extraordinary invigoration for me, I am thinking of getting rich, in order to be able to repeat these trips [to the lands of antiquity]. A congress on Italian soil! (Naples, Pompeii.)" This new hobby, destined to become a lifelong obsession eventuating in the collection of thousands of pieces, seems restitutive to the loss of his father and a solace for the anticipated future of solitary research.

Freud made clear in his next letter to Fliess that the appeal of these recent theoretical ideas arose not so much from their intrinsic merit as from the prospect of uniting their work.

> My inner joy in suddenly being struck by an idea obviously was related not to the latent proofs but to finding a common ground for the work we share. I hope it will go so far that we can jointly build something definitive on it, and thereby blend our contributions to the point where our individual property is no longer recognizable. After all, I can collect facts only in the psychic sphere, you in the organological one; the in-between areas will require a hypothesis.[26]

The desperate attempt continued with speculations concerning the distribution of Fliess's 28-day feminine and 23-day masculine sexual substances, which Fliess believed were present in persons of either sex. "[Perhaps the gestation] periods themselves, rather than the breakthroughs, [should] be numbered multiples. The same must apply to the 28[-day] p. I have not yet tried this new calculation. (Just done;

doesn't work.) The principal idea in this attempt seems to me to be the different deployment of the two substances. . . . Both substances are released simultaneously every day." Perhaps, Freud reasoned, abnormal levels of production and accumulation led to the various psychopathologies. Having for the time being exhausted his calculations, Freud wrote, "Hidden deep within this is my ideal and woebegone child—metapsychology."

"You may," he added, "be interested to hear how I arrived at [the new idea]. I noticed that on certain dates, which clearly recur every 28 days, I have no sexual desire and am impotent—which otherwise is not yet the case, after all. Then, when the matter occurred to me, I had a happy day without really knowing why, a sort of blissful aftertaste like after a beautiful dream." He concluded, "It seems plausible to regard the periodic melancholia/mania as a temporal separation of the otherwise simultaneous release of pleasure and unpleasure," and then added a more likely explanation for the fluctuations: He was again having doubts about the seduction theory, and although he had not yet succeeded in finishing a case based on the new premises, he had the feeling that something important was missing.

## A Brief Reinvigoration
## and a Curious Descent into Demonology

During the first months of 1897, Freud's mood lifted and his creativity returned. He felt "much more stable," believing that his "critical age" had now passed.[27] In his January 3, 1897, letter of New Year's greetings to Fliess, Freud confidently predicted that great discoveries awaited them both. "Give me another ten years, and I shall finish the neuroses and the new psychology. You probably will need less time for your organology. In spite of the complaints you allude to, no New Year has ever found both of us as rich and as ripe. When I happen to be without anxiety, I am still ready to take on all the devils; and you have never known anxiety." Although certainty regarding the critical etiological periods for the neuroses eluded him, he wrote, everything seemed to be pointing to the first three years of life.

On January 11, 1897, Freud was "in the full swing of discovery," offering "red-hot" new ideas on the determination between psychosis (i.e., earlier seduction, in the first one and a half years) and neurosis and on the nature of perversion. The next day he wrote again, expressing full confidence in his new ideas, a confidence that continued on January 17. So determined was he to find independent confirmation of his childhood seduction hypothesis that he had turned to the medieval theory of demonic possession. "[The victims'] confessions under torture [were] so like the communications made by my patients in psychic treatment," he told Fliess. The victims of the ecclesiastical torturers, Freud reasoned, were reenacting repressed experiences of sexual assault, and so, by reversing the roles, were their torturers.

By January 24, Freud, encouraged by Fliess, was finding connections everywhere. *Infantile Paralyses* was finished, and Freud's imagination was free to revel in witchery.

> The idea of bringing in witches is gaining strength. . . . Their "flying" is explained; the broomstick they ride probably is the great Lord Penis. The secret gatherings, with dancing and entertainment, can be seen any day in the streets where children play. I read one day that the gold the devil gives his victims regularly turns into excrement; and the next day Mr. E., who reports that his nurse had money deliria, suddenly told me (by way of Cagliostro—alchemist—*Dukatenscheisser* [one who defecates ducats]) that Louise's money always was excrement. So in the witch stories it is merely transformed back into the substance from which it arose. . . . The story of the devil, the vocabulary of popular swearwords, the songs and customs of the nursery—all these are now gaining significance for me. . . .
>
> I am beginning to grasp an idea: it is as though in the perversions, of which hysteria is the negative, we have before us a remnant of a primeval sexual cult, which once was—perhaps still is—a religion in the Semitic East (Moloch, Astarte). . . .
>
> I dream . . . of a primeval devil religion with rites that are carried on secretly, and understand the harsh therapy of the witches' judges. Connecting links abound.

Freud was treating a Mr. E. throughout this critical period in his own personal development and in the development of his ideas. Herr E. suffered from an obsessive-compulsive illness in which an irrational fear that he might kill people made him afraid to go out in the streets. Mahl thinks this may be the patient from whom Freud first learned of the Oedipus complex.[28] We shall have more to say about this important patient later.

Although for the moment his hypothesis about paternal seduction seemed secure in the etiology of hysteria, Freud was having doubts about the choice of neurosis being based on developmental periods. He wrote also that the medical school had passed him over for promotion to *Extraordinarius,* or adjunct associate professor, in favor of a younger man.[29] He told Fliess that the news left him cold, though he thought it might hasten his final break with the university. In fact, the medical school faculty, adopting the recommendation of Krafft-

Ebing, Nothnagel, and others, had on June 12, 1897, recommended that Freud be promoted; it was the ministry that did not act on
the recommendation and would not until Freud got it to do so in
1902.[30]

In his next combined letter of February 8 and 11, 1897, Freud
felt that the progress of his work was "splendid." His progress may
have been encouraged by what he had taken to be a criticism from
Breuer, who could not "let any opportunity go by when there is a chance
of spoiling the most harmless state of contentment." Breuer had received
a copy of Freud's newly published *Infantile Paralyses* and had paid
Martha a visit during which he had inquired as to "how the publisher
[might] have reacted to the unanticipated size of this work." Actually,
Freud *was* feeling sensitive about the length of his book, since it had
exceeded the size prescribed for Nothnagel's series.

Meanwhile, Freud had stopped trying to connect his childhood
periods in mental development to Fliess's numerology. "I have long
since given up my attempt, never intended seriously, to play on your
flute. I would rather have you present a concert to me at [our Congress at] Easter." His practice had increased, and he was working hard
at psychotherapy. He had had —"a rarity" these days—two days of
bad mood. The increased work and low spirits had interfered with
new theorizing. "Even the chronological relationships [had] become
uncertain," though the seduction hypothesis had garnered a surprising confirmation. "Unfortunately, my own father was one of these per-
verts and is responsible for the hysteria of my brother (all of whose
symptoms are identifications) and those of several younger sisters. The
frequency of this circumstance often makes me wonder." He would
be bringing "a lot of strange material" to the next congress.


## Running Aground

Freud's doubts about the seduction theory grew more serious in the
spring of 1897 as he approached his 41st birthday, and his prolonged
good mood, which had begun in January, sagged. In March his daughter Mathilde came down with diphtheria, and then in April it appeared
that his son Martin had also contracted the disease. Mathilde rebounded
quickly and Martin's illness proved innocuous, but the toll on Freud
was substantial. About children and work, he wrote, "Much joy could
be had from the little ones if there were not also so much fright. On
these occasions I notice with sorrow how far down the overwork and
tension of the last years have brought me."[31]

He was still working 10 to 12 hours a day at his private practice and at the beginning of March was struggling "with the difficulties of treatment and of understanding, which depending on [his] mood [appeared to him] larger or smaller."[32] On March 29 Freud wrote Fliess of having just ended a week of "misery" during which "work [had been] a terrible torture." Fortunately, he joked, he had not encountered Breuer, who might have advised him to emigrate. Though now feeling refreshed, he felt discouraged that he had yet to bring a single analytic case to completion.

On April 6 Freud related a divergent insight that presaged the demise of the seduction theory. "The point that escaped me in the solution of hysteria lies in the discovery of a different source." This different source was "hysterical fantasies," which functioned in the manner of screen memories—later fantasies that served as screens on which were projected condensed versions of things the child had earlier heard but had not understood. All in all, he was exhausted and looked forward eagerly to their Easter congress.

The Easter congress at Nuremberg turned out to be more complicated than Freud had anticipated. Fliess had not been interested in Freud's witch theories, and, worse, in the midst of Freud's worries about his seduction theory, Fliess had gratuitously pressed upon him the emendation that grandfathers, not fathers, were the more likely culprits. Fliess also stressed the role of bisexuality in one of Freud's cases, and this idea made a great impression on Freud, further opening the door to a recognition of his own femininity.[33] After the congress at Nuremberg Fliess resumed his travels, and Freud was for a time uncertain as to where to write to his friend about the new and unsettling ideas that were now occurring to him about his theory of neurosis. He was annoyed about these matters and told Fliess so in his first postcongressional letter of April 28. The letter ended with an account of a new case of hysteria in which the seduction hypothesis appeared valid, though Freud admitted being "still in doubt about matters concerning fathers [paternal seduction]."

Having expressed some of his hostility toward Fliess, Freud was then free to feel the salutary aftereffects of their congress. On May 2, a few days before his 41st birthday, Freud had heard from Fliess and felt fully renewed. Freud reported in response that he had been "in a continual euphoria and [had] been working like a young man." He enclosed with this letter a draft consolidating his theoretical acquisitions. The screen memory idea continued to illuminate. He had gained "a sure inkling of the structure of hysteria," confiding that "everything goes back to the reproduction of scenes." He believed that he had found a way of integrating the roles of seduction and fantasy in the creation of neurosis. His theory now held that all three neuroses—

hysteria, obsessional neurosis, and paranoia — stemmed from the same source; namely, infantile seduction. As Freud closed this last letter of his 41st year, he remarked that he had "become noticeably anxious this year."

Fliess returned to Berlin refreshed from his travels, and Freud now called fully once again on his friend's receptive powers. Without such an audience, he told Fliess on May 16, 1897, he could not work properly. He wrote Fliess that he still felt something important was missing from his explanation of hysteria and that he was waiting for new *Schübe* to complete the theory. *Schub,* or *Schübe* in the plural, was a biological term in Fliess's theory that Freud began to use now to refer to creative thrusts from his unconscious. Freud wondered if he should turn his attention to writing about dream interpretation, an area in which he felt he knew exactly what he was doing — indeed, he delighted in the fact that no one else understood the meaning of dreams. Yet he was not really able to shift his focus from the scientific problems that seemed more important to him. "No matter where I start," he lamented, "I always am right back with the neuroses and with the [psychic] apparatus," that is, with the problems of neurotic etiology and the neuropsychological theory of the mind. It certainly is neither personal nor objective indifference," he continued, "if I cannot get my pen to write anything else." Things were "fermenting and bubbling; [he was] only waiting for a new thrust."[34] Note the passive-receptive stance that Freud was now taking toward his own creativity. He was finding himself having to wait for his creative ideas to occur to him; they appeared and disappeared on their own.

Fliess had asked Freud to attempt a draft of his entire theory of neurosis, but Freud did not feel ready to attempt it. "I believe," his letter of May 16 went on, "what prevents me is an obscure expectation that shortly something essential will turn up." While his hand was stayed by doubts and uncertainties about neurosis and the psychic apparatus, he remained certain that he had unraveled the mystery of dreams. "On the other hand," he continued, "I have felt impelled to start working on the dream, where I feel so very certain." This was Freud's first mention of the possibility of writing a treatise on dreams.[35]

Meanwhile Freud's theory of neurosis was taking on water. "A proud ship was wrecked for me a few days after my return. My banker, who was furthest along in his analysis, took off at a critical point, just before he was to bring me the last scenes [of seduction]. This certainly also damaged me materially, and convinced me that I do not yet know everything after all about the mainspring of the matter."[36] At the end of the letter Freud wrote, "During the past few days I had all sorts of fine ideas for you, but they have disappeared again. I must wait for the next thrust which will bring them back." The wait was not long, for the next letter, on May 25, contained "a thrust of ideas which arouse great hope in me." A theoretical draft concerning the relations between scenes of actual seduction and fantasies accompanied the letter.

On May 31, 1897, Freud described the wish to put an end to his "ever-recurring doubts" about paternal seduction and included another theoretical draft based on the *Schübe* described in his letter of the 25th. The theoretical draft that accompanied this letter of May 31, 1897, contained ideas that would prove incompatible with the seduction theory as well as key elements in the concept of incestuous fantasy that would replace it. Indeed, their potential importance against the seduction theory suggests that unconsciously Freud perceived that the sinking ship from which scraps had washed ashore was his seduction theory of neurosis.

The first of these "scraps" was the realization that death wishes toward the same-sex parent are a constituent feature of neurosis. A second was that a fantasy can be the starting point in a sequence of psychodynamic events, and a third was that "symptoms, like dreams, are *the fulfillment of a wish*." A fourth "scrap" was the idea that humankind had evolved out of a natural condition of incest and that its horror among civilized people arises from the recognition that it is anti-social—absent its prohibition "the members of a family remain together permanently and become incapable of joining with strangers."[37] Freud knew these insights were "only premonitions" but added, "Something has come of everything of that sort; I have to take back only the bits of wisdom I wanted to add to the Pcs [preconscious system]." He could feel that more was coming. "Another presentiment tells me, as though I already knew—but I know nothing at all—that I shall very soon uncover the source of morality." With so much happening inside, his isolation was both painful and wonderful. "Thus, the whole matter is still growing in my expectation and gives me the greatest pleasure. If only you were nearer, so that I could tell you about it more easily."

Freud wrote in this letter of being overtaken by summer vacation lassitude and of no longer wanting to work on anything. He then related an "overaffectionate" dream about his daughter Mathilde. Freud interpreted the wish element in the dream as wanting to catch a father "as the originator of neurosis" and thus put an end to his tormenting doubts about the seduction theory.

## The Crisis Begins

Freud's inability to make up his mind about neurosis left him regressively vulnerable to the summer doldrums, and he received no new *Schübe* following those of May 25. He had gotten close to recognizing the Oedipus complex in general and his own in particular, but he was not ready to put it together. During this summer Freud became less inclined to correspond with his friend and reneged on their next congress. He seemed to want to resolve his doubts about neurosis alone without discussing them further with Fliess. When he did write, he told of having undergone peculiar psychological experiences and strange states of mind.

On June 18 Freud told Fliess that he was in a state of "fathomless and bottomless laziness, intellectual stagnation, summer dreariness, vegetative well-being. . . . Since the last thrust nothing has stirred and nothing has changed. . . . In times like these my reluctance to write is downright pathological." He was looking forward to a summer congress, though he would have nothing to bring to it and seemed oddly unable to plan it. "I am very much longing for the end of the season. I plan to be in Aussee again June 26 to 29. Gradually we might begin to tackle the question when we can see each other this summer. I need a new impetus from you; after a while it gives out on me. Nuremberg got me going for two months."

As noted, the medical school faculty had recommended Freud for a professorship on June 12. He did not know that the ministry would ignore the recommendation. On June 22, in response to teasing from Fliess, he joked that his friend would have to call him Herr Professor at their next congress. "I mean to be a gentleman like other gentlemen," he wrote. But the joking tone quickly faded. "The truth is," the letter continued, "that we keep pace wonderfully in suffering, but less so in creativity. *I have never before even imagined anything like this period of intellectual paralysis. Every line is torture* [Italics added]." He felt that his senses were open, but that he understood nothing. He awaited their next congress "stupidly expectant in the face of your disclosures." Fliess had offered an observation that seemed to shed light on the dramatic oscillations in Freud's creativity, and now Freud replied:

> Your remark about the occasional disappearance of periods and their reappearance above ground struck me with the force of a correct intuition. For this is what has happened with me. Incidentally, *I have been through some kind of neurotic experience, curious states incomprehensible to consciousness. Twilight thoughts, veiled doubts, with barely a ray of light here or there.*[38] [Italics added]

He concluded his letter, "Otherwise I am dull-witted and ask your indulgence. *I believe I am in a cocoon, and God knows what sort of beast will crawl out* [Italics added]."

The next letter, on July 7, began:

> I know that at the moment I am useless as a correspondent, with no right to any claims, but it was not always so and it will not remain so. *I still do not know what has been happening in me. Something from the deepest depths of my own neurosis set itself against any advance in the understanding of the neuroses, and you have somehow been involved in it.* For my writing paralysis seems to me designed to inhibit our communication. I have no guarantees of this, just feelings of a highly obscure nature. Has nothing of the kind happened to you? [Italics added]

These resistances and other psychological disturbances appear to have resulted from a mid-life activation of Freud's Oedipus complex. Yet at the same time, there had been "all kinds of advances" in his theoretical work. Dreams, he now saw, "contain *in nuce* [in a nutshell] the psychology of the neuroses in general," but he still could not focus his scientific energies on them. In the midst of other theoretical conundra—such as the biological bases for mental phenomena, a subject on which he had made no progress and would simply have to rely on Fliess—he felt most certain about his explanation for dreams, yet *his* scientific dream remained detached from it.[39] On July 20 he was again

> out of the clouds and very curious. At the same time my special [Fliessian] dates that had been on the decline have appeared again (July 17 feminine menstruation in its most developed form, with occasional bloody nasal secretion before and afterward).[40] The relative quiet and several minor solutions were very good for me. . . . I [did not] comply with your wish to prepare a preliminary account of the hysteria matter. I am letting things simmer.

The next three letters concerned themselves largely with attempts to coordinate the vacation plans of the two families so that a congress might occur. At least until the last of these letters, Freud was feeling much better, as he generally did while on vacation. After the most elaborate efforts to arrange a meeting, the two men agreed on a plan. Then Freud suddenly reneged. The next day, August 14, he explained his reasons for canceling the arduously agreed-upon plans. "I must keep reminding myself that I did do a good deed yesterday by canceling; otherwise I would regret it too much. But I believe it really was so."

Freud next offered extensive, detailed explanations for having canceled, all purportedly arising from his concern that in the abandoned plan the Fliesses would have had to bear too many sacrifices.

Certainly the travel plans of the two families were complex, but a plan had been agreed upon. Moreover, Freud's explanation for abandoning it was so elaborate as to bespeak a disinclination to discuss science with his friend while he remained confused about the seduction theory. Clues appeared as he made first mention of the progress of his ideas. "This time you are losing nothing at all [by not hearing] my tales. Things are *fermenting* in me," he wrote, but nothing had yet been brought to conclusion. He felt "very satisfied with the psychology, tormented by grave doubts about [his] theory of the neuroses, too lazy to think, and [had] not succeeded here in diminishing the agitation in [his] head and feelings; this can happen only [on vacation] in Italy." Apparently, doubts about the seduction theory were associated in Freud's mind with becoming independent of Fliess, an eschewing of a dependence that Freud had repeatedly said he required and enjoyed. Thus he felt anxious about the scientific status of his new ideas and, apparently, guilty about the new independence.

The August 14 letter continued:

> After having become very cheerful here, I am now enjoying a period of bad humor. The chief patient I am preoccupied with is myself. My little hysteria, though greatly accentuated by my work, has resolved itself a bit further.[41] The rest is still at a standstill. That is what my mood primarily depends on. The analysis is more difficult than any other. It is, in fact, what paralyzes my psychic strength for describing and communicating what I have won so far. Still, I believe it must be done and is a necessary intermediate stage in my work.
>
> Now, my cordial greetings to you both, and let the brief disappointment soon be followed by new hope, just as it did in our case.
> Your
> Sigm.[42]

Freud's next letter, written August 18, continued to exude a worry over bad motives:

> Just received your letter, which proved me right: [You wrote of suffering] journeys by carriage, migraine, and August heat. I am pleased that I could at least spare you some discomfort; but it was not done gladly. My cancellation certainly did not have any neurotic motives, but something like a superstition. . . . I saw that you were willing to make every possible sacrifice, and yet what might have been arranged would not have matched the long-cherished expectation.

There followed a small effort toward making a meeting possible. "I am aware recently of having somewhat curtailed my correspondence with you, just because there was the prospect of our getting together. Now that it no longer exists—in my thoughts—I think I want to have the way open again to the old, unjustly scorned technique of exchanging ideas [by letter]."

Sigmund and Martha were looking forward to their trip to Italy, despite being discomfited by reports of train accidents. Fliess knew of his friend's travel phobia, and Freud expected him to laugh at its current exacerbation.[43] Nonetheless, Freud confessed, "[I have] new anxieties which come and go, but in between last for half a day. Half an hour ago I was pulled out of my fear of the next train accident when the thought occurred to me: W. and I. also are traveling, after all." The ambivalent thought that Wilhelm and his wife, Ida, were also in danger had soothed him. "But," he warned, apparently referring to Frau Fliess, "this must remain strictly between us." The letter went on, "You promised me, by the way, a congress on Italian soil, of which I shall remind you in due time. It is sad how little we have succeeded in overcoming the space between us."

His final letter from the summer of 1897, and from the secure days of the seduction theory that bound him to Wilhelm, was sent from Siena on September 6. "As you know, in Italy I am seeking a punch made of Lethe [the river where the dead drank to achieve forgetfulness]; here and there I get a draft. One savors the strange kind of beauty and the enormous creative urge; at the same time my inclination toward the grotesque, perverse-psychological gets its due. I have much to tell you about (which from now on will be a catchword between us)."

He would tell him that the seduction theory had come apart.

# CHAPTER NINE

## Lost
### (Ages 41–43)
### THE MID-LIFE CRISIS

FREUD was drawn down into the depths of his mid-life transition during the fall of 1897, when he was 41. The crisis began with his initial renunciation of the seduction theory in September 1897 and ended in September 1899 with the completion of *The Interpretation of Dreams*. The changes in Freud's dream and his creative work during these two years were complexly intertwined. I shall summarize them here before proceeding to examine them in detail.

As we have seen, Freud felt certain that he understood the meaning of dreams.[1] As early as September 23, 1895, he had written Fliess of having had a dream that supplied "the funniest *confirmation* of the conception that dreams are motivated by wish fulfillment [Italics added]," suggesting that he had mentioned the idea to his friend even earlier, perhaps during a congress. Nonetheless, the discovery appeared in the letters as though it had been created all at once and he had come to it entirely on his own. There was subsequently none of the usual exchange of ideas between the two men, and Freud never revised nor departed from the concept. Throughout his torturous work on neurosis the dream explanation, though given little attention, was always in hand. It was a scientific problem of questionable value in general psychology, and it had little clinical significance to Freud then.

The large theoretical problem that was tightening its hold on Freud—the problem on which he was coming to believe the realization of *his* dreams depended—concerned the origin of neurosis. Neurosis was a problem that was connected both to science and to treatment; its solution could thus realize both aspects of Freud's dream and help to integrate his identity. By contrast, dreams were normal phenomena, and interpreting them did not seem to meet pressing clinical needs. In Freud's mind dream interpretation was so far removed from practical use that it had the status of the kind of folk wisdom beloved of lay audiences, that is, lecture material, as he laconically put it, that "was acclaimed enthusiastically by the Jews" who gathered in reading circles to discuss popular psychology.[2] One could not, Freud lamented to Fliess, make a living from it.[3]

The developmental task Freud now faced could not be met simply by generating insights about wish fulfillment. He needed to find a more complex edition of his dream, one that would permit him to integrate his identity, including his own femininity. This meant giving up the narrowly scientific dream of his youth, the psychology for neurologists, and forming a new version that would animate his work on the dream book and give him a solid internal base as a person. In between the old and the new versions of his dream stood a harrowing period of developmental work, involving loss, mourning, and personality fragmentation. Shifting his focus from neurons to wishes meant reshaping his dream from a narrowly masculine "hard" science version to a broader, more feminine "soft" science one. As Freud grew comfortable with a more feminine subject matter and a more feminine way of working, he was able to see that his work on *The Interpretation of Dreams* would also illuminate the problem of neurosis, albeit in purely psychodynamic terms. Thus by the time he finished writing the book both aspects of his dream, the scientific and the clinical, had become integrated in the work, but the developmental labor required to value the dream book took a long time. This work occurred on unconscious as well as conscious levels.

## The Letter of September 21, 1897

Freud announced to Fliess on September 21, 1897, that his solution to the riddle of neurosis had collapsed. "I want to confide in you immediately," he wrote, "the great secret that has been slowly dawning on me in the last few months. I no longer believe in my *neurotica* [theory of the neuroses]." Since Fliess had supported the theory, Freud felt he owed him a full explanation. The first set of reasons Freud offered had to do with the therapeutic aspect. The seduction theory had not enabled him to complete a single treatment. Patients who had previously been engaged in analysis left upon its introduction, and even with the partial successes Freud could not escape noticing that the results could be explained in other ways. The second set of reasons was conceptual. Freud had discovered that hysteria was even more prevalent than he had imagined. This meant that the incidence of paternal seduction would have to be incredibly high to account for it, since epidemiologically, not every instance of molestation could be expected to produce a neurosis. The third set of reasons was empirical. Where was one to find reliable evidence of so distant an event as childhood molestation when the unconscious did not distinguish between reality and fantasy? And even if the unconscious mind *could* make such distinctions, the antipathy between the conscious and unconscious minds was so powerful that even in psychosis such childhood secrets did not appear unmistakably. How could one hope that treatment would reduce this antipathy to the point where the patient's conscious mind could gain access to the unconscious memories?

These considerations had grown so weighty that Freud considered giving up the hope both of curing neurosis and of solving the riddle of its origins. Yet he had pinned his dream on seduction. "The expectation of eternal fame was so beautiful, as was that of certain wealth, complete independence, travels, and lifting the children above the severe worries that robbed me of my youth. Everything depended upon whether or not hysteria would come out right." Paradoxically, rather than feeling ashamed or defeated, Freud had instead a feeling of having won a victory and of pride in his intellectual scrupulousness. Paraphrasing Hamlet, he would adopt the motto "To be cheerful is everything." Yet he also recalled the Jewish quip "Rebecca, take off your gown; you are no longer a bride," which seemed applicable to his reduced hopes.[4]

A terrible blow had been struck to his dream, yet Freud felt excited, perhaps by the prospect of a triumph over the tyranny of the biological. The narrow positivist scientific training of his youth had constrained him, and now that he had given himself completely to the problem of the neuroses, it was rendering him incompetent. It prevented him from putting together into large, satisfying, useful explanations the strands of psychological explanation that he had held in his hands for more than two years. To overcome these "hard science" constraints on his thinking and imagination meant also to triumph over the internalized mentors and requisite others, from Brücke to Fliess, who personified them in his imagination and who had inspired, driven, and controlled him throughout his youth. It was also true that while he had lost neurosis, he still had his other scientific acquisitions. "In this collapse of everything valuable," he wrote, "the psychological alone has remained untouched. The dream stands entirely secure, and my beginnings of the metapsychological work have only grown in my estimation."[5] But devoid of their organic connections and clinical implications, how much could he value these endeavors?

In the midst of writing this letter and the anxiety about his friend's reaction to it, a note from Fliess arrived and moved Freud to propose a quick reunion, perhaps in an attempt to make up for backing out of the August congress and for quitting the seduction theory. Freud was writing his letter on a Tuesday and went to Berlin the following weekend for a two day visit. He came back reassured; perhaps he was not yet scientifically beyond the pale after all.

## Developmental Injury and Regression

Freud's giddiness about his newfound freedom soon devolved into disorientation. Indeed, the loss of the seduction theory was a serious blow to his dream and one that required strenuous reparative efforts. In the month of October 1897 Freud, now 41, immersed himself deeply in self-analysis. Dreams pressed more urgently upon his waking consciousness, and he carefully analyzed the associations and memories to which they gave rise. Occasionally he asked his mother for details of his infancy and early childhood, which she amply provided. Patients helped by staying away in droves so that he could devote the unused analytic hours to himself.

The compelling currents now let loose in his psyche were endogenous, yet Freud permitted himself to be captured by them. He needed this sort of developmental work badly since he had lost the means for the realization of his dream and was in the midst of the emotional resonances of the first anniversary of his father's death. Both were losses that made him feel small. After the satisfaction over winning a degree of freedom from his scientific prejudices faded, Freud felt humiliated and impotent, as though he were once more a little boy competing with grown men.

During that October Freud's dreams brought back mortifying memories of his envy and rivalry toward Julius and Jacob, including his terror about his mother's absence while she gave birth to his sister Anna and Philipp's sadistic attempt to find her in a wardrobe, a joke that took advantage of his helplessness. He also recalled feeling incompetent in relation to his nursemaid, and this feeling he now reexperienced therapeutically with patients as he proceeded with their treatment bereft of an etiological theory. Freud uncovered, too, his impotent adolescent love for Gisela and Pauline and realized that his experiences had been so painful that he had repressed and defensively transported the memories from adolescence even further into the past, into the antiquity of childhood. All in all, he felt like a doubting Hamlet whose pride must rest on being enthusiastic and ready rather than on the tangible accomplishments of a mature scientist.

While Freud occasionally managed a sense of discovery and intellectual mastery, at all times he realized the tremendous value of the self-analysis and tried to accept it as one of the sacrifices of the peculiar new science to which he was giving birth. On October 3, 1897, he wrote Fliess:

> There is still very little happening to me externally, but internally something very interesting. For the last four days my self-analysis, which I consider indispensable for the clarification of the whole problem [of neurosis], has continued in dreams and has presented me with the most valuable elucidations and clues. At certain points I have the feeling of being at the end, and so far I have always known where the next dream-night would continue.[6]

A week and a half later, on October 15, 1897, Freud wrote, "My self-analysis is in fact the most essential thing I have at present and promises to become of the greatest value to me if it reaches its end." Unhappily but usefully, Freud was having to learn firsthand about the inextricable connection between progress and resistance in analysis: "In the middle of it, it suddenly ceased for three days, during which I had the feeling of being tied up inside (which patients complain of so much), and I was really disconsolate." Freud was about to fit the final piece to the puzzle of the Oedipus complex. For 25 years he had been remembering that scene about being separated from his mother and crying desperately and his half-brother Philipp opening the wardrobe to look for her. Why had his brother performed this incomprehensible act? Analyzing his dreams and associated memories now made the explanation clear. *He* had demanded that Philipp open the *Kasten* (box), because he knew that his brother had recently had the nursemaid arrested for stealing—had had her *eingekastelt* (boxed up)—and thought that Philipp had done the same thing to his mother. After telling Fliess of this insight, Freud proceeded in an off-handed and dispirited way to announce his discovery of the Oedipus complex:

> So far I have found nothing completely new, [just] all the complications to which I have become accustomed. It is by no means easy. Being totally honest with oneself is a good exercise. A single idea of general value dawned on me. I have found, in my own case *too*, [the phenomenon of] being in love with my mother and jealous of

my father, and I now consider it a universal event in early childhood. . . . If this is so, we can understand the gripping power of
*Oedipus Rex.*[7] [Italics added]

By the end of October Freud was fully immersed in developmental work, choosing violent verbs and Faustian imagery to describe it.[8]
On October 27 he wrote of having been *"whirled* back" with "an
elemental force" to the prehistory of his childhood. "*Gripped* and *pulled*
through ancient times" by the rapid movement of associations, his
moods were as changeable as "the landscapes seen by a traveler from
a train [Italics added]."[9] Memories of first loves and friendship were
coming back "and also first fright and discord. Many a sad secret of
life is here followed back to its first roots; many a pride and privilege
are made aware of their humble origins."

Freud continued to learn about resistance firsthand, helplessly going through what he had seen his patients go through, "days when I
drag myself about dejected because I have understood nothing of the
dream, of the fantasy, of the mood of the day; and then again days
when a flash of lightning illuminates the interrelations and lets me understand the past as a preparation for the present." He was gaining
new clinical insights about resistance, thinking it a sort of moral de-
generacy arising from the masturbatory pleasure-seeking period of infancy that preceded the onset of repression. "I dig it out by my work;
it struggles; and the person who initially was such a good, noble human being becomes mean, untruthful, or obstinate, a malingerer—
until I tell him so and thus make it possible for him to overcome this
[infantile] character."[10]

## A Shattered Dream and a Year of Crisis

After the beginning of November 1897 Freud's self-analysis slowed
to a "trickle," and he was now deep in a developmental crisis.[11] He
could see no way to realize his dream or to change it. This period of
crisis would be broken in February, would resume in March, and would
continue for the remainder of 1898.

On November 10 Freud wrote Fliess of being lost theoretically
and very bored. "I shall force myself," he added, "to write the dream
in order to come out of it."[12] Note that Freud would have to *force*
himself to write *The Interpretation of Dreams;* the book did not emerge
from the creative abundance freed by the abandonment of the seduction theory and the discovery of the Oedipus complex. Indeed,
though he collected dreams and gave some lectures in the next three

months, Freud was unable to summon the creative spirit to begin the book.

December 1897 found Freud unable to move his self-analysis forward and forced to wait passively for new creative developments. Although he was having ideas that seemed to connect his clinical and scientific goals, they were fleeting.

> Every now and then ideas dart through my head which promise to realize everything, apparently connecting the normal and the pathological, the sexual and the psychological problem, and then they are gone again and I make no effort to hold onto them because I indeed know that neither their disappearance nor their appearance in consciousness is the real expression of their fate. On such quiet days as yesterday and today, however, everything in me is very quiet, terribly lonely. I cannot talk about it to anyone, nor can I force myself to work, deliberately and voluntarily as other workers can. I must wait until something stirs in me and I become aware of it. And so I often dream whole days away.[13]

Freud's thoughts then turned to the next congress, proposed for December in Breslau. Though he wished for a meeting in Italy, this year's poverty made that out of the question. Besides, he had learned that his wish to visit Rome was neurotic, based on an adolescent identification with Hannibal. He recalled that Breslau, too, had childhood significance: Traveling with his family from Freiberg to Leipzig at three years of age, on the move that would take them to Vienna, the gas flames in the station had reminded him of spirits burning in hell. "My travel anxiety, now overcome," he added, "also is bound up with this."

On December 12 Freud told Fliess that he was eagerly looking forward to hearing the latest developments in his work at their next reunion. For himself, he would have nothing to bring, other than the "crazy" thoughts he had been harboring for months. In reality, these included genuine insights into the origins of religion, but they were so far away from his dream of real scientific discovery that he had to disparage them. He considered the ideas "*meschugge*" (crazy) and applied to them a gruesome term of failed gestation—"*Ausgeburt*" (deformed, evil offspring).[14] "I have gone," he wrote, "through a desolate and foggy period and am now suffering painfully from [nasal] suppuration and occlusion; I hardly ever feel fresh. If this does not improve, I shall ask you to cauterize me in Breslau."

Freud reported in this letter that recent clinical evidence had once again restored his confidence in the seduction theory. In his next letter, written December 22, he was able to add additional confirmatory detail, and he was "in good spirits again." He ended the letter with a quote from Goethe, which he proposed to use as his new clinical motto: "What has been done to you, you poor child?" This renewed faith in his theory abated the crisis caused by the blow to his dream earlier in the year. As December 1897 drew to a close, Freud also benefited from a congress with Fliess, which freed the stalemated pressures that had been growing within.

## Deserted by the Feminine

There was little feminine imagery in Freud's letters during these first months of his mid-life crisis. When his femininity did make an appearance, it was largely in negative terms, such as *Ausgeburt*. Thus in October he wrote that a Fliessian 28-day feminine period had blocked his self-analysis. He was tempted to blame the feminine for all repression, but he was so preoccupied with his self-analysis that he had not had time to test out his hypothesis that the feminine aspect of personality was responsible for repression in both sexes. Fliess, by contrast, had proposed that men repress the feminine parts of their natures whereas women repress their masculine parts.[15] On November 14 Freud wrote Fliess that he had given up the attempt to explain libido as masculine and its repression as feminine, implying that he was abandoning the whole line of explanation.

Freud was lost, and if the feminine was helping him at all, it was doing so at a deeply unconscious level. Recall from Chapter One his dream about old Brücke and the long journey to the small wooden house with the boards, or slumbering children, that would help him bridge the chasm from the window to what lay beyond. It was at some point during these years when he was struggling to write *The Interpretation of Dreams* that Freud had this dream. He thought that the guide who helped him during his long, weary journey was based on the female guide in Haggard's novel, entitled *She*. Associating to the dream, Freud recalled that in the novel "the guide, instead of finding immortality for herself and the others, perishes in the mysterious subterranean fire."[16]

A December congress in Breslau briefly revived Freud's femininity. Fliess had proposed that all left-handed people were latently homosexual and that ambidextrous people were bisexual. Afterward, Freud wrote his friend, "Back home and in harness again, with the delicious aftertaste of our days in Breslau. Bi–bi [bilaterality–bisexuality] is ringing in my ears, but I am still feeling too well for serious work."[17]

> What I want now is plenty of material for a mercilessly severe test
> of the left-handedness theory; I have needle and thread ready [a Flies-
> sian test for left-handedness]. Incidentally, the question that fol-
> lows from it is the first in a long time on which our hunches and
> inclinations have not taken the same path.
>     I have not yet found the time to have a word with my female
> side.
>     My nose is behaving itself and conveys its thanks.[18]

Within a few days the jokes had gone sour.[19] Fliess was not
amused by Freud's jokes about his theory, and Freud was forced to
state his objections straightforwardly. "I literally embraced your stress
on bisexuality," he offered, "and consider this idea of yours to be the
most significant one for my subject since that of 'defense.' " Both of
them, Freud continued, believed that bisexuality formed part of the
basis for repression. It was only the attempt to connect bisexuality to
bilaterality to which Freud objected. If his consciousness had not been
clouded in Breslau by a postoperative reaction, Freud wrote, he would
certainly have objected to Fliess's assertion that "each of the two halves
[of the body] probably contains both kinds of sex organs." The letter
continues: "I had the impression, furthermore, that you considered me
to be partially left-handed; if so, you would tell me, since there is nothing in this bit of self-knowledge that might hurt me." In reality, Freud
insisted, he had never been able to tell his right from his left and therefore could never have felt a preference. "Rather I could say that years
ago I had two left hands." No "organic feeling" had ever told him which
of his hands was which, and he wondered if that were not true for
others. "I used to test this," he wrote, "by quickly making a few writing movements with my right hand. As far as other people are concerned, I must to this day work out their position and so on. Perhaps
this fits in with your theory; perhaps it is connected with the fact that
I have an infamously low capability for visualizing spatial relationships."

As for his self-analysis, he was collecting wild dreams and "groping about . . . in the dark." And as for creative theoretical work, Freud
had done no writing on neurosis or dreams since his *Schub*-inspired
draft on "The Architecture of Hysteria," sent to Fliess on May 25, 1897,
the credibility of which had been damaged over the summer.

## A Genuine Breuer

In mid-January 1898 Freud succeeded in jump-starting his stalled
creativity by provoking a galling act of Breuerian generosity.[20] "What
I am writing now," he began his account of the event to Fliess, "is sheer

craziness." Freud still owed Breuer money from the loans received while a medical student. Only this month had Freud, at 41 years of age, been able to make the first installment of 500 florins. Breuer returned 350 with a receipt for 500. He told Freud he had imagined that the debt had already been paid; besides, he insisted, Freud had undercharged him for the treatment of his niece two years earlier. Freud sent the 350 back and wrote that the niece's treatment was an entirely separate matter and that truly he could now afford to begin repaying the loan. Breuer countered by agreeing to keep the 350, so long as Freud accepted his receipt for 850 florins. "All this," Freud concluded his account to Fliess, "[was done] with the greatest lack of logic, with disdainful condescension and deeply hurt feelings, as well as an unabated need to do good. Just expand a little on this abbreviated [description of the] affair. It is genuine Breuer. It is enough to make one extremely ungrateful for good deeds."

Nonetheless, Freud was in good spirits and wrote, "All sorts of little things [are] teeming; dream and hysteria fit together ever more neatly. . . . One must take it as it comes and be glad that it comes at all. . . . All sorts of other things keep dawning on me and always everything earlier is forgotten. It is too soon to summarize." Freud closed by saying that a recent addendum from Fliess concerning the role of the left foot had softened his objection to the "Bi–Bi" theory.

By the 22nd of January 1898 Freud's good spirits and creativity had vanished, and his anger toward Breuer had been refueled by a rumor that his former mentor had criticized the way Freud conducted his financial affairs. "This nasty habit of my [mental] organization suddenly to rob me of all my mental resources is for me the hardest thing in life to bear," Freud wrote. The only noteworthy intellectual occurrence had been a confirming of the Bi–Bi theory. Freud had succeeded in unbuttoning his clothes with his left hand, passing (or failing) another Fliessian test for latent homosexuality. "The button business," he acknowledged, " . . . stands out like an oasis in the desert."


## A Hiatus

By the end of January 1898 Freud's three months of desultory intellectual wandering and resistance to his self-analysis were lifting. He had finally succeeded in beginning the dream book. The 29th of January had been a day of "wild joyfulness" over progress in dream interpretation and self-analysis. In early February he was "for no accountable reason in a splendid mood." He wrote Fliess, "[I] have found my daytime interest. I am deep in the dream book, am writing it fluently, and enjoy the thought of all the 'head shaking' over the indiscretions and audacities it contains." In particular, he imagined that Breuer would disapprove and was warmed by the prospect. He was also beginning to read the arid literature on dreams. "As for the rest, everything is still in a state of latency. My self-analysis is at rest in favor of the dream book."[21]

As March 1898 neared, Freud's practice increased after being way down since the previous summer. He had not heard from Fliess and not only missed his "Other" but feared the silence was ominous. He had been extraordinarily productive in working on the dream treatise — indeed, Freud now referred to it for the first time as not just a dream (*Traum*) but a book (*Traumbuch*) — and had completed several chapters. "It is turning out nicely and leads me far more deeply into psychology than I had imagined."

Further into psychology meant further away from the organic but closer to other large scientific problems as well as toward the humanistic interests of his youth. Connected as Fliess was to biology, Freud's growing sense of independence stimulated concerns about an alienated Other. "All of the new formulations," his letter continued, "are at the philosophical end; absolutely nothing has come up at the organic–sexual one."[22] He hoped not to come to the Easter congress "completely empty-handed."

By March 5, 1898, Freud had not yet heard from Fliess and was worried that he must be sick. Meanwhile, "a whole section of the dream book" had been completed. Yet despite the rapid progress of the book during February, on March 10 Freud was still worrying about the absence of biological ideas. The book had come to "a halt again."

> Meanwhile the problem has deepened and widened. *It seems to me that the theory of wish fulfillment has brought only the psychological solution and not the biological*—or, rather, metapsychical— one. (I am going to ask you seriously, by the way, whether I may use the name metapsychology for my psychology that leads behind consciousness.) Biologically, dream life seems to me to derive entirely from the residues of the prehistoric period of life (between the ages of one and three)—the same period which is the source of the unconscious and alone contains the etiology of all the psychoneuroses, the period normally characterized by an amnesia analogous to hysterical amnesia.[23] [Italics added]

It still seemed to Freud that psychological explanations devoid of organic underpinnings were scientifically so exotic that one would have to ask a biologist what to call them. Freud was now considering the hypothesis that what was *seen* during the critical first three years of life produced dreams, what was *heard* produced fantasies, and what was *experienced sexually* produced neuroses. Thus he tried once again to find a place for his physicalist seduction hypothesis in the new theorizing about dreams.

In mid-March 1898 Freud reluctantly sent his growing dream manuscript to Fliess. "The idea occurred to me that you might like to read my dream study but are too discreet to ask for it. It goes without saying," Freud felt it necessary to add, "that I would have sent it to you before it goes to press."[24] Fliess responded with praise for the manuscript. This was a great relief to Freud and led to a renewal of mentorial vows, with Freud gushing about the superiority of Fliess to Breuer and his relief at being rid of his former mentor. "I hope," Freud wrote, "you will tell me more about many particular points when we meet. You shall not refuse me the duties of the first audience and supreme judge."[25] The beginning of April found him productively preoccupied with the dream book, without thought or interest in any other scientific matter.[26]

Yet Freud remained insecure about the scientific value of the project. After April he did not again refer to it as anything more than a dream until a year and a half later when it was nearly completed. He referred to it as a *Traumbuch* on April 3 and as *Traummaterial* on April 27.[27] After that the book is returned to the status of a *Traum* and is not again elevated to that of a book, work, study, or manuscript until his letter to Fliess on August 1, 1899, some 15 months later.

## Eight More Months of Developmental Crisis

The Easter congress had to be canceled because of Frau Fliess's ill health. Instead, Freud went to Italy with his younger brother Alexander. Though he began the trip without much enthusiasm, Freud enjoyed himself hugely.[28] This act of holiday independence from Fliess was followed by eight months of creative desolation. Indeed, the creative achievements of February and March proved merely an interruption in the developmental crisis that had begun in 1897. Now once more there would be no self-analysis, no inspiriting feminine imagery, and little creatively unencumbered work on the dream book. Altogether it would be a period of difficulty that would not end until the two men had a successful congress at the end of the year in December.[29]

Meanwhile, by the end of April 1898 disconfirmatory data had beset the seduction theory once more. Freud wrote Fliess that he had "defined the etiology too narrowly; the share of fantasy in it [was] far greater than [he] had thought in the beginning." By May 1, 1898, just before his 42nd birthday, it was apparent that the stimulative effects of the holiday with his brother had dissipated. "I feel parched," he wrote, "some spring within me has gone dry and all sensibilities are withering." The free time left to him by his practice, now flagging again, was simply being wasted. He was "completely involved in the dream book and completely stupid about it."[30] It had been five months since their last reunion, and he felt badly in need of the congressional stimulation now in the offing for the end of May. His work on the dream book had slowed, and he needed help. Along with this letter Freud sent a chapter of the dream book.

By mid-May Fliess had returned the chapter with encouraging comments. Freud's spirits were lifted, and he sent his friend another chapter. "I shall change whatever you want," he wrote, "and gratefully accept contributions. I am so immensely glad that you are giving me the gift of the Other, a critic and reader—and one of your quality at that. I cannot write entirely without an audience, but do not at all mind writing only for you." Fliess had renewed his friend's strength, and Freud, now feeling that he could "withstand anything," wrote, "The habit of working on the dream [book] is—after the [work on the etiology of] hysteria torture—extremely good for me."[31] This restorative, too, was short lived. On the 24th of May, Freud was obsessed with the dream book and extraordinarily "constricted."

## Fliess Exercises His Authority

Freud then sent Fliess a dream whose content was so embarrassingly personal and so revealingly analyzed that Fliess advised against its publication. We do not know what the content was. Freud thanked Fliess for the advice, accepted it, and then felt resentful for several months. "So the dream is condemned," he wrote. "Now that the sentence has been passed, however, I would like to shed a tear over it and confess that I regret it and that I have no hopes of finding a better one as a substitute." How could a vivid specimen be found that wouldn't be incriminating? "As you know," he continued, "a beautiful dream and no indiscretion—do not coincide. Let me know at least which topic it was to which you took exception and where you feared an attack by a malicious critic." Freud also felt that something essential was missing from the theory in the dream book. He was finding it "wretchedly difficult to set out the new psychology insofar as it [pertained] to the dream." He admitted, "I am stuck at the relationship of the two systems of thinking; I must deal with them in earnest. For a while I again shall be of no use to anyone. The tension of uncertainty makes

for an infamously unpleasant state, which one feels almost physically."[32]

On June 20, 1898, Freud wrote Fliess that he continued to have
difficulty working out the psychological theory for dreams and that
he was "mourning" the expurgated dream. He was still unable to keep
his attention turned from neurosis. "The psychology," he wrote, "is
proceeding in a strange manner; it is nearly finished, composed as if
in a dream and certainly, in this form, not fit for publication, nor intended for it, as the style shows. I feel very timid about it. All its themes
come from the work on neurosis, not from that on dreams."

At the end of the first week of July Freud sent a carelessly written
draft of the psychology to Fliess and claimed that he had not written
"a single paragraph knowing where [he] would end up." He was becoming comfortably lazy. At the end of the month Freud was on vacation in Aussee and, in a state of "peasant" mindlessness, having
difficulty writing.[33] In late August 1898, while Freud was still on vacation, Fliess evidently sent news of a theoretical breakthrough in his
own work. Freud wrote back congratulating him on "the happy news
of the unlocking of the mysteries of the universe and of life, of intellectual successes more beautiful than one could dream of," and stating
"I rejoice once again that eleven years ago I already realized that it
was necessary for me to love you in order to enrich my life."

## Doubts about Seduction Deepen

Freud was getting bored with vacation life and had decided to attempt
a connection between his own ideas about psychology and those in
the literature on dreams. At the same time, he wrote, "I am becoming
ever more doubtful about the work on hysteria; its value seems smaller,
as though I had left out several major factors, and I really dread having to take it up again."[34] Five days later a sense of despair had developed over the inadequacy of his work on neurosis. Freud was 42.

> In the inactivity here and in the absence of any fascinating novelty,
> the whole business [of hysteria] has come to weigh heavily on my
> soul. My work now appears to me to have far less value, and my
> disorientation to be complete; time — another entire year has gone by
> without any tangible progress in the theory — seems incommensurate
> with what the problem demands. *Moreover, it is the work on the
> success of which I have staked my livelihood.*[35] [Italics added]

Fliess apparently then complained about the absence of a biological basis in Freud's developing theory of psychology.[36] On Septem-

ber 22 Freud replied, "I am not at all in disagreement with you, not at all inclined to leave the psychology hanging in the air without an organic basis." Freud still believed, as much as Fliess did, that a psychological explanation without a biological foundation was hopelessly incomplete. "But apart from this conviction," he complained, "I do not know how to go on, neither theoretically nor therapeutically, and therefore must behave as if only the psychological were under consideration. Why I cannot fit it together [the organic and the psychological] I have not even begun to fathom." Freud ended this letter by describing an opportunity that had arisen to travel free to Berlin, which he was declining. In his next letter he expressed surprise that Fliess was disappointed and offered rationalizations for his decision not to visit. Concerning his theoretical work, he was as helpless as "an ox on a mountain."[37] A new case appearing within the yawning vacancy of his practice had failed to resolve doubts about seduction.

## The Second Anniversary of Jacob's Death

Then in October 1898, during the month of the second anniversary of his father's death, "an avalanche" of patients descended on him.

> The treatments start at nine o'clock—before that two short calls—and last until one-thirty; from three to five a pause for consulting hours, the office being alternately empty or full; from five to nine treatments again. . . . Naturally, I am speechless and half-dead in the evening. But Sunday is almost free. [Working on theory,] I move things around, test them, and make changes here and there; I am not entirely without new leads. If I happen to hit on anything, you shall hear about it. Half of my patients now are men of all ages, fourteen to forty-five years.[38]

By October 23 the press of clinical business had lightened, and Freud had more time to think. "Once again there [was] a glimmer of light on the horizon." It seemed to him now that this year he would "be in a position to find [his] way back to the truth from grave errors."

Masson thought that since Freud was talking about finding his way back to the truth, he must have been referring to the seduction theory.[39] However, as we have seen by closely following the vicissitudes of his belief in the theory over the 13 months since he initially abandoned it in September 1897, there had been movement toward as well as away from the theory. In fact, during the previous five months, since the spring of 1898, Freud's belief in the theory had been at a low whereas, at the same time, his long-held belief in wish fulfillment as the central mechanism in dreams had survived extensive research and thought. This makes it seem likely that by finding his way back, Freud meant continuing on the path that emphasized the key role of fantasy in neurosis. Masson acknowledges that against his interpretation stands Freud's declaration to Fliess on November 7, 1899, regarding his theory of neurotic etiology: "Last year's gain, fantasies, have stood the test splendidly."

## Still in the Dark

Nevertheless, the unifying solution continued to elude Freud. His letter of October 23, 1898, went on: "As yet there is no light. . . . The dream [book] is lying still, immutably; I lack the incentive to finish it for publication, and the gap in the psychology as well as the gap left by the [removal of the] thoroughly analyzed sample [dream] are obstacles to bringing it to a conclusion which so far I have not been able to overcome. In other respects I am completely lonely." The "gap in the psychology" referred to the missing biological connections. "If ascertaining the few points required for explanation of the neuroses entails so much work, time, and error, how can I ever hope," he lamented, "to gain an insight into the whole of mental activity, which was once my proud expectation?"

Though Freud wrote of longing for a congress, he ignored his friend's report of his surgery and, on discovering his error later in the month, declined to use Fliess's illness as a reason to visit: "If you needed anything other than rest and I were in a better mood and better general physical condition, I would have used the holidays for a trip to Berlin; but since I have a cold and am engrossed in my own expectations, I would bring you neither invigoration nor enjoyment. I am completely focused on one subject [the dream book]."[40]

A week later Freud had a large furuncle removed from his scrotum. His postoperative recovery was uneventful. Fliess's was not, and by the end of November Freud, under the self-imposed requirement of analytic honesty, had to confess that he resented Fliess for his suffering. "It is very unreasonable of me, nor do I understand it fully; I am relating it to you as a phenomenon that evidently I am angry with you because you are doing poorly." Freud hoped to learn that his friend was now doing better, and he wanted to visit him at Christmas, "but harmlessly without a manuscript, even without any inquisitiveness on my part, simply to see you and chat with you. . . . I hope you understood that my furuncles were trumpeted so much only as a damper."[41]

In early December Freud was subjecting himself to the "horrible punishment [of] those who write." He was reading the literature on dreams, and it was making him stupid. Tucked into this scholarly far-rago, Freud was finding it hard to remember his own ideas.[42] The reading was an "awful tedium," and he was looking forward with great excitement to the congress, now planned and only days off.[43] "Rare-ly," he wrote on December 20, 1898, "have three months of separa-tion seemed as long to me as these last ones."

## The Dream Solves the Problem of Neurosis

By January 3, 1899, the meeting had occurred and Freud was irradi-ated with postcongressional insight:

> After the fall of the meteor gleams a light that brightens the gloomy sky for a long while thereafter. For me it is not yet extinguished. In this brightness, then, I suddenly glimpsed several things, and then even the first professional vexations of the New Year could not dis-turb my good mood.
>
> In the first place, a small bit of my self-analysis has forced its way through and confirmed that fantasies are products of later peri-ods and are projected back from what was then the present into earlier childhood; the manner in which this occurs also emerged.

Now, just as with the original renunciation of the seduction theory, self-analytic activity led again, this time decisively, to its abandonment. The developmental work of his self-analysis was helping Freud to ac-cept psychology as a suitable domain for the realization of his dream. He was saving the details for an Easter congress and offered now only an epigram: "To the question 'What happened in earliest childhood?' the answer is, 'Nothing, but the germ of a sexual impulse existed.' "

The self-analytic insight concerned the screen memories (discussed in Chapter Three) in which Freud used a fictive patient to recount his own Freiberg memories of playing in the meadow with his cousins John and Pauline and of later, during adolescence, falling in love with Gisela. In January 1899 Freud was just beginning to work on his "Screen Memories" paper, and in this work he realized that the meadow memory had been created at 20 to screen sexual wishes directed at Gisela and Pauline.[44]

This self-analytic finding now confirmed the sort of nagging doubt mentioned in the September 1897 letter to Fliess, when Freud initially rejected the seduction theory. "It seems once again arguable," he had written then, "that only later experiences give the impetus to fanta-sies, which [then] hark back to childhood,"[45] that is, that memories of childhood seduction are created later in life. In the "Screen Memories" paper, he concluded that what had happened in his own mind invariably happened in hysterical patients, too, that memories of childhood seduction are fictions that are created during adolescence and projected backwards for defensive reasons.

The following day, on January 4, as he described in a letter to Fliess, Freud's illumination burned on brightly even as his energy flagged:

> I got tired yesterday, and today I cannot go on writing along the lines I intended because the thing is growing. There is something to it. It is dawning. In the next few days there certainly will be some additions to it. . . . I want to reveal to you [now] only that *the dream schema is capable of the most general application, that the key to hysteria as well really lies in dreams.* [Italics added]

The pivotal insight that Freud had won from his long period of developmental struggle and crisis was not simply that wishful fantasies were the source of neurosis. He had had that idea since May 31, 1897, when he told Fliess that "symptoms, like dreams, are *the fulfillment of a wish.*"[46] The recent self-analytic work had confirmed this already existing hypothesis. More importantly, he now saw that dreams and neurotic symptoms shared a common *mechanism.* Now he understood why he had not been able to finish the dream book. "If I wait a little longer," he wrote, "I shall be able to present the psychic process in dreams in such a way that it also includes the process in the formation of hysterical symptoms. So let us wait." Freud sensed with patient confidence that he was on the correct path to solving in a single unifying scheme three of the research problems that preoccupied him — the origins and mechanisms of neurosis, the nature of the psychic apparatus, and the meaning of dreams. Freud's confidence would carry through until their next congress at Easter.

Yet over this happy prospect loomed the ambivalently avoided, fateful disharmony with Fliess. For only one — *wishful fantasy or biological period* — could prove the fundamental psychological cause. Freud closed his January 4th letter in the defensively jocular tone of a man trying to make light of a victory over a friend:

> Now look at what happens. Here I live in ill humor and in darkness until you come; I get things off my chest; rekindle my flickering flame at your steadfast one and feel well again; and after your departure, I again have been given eyes to see, and what I see is beautiful and good. Is that only because the [Fliessian] special date had not yet come? Or could not one of the many days available

for all purposes be fashioned into the special date by means of the psychic influences affecting the one who is waiting? Must not some place be left for that, so that the [dynamic] force is not ruled out by the time [element]?

Later on in January Freud wrote Fliess of "advances in the wish theory" and of "the certainty that [he had] put [his] finger on an important nodal point" and of setting a case right "with the key of fantasy," as opposed to actual seduction.[47] At the end of the month, he was "still living on" their last congress:

The light has not gone out since then; bits of insight are dawning now here, now there—a genuine reinvigoration by comparison with the desolation of last year. What is rising out of the chaos this time *is the connection to the psychology contained in the* Studies on Hysteria—*the relation to conflict, to life: clinical psychology,* as I should like to call it. Puberty is becoming ever more central; fantasy as the key holds fast.[48] [Italics added]

## Falling in Love with *The Interpretation of Dreams*

In early February 1899 Freud, exhausted from his clinical labors, complained about the slow pace of his theoretical work and the general awfulness of life in Vienna. "I am still perfectly serious about a change of profession and residence, in spite of all the improvements in my practice and income. . . . Fate . . . has simply forgotten your friend in his lonely corner," he wrote to Fliess.[49] Yet the overall tone was really one of resigned contentment. By the 19th, Freud imagined work had turned into a "neoplasm" that was consuming the entire organism of both men, "a sort of neoplastic tissue infiltrating the human and finally replacing it." He reported happily, "I have turned completely into a carcinoma. The neoplasm in its most recent stages of development likes to drink wine. Today I am supposed to go to the theater; but this is ridiculous—like an attempt to graft onto the carcinoma. Nothing can adhere to it, so from now on the duration of my life span is that of the neoplasm."

He was happy because his research on the dream book, which had seemed like a detour, was solving the problem of neurosis and opening up all of psychology, too. His January insight about the central, determining role of wishes was being sustained by additional thought and evidence and was proving to be powerfully synthetic as well. His new idea had made it possible to understand that neurotic symptoms were compromise formations built between wishes and the defenses against them.

My last generalization has held good and seems inclined to grow
to an unpredictable extent. Not only dreams are wish fulfillments,
so are hysterical attacks. This is true of hysterical symptoms, but
probably applies to every product of neurosis. . . . I believe I now
know what determines the distinction between symptoms that make
their way into waking life and dreams. It is enough for the dream
to be the wish fulfillment of the repressed thought, for dreams are
kept at a distance from reality. But the symptom, set in the midst
of life, must be something else besides: it must also be the wish fulfillment of the repressing thought.

"A symptom," he continued, "arises where the repressed and the
repressing thought can come together in the fulfillment of a
wish. . . . This key opens many doors."[50]

## Saved from Error

By March Freud was increasingly feeling the benefits of his successful
work in refashioning his dream. On March 2, 1899, he wrote that
"things [were] going almost uniformly well" for him and that he was
waiting impatiently for Easter to show Fliess all the new material about
wish fulfillment. These ideas were breathing new life into old cases
and were being eagerly applied to new ones.

The realm of uncertainty is still enormous, problems abound, and
I understand theoretically only the smallest fraction of what I am
doing. Yet every few days things become clearer—now here, now
there; I have become modest and count on long years of work and
patient collecting, with the help of a few useful ideas after vacation
and our meetings.

The next day he wrote Fliess, "The main result of this year's work
appears to me to be the surmounting of fantasies; they have indeed
lured me far away from what is real." It seems that the fantasies Freud
referred to here were patients' about seduction and that surmounting
them meant recognizing them as such rather than regarding them as
memories of actual events.[51] The clearing up of his theory was also
clearing up his head. "Yet all this work has been very good for my
own emotional life," he continued. "I am apparently much more normal than I was four or five years ago."[52]
    Foreshadowing the future, enrollment in Freud's lectures had gone
up and medical students were seeking him out for treatment. Yet he
sensed that all this was premature. Much wearying work remained

to be done and further disillusionments borne. Nonetheless, Freud's belief that he had rescued himself from error and had regained the correct path held steady. At the end of March 1899, just prior to the Easter congress, he wrote Fliess, "You will doubtless confirm [when shown the new findings] that it has begun to dawn in my darkness since fall. I have emerged from several blind alleys."

## A Congress No Longer Avails

This congress, convened in Innsbruck, did not, however, have the prolonged and sanguine effects Freud had come to expect. Instead, it produced six weeks of postcongressional gloom. "Since [the congress]," Freud wrote his friend on April 24, 1899, as he approached his 43rd birthday, "I have been ill-humored, at odds with my work and everything connected with it." Could it be, Freud wondered, that these storm clouds were "harbingers of birth," as Fliess had apparently characterized a migraine headache Freud had suffered in Innsbruck? By the end of May 1899 Freud had recovered from the mild depression that had followed him since Easter. This depression had occurred in conformance with a "28 + 28/2" day Fliessian period and had given "way to an unfounded sense of well-being." He had finished his essay on screen memories and liked it very much. His waiting room was empty: "I would like to imagine that it is possible to introduce the dream [book]; I do not yet know how. If in June and July things continue as they are now, with two and a half patients a day, I shall have to write it. What else would I do with my time?"[53]

The dream book had entered its final phase. It was "suddenly taking shape, without any special motivation, but this time [he was] sure of it." Still annoyed about the vetoed dream, Freud now asserted that no more censorship would be allowed.

> I have decided that I cannot use any of the disguises, nor can I afford to give up anything because I am not rich enough to keep my finest and probably my only lasting discovery to myself. . . . So the dream [book] will be. . . . Unfortunately, to frighten one off, the gods have placed the literature before the presentation. The first time I got stuck in it. This time I shall fight my way through. . . . No other work of mine has been so completely my own, my own dung heap, my seedling and a *nova species mihi* [my own new species] on top of it.[54]

It had initially been Fliess who insisted that Freud review the existing literature. In June Freud was again reading dutifully, working on the first chapter, which would contain that review. This was depressing work and tended to submerge and obscure his own ideas. Yet he found he could integrate much of it in his own terms. Unifying the various explanations offered by other writers, Freud saw that the dream could be seen to fulfill a single, underlying wish—the wish to sleep—doing so through an infinite variety of means.[55]

## A Summer of Happiness with the Dream

At the end of June 1899 the Freud family enjoyed a lovely brief vacation in Bavaria. It reminded Freud of the first congress with Fliess nine years earlier, which had included a walking tour to Berchtesgaden. At the railroad station there Freud reminded Fliess that he had "witnessed one of [his] finest attacks of travel anxiety."

> In the visitors' book on the Hirschbühel you are described in my own handwriting as a "universal specialist from Berlin." Between Salzburg and Reichenhall you were, as usual, blind to the beauties of nature and instead raved about the Mannesmanns' tubes [a new industrial invention]. At the time I felt somewhat overwhelmed by your superiority; this I felt distinctly.[56]

On July 8 Freud sent Fliess a proof of the first page as a gesture of appreciation for his help. The publisher was setting *The Interpretation of Dreams* into type even as it was being written. There was an illness in Fliess's family and Freud offered to come and help out. He went ahead and made plans to visit before hearing from Fliess, then postponed the trip when news from intermediaries made it seem unnecessary.[57] Finally, Fliess wrote to say that the need for Freud to visit had passed but that the opportunity for a congress was appealing nonetheless. Freud begged off, saying that he was too tired and irritable to offer Fliess the sort of audience his new biological findings deserved. September, he suggested, would be better.[58]

Meanwhile, the first chapter had been finished, and this led Freud to look back on the year with satisfaction: "On the whole it was a year that was triumphant and that resolved doubts."[59] He was referring to ridding himself of the seduction theory and putting wish fulfillment in its place, thereby advancing his theoretical understanding of psychology across a broad front. New projects, such as *The Psychopathology of Everyday Life,* to be published in 1901, had already begun to gestate in his imagination.

## Fliess as Research Assistant

On July 22, 1899, Fliess apparently asked to read the material *before* it went to the printer. Freud allowed himself to be confused by the request, at the same time begging off on the grounds that it would be too much work for his friend. "Now, I do not understand what you want to see, and when. Am I to send you this first chapter? And then the continued revisions, before I send them to the printer? You would be taking on a great burden without any pleasure if you still took pains with it." The dream research had risen so far in his estimation that Freud now believed it had succeeded in "placing the neuroses and psychoses in [the sphere of] science by means of the theory of repression and wish fulfillment."

In August Freud began to rain down a torrent of printer's proofs upon Fliess. "I am sending you the first proofs of the introductory (literature) chapter in two envelopes at the same time," he wrote. "If there is anything you object to, send me that page with your remarks; there is still time to use them, until the second or third proofs." The dream was now, for the first time since the end of April 1898, no longer merely a dream but a reality; it had become a *Traumarbeit* (a work on dreams) and, later in the same letter, a *Traumbuch* (a dream book).[60]

On August 1, 1899, enjoying work on the book while vacationing in Riemerlehnen, Freud found occasion to throw another Breuerian log on the fire and to warm his hands contemplating it. Breuer, he had been told, had objected to a missing connection between death and sexuality in Freud's recent essay, "The Psychical Mechanism of Forgetfulness." Angered, Freud relished the fantasy of upsetting Breuer by offering such abundant connections in the dream book as to be indiscreet. Even so, Freud imagined that if the book won him a promotion in the university, Breuer would come crawling. "The farther the work of the past year recedes," he wrote, "the more satisfied I become." Then, immediately, as if this were a repudiation of the seduction theory and that doing so had hurt his friend, he added, "But bisexuality! You are certainly right about it. . . . We have a lot to discuss on this topic."

Freud was in the full swing of completing his book with the spheres of psyche, work, and family in near-perfect relation.

> Things are incomparably beautiful here; we take walks, long and short, and all of us are very well, except for my occasional symptoms. I am working on the completion of the dream book in a large, quiet, ground-floor room with a view of the mountains. My old and grubby gods, of whom you think so little, take part in the

work as paperweights for my manuscripts. The loss of the big dream
that you eliminated is to be compensated for by the insertion of
a small collection of dreams. . . . Only the last, psychological chapter needs to be reworked, and that I shall perhaps tackle in September and send you in manuscript form or—bring with me [to the
proposed congress]. It occupies my full interest.

On August 6 he wrote Fliess that it was unnecessary for him to
return the proofs he had been sent: "Since you did not take exception
to anything in Chapter 1, I shall finish it in the galleys. Nothing else
has yet been set in type. You shall receive the proofs as soon as they
arrive and the new parts will be marked in them." Freud was avoiding
Breuer, who was vacationing nearby, and was feeling very satisfied
with his work. "Conditions are ideal for me here," he reported, "and
I feel correspondingly well. I take walks only in the morning and the
evening; the rest of the time I sit at my work. One side of the house
is always delightfully shady when the other is blazing hot." He finished
his letter by thanking Fliess for his help with "the Egyptian dream book."
By calling the book Egyptian, Freud was toying with his critics in advance, saying that his theory might seem to them to be prescientific,
but with it he could divine fate.

The idyll of psyche, work, and family was still going on in mid-
August.

I have been here for four weeks now and lament that this lovely
time is passing so quickly. In another four weeks my vacation will
be over, and it is not enough for me. I work wonderfully well here,
in peace . . . in a state of almost total wellbeing; in between I run
out for walks and enjoy the mountains and woods. . . . I am completely immersed in my work. . . .
    Please send back only the proofs to which you take exception
and write your comments in the margin. Also, later on, when it
is possible for you, correct any quotations or references; I have no
literary sources available here, of course.[61]

On the 27th of August Freud could think of "nothing but the
dream," being "completely useless in all other respects." He had rushed
a stack of pages to the printer, and it was now necessary for him to
immediately turn his attention to the very difficult psychological chapter. "What would you think," he suggested, "of ten days in Rome at
Easter . . . if all goes well, if I can afford it, and have not been locked
up, lynched, or boycotted on account of the Egyptian dream book?"
    Having failed to secure promotion by traveling the high road of
neurology, Freud had determined with this book—as he avowed

in its inscription—to shake up the infernal regions. But that immortal figure, Amalia's defiant, heroic little boy inside, was growing frightened now as the time neared for the reaction he hoped the book would provoke. This childish part of him still sought Fliess's protection.

> I am completely into the dream [book], am writing eight to ten pages a day, and have just got over the worst in the psychology—it was agonizing. I do not even want to think about how it has turned out. You will tell me whether it can stand at all, but in the galley proofs; reading the manuscript is too much drudgery, and everything can still be changed. . . . I am afraid it is—bunk. . . . And then they'll really let me have it! When the storm breaks over me, I shall escape to your guest room. You will find something to praise in it in any event, because you are as much on *my* side as the others are *against* me. . . .
>
> I have just now received sixty galleys, which I am sending to you in the same mail.

## *The Interpretation of Dreams* Completed

On September 11, 1899, Freud sent the entire manuscript of *The Interpretation of Dreams* to the publisher. After a momentary elation he felt depressed. He was certain that his conclusions were correct, but he was appalled at the bad writing: "The style . . . was quite incapable of noble, simple expression and lapsed into facetious circumlocutions straining after metaphors." This depression became a deep depression when Freud was asked by Fliess to contemplate a trip to Berlin. "*Meschugge,* as you see," he responded, "and at present I am obviously unbearable, would talk only about dreams. . . . So let me go on wavering [about planning a congress] for a while." To further darken Freud's mood, the entire Breuer family had now gathered nearby at Berchtesgaden and had to be avoided.

The next week there were torrential rains that caused flooding, disrupted communication and travel, and made a trip to Berlin impossible. Freud was still in a bad mood from completing the manuscript, and this led directly to thoughts about Breuer. "Fall has really started," he wrote, "and Breuer is just as much locked in here as I am, so that we are bound to meet daily, on which occasions the ladies on both sides make a great show of tenderness to each other. Another reason to wish one were somewhere else."[62]

By September 21, his vacation over, Freud was back in Vienna and still bothered about the poor writing in the dream book. "Somewhere inside me there is a feeling for form, an appreciation of beauty as a kind of perfection; and the tortuous sentences of my dream book, with their parading of indirect phrases and squinting at ideas, deeply offended one of my ideals.[63] Nor am I far wrong in regarding this lack of form as an indication of insufficient mastery of the material." Freud hated to ask his friend to read such inadequate stuff but wrote, "Unfortunately I cannot do without you as the representative of the Other — and again have sixty more pages for you."

## Dispelling the Mentorial Demons

Freud included in this packet a collection of dreams that included the well known "non vixit" dream. In this dream, he told Fliess, he had been delighted to outlive him.

> *I had gone to Brucke's laboratory at night, and, in response to a gentle knock on the door, I opened it to* (the late) *Professor Fleischl, who came in with a number of strangers and, after exchanging a few words, sat down at his table.* This was followed by a second dream. *My friend Fl.* [Fliess] *had come to Vienna unobtrusively in July. I met him in the street in conversation with my (deceased) friend P., and went with them to some place where they sat opposite each other as though they were at a small table. I sat in front at its narrow end. Fl. spoke about his sister and said that in three-quarters of an hour she was dead, and added some such words as "that was the threshold." As P. failed to understand him, Fl. turned to me and asked me how much I had told P. about his affairs. Whereupon, overcome by strange emotions, I tried to explain to Fl. that P. (could not understand anything at all, of course, because he) was not alive. But what I actually said—and I myself noticed the mistake—was, "*NON VIXIT*" [he had not lived].*[64] I then gave P. a piercing look. Under my gaze he turned pale; his form grew indistinct and his eyes a sickly blue—and finally he melted away. I was highly delighted at this and I now realized that Ernst Fleischl, too, had been no more than an apparition, a "revenant"* [a ghost or, literally, one who returns]; *and it seemed to me quite possible that people of that kind only existed as long as one liked and could be got rid of if someone else wished it.*[65]

Discussing this dream in *The Interpretation of Dreams*, Freud warned the reader that he would not do in waking life what he had done in the dream. He would not analyze it fully because that would be "sacrificing to [his] ambition people whom [he] greatly [valued]."[66] Of the associations that Freud did offer, the first was to that signal moment in his professional beginnings when Brücke had confronted him about his tardiness. The young Freud had then been obliterated by his senior's "terrible blue eyes," reduced "just as P. was in the dream, where, to [Freud's] relief, the roles were reversed."[67]

As the dream book went to press, Freud dreamed of the professional superego figures of his youth: most importantly, Brücke, but also Fleischl, Paneth, and, most recently, Fliess. What would they think of him, a promising neurophysiologist who had written an Egyptian dream book? What searing criticism would a betrayed and disappointed Brücke have directed his way? Freud was learning that scientific bullies could be faced down but not without tremendous soul-wrenching effort, and not completely. The alternative was never to have lived.

The sense of being scientifically empty persisted during the next few weeks; then Freud's mood rallied as his love for the dream book returned.[68] New *Schübe* appeared concerning a theory of sexuality. Not to be completed until 1905, the *Three Essays on the Theory of Sexuality* would join *The Interpretation of Dreams* as the second and final pillar of the new psychoanalytic science. Freud's unconscious was germinating contentedly now, as the developmental work on his mid-life crisis neared an end.

## CHAPTER TEN

# Finding a New Way Home
## (Ages 43–45)
### THE FINAL PHASE
### OF THE MID-LIFE TRANSITION

*T*HE *Interpretation of Dreams* did not do well. It received more attention in popular periodicals than in professional ones, and in the latter its reception was mixed. Only 351 copies were sold in the first six years, and a second printing was not needed until 1909. By comparison, Darwin's *Origin of Species* sold out its entire first edition of 1,250 copies on the first day.[1] Ironically, the poor reception accorded his dream book helped Freud reduce the domain of youthful illusion that still complicated his transition to middle age; increasingly, he felt prepared to accept his fate, whether it brought scientific fame or not. This relaxation of the tyranny of his dream complemented the ongoing changes in his relationship to his unconscious creativity: No longer was he tormented by its failure to produce insights on time. In fact, Freud did no writing at all for the first year after completing *The Interpretation of Dreams.* When he did begin to write again, he entertained himself with an analysis of ephemera, resulting in *The Psychopathology of Everyday Life,* and was content to allow the theory of sexuality, his next major theoretical work, a slow, luxurious growth.[2] Thus, the final two years of Freud's mid-life transition were characterized by an equanimity remarkable for both its novelty and its resilience.

Freud was also groing more independent of Fliess; by the summer of 1900, following a congress at Achensee, near Innsbruck, the active period of their friendship was at an end. Although it appears that Fliess withdrew first, Freud accepted this perfection of his professional isolation without strong objection. At the same time, Freud's relationship with his sister-in-law Minna grew more intimate. Her fiancé, Schönberg, had died in 1886, and Minna, long a favorite of Freud's, by 1894 was considered a confidante.[3] She was a frequent visitor to the Freuds' home in the role of maiden aunt, and she joined the family permanently in 1895.[4] Minna was interested in psychoanalysis and more intellectual than Martha generally, and Freud now came to rely on her as he had on Fliess. This represented a further step in his ability to enter into intimate, sublimated relations with women and in the integration of his own femininity. Indeed, sustained close relationships with women would become a striking feature of the second half of Freud's life.[5]

During the winter of 1900 Freud suffered a recrudescence of his mid-life crisis. In the silence following the publication of his dream book, he had turned once again to the problem of neurosis for the fulfillment of his dream. His longtime patient, Herr E., looked as though he were about to provide memories that would confirm a new etiological theory concerning sexuality. While the exact nature of Freud's new hypothesis remains unknown, the confirmatory evidence failed to appear, and again Freud found himself floundering amidst collapsed certainties. This time however, he was better able to set his hopes aside. He was then able to see that the problem in E.'s treatment arose not so much from unabreacted childhood memories as from a reluctance to end his treatment; that is, the problem arose from a transference to Freud himself.

Freud might have considered the process of analyzing the transference relationship, compared to the good, hard clinical science of identifying the neurological bases of symptoms and alleviating them, to be "woman's work." This increasing appreciation of the clinical importance of the relationship between himself and his patients was another reflection of a greater acceptance of his femininity. To be sure, there would be other therapeutic setbacks, such as mistakes in diagnosis and the premature termination of his treatment of Dora, toward which we shall shortly turn, but with his focus shifting from symptoms to the transference relationship, Freud's clinical confidence and mastery now grew qualitatively.

During this final phase of the transition, Freud conquered his inhibition about visiting Rome and did so in the summer of 1901. On his return in the fall from this symbolic triumph, Freud succeeded in lowering himself to the grubby, unheroic business of finally getting promoted to professor, exploiting the time-honored means of personal influence. The promotion was at last secured late in March 1902, as Freud neared his 46th birthday. It was plain to him then that his own youthful arrogance had prevented him from winning it sooner.[6]

## Patiently Awaiting New Developments

On October 11, 1899, Freud wrote Fliess that "something [was] at work on the lowest floor." He was 43.

> A theory of sexuality may be the immediate successor to the dream book. Today several very strange things occurred to me, which I do not yet properly understand at all. As far as I am concerned, there is no question of deliberation. This method of working moves along by fits and starts. God alone knows the date of the next thrust, unless you have figured out my formula. If more comes along, we shall scarcely be able to avoid discussion and collaboration. Wild things, by the way, some of which I already surmised during the stormy first epoch of productivity.

He ended by quoting Goethe's *Faust,* "Again ye come, ye hovering forms." At the end of the month Freud was in good spirits despite having been intellectually lazy. His new scientific stirrings remained "unborn."[7] On November 4 *The Interpretation of Dreams* came out, a day, he told Fliess, that was punctuated by a "gorgeous migraine" that dissipated the ill humor that had prevailed the day before. New thoughts about a theory of sexuality were coming at a "leisurely" pace, but obscurities concerning the "female aspect . . . [made him] distrust the whole thing."[8]

Since Freud's practice was down, he was especially grateful in early November to receive a referral from Fliess of a German woman for whom, as he often did with foreign patients, he busied himself in finding lodging and nursing care. The outrage that Freud had feared and hoped the dream book would provoke had not occurred. In fact, there had been little reaction of any kind. Business was so bad that he and Martha were considering moving to the outskirts of Vienna, yet he was not dispirited. Freud's new thoughts on the sexual theory were bubbling, and the previous year's replacement of seduction with fantasy had "stood the test splendidly."[9] On November 19, Freud remained buoyant and regarded his germinating science with patient maternity. "With regard to the sexual theory," he told Fliess, "I still want to wait. An unborn piece remains attached to what has already been born."

One month after the dream book's publication Freud wrote that it had "not yet occasioned any outcries," adding dubiously, "Sales so

far supposedly are satisfactory." He had become aware of a change
in the pattern of his moods: "I have actually profited from my mild
depressions since they have begun to occur periodically; during the
interim periods I feel more consistently well than ever before." He knew
any such periodicity would peak Fliess's interest. "Otherwise," he wrote,
"things are slumbering and preparing themselves. *Sexual Theory and
Anxiety* is the title of my next work, which deep down must have
progressed further than I know because I feel so very confident." He
was glad to hear that Fliess's work was, by contrast, "progressing clearly
and lucidly, in full light" but declared, "This way of working doubtless would not suit my subterranean matter."[10]

Around the beginning of December Fliess visited Freud in Vienna. After the visit Freud wrote, on December 9, 1899, of new thoughts
about the choice of neurosis. His now discredited earlier attempt had
been to relate the different forms of psychopathology to the age at which
sexual molestation occurred. Now he began to relate it to stages in
the maturation of the child's own sexuality. Here, clearly, was the beginning of a developmental psychopathology based on the epigenetic
unfolding of the child's own libido, a view destined to endure as Freud's
mature theoretical position.

Despite economic privation, professional isolation, and the neglect
that greeted his dream book, as Christmas 1899 approached, Freud
remained cheerful. He was particularly excited about the near prospect
of a clinically and theoretically triumphant end to his long treatment
of Herr E. On December 21 Freud wrote Fliess:

> You are familiar with my dream which obstinately promises the
> end of E.'s treatment (among the absurd dreams [in *The Interpre-
> tation of Dreams*]), and you can well imagine how important this
> one persistent patient has become to me. It now appears that the
> dream will be fulfilled. I cautiously say "appears," but I am really
> quite certain. Buried deep beneath all his fantasies, we found a scene
> from his primal period (before twenty-two months) which meets
> all the requirements and in which all the remaining puzzles con-
> verge. It is everything at the same time—sexual, innocent, natural,
> and the rest. I scarcely dare believe it yet. It is as if Schliemann had
> once more excavated Troy, which had hitherto been deemed a fa-
> ble. At the same time the fellow is doing outrageously well. He
> demonstrated the reality of my theory in my own case, providing
> me in a surprising reversal with the solution, which I had over-
> looked, to my former railroad phobia. For this piece of work I even
> made him the present of a picture of Oedipus and the Sphinx. My
> phobia, then, was a fantasy of impoverishment, or rather a hunger
> phobia, determined by my infantile greediness and evoked by my
> wife's lack of a dowry (of which I am so proud). . . .
>
> So I am growing older, patiently awaiting further developments.

Though he never explained this new theory to Fliess, it is clear that Freud was trying once again to find the cause of neurosis in sexual memories from earliest childhood. Perhaps the poor response to *The Interpretation of Dreams* had led Freud to revive the seduction theory. Three days later he wrote his friend, "In regard to the sexual theory, just be patient. It will assuredly come. Out of context it sounds so wild. I believe I have once again found something about anxiety." He had learned not to force it. He continued: "(There still are strange ebbs and flows; at times they carry me to the crest of certainty, and then everything flows away again and I am back on dry land. I do believe, however, that the sea is gaining). Following your advice, I am letting it grow naturally."

## A Recrudescence of the Mid-Life Crisis

By January 8, 1900, doubts about the new theory had arisen. Commenting to Fliess on a "stupid" review of his dream book, Freud remarked that he did not count on recognition in his lifetime. Clinically, his subject matter once again seemed "obscure." "All I seek," he wrote Fliess, "is quiet and some material comfort. I am not working, and there is silence in me. If the sexual theory comes, I shall listen to it. If not, then not." In order to sustain the spirit necessary to be clinically effective, he was finding it necessary to divert his attention from theoretical conundra. "In the evenings I read prehistory and the like, without any serious purpose; otherwise my only concern is to bring my cases, in good spirits, closer to a solution." He still hoped that E. would come through with the theoretically crucial scenes. "In E.'s case, the second genuine scene is coming up after years of preparation; and it is one which may *perhaps* be confirmed objectively by asking his elder sister. Behind it a third, long-suspected scene approaches."

For most of January 1900, the children were sick and Freud's practice remained low. In a brief note to Fliess on January 12 about his work, Freud said only, "No new case. Bleakness otherwise." On the 26th of the month Freud wrote, "Nothing is happening, really. When I remind myself that I have had only one new case since May 1899 . . . and that again I am to lose four patients between April and May, I am not exactly in a cheerful mood. How I shall manage I do not yet know, but I am determined to stick it out." His book was still being ignored, and he had "given up as hopeless the project of finding summer work" to supplement his diminished income. His treatments were going well and no longer taxed him as heavily as before. "New ideas," he told Fliess, "come slowly, but there never is total stillness." Instead of the long-awaited, decisive confirmation, Herr E. had presented fresh obscurities. "In the case of E., there is again a delay and a darker region, but the earlier findings still stand. I am collecting material for the sexual theory and am waiting for a spark to set the accumulated material on fire."[11]

By February 1, 1900, Freud's mood had darkened. He was feeling more keenly his separation from Fliess and longed to live in Berlin, where he imagined his practice would prosper and his ideas would meet with less prejudice. It was in this letter that Freud made his oft-quoted remark about not being a scientist but a "conquistador." These people, he noted, were honored only if they discovered something of great importance. For himself, his luck had gone bad. "I no longer discover anything worthwhile." In the next paragraph Freud referred to a "kind" but "diffuse" review of *The Interpretation of Dreams* in a lay periodical, and near the end of the letter he admitted being, like one of his patients, ready to "explode with rage."

What had happened? The illness in his children, the separation from his friend, his financial straits—all had been accumulating into a solid winter depression. But more crucially, the absence of appreciative response to his book from the scientific community had turned Freud's ambitions once again back toward solving the problem of neurosis. E.'s case in particular had promised to end in a combined scientific and clinical breakthrough. Freud had been in avid, then cautious, expectation of confirmatory evidence since December. By the end of January he saw that the solution so nearly at hand was illusory. On February 1 he was ready to explode. By the 12th he had had to conclude that once again his views on the etiology of neurosis were in error.

In that letter of February 12, 1900, Freud told Fliess that his practice had picked up and that his depression was beginning to lift. "If I could only tell you," he lamented to Fliess, "what constant changes my thoughts undergo in relation to my work, that is, what errors I still find to correct, and how difficult it all is, you would probably make allowances for the neurotic fluctuations in my self-confidence, especially if you also took into account my life's worries."[12] He concluded his letter, "On the whole I am farther away from Rome than at any time since we met, and the freshness of youth is very markedly on the decline. The journey is long, the stations at which one is thrown out are very numerous, and we are left with 'if I can stand it.'"

Toward the end of February the crisis passed, though the healing continued through March. On February 22 Freud announced that a "splendid migraine" had completed his recovery, and on March 11, 1900, he was ready to tell Fliess more about what had happened. Acknowledging that a separation was occurring between them, Freud made it explicit that he had decided to write less often, and he reported that he had been surprised to find how comfortably the previous three weeks had gone by since his previous letter. The children had been well, as he had been; his practice was up; and his patients were prospering. He had been "virtually cut off from the outside world; not a leaf [had] stirred to reveal that *The Interpretation of Dreams* [had] had any impact on anyone." Then he summarized the recent history of his own case:

> After last summer's exhilaration, when in feverish activity I completed the dream [book], fool that I am, I was once again intoxicated with the hope that a step toward freedom and well-being had been taken. The reception of the book and the ensuing silence have again destroyed any budding relationship with my milieu. My second iron in the fire is after all my work [on neurosis]—the prospect of reaching an end somewhere, resolving many doubts, and then knowing what to think of the chances of my therapy.[13] *Prospects seemed most favorable in E.'s case—and that is where I was dealt the heaviest blow. Just when I believed I had the solution in my grasp, it eluded me and I found myself forced to turn everything around and put it together anew, in the process of which I lost everything that until then had appeared plausible. I could not stand the depression that followed.* Moreover, I soon found that it was impossible to continue the really difficult work in a state of ill humor and lurking doubts.[14] I really believed I would have to give up on the spot. I found a way out by renouncing all conscious mental activity so as to grope blindly among my riddles. Since then I am working perhaps more skillfully than ever before, but I do not really know what I am doing. . . . In my spare time I take care not to reflect on it. . . . As soon as I am free of my trade, I live like a pleasure-seeking philistine. . . . So I vegetate harmlessly, carefully keeping my attention diverted from the subject on which I work during the day. Under this regimen I am cheerful and equal to my eight victims and tormentors [patients]. [Italics added]

In his letter of March 23, 1900, Freud filled in more of the missing details concerning the crisis. He noted again the problem of the dream book's poor reception, which had grown in his mood over the past few months.

> Its reception has certainly not given me any joy. Understanding for it is meager; praise is doled out like alms; to most people it is evidently distasteful. I have not yet seen a trace of anyone who has an inkling of what is significant in it. I explain this by telling myself that I am fifteen to twenty years ahead of my time. Then, of course, the usual qualms associated with forming a judgment about oneself set in.

There has never been a six-month period in which I so constantly and so ardently longed to be living in the same place with you and that which is yours as the one that has just passed. *You know that I have been going through a deep inner crisis;* you would see how it has aged me. [Italics added]

Freud then acknowledged how moved he was that Fliess had proposed an Easter congress—a proposal he nonetheless found himself disinclined to accept. There were "inner reasons" that militated against it:

An accumulation of imponderables, which, however, weigh heavily on me (from the natural habit of madness, you will perhaps say). Inwardly I am deeply impoverished, I have had to demolish all my castles in the air, and I am just now mustering enough courage to start rebuilding them again. During the catastrophic collapse you would have been invaluable to me; in the present stage I would scarcely be able to make myself intelligible to you. I conquered my depression with the aid of a special diet of intellectual matters and now, thanks to the distraction, it is slowly healing. If I were with you, I could not avoid trying to grasp everything consciously and describe it all to you; we would talk reason and science; your beautiful and positive biological discoveries would arouse my innermost (impersonal!) envy. The upshot would be that I would go on complaining to you for five days and return all upset and dissatisfied to my summer, for which I shall probably need all my composure. No one can help me in the least with what oppresses me; it is my cross, I must bear it; and God knows that in adapting to it, my back has become noticeably bent.

## Out of the Wreckage a New Therapeutic Mastery

By April 4, 1900, Freud's clinical competence had resumed its growth. His patients were progressing well, and E., was expected to "terminate treatment at Easter," Freud announced to Fliess adding, "having benefited enormously, I hope." He still did not understand the attendant theoretical problems fully, but his clinical skill grew nonetheless. During a trial period he had correctly diagnosed and referred out a paranoid patient who was unsuitable for analysis.[15]

On April 16 Freud wrote Fliess that the case of Herr E. had been successfully terminated:

E. at last concluded his career as a patient by coming to dinner at my house. His riddle is *almost* completely solved; he is in excellent shape, his personality entirely changed. At present a remnant of the symptoms is left. *I am beginning to understand that the apparent endlessness of the treatment is something that occurs regularly and is connected with the transference.* . . . I could have continued the treatment, but I had the feeling that such prolongation is a compromise between illness and health that patients themselves desire, and the physician must therefore not accede to it. The asymptotic conclusion of the treatment basically makes no difference to me, but is yet one more disappointment to outsiders. [Italics added]

Five years earlier, in the *Studies on Hysteria*, Freud and Breuer had been so focused on symptoms that they tried to eliminate them one by one. Now Freud saw that his treatment changed the personality as a whole, even though the parts, including some symptoms, remained the same. He was moving from the neurologist focused on symptoms of pathology to the psychoanalyst concerned with the whole person. He was also learning that symptoms do not arise simply from childhood events or even from fantasies but also function as an expression of the relationship between analyst and patient.

In his next letter to Fliess at the end of April Freud, his mood reflecting the arrival of spring, described having overcome mistakes in technique with another patient: "The trees in front of my window have delicate reddish leaves. I am curious about what spring will bring forth in you; I am content with a mood of equanimity and physical well-being."[16] On May 7, 1900, the day after his 44th birthday, Freud wrote Fliess:

I would have no objection to the fact of splendid isolation if it were not carried too far and did not come between you and me as well. On the whole—except for one weak point, my fear of poverty—I have too much sense to complain and at present I feel too well to do so; I know what I have and I know, in view of the statistics of human misery, how little one is entitled to. But no one can replace for me the relationship with the friend which a special—possibly feminine—side demands, and inner voices to which I am accustomed to listen suggest a much more modest estimate of my work than that which you proclaim. . . . It will be a fitting punishment for me that none of the unexplored regions of psychic life in which I have been the first mortal to set foot will ever bear my name or obey my laws. . . . Yes, I really am forty-four now, an old, somewhat shabby Jew. . . .

In general, things are stirring somewhat.

The number of Freud's letters to Fliess per annum now began a steep descent from the concluding year's 46 to 23.

Nine days later, in the midst of an epistolary silence from Fliess,

Freud wrote him to describe another clinical success. Despite the transparency of its etiology, this had been his "most difficult case," which until recently had completely stymied him.

> For four years I could not get close to it. Moreover, it was the only case Breuer sent me. He kept sending the girl back to me whenever I had chased her away in utter despair. Last year I finally began to get on good terms with her, and this year at last I succeeded. I found the keys; that is to say, I could convince myself that the keys found elsewhere fitted her and, as far as the short time (December until now) permitted, I have deeply and fundamentally influenced her condition. She took leave of me today with the words,"What you have done for me is invaluable."

On hearing the news of her marvelous recovery, Breuer had exclaimed to the girl, "So he is right after all!" Freud recognized from his annoyance at Breuer's continuing doubts that the separation from his former mentor was incomplete.[17] As for the dream book, it now seemed clear to Freud that it was not going to receive serious attention.

By May 20, 1900, Freud had fully regained his clinical balance. "Yesterday," he wrote Fliess, "the fourth patient [the last of those Freud expected to lose that spring] said good-bye on the most cordial terms, in excellent shape, with Böcklin's *Selected Paintings* as a parting present. This case gave the greatest satisfaction and is perhaps complete. So things have gone well this year. I have finally conquered. But what am I going to do now? I still have three and a half persons—that is, sessions—a day. Not enough toys for the whale."[18]

Freud wrote only four letters to Fliess during the summer of 1900, which ended with their final meeting at Achensee. His spirits and his sense of clinical confidence remained high despite having made a dramatic diagnostic mistake. In June he had described the case to Fliess as "beautiful—a thirteen-year-old girl whom I am supposed to cure instantly, and who for once shows me on the surface what I usually endeavor to unearth beneath superimposed layers."[19] He did not describe the mistake to Fliess but instead wrote of it later in *The Psychopathology of Everyday Life* as an example of the unconsciously motivated forgetting of unpleasant knowledge: Six months after treating the girl, Freud had been astounded to find that he could not remember the patient at all.

> My bewilderment grew when I turned the pages [of my appointment book] and discovered that I treated the case in a sanatorium and made daily visits over a period of weeks. A patient treated under such conditions cannot be forgotten by a doctor, after scarcely

six months. . . . Finally the record of the fees I had received brought back to me all the facts that had striven to escape from my memory. M — l was a fourteen-year-old girl, the most remarkable case I had had in recent years, one which taught me a lesson I am not likely ever to forget and whose outcome cost me moments of the greatest distress. The child fell ill of an unmistakable hysteria which did in fact clear up quickly and radically under my care. After this improvement the child was taken away from me by her parents. She still complained of abdominal pains which had played the chief part in the clinical picture of her hysteria. Two months later she died of sarcoma of the abdominal glands. The hysteria, to which she was at the same time predisposed, used the tumour as a provoking cause, and I, with my attention held by the noisy but harmless manifestation of hysteria, had perhaps overlooked the first signs of the insidious and incurable disease.[20]

By July 1 Freud had become so wearied of his work and in need of a vacation that he felt "dull, irritable, and morose." On the 10th, the two friends secured plans for an August congress. Freud looked forward to hearing the progress in Fliess's ideas, he wrote, though he could not guarantee much in return. He reported that he was "totally exhausted by [his clinical] work and everything connected with it that [was] germinating, enticing, and threatening," admitting, "The big [theoretical] problems are still wholly unresolved. Everything is in flux and dawning, an intellectual hell, with layer upon layer; in the darkest core, glimpses of the contours of Lucifer-Amor."

## Writing Ephemera While the New Theory Germinates

The two men quarreled ominously at their August congress in Achensee, yet Freud returned from his vacation feeling "outrageously merry."[21] His first letter after the congress made no reference to any difficulty, and their argument would not resurface until the following May. The letter of September 14, 1900, begins, "Astonished that you stayed away longer than we did. I have been in Vienna since September 10. I am very glad you had such a good time. It was extremely nice for me, too." Indeed, Freud had arrived back in Vienna in fine spirits and had eagerly resumed work the same day. After parting from Fliess in Achensee, he had traveled south with various family members, including Minna, who was sick. "On September 8 I took Minna to Merano," he wrote, "where she is supposed to stay for either a few weeks or a few months to cure her pulmonary apicities [inflammation]. I believe I have told you that the recurrence of this affliction, for which she was sent to Sicily at the age of seventeen, casts a shadow on the immediate future."

This was the first time Freud expressed concern about his sister-in-law's health. Fliess seems to have taken an interest in the matter; though writing less often, he made a point of asking about her. These letters now reveal a deepening of the intimacy between Freud and Minna, perhaps to mitigate the increasing distance from Fliess. Ten days later Freud told Fliess that he had begun writing again. This new project, the first in the year since completing *The Interpretation of Dreams,* was *The Psychopathology of Everyday Life.*

Freud remained in good spirits in October 1900. *The Psychopathology of Everyday Life* was moving along, and he had begun writing his essay "On Dreams," a distillate of the dream book that he had promised for a summer issue of the journal *Grenzfragen des Nerven- und Seelenlebens* (Boundary Questions between Neurology and Psychology).[22] In late October he was having a "quieter time" and recalled having sent his friend "the firstborn of the dream book" the year before.[23] A month later Freud finally heard from Fliess after the long hiatus in the correspondence from Berlin. Fliess had not written because of family troubles, including the paranoid mental illness of his mother. In fact, both men were following a plan of writing less. "I myself," Freud wrote, "would not have waited so long with my inquiry if I had not promised myself at the beginning of this year's exchange of letters to refrain under all circumstances from complaining to you so much."

Freud told Fliess that Minna had settled on Oscar Rie to be her physician. Her symptoms, which included a high pulse rate, were as obscure as they were worrisome. With regard to his own work, "it [was] certainly not a time of harvest, of conscious mastery," although "on a subterranean level it [was] probably proceeding quite well." What was missing was "the organization and the detailed elaboration." Freud no longer saw any prospect of shortening the duration of treatment or of expanding the range of its application. He was not sure when he would be able to make a definitive presentation of his theoretical position on neurosis; moreover, it was not clear that anyone wanted it. He had resigned himself, he wrote, to living like someone who speaks a foreign language or is the first, or last, member of his tribe.[24]

Nevertheless, it was "a lively time," one that brought Freud an attractive new patient. He described Ida Bauer, later the famous "Dora," to Fliess as "an eighteen-year-old girl, a case that has smoothly opened to the existing collection of picklocks."[25] Eleven weeks later she quit.

## Dora

The case of Dora is important because it is the first lengthy account of an analysis from Freud at a time when he was gaining mastery of his clinical technique. It is also important because its failure helped Freud secure the hold he had gotten from Herr E. on the importance of transference. Dora, Freud wrote in "Fragment of an Analysis of a Case of Hysteria" (1905), was "in the first bloom of youth," a "girl of intelligent and engaging looks."[26] She suffered from hysterical cough and loss of voice and had recently become so angry at her parents, particularly her father, that she had threatened to kill herself. Her worried and guilty father brought her to Freud for treatment. Over the course of her brief analysis Freud learned that the girl suffered from multiple sexual conflicts.

Dora's father was having an affair with Frau K., a woman to whom Dora herself had long been possessively devoted. Oedipally attached to her father, Dora envied *each* of the lovers and felt betrayed by both. Frau K.'s husband was himself attracted to Dora, and Dora's father seemed willing to sacrifice her to Herr K. in return for his tolerating the affair with Frau K. Herr K. had made sexual advances toward Dora—a kiss at the lake and other importunities—but Dora's father had dismissed her charges against him as adolescent fantasy. In truth, Dora *was* enamored of Herr K. and fantasized marrying him, but she had recently become embittered after discovering that he had been having an affair with a governess and had made love to the governess using exactly the same words he had spoken to her at the lake. Before long, she became disappointed with Freud, too, and quit her treatment without notice after having made only a beginning in exploring her conflicts.

Because Freud's new sense of clinical mastery was a product of deep developmental changes, the clinical failure with Dora had no active theme in his mind to join and thus remained merely a disappointing event, as had the diagnostic error with the 13-year-old girl the previous summer. Nevertheless, Freud had felt drawn to Dora and had held high hopes for her treatment, and he regretted its abrupt, surprising, and unsatisfactory end. Perhaps the attractive adolescent reawakened a portion of his unrequited love for Gisela. If so, the writing of Dora's case in an astonishingly fast three weeks may have been yet another attempt to master this sort of loss through intellectual means. It was also true that Freud, after a long hiatus, had begun to write again and was content to find his hand turning easily to minor project such as *The Psychopathology of Everyday Life* and "Dreams and Hysteria [Dora]" while the theory of sexuality continued its long germination.

Nonetheless, the failure did help Freud to understand yet more deeply the technical conundrum posed by transference. While he had written the case with extraordinary speed and had had no difficulty getting it accepted for publication, he withdrew the case and did not publish it for another four years. At that later point, he added a postscript in which for the first time he took up in detail the problem of transference in psychoanalytic treatment. Then, presumably after a few more years of learning about the matter, he wrote that in Dora's case he had "not succeed[ed] in mastering the transference in good time" and that his failure to do so had led to the abrupt termination.[27]

He had been aware in the beginning of the case, Freud averred in his postscript, of replacing Dora's father in her imagination. But he faulted himself for being deaf to a warning in the first of her dreams that she must leave his treatment as well as Herr K.'s house. And there had been, he now realized, further ominous signs of the transference in a second dream. Instead, he lamented, "transference took me unawares, and, because of the unknown quantity in me which reminded Dora of Herr K., she took her revenge on me as she wanted to take her revenge on him, and deserted me as she believed herself to have been deserted by him. Thus," he concluded, "she acted out an essential part of her recollections and phantasies instead of reproducing it in the treatment."[28]

The Dora case has spawned a literature of victimology, written by analysts and nonanalysts alike, in which Freud's frank, pellucid account of the case has allowed scholars and clinicians to demonstrate the superiority of their insight.[29] Some psychoanalytic purists like to believe that the technical problem posed by the transference can be solved doctrinally and have faulted Freud for not having interpreted it right away. Yet balancing historical exploration and transference analysis in the here-and-now in any given case remains a clinical dilemma that is best solved empirically; the most productive balance between the two foci has to be groped for anew with each patient. Freud summarized the dilemma wisely when he wrote in the postscript to the "Fragment" that early attention to the transference distorts a case whereas ignoring it leaves the work vulnerable to surprising disruptions.

Commentators have tended to forget that the essay was written as a follow-up to the dream book. Its stated purpose was to show how dreams are interpreted, not how psychotherapy is conducted. Consequently, exchanges between Freud and his patient were condensed, making him seem intellectualist, didactic, and argumentative. It is true that, as Freud later said, early psychoanalytic technique erred in these ways, but the account he presented in the "Fragment" exaggerated them. Critics have also failed to take sufficiently into account the extraordinary brevity of the analysis and the fact that Freud mistakenly imagined he had many more months in which to work. Had Freud in this 11-week psychoanalysis done all of the transference interpretation critics fault him for not doing, he would have been even more deductive, precipitous, and overbearing. As for the bullying, critics—imagining collaboration and contention to be antithetical—have missed the strength of the collaborative engagement between the insistent Freud and the contentious Dora, a productive engagement that is apparent even as they analyzed her decision to terminate. A deep respect for his young patient's rights and her dignity was inherent in Freud's refusal to try to argue Dora out of her decision.[30]

On April 1, 1902, 15 months after the treatment had ended, Dora reappeared. Since the termination with Freud, she had gotten better. One of Herr K.'s children had died, and she had taken the occasion to visit the Ks., who received her as though there had been no estrangement. Dora confronted Frau K. about the affair with her father, and the woman admitted it. In addition, Dora got Herr K. to confess that he had made sexual advances toward her, and she had the satisfaction of taking this admission to her father. She then abandoned relations with the K.s entirely.

The previous October, 1901, on the anniversary of the beginning of her treatment with Freud, Dora lost her voice again. On inquiry, Freud learned that this had been a reaction to a traumatically wonderful event. One day she had bumped into Herr K. on a busy street. Herr K. had stopped, transfixed, as though fighting for words, and had been run over by a carriage. Because or despite the fact that Herr K. survived, the aphonia had passed and was not the occasion for Dora's current visit to Freud. A fortnight earlier Dora had developed a facial neuralgia, and it was for this that she now sought her former analyst's help. Freud was wary. "One glance at her face . . . was enough to tell me that she was not in earnest over her request." Finally, Freud "could not help smiling" as he showed Dora that her neuralgia had been occasioned by her reading in the newspaper of his promotion to Professor.[31] Freud interpreted the symptom to Dora as a punishment for having slapped and lost her lover and for having abandoned and lost her analyst. "I do not know," he wrote, "what kind of help she wanted from me, but I promised to forgive her for having deprived me of the satisfaction of affording her a far more radical cure for her troubles." Later Freud heard that Dora had married, "reclaimed," he noted with mordant satisfaction, "by the realities of life."[32]

## A Dear and Faithful Patient

Again there was a long lapse in Fliess's correspondence. Finally, on January 1, 1901, Freud had a letter from his friend, and he responded to it immediately. Freud had correctly imagined that the silence issued in part from Fliess's trials with his mother's mental illness, and with this knowledge he had "tolerated [his] deep loneliness with relative calm." Meanwhile, he wrote, *The Psychopathology of Everyday Life* was proceeding nicely and his patients were doing well. Dora had quit treatment the day before, but Freud made no mention of it. Minna remained unchanged and her diagnosis unclear. Finally he put the question to Fliess directly: "Let me just ask you: Should we wait with our exchange of letters until a time when neither of us has any hardships? And would this not mean asking too much and showing too little friendship?"

Apparently receiving no response from his friend, Freud wrote Fliess again on January 10, 1901, of being "mentally rather lively," having already begun writing about Dora in addition to *Everyday Life*.[33] Two weeks later he finished writing Dora's case.

> I finished "Dreams and Hysteria" yesterday, and today I already miss a narcotic. It is a fragment of an analysis of a case of hysteria in which the explanations are grouped around two dreams; so it is really a continuation of the dream book. In addition, it contains resolutions of hysterical symptoms and glimpses of the sexual-organic foundation of the whole. It is the subtlest thing I have written so far and will put people off even more than usual. Still, one does one's duty and does not write for the day alone. The essay has already been accepted by Ziehen, who does not realize that I shall soon inflict the "Psychopathology of Everyday Life" on him as well. How long Wernicke will put up with these cuckoo's eggs is his business.[34]

By January 25, 1901, Minna's condition had reached a crisis. Freud wrote Fliess, "There is no doubt of the existence of an intestinal ulcer. But was it really an embolism?" Other dark possibilities presented themselves. "Rie claims to have noticed impure heart sounds throughout those days. She takes only milk now; pain rules her days. I have all sorts of fears about what the future will bring."

By the end of January Fliess had written again and asked about Minna's health. Freud reported that beyond the existence of an ulcer Minna's diagnosis remained obscure. Nonetheless, he and Martha were both encouraged by the recent improvement in her overall condition. About his writing Freud expressed the hope that "Dreams and Hysteria" would please Fliess. "Bisexuality is mentioned [in it] and specifically recognized once and for all, and the ground is prepared for detailed treatment of it on another occasion. It is a hysteria with tussis nervosa and aphonia, which can be traced back to the character of the child's sucking, as the principal issue in the conflicting thought processes is the contrast between an inclination toward men and an inclination toward women." *Everyday Life,* he added, was half finished, his practice down, and his finances worrisome. "In the midst of the present and material depression," he wrote, "I am tormented by the temptation to spend this year's Easter week in Rome." But he had neither the money nor the sense of accomplishment to justify it. "Let us hope for better times," he ended his letter. "I ardently wish that you may soon have such times to report."[35]

Fliess must have wondered about this invitation to visit Rome, for Freud withdrew it and explained himself in his next letter.[36] It had merely been an escape into "the most beautiful of my former fantasies," he wrote, a congress—which Fliess had once promised—on "classical soil." In fact, Freud realized, "the congresses themselves have become relics of the past." Otherwise, *Everyday Life* was nearly finished, marred, though it was, by "a certain dullness."[37] The nature of Minna's illness, while clearly not "neurotic," remained obscure, even though the ulcer had healed and she continued to improve generally.

In early March 1901 an opportunity arose to visit Berlin in connection with a patient, but nothing came of it other than a wishful dream of seeing Fliess and his children, whom Freud had never met. Both *Everyday Life* and "Dreams and Hysteria" had been accepted for publication. [38] Minna was decidedly better. On March 24 Freud was pleasantly surprised to receive from Fliess a favorable newspaper review of *The Interpretation of Dreams,* which had appeared in the Berlin *Tag* [Day]. "Does this mean," Freud quipped, "that perhaps its 'day' has come?" Some of the children were sick, others were thriving, and Minna was about to go to Edlach to begin hydrotherapy for the remainder of her mysterious illness. Happiness, Freud mused, must be found to obtain whenever fate fails to carry out all her threats at once.

On May 6, 1901, Freud turned 45. This year would see another drop in the frequency of his correspondence with Fliess, from the previous year's 23 to 12. On May 8 Freud thanked Fliess warmly for having sent birthday wishes. "Your letter gave me by no means the least pleasure, except for the part about magic, which I object to as a superfluous plaster to cover your doubt about 'thought reading.' I remain loyal to thought reading and continue to doubt 'magic.' " "Thought reading" referred to a dismissive remark Fliess had made about Freud's interpretative method during their congress the previous summer at Achensee. This is the first mention of the argument the two men had had, but Freud chose not to pursue it. Minna, he reported, was feeling better at Edlach, despite experiencing sequelae of what Freud believed to be genuine cardiac changes.

Freud went on to say that he "had made peace with [his] circumstances" and was contenting himself with "a fragment of a Pompeiian wall with a centaur and faun" in place of his longing for Italy, that piece of statuary fortifying him in the solitude of his study. Minna had left Edlach on June 8 to stay with her mother in Reichenhall. Freud told Fliess that he was satisfied with her improvement, however incomplete, as it so exceeded his expectations. His psychoanalytic patients also continued to improve. Even the children had laid illness aside for a while. He was correcting the proofs of *Everyday Life* and finding little pleasure in what he had wrought. Doubts had arisen about publishing "Dreams and Hysteria," but what these were, he did not tell Fliess. The important theoretical problems concerning the sexual theory, which had been growing since October 1899, required further gestation. "Progress in my work," he concluded his letter, "is apparently to be expected only by a more-than-thousandfold repetition of the very same impressions, and I am quite ready to submit to them. So far everything proves to be correct, but I cannot yet survey the full extent of the riches and cannot master them intellectually."

## Not All Wishes Can Be Fulfilled

In his next letter, of June 9, 1901, written in response to one from Fliess, Freud made clear his own sense of having completed a period of transition. In it evidence of mid-life disillusionment was strong. His review of the period now ending began with a reminder of the time during his late 30s that had led into it: "You have reminded me of that beautiful and difficult time when I had reason to believe that I was very close to the end of my life [because of cardiac disease], and it was your confidence that kept me going. I certainly behaved neither very bravely nor very wisely. I was too young, my instincts still too hungry, my curiosity still too great to be able to remain indifferent." But that was then. "I am more humble now, and more ready to bear what will come. There is no doubt that not all wishes can be fulfilled. Some things for which I fervently strove have already become impossible; *why should I not have to bury a new hope each year* [Italics added]?" He ended his letter by eschewing complaint: "I have been quite satisfied with my mood for many weeks now."

During the summer of 1901 Freud's spirits remained good. He had visited Minna in Reichenhall and found her health improved. His gratitude over her recovery led him to wax rhapsodic about the surrounding countryside.[39] He had taken a trip to "nearby Thumsee, and fallen in love with the little place: Alpine roses right down to the road, the small green lake, glorious woods all around, with strawberries, flowers, and (I hope) mushrooms as well. So I inquired about the possibility of getting accommodations at the only inn. . . . Apart from the attractions of the place, it is especially important for me to stay close to my dear patient."

Freud was still working to consolidate his new clinical mastery. On July 5 he wrote, "My . . . clients are doing extremely well this year, though there were fewer than last year. Thanks to less drudgery, I feel incomparably better than at the same time [last year]." He could now regard as "an outstanding success" a patient who continued to have symptoms of "sensations and visions." This "shabby remnant" bothered neither himself nor his patient. "You know," he explained to Fliess, "that during my therapy the patient's general condition changes in every respect; in the process the symptoms, which require a certain degree of attention to subsist, gradually begin to shrink." That the proper focus of psychoanalytic treatment was the patient's entire personality, not the particular—even colorful—symptoms that had so concerned him as a young neurologist, was the crucial insight that had allowed him to conquer the crisis that occurred in his treatment of Herr E. the year before.

## The Quarrel with Fliess Finally Surfaces

Amidst the dearth of correspondence during that summer of 1901, Freud wrote one letter to Fliess that many years later he characterized as very important in the history of their relationship.[40] It was written on August 7, 1901, while he was vacationing with the family back in Thumsee. Fliess had voiced an insultingly low opinion of Freud's friend Oscar Rie, physician to his children and to Minna and married to Fliess's sister-in-law. Freud disagreed strongly and added, "There is no concealing the fact that the two of us have drawn apart to some extent," adding that they were now in disagreement about Breuer, too. "I no longer despise him and have not for some time; I have felt his strength. If he is dead as far as you are concerned, then he is still exerting his power posthumously. What is your wife doing other than working out in a dark compulsion the notion that Breuer once planted in her mind when he told her how lucky she was that I did not live in Berlin and could not interfere with her marriage?" Evidently, Breuer's suggestion that Freud would come between her and her husband had lately grown active in Frau Fliess's imagination, but Fliess had not made the connection. "In this you too have come to the limit of your perspicacity; you take sides against me and tell me that 'the reader of thoughts merely reads his own thoughts into other people,' which renders all my efforts valueless."[41] The resentment he had contained for nearly a year warming, Freud continued, "If that is what you think of me, just throw my 'Everyday Life' unread into the wastepaper basket. It is full of references to you — manifest ones, for which you supplied the material, and concealed ones, for which the motivation goes back to you. The motto, too, was a gift from you. Apart from anything that might remain of the content, you can take it as a testimonial to the role you have played for me up to now."

Referring to Breuer, Freud continued:

> I do not share your contempt for friendship between men, probably because I am to a high degree party to it. In my life, as you know, woman has never replaced the comrade, the friend. If Breuer's male inclination were not so odd, so timid, so contradictory — like everything else in his mental and emotional makeup — it would provide a nice example of the accomplishments into which the androphilic current in men can be sublimated.

Freud ended his letter exclaiming, "And now, the main thing! . . . My next work will be called 'Human Bisexuality.' It will go to the root of the problem and say the last word it may be granted me to say — the last and the most profound." For the moment, he had only a central insight based upon the idea "that repression, [the] core problem, is possible only through reaction between two sexual currents." Reminding Fliess of an earlier conversation — when Freud had asserted that *the* solution lay in sexuality, Fliess had corrected him, insisting that it lay in *bi*-sexuality — Freud freely admitted, "The idea itself is yours."

> Perhaps my sense of honesty will force me to ask you to coauthor the work with me; thereby the anatomical-biological part would gain in scope, the part which if I did it alone, would be meager. I would concentrate on the psychic aspect of bisexuality and the explanation of the neurotic. That, then, is the next project for the immediate future, which I hope will quite properly unite us again in scientific matters as well.

Thus even as the relationship was ending, Freud tried once more to unite psychology to biology and himself to his friend. The hopes that had been there at the beginning remained at the end, but only vestigially. He had changed, and the wishes that had once burned so brightly were now merely wistful. Freud's mid-life transition was over.

CHAPTER ELEVEN

# A Wider Realm
## (Age 45 and After)
### THE ENTRY INTO MIDDLE AGE AND BEYOND

FREUD now underwent a period of rapid change as he entered middle age. Important decisions followed in quick succession. In August 1901 he visited Rome for the first time. On his return to Vienna in September he set to work to win his overdue promotion to professor. By March 1902 he had secured it. That fall, taking the suggestion of Wilhelm Stekel, a former patient and fellow psychiatrist, Freud invited a small group of physician pupils to meet regularly with him in his home for a discussion of psychoanalytic ideas. By 1904, when he was 48, the group was host to several international guests, and by 1906 it had changed its name to the Vienna Psychoanalytic Society, the first of the many psychoanalytic societies to come. In 1905 Freud finished writing the long-germinating *Three Essays on the Theory of Sexuality*, which joined *The Interpretation of Dreams* to form the foundation of the new psychoanalytic science. With the creation of the International Psychoanalytic Association in 1910, Freud's ideas were transformed from a theory into a movement.

By age 45 a change in Freud's personality had become notable. Jones wrote that by that age Freud had secured a full maturity rarely reached by anyone. Because I believe that development continues throughout middle age and beyond, I would not put it that way. Nonetheless, the heroic boyishness that had been so marked a feature of Freud's professional strivings during his late 30s and early 40s had largely disappeared, though not entirely. He developed the *gravitas*

237

that Cicero thought intrinsic to middle age, and, as has also been said of Samuel Johnson at 48, *gravitas* remained a steady and enduring quality of his from about age 48 on.

## End of the Relationship with Fliess

Freud's relationship with Fliess was effectively over in 1902. During that year Freud wrote two letters, the following year one, and in 1904, when he was 48, three. There were no letters after that. The relationship officially ended in 1904 over the plagiarism of Fliess's ideas about bisexuality by the friend of a patient of Freud's. In fact, as we have seen, a breach had formed between the two men following an argument in August of 1900 about the respective value of each other's work. Yet this cause, too, must be understood developmentally. For Freud, the relationship was developmentally exhausted by 1900. He no longer needed a fellow conquistador with whom to tilt at windmills; actually, he needed the opposite—a measure of disillusionment that would permit him to get clearer about himself, his dream, and his work in order to build a life suited for authentic growth as a middle-aged man.

It is possible, as has been suggested, that it was Fliess's envy over Freud's publication of his book on dreams, in the absence of any similar accomplishment of his own, that led him to withdraw from the relationship. A year and a half younger than Freud, Fliess may have been entering his own mid-life transition in 1900. If this were the case, he may also have needed less adolescent fantasizing and greater isolation; we do know that it was Fliess who first increased the distance between the two men. And Fliess did not succeed in publishing the great (in a personal, developmental sense, not in an objective scientific or scholarly one) work of his mid-life transition, *The Course of Life,* until 1906, when he was 48.[1]

## Last Letters to Fliess

Late in the summer of 1901 Fliess responded to Freud's invitation to coauthor a work on sexuality by complaining that while his friend undervalued his work, he threatened to steal his ideas. After his return from Rome Freud wrote Fliess on September 19, 1901, denying both charges and renewing his own. He was still nettled by Fliess's having said that his interpretations were merely projections of his own thoughts onto others. "For whom do I still write?" he asked. "If as soon as an interpretation of mine makes you uncomfortable, you are ready to agree that the 'reader of thoughts' perceives nothing in the other but merely projects his own thoughts, you really no longer are my audience either and must regard my entire method of working as being just as worthless as the others do."[2]

Even with the increased emotional distance and the diminution in the frequency of the correspondence, Fliess continued to send Freud patients in 1901, and both men exchanged occasional news and pleasantries in 1902. Fliess referred a Mrs. D. for treatment in September 1901, and in November Freud reported that the patient was doing well. "You are surely entitled to hear from time to time how matters stand with your patient. . . , " he wrote. "You have indeed selected a case for me that is made to order for this therapy. I can say that so far it has gone extremely well. . . . Once again . . . everything falls into place, at least according to my more recent conceptualization, and the instrument responds willingly to the instrumentalist's sure touch."[3] Despite the breach between himself and his friend, Freud's clinical confidence held firm and contributed to his newfound equanimity. In December 1901 he told Fliess that amid misfortunes and bad luck, he was "continuously practicing endurance."[4]

In January 1902 Fliess again sent Freud a positive review of the dream book that had been published in a lay periodical. Freud had been able to find only two reviews of his book in professional journals and both had been negative. So, amidst the gloom of family illness—Freud's son Ernst and his daughter Anna had scarlet fever, and one of his sisters was very ill—Fliess's clipping was very welcome.

## A First Bow to Authority

In March Freud had better news to report. He had finally secured his professorship. On March 11, responding to a letter from Berlin, he told Fliess how he had done it. His letter began, "Just imagine what an 'excellency' [the minister of education] can accomplish! He can even bring it about that I once again hear your dear voice in a letter."[5] But lest Fliess think that the promotion had been awarded for merit, Freud's "harmful urge to honesty" demanded that a truer account be given. "When I came back from Rome, my enjoyment of life and work was somewhat heightened and that of martyrdom somewhat diminished."

> I found my practice had almost melted away; I withdrew my last work from publication [presumably Dora] because just a little earlier I had lost my last audience in you. I could foresee that waiting for recognition might take up a good portion of my life and that in

the meantime none of my fellow men would bother about me. And I did want to see Rome again, take care of my patients, and keep my children in good spirits. So I made up my mind to break with strict virtue and take appropriate steps, as other humans do. One must look somewhere for one's salvation, and I chose the title as my savior."[6]

Freud had contacted his former teacher, Exner, who intimated that someone had discouraged the minister of education from acting on the promotion that the medical school faculty had long since recommended and that personal influence would be necessary to counteract the opposition. Freud then sought out a friend and former patient, Frau Gomperz, who was pleased to speak to the minister on his behalf. To Gomperz the minister expressed both surprise at the delay and ignorance of the existence of the candidate. It was necessary for Freud to renew his application and to get Nothnagel and Krafft-Ebing—none too soon, as they were both about to retire—to resubmit it. They did so quickly, yet the minister avoided Gomperz and her subsequent inquiries about the promotion.

It is worth noting that while Freud deserved the promotion on scholarly grounds, he finally received it as a result of his clinical mastery. For at this point a current patient of Freud's, Marie Ferstel, learned of the problem. Ferstel was married to the newly appointed consul general for Berlin and was concluding a highly successful treatment with Freud. Without Freud's urging, she took it upon herself to importune the minister of education and insist that the doctor who had cured her be promoted to professor. Frau Ferstel offered the minister a valuable painting for the gallery he was planning to establish, and the deal was done. Freud had made, as he put it, his "first bow to authority."[7]

One day [Ferstel] came to her session, beaming and waving an express letter from the minister. So it was accomplished. . . . Public acclaim was immense. Congratulations and flowers already are pouring in, as though the role of sexuality has suddenly been officially recognized by His Majesty, the significance of the dream certified by the Council of Ministers, and the necessity of a psychoanalytic therapy of hysteria carried by a two thirds majority in Parliament.[8]

But Freud did not restrict his contempt to the ministry and to sycophantic well-wishers: "In the whole affair there is one person with very long ears who has not been sufficiently appreciated in your letter, and that is myself. If I had taken the few steps three years ago, I would have been appointed three years earlier and been spared all sorts of things. Others are that clever without first having to go to Rome."[9] The defiant isolation he had begun 15 years earlier on his return from Paris and Charcot with his announcement about male hysteria, and the consequences-be-damned stance he had adopted toward his profession in the last five years with his absurd insistence that *all* hysterics had been sexually molested by their fathers, were being replaced by a worldlier maturity. Freud's defiance and his capacity to work in isolation, if need be, remained, but he was now willing to enter more fully into the world and dirty his hands in the affairs of men.

Following the announcement of his promotion, there is not extant a substantive letter from Freud for two years. It seems likely that during the cooled and declining correspondence Fliess lost or threw away a few letters written to him by Freud in 1903. In the interim Freud had created a new realm for himself and a new entry life structure for middle age.

On April 26, 1904, Freud wrote Fliess for the first, or one of the first, times since 1902. He was just about to turn 48:

> If I am writing to you again after such a long interval, you surely will assume that I am prompted not by an emotional impulse but by a practical motive. And so it is. . . . Several competent young physicians who—I do not want to be secretive with you— belong to the circle of my pupils plan in the near future to attempt publication of a scientific journal that will be devoted to the "biological and psychological exploration of sexuality."[10]

His students would be asking Fliess to collaborate, and Freud was writing to encourage him to do so. The journal was timely, Freud wrote, because "everywhere the signs of agreement with my views are increasing." He had recently read a "stunning" review by the Swiss psychiatrist Eugen Bleuler in the *Münchener medizinische Wochenschrift* praising his studies on hysteria and dreams. It now seemed possible to Freud that recognition would come during his lifetime; a promising harbinger of this was the fact that he was "beginning to have better student material at [his] disposal."[11]

Fliess, in one of the few letters that we have from him, replied immediately. "I was very glad to hear from you," he wrote, "even though, by your own statement, your lines were not motivated by any emotional impulse. I was especially pleased about the news that you are gaining more recognition."[12] Fliess declined to contribute to the new journal, because his hands were full with his own book. He wondered what had happened to *Jokes and Their Relationship to the Unconscious,* material for which Freud had sent him "exactly a year ago."[13] The letter ended cordially, as was the tone of Freud's next letter to Fliess in July 1904, congratulating him on his sister-in-law's upcoming marriage. This would bring Fliess to Vienna, but the Freuds intended to leave on vacation the evening before.

## A Reason to End It

The final exchange of four letters, two from each man, occurred later that month. Fliess had seen Otto Weininger's *Geschlecht und Charakter* (Sex and Character), the first portion of which dealt with ideas about the biological basis of bisexuality. Weininger had quoted a man by the name of Swoboda, who Fliess thought was one of Freud's pupils. Fliess wrote Freud requesting an explanation.[14] Freud responded blandly that Swoboda had not been his student but his patient and that bisexuality came up in every treatment. Nonetheless, he agreed with Fliess's surmise that Weininger was "a burglar with a key he picked up" from Swoboda.

On July 26 Fliess confronted Freud with an unpleasant fact: Their mutual friend Oscar Rie had told him that when Weininger showed Freud a prepublication draft of his manuscript, Freud had advised against publication only on scientific grounds, offering no objection on the grounds that the ideas belonged to Fliess. Further, not only had Freud failed to arrest the burglar, Fliess complained, he had next failed to warn him of the crime in progress. Fliess also expressed surprise and dismay that Freud was using the idea of bisexuality routinely in his treatments, and he recalled for Freud that they had discussed bisexuality for the first time in Nuremberg in 1897.

> While I was still lying in bed . . . you told me the case history of the woman who had dreams of gigantic snakes. At the time you were quite impressed by the idea that undercurrents in a woman might stem from the masculine part of her psyche. For this reason I was all the more puzzled by your resistance in Breslau to the assumption of bisexuality in the psyche. In Breslau I also told you about the existence of so many left-handed husbands among my acquaintances, and from the theory of left-handedness I developed for you an explanation which down to *every detail* corresponds to Weininger's (who knows nothing about left-handedness). To be sure, you rejected left-handedness itself and, as you yourself admitted most candidly, forgot our bisexual discussion for some time.[15]

Fliess concluded his letter generously by writing, "Both of us would no doubt have wished for a better reason to correspond than arguing about a *robber*. May the future bring it to us."

The candid admission that Fliess referred to was Freud's in *The Psychopathology of Everyday Life,* where he had written:

> One day in the summer of this year [1901] I remarked to my friend Fl., with whom I have a lively exchange . . . of scientific ideas: "These problems of the neuroses are only to be solved if we base ourselves wholly and completely on the assumption of the original bisexuality of the individual." To which he replied: "That's what I told you two and a half years ago at Br. [Breslau] when we went for that evening walk. But you wouldn't hear of it then." It is painful to be requested in this way to surrender one's originality. I could not recall any such conversation or this pronouncement of my friend's. . . . In the course of the next week I remembered the whole incident, which was just as my friend had tried to recall it to me; I even recollected the answer I had given him at the time: "I've not accepted that yet; I'm not inclined to go into the question."[16]

On July 27 Freud wrote back, "I see that I have to concede to you more right than I originally was prepared to; I am taken aback by my having forgotten how much I had complained about my pupil Swoboda and by my glossing over Weininger's visit to me (which, however, I had not forgotten)." Oscar Rie's account was correct, Freud wrote, though the book that Weininger had shown him was in important ways different from the one published. Nonetheless, Fliess's ideas were unmistakable in it, and Freud admitted that his forgetting the conversation with Weininger must have resulted from an unconscious feeling of guilt about his own role in the affair.

In his own defense, however, Freud pointed out that it would not have made sense for him to arrest the thief. Ideas, after all, cannot be "patented"; moreover, the general idea of bisexuality was becoming common in medical writings. He had feared since *The Psychopathology of Everyday Life* that the two friends might have occasion to regret the unrestrained openness of their previous conversations and had tried to forget the details of Fliess's remarks about bisexuality, using only the general notion in his interpretations to patients. "At that same time," Freud wrote, "I evidently reproached myself dimly, as I do today in complete clarity, for my generosity or carelessness with your property." However, he insisted, the damage would not be great, since the shoddiness of Weininger's work would ensure its obscurity. Freud added:

> You are not alone in regretting — I do too — that this incident in which you reproach me has reawakened a long-dormant correspondence. It is not my fault, however, if you find the time and the inclination to exchange letters with me again only on the occasion

of such petty incidents. The fact is that in the past few years—
"Everyday Life" is the dividing line—you have no longer showed
an interest in me or my family or my work. By now I have gotten
over it and have little desire for it any longer; I am not reproaching
you and ask you not to reply to this point.

As for the future, Freud was anxious to avoid another misunderstanding with his former friend:

I trust you will still be so kind as to help me out . . . by reading
the remarks on bisexuality in the proofs of my just completed
"Essays on the Theory of Sexuality" and changing them to your
satisfaction. It would be easier to postpone publication until you
have surrendered your biology to the public. But I do not know
when this will be. . . . There is so little of bisexuality or of other
things I have borrowed from you in what I say, that I can do justice
to your share in a few remarks. I must only be sure that you agree
with them and do not find grounds in them for reproaches later on.

There would be no later on—no more letters, no more congresses, and
no more shared flights of heroic fancy.

## The Dream Book Brings Disillusionment
## and a Wider Realm

Freud's dream book *had* brought him better students, or at least more
ambitious ones. Later that year Freud invited four of these physician-
students—Max Kahane, Rudolf Reitler, Wilhelm Stekel, and Alfred
Adler—to join him to discuss his work at his home on Wednesday evenings.[17] The group gave its meeting the title "Psychological Wednesday Society." Stekel reported the meeting in the Sunday edition of the
*Neues Wiener Tagblatt*. The group grew and welcomed such international guests as, among others, Carl Jung and Ludwig Binswanger from
Switzerland, Karl Abraham from Berlin, A. A. Brill from America,
and Ernest Jones from England. By 1906, when Freud was 50, there
were 17 members, and the group hired a secretary, a young machinist
and gifted autodidact, Otto Rank. By 1908 the group had grown to
22 members, though far fewer attended any given meeting. On April
15, 1908, it adopted its permanent name: the Vienna Psycho-Analytical
Society.[18]
    Freud was lucky that his book had produced so little reaction be-

yond the interest of gifted students. Had it stimulated the widespread fierce resistance he had fantasized, it might have delayed his giving up the more puerile aspects of the heroic conquistador fantasy; prolonged his comradeship in imaginary battle with his co-belligerent, Fliess; and postponed his growing up. The nonreaction to the dream book ushered in the process of mid-life disillusionment through which the tyranny of the youthful dream was lessened. Freud did little research between ages 45 and 49 and was content to let his next great creation, the *Three Essays on the Theory of Sexuality,* grow at its own speed. Across the entire span of Freud's research career, from age 20 to 82, this cessation in output was equaled only once—in the years between ages 77 and 81.

After the lull during his late 40s, Freud's 50s would be far and away his most productive as a writer.[19] In quantitative terms, his output then exceeded by nearly 50 percent that of the adjacent decades of his 40s and 60s, and the troughs that at times characterized his creative productivity disappeared entirely. Freud later referred to the 50s as the "best decade" of the life cycle. During this decade his identity as a scientist and clinician expanded to include that of biographer. He wrote *Little Hans* and *The Rat Man* at 53, *Leonardo Da Vinci* at 54, *Schreber* at 55, and *The Wolf Man* at 58. He also wrote the papers on therapeutic technique, which, three quarters of a century later, we can say are not only elegant in their simplicity but timeless in their clinical wisdom. Foreshadowing the speculative psychohistorical and social psychological works that would flower in his old age, Freud at 56 wrote *Totem and Taboo* and at 59 the *Papers on Metapsychology* (the pure psychology), including *Mourning and Melancholia,* in which the ego's relations with its own internal objects was emphasized for the first time. As the era of his middle age neared a close, Freud wrote his *Introductory Lectures.* These lectures, delivered at 59, 60, and 61, were expressly culminating. He intended them to bring his career as a lecturer at the University of Vienna to an end. With graceful mastery, he set forth in them the essence of what he had learned about the mind over the era of his middle adulthood.

I have not closely studied the years of Freud's early 60s, so I do not know if it is possible to identify a transitional period there as our theory of the life cycle and its eras would indicate. Anzieu alluded to a crisis occurring at around this point, similar in magnitude to that of Freud's early 40s, and Jones wrote of important changes in Freud's personality occurring after the mid-life transition.[20] It is clear that Freud embarked on a brand-new era of creative work beginning in his early to mid-60s. Concluding *The Introductory Lectures* at 61, Freud in the final era of his life reached beyond clinical psychiatry and biography to social theory and to the vast psychoanalytically uncharted domains of the ego, society, and history. He wrote *Beyond the Pleasure Principle* at 64, *Group Psychology and the Analysis of the Ego* at 65, *The Ego and the Id* at 66, *The Future of an Illusion* at 71, *Civilization and Its Discontents* at 73, and *Moses and Monotheism* at 81, as he began the transition from life to death.

Could this sort of fresh creativity have been possible in late adulthood without intensive developmental work in the years around 60 during the transition to old age? It does not seem that the discipline and profession of psychoanalysis that Freud built in his 40s could have been created without the work of his mid-life transition. Yet the prospect of ceaseless developmental challenge does not please us. There is an almost irresistible temptation to yield to one's own age parochialism and assume that after the current battle has ended, a flat terrain free of psychological travail will follow. That such a featureless developmental landscape appeals is testimony to how wearying we each find our own lot, no matter how enviable it may appear. In truth, everything we can bear to know from our own lives and the study of others' tells us that this cannot really be so. At 65 Freud gave testimony both to the illusion and to the underlying reality when he wrote his son Ernst that "*das ruhige Alter scheint auch so eine Fabel zu sein, wie die glückliche Jugend*—a peaceful old age appears to be as much of a fable as a happy youth."[21]

# Notes

## Acknowledgments and Preface

1. I am also indebted to Darius Ornston and his contributors for their excellent book, *Translating Freud*, which deepened my understanding of the difficulties involved in translating Freud's German into English.

2. See Ornston, ibid.

3. Bernice Neugarten poineered studies in adult development before the subject became popular. See her book *Personality in Middle and Late Life* as well as her article "A Developmental View of Adult Personality" and subsequent works.

4. In his studies of self-actualized people Abraham Maslow was unable to find a single person who had achieved this high level of psychological development prior to the end of the mid-life transition. See Maslow, *Toward a Psychology of Being*, p. 130.

## Chapter One

1. Letter to Fliess, September 21, 1897, in Jeffrey Masson (ed.), *The Complete Letters of Sigmund Freud to Wilhelm Fliess.*

2. Peter Gay, *Freud: A Life for Our Time*, p. 89.

3. Ibid., p. 96.

4. Ibid.

5. Ibid., p. 100.

6. The letters span the years 1887 to 1904, with 71 percent written when Freud was between ages 39 and 45.

7. Masson, op. cit., p. 405.

8. George Mahl, "Explosion of Discoveries and Concepts: The Freud–Fliess Letters," Chapter 4 in *A First Course in Freud*, p. 33.

9. Masson, op. cit., p. 261.

10. Sigmund Freud, *The Interpretation of Dreams,* in James Strachey (ed.), *The Standard Edition of the Complete Psychological Works of Sigmund Freud* (hereafter cited as *SE*), vol. 4, p. 206.

11. Ibid., vol. 5, pp. 452–455.

12. Ibid., p. 454.

13. Among comtemporary psychoanalysts, Robert Nemiroff and Calvin Colarusso have been the leading exponents of an adult developmental point of view toward psychopathology and treatment. See their book *The Race against Time.* For clinically sensitive experimental studies of adult development, see Harvey Peskin's "Uses of the Past in the Adult Lifespan."

14. These ideas and perspectives informed my study (1984) of the depressive crisis that the 18th-century English writer Samuel Johnson suffered during his 50s. By its end I was led to propose that transitional periods in themselves promote superego–ego splitting, sadistic superego attack, and masochistic ego regression, as well as—when development proceeds successfully—the maturing of both intrapsychic agencies. My study of Freud had led me to revise this hypothesis by limiting the notions of superego attack and ego regression to occasions of crisis brought about by the blocking of normal development.

15. Roger Gould independently found a similar age-linked sequence of developmental periods using questionnaire data from a large sample of men and women; see his book *Transformations.* For a study of age-linked periods in the evolution of ego defense mechanisms, see George Vaillant's *Adaptation to Life.*

16. A conception of the ages of life has been a predominant feature in man's thinking about himself for at least three millennia. The historian Philippe Ariès writes in *Centuries of Childhood* that it is hard for contemporary persons to grasp the tremendous meaning the concept of the ages of life held for the ancients. In the hands of the Greek philosophers it formed part of a larger system for the explanation of nature. From time to time there has occurred an epoch in which people lose interest in the perspective, and we may be emerging from one of those now.

17. G. Acsádi and J. Nemeskéri, *History of Human Life Span and Mortality.*

18. Ibid., p. 170.

19. The leading researcher in anthropological studies of adult development is David Gutmann, author of "The Cross-Cultural Perspective: Notes Toward a Comparative Psychology of Aging" and other works.

20. See Harvey Lehman's *Age and Achievement* and Dean Simonton's *Genius, Creativity, and Leadership.*

21. See Levinson on the developmental tasks of the novice phase.

22. Teiresias's prophesies in Book XI of the *Odyssey* that Odysseus will live a long middle age full of unexpected adventures and die an old man far from his home.

23. See my "The Accursed Correspondence: The Freud/Jung Letters."

24. See my "Samuel Johnson's Breakdown and Recovery in Middle-Age: A Life-Span Developmental Approach to Mental Illness and Its Cure" and "Freud's Mid-Life Crisis."

25. Truman Capote, *Other Voices, Other Rooms.*

26. James Baldwin, review of *The Arrangement,* by Elia Kazan, *New York Review of Books,* 23 March 1967, p. 17.

27. He did so in a letter written to Fliess at age 32. Masson, op. cit., p. 24. Cf. Michael Schröter (ed.), *Sigmund Freud: Briefe an Wilhelm Fliess, 1887–1904,* p. 11.

28. Max Schur (*Freud: Living and Dying,* p. 97 n. 2) renders *Mittelelend* as "the pain of ovulation" in *"und bin seither sehr faul gewesen, weil sich das zur intensiven Arbeit notige Mittelelend nicht einstellen will"* (Schröter, op. cit., p. 191). Schur translates this "and have been very lazy ever since, for that state of semi-misery which is essential for intensive work will not re-establish itself" and considers the unusual word *"Mittlelend"* to be a pun alluding to *Mittelschmerz,* the pain some women feel at ovulation. I interpret *"Ich bringe nichts als zwei offene Ohren und einen zur Aufnahme geschmierten Schlafenlappen"* as vaginal. The connotation is not necessarily sexual. Cf. Schröter, op. cit., p. 204.

29. S. Freud, *The Interpretation of Dreams, SE,* vol. 5, p. 453.

30. Daniel and Judy Levinson, personal communication, 1990.

31. Richard Wollheim, *Sigmund Freud,* p. xxxix.

## Chapter Two

1. Masson, op. cit., p. 129.

2. J. B. Bury, *The Idea of Progress.*

3. Nietzsche was one of the few who saw that natural selection had cut the moral ground out from under Western civilization. Take divinity out of Christianity, he argued, and the whole superstructure collapses.

4. Priscilla Robertson, *Revolutions of 1848.*

5. P. G. J. Pulzer, "The Development of Political Antisemitism in Austria," p. 430.

6. Roger Morgan, "Avant-Garde Intimations." Hannah Decker (*Freud, Dora, and Vienna 1900,* p. 22) makes the relative growth of the Jewish population even more dramatic: According to her research, the general population quadrupled between 1857 and 1910 while the Jewish community increased 28 times from roughly 6,000 to 175,000.

7. P. G. J. Pulzer, p. 437, op. cit.

8. Marianne Krull, *Freud and His Father.*

9. Rabbi J. Heshel, "The History of Hassidism in Austria."

10. Renée Gicklhorn, "The Freiberg Period of the Freud Family," p. 39.

11. Krüll, op. cit., pp. 91, 100.

12. Ibid., p. 95.

13. Cf. William McGrath's "How Jewish Was Freud?" For depictions of Freud that emphasize his Jewishness, see Jerry Diller's *Freud's Jewish Identity* and David Blatt's "The Development of the Hero: Sigmund Freud and the Reformation of the Jewish Tradition."

14. The upper floor appears to provide about 1,100 square feet of living space.

15. Krüll, op. cit., p. 98.

16. Roger Morgan, op. cit.

17. Krüll, op. cit., p. 73.

18. Ibid., p. 98.

19. Ibid. See also Martin Freud, *Sigmund Freud: Man and Father,* p. 11.

20. Ernest Jones, *The Life and Works of Sigmund Freud,* vol. 1, p. 3.

21. M. Freud, "Who Was Freud?," p. 202.

22. M. Freud, *Sigmund Freud: Man and Father,* p. 11

23. Ibid., p. 11.

24. M. Freud, "Who Was Freud?," p. 202. For Amalia's brothers' involvement, see Alexander Grinstein, *Freud at the Crossroads,* p. 64.

25. The name Sigismund is German; Schlomo is a Hebrew name, after the paternal grandfather. From age 16 on, with occasional exceptions, Freud used Sigmund. See Walter Boehlich (ed.), *The Letters of Sigmund Freud to Eduard Silberstein.*

26. Krüll, op. cit., p. 116.

27. Gicklhorn, op. cit., p. 41.

28. The evidence for a general economic downturn, rather than individual imcompetence, to account for Jacob's business reversals and the necessity of leaving Freiberg is unclear. Cf. Krüll, op cit., pp. 143–144.

29. His grown children, Philipp and Emanuel, immigrated to Manchester, England. It is possible that they left to avoid being called up to fight in the war against Sardinia. Krüll, op. cit., p. 145.

30. M. Freud, *Sigmund Freud: Man and Father,* p. 20.

31. Ernest Freud, Lucie Freud, and Ilse Grubrich-Simitis (eds.), *Sigmund Freud: His Life in Pictures and Words,* p. 12.

32. Ernst Freud (ed.), *The Letters of Sigmund Freud,* p. 86.

33. See Heller's "Freud's Mother and Father: A Memoir."

34. M. Freud, *Sigmund Freud: Man and Father,* p. 12.

35. The letter is dated February 2, 1886. Ernst Freud, *The Letters of Sigmund Freud,* p. 202.

36. Like Nietzsche, Freud insisted on a sharp distinction between inhibition and morality. For both thinkers, a man cannot be considered virtuous unless he has the ability to be evil.

37. Heller, op cit., pp. 418–421.

38. M. Freud, *Sigmund Freud: Man and father,* p. 19.

39. Anna Freud Bernays, "My Brother, Sigmund Freud," p. 140.

40. M. Freud, *Sigmund Freud: Man and Father,* pp. 11–12. For his part, Freud often arrived constipated; see Jones, op. cit., vol. 2, p. 391, and Paul Roazen, *Freud and His Followers,* p. 46. Freud's mother died when he was 74. He did not attend the funeral and expressed relief because he had not wanted her to suffer the pain of his dying first; see Roazen, op. cit., pp. 40–41.

41. As Amalia liked to call him; see Heller, op. cit.

42. Sigmund Freud, *New Introductory Lectures, SE,* vol. 22, p. 3.

43. Roazen, op cit., p. 46.

44. Ibid., pp. 41–42.

## Chapter Three

1. Ernst Freud, *The Letters of Sigmund Freud,* p. 401.
2. Schröter, op cit., pp. 288–289. See also Masson, op. cit., p. 268.
3. Masson, op. cit., pp. 271–272.
4. Sigmund Freud, *The Psychopathology of Everyday Life, SE,* vol. 6, p. 51 n. 2.
5. Sigmund Freud, *Leonardo Da Vinci and a Memory of His Childhood, SE,* vol. 11, pp. 78–79.
6. Sigmund Freud, "Screen Memories," *SE,* vol. 3. p. 309 n. 1. See Masson, op. cit., p. 338 n. 1 Bernfeld discovered the ruse; see his "An Unknown Autobiographical Fragment by Freud."
7. S. Freud, "Screen Memories," *SE,* vol. 3, pp. 312–313.
8. In another letter to Fliess some two months later, on December 3, 1897, Freud revealed that at least some part of this trip from Freiberg to Leipzig and from there to Vienna had brought the fires of hell to his childish imagination: "Breslau also plays a role in my childhood memories. At the age of three years I passed through the station when we moved from Freiberg to Leipzig, and the gas flames which I saw for the first time reminded me of spirits burning in hell. . . . My travel anxiety, now overcome, also is bound up with this."
9. Jones, op. cit., vol. 1, p. 15.
10. Other parts were lovely. See Arthur Schnitzler, *My Youth in Vienna.*
11. Decker (op. cit., p. 24) asserts that the Freuds moved a sixth time during these years but neither specifies where nor documents it.
12. For more about the help provided by Amalia's family, see E. Freud, *The Letters of Sigmund Freud,* p. 42, and Bernfeld, "Sigmund Freud, M.D., 1882–1885," p. 207.
13. Things may have started to improve earlier. Apparently, the Pfeffergasse apartment was large enough to offer the prospect of boarding two of Freud's classmates, the Silberstein brothers. See Boehlich, *The Letters of Sigmund Freud to Eduard Silberstein,* p. xv.
14. Krüll, op. cit., p. 95.
15. Jones, op. cit., vol. 1, p. 19. Krüll (op. cit., p. 160) offers a somewhat different translation. Some writers believe that Jacob was urging his son to return to Judaism. See McGrath's "How Jewish Was Freud?" Freud made this Bible a permanent part of the study he established that year at 19 Berggasse. He took it with him in 1939 when the Nazi occupation of Vienna forced him to immigrate to England.
16. Bernays, op. cit., p. 141. Freud's initial lessons in German came from his mother.
17. S. Freud, *The Interpretation of Dreams, SE,* vol. 4, p. 216.
18. Krüll, op. cit., p. 151.
19. S. Freud, *The Interpretation of Dreams, SE,* vol. 4, p. 197.
20. S. Freud, *The Psychopathology of Everyday Life, SE,* vol. 6, pp. 219–220.
21. Fritz Wittels, *Sigmund Freud: His Personality, His Teaching, and His School,* p. 60.

22. McGrath, op. cit., p. 59.

23. Sigismund Freud: Student of Law. William J. McGrath, *Freud's Discovery of Psychoanalysis.*

24. This rendering of the Gisela Fluss affair conforms to the most recent scholarly account provided by Boehlich. Some earlier versions differ. Cf. Gay, op. cit., and Ronald Clark, *Freud: The Man and His Cause.*

25. See Freud's letter to Silberstein of January 30, 1872, in Boehlich, op. cit., p. 4.

26. Ernst Freud, "Jugendbriefe Sigmund Freuds," p. 774. The German is *"Wir beide waren nur ein an Wichtigkeit und Geist verschwindend kleiner Bruchteil einer großen Gesellschaft deren Perle „Ichthyosaura" war."* Cf. the differing translation in Ernst Freud, "Some Early Unpublished Letters of Freud," p. 422. See Freud's letter to Silberstein of August 17, 1872, for Emil's role in the affair in Boehlich, op. cit., p. 11.

27. Boehlich agrees with Eissler that the nickname comes from a popular poem of the time, *Der Ichthyosaurus* by Josef Victor von Scheffel. See Boehlich, op cit., pp. 195–197, and Kurt R. Eissler, "Creativity and Adolescence," p. 470.

28. See Freud's letters to Silberstein of March 25 and July 27, 1872, in Boehlich, op. cit., pp. 5–6.

29. S. Freud, "Screen Memories," *SE,* vol. 3, pp. 312–313.

30. Boehlich, op. cit., p. 12.

31. Ibid., p. 18.

32. Ibid., p. 16. The original of this letter is missing and may have been destroyed by Silberstein in keeping with Freud's wishes. The translation is from a photograph that is not in every respect clear.

33. Ibid., pp. 18–19, p. 19 n. 1.

34. Ibid., p. 90, p. 91 n. 10.

35. Scholars (cf. Clark) have disagreed about the intensity of Freud's feelings for Gisela. I originally derived the interpretation offered here from the scantier evidence available in the Heinz Stanescu's "Young Freud's Letters to His Rumanian Friend, Silberstein" and other materials. I then found my interpretation confirmed by Boehlich's more recent publication of the complete set of letters. See also Mahl, "Explosion of Discoveries and Concepts: The Freud–Fliess Letters."

36. E. Freud, "Some Early Unpublished Letters of Freud," pp. 424, 426.

37. Ibid., pp. 420–421.

38. Ibid., p. 421.

39. Ibid., p.422.

40. Ibid., pp. 422–423.

41. Ibid., p. 424.

42. S. Freud, "Screen Memories," *SE,* vol. 3, p. 313.

43. Kurt R. Eissler, op. cit., p. 469.

44. Sigmund Freud, *Notes upon a Case of Obsessional Neurosis, SE,* vol. 10, p. 280.

45. The essay was probably written by a friend of Goethe's, the Swiss theologian Tobler (see Clark, op. cit., p. 28). Though Goethe had not writ-

ten the essay, the mistaken attribution was understandable: So congenial were its tones that even Goethe thought that he might once have had a hand in writing it.

46. Gay, op. cit., p. 24.

47. Reprinted in Fritz Wittels, *Freud and His Time*, pp. 31–34.

48. Sigmund Freud, "The Question of Lay Analysis," *SE*, vol. 20, p. 8. The writing was completed in 1924. See George F. Mahl's "The Chronology of Freud's Writing His Psychological Works" and also *SE*, vol. 5, p. 441.

49. See Freud's March 6, 1874, letter to Emil Fluss in E. Freud, "Some Early Unpublished Letters of Freud," p. 427.

50. Sigmund Freud, Postscript to "The Question of Lay Analysis," *SE*, vol. 20, p. 253: "In my youth I felt an overpowering need to understand something of the riddles of the world in which we live and perhaps even to contribute something to their solution.'

51. E. Freud, "Jugendbriefe Sigmund Freuds," p. 775.

52. In Freud's first research, at 20, he succeeded in discovering the hidden testicles of the eel by dissection. At 41, deep in a mid-life crisis, Freud had a dream that refers to this critical moment of hearing Brühl's reading on nature and choosing a career. He reported and analyzed it in *The Interpretation of Dreams, SE*, vol. 5, p. 439.

## Chapter Four

1. After a break of 29 years, an additional and final letter was written on April 28, 1910. See Boehlich, op. cit., app.

2. Boehlich dates Silberstein's return to Vienna as "winter semester" of 1875, by which he may be referring to what we would call the fall semester. The correspondence from Freud continues into October 1875 and then stops for six months (until Freud is in Trieste), presumably because Silberstein is close at hand. It is apparent from the letters that Silberstein was not in Vienna in the first months of 1875; see Boehlich, op. cit., p. xiv.

3. Thus, from halfway through Freud's 19th year on, both he and his friend were usually in Vienna and correspondence during the academic year was largely unnecessary. Some of what little correspondence there may have been could have been burned. Freud had spoken cheerfully of this prospect as late as his letter to Silberstein on September 7, 1877; see Boehlich, op. cit., p. 167.

4. Ibid., p. 89.

5. Ibid., p. 92.

6. Ibid., p. 83.

7. As Freud told Silberstein in his last letter to him, written on his 54th birthday; ibid., p. 185.

8. S. Freud, "Screen Memories," *SE*, vol. 3, pp. 312–313.

9. Boehlich, op. cit., p. 24.

10. Ibid., p. 25.

11. Ibid., p. 26.

12. Ibid., p. 28.
13. Ibid., p. 32.
14. Ibid., pp. 32–33.
15. Ibid., p. 36.
16. Ibid., pp. 36–37.
17. Ibid., p. 41.
18. Ibid., p. 41. It is possible that the picture Freud wanted was of Silberstein; he asked his friend to send one on other occasions.
19. According to Arthur Schnitzler, op. cit., expressions of anti-Semitism were uncommon and considered ridiculous during the liberal Vienna of the 1860s and 70s but then became public and acceptable again in the 1880s.
20. Boehlich, op. cit., pp. 47–48.
21. Ibid., p. 54.
22. Ibid., p. 61.
23. Ibid., pp. 70–71.
24. Ibid., pp. 72–73.
25. Ibid., p. 77.
26. Ibid., p. 79.
27. Contrary to McGrath's portryal of the adolescent Freud as a political enthusiast, Freud rarely mentions politics in his letters to Silberstein. Moreover—and contrary to Carl Schorske's notion that Freud created psychoanalysis out of political disappointment—there is even less (if less be possible) interest expressed in politics in his later letters to Wilhelm Fliess. Indeed, Freud did not register to vote until he was 50. The Wolf Man, whom Freud analyzed in his mid- to late 50s and then again at 61, also reported that Freud was completely uninterested in political issues. See Muriel Gardiner (ed.), *The Wolf-Man,* p. 147; Eli Zaretsky's *Psychoanalysis: From the Psychology of Authority to the Politics of Identity,* chap. 1; McGrath's *Freud's Discovery of Psychoanalysis;* and Schorske's otherwise brilliant *Fin de Siècle Vienna: Politics and Culture.*
28. Boehlich, op. cit., p. 78.
29. Ibid., p. 80.
30. See ibid., pp. 81, 84.
31. Ibid., pp. 83–84.
32. Boehlich appears to have made an error in rendering the German *"man spricht allgemein davon"* as "it is generally mooted" rather than as the more obvious "it is generally said" (Boehlich, *Sigmund Freud: Jugendbriefe an Eduard Silberstein 1871–1881,* p. 97, and Boehlich, op. cit., p. 84).
33. Boehlich, *The Letters of Sigmund Freud to Eduard Silberstein,* p. 84.
34. Ibid.
35. Ibid., p. 87. The Lessing Freud refers to may have been Gotthold, the 18th-century German essayist and playwright whose tragedy "Miss Sara Sampson" was considered a classic of German literature.
36. Freud's Vienna may have been virtuous, but it was an erotic paradise for his contemporary Arthur Schnitzler, according to his *My Youth in Vienna.* In the latter's account, prostitutes were everywhere, lower-class women were readily available for amorous intrigues with gentlemen, bored wives

were available to the daring, and even single middle-class girls could be had with some subtlety and perseverance. Freud's Vienna appears to have been created out of large and roughly equal measures of inhibition, sublimation, and professional ambition.

37. Boehlich, *The Letters of Sigmund Freud to Eduard Silberstein*, p. 90.

38. Ibid., pp. 91–94.

39. Ibid., p. 96.

40. Boehlich, *The Letters of Sigmund Freud to Eduard Silberstein*, p. 95.

41. James R. Barclay, "Franz Brentano and Sigmund Freud," p. 8.

42. Boehlich, *The Letters of Sigmund Freud to Eduard Silberstein*, p. 104.

43. Ibid., p. 102.

44. Ibid., p. 104.

45. Ibid.

46. Ibid., p. 106.

47. Ibid., p. 109.

48. Ibid.

49. Ibid., p. 109.

50. Ibid., p. 111.

51. Sigmund Freud, *The Future of an Illusion, SE*, vol. 21, p. 32.

52. Boehlich, *The Letters of Sigmund Freud to Eduard Silberstein*, p. 111.

53. McGrath, *Freud's Discovery of Psychoanalysis.*

54. Boehlich, *The Letters of Sigmund Freud to Eduard Silberstein*, p. 104.

55. Ibid.

56. Ibid., pp. 94–95, p. 95 n. 2.

57. Ibid., p. 99.

58. Ibid., p. 101.

59. Ibid., p. 123.

60. Ibid., p. 127. The declaration about the change in his dream paralleled his later one to Fliess about abandoning the seduction theory. That letter, too, was written in September during an important transitional period in his development and sent to his closest friend as soon as he had unpacked from vacation. Then he had written Fliess, "And now I want to confide in you immediately the great secret that has been slowly dawning on me in the last few months" (Masson, op. cit., p. 264).

61. Bernays, op. cit., p. 145.

62. This is excerpted from a longer quote purported to be from a letter to Martha on August 16, 1882, at the beginning of their engagement (Jones, op. cit., pp. 178–179). There is no letter from August 16 in Ernst Freud's *Letters of Sigmund Freud* or in the German *Sigmund Freud: Briefe 1873–1939,* edited by Ernst and Lucie Freud. Nor can I find this passage in the letters adjacent to August 16 or elsewhere in these volumes. Gay reprints the same quote and gives only the aforementioned Jones citation for it.

63. Without the concept of the dream — its origins, evolution, and on-going developmental significance — McGrath (*Freud's Discovery of Psycho-*

*analysis*) see Freud's fantasy of becoming a famous doctor as a regressive withdrawal from the competitive world of Viennese science to the "safety" of practical aims.

64. Boehlich, *The Letters of Sigmund Freud to Eduard Silberstein*, pp. 123, 127. Freud characterized both nieces—19-year-old Pauline and 17-year-old Bertha—by these adjectives.

65. Ibid., p. 129, and McGrath, *Freud's Discovery of Psychoanalysis*, pp. 133, 149.

66. S. Freud, "Screen Memories," *SE*, vol. 3, entire essay and p. 314 in particular.

67. Boehlich, *The Letters of Sigmund Freud to Eduard Silberstein*, p. 127.

68. Ibid, pp. xx–xi, 138.

69. Ibid., pp. 134–138.

70. Ibid., p. 188.

71. Ibid., p. 138.

72. Boehlich's conclusion that Freud pretended that Gisela had married in a desperate attempt to bury the ghost seems less plausible that the supposition that Freud's informant had simply been in error.

73. Jones, op. cit., vol. 1, p. 33 n. e.

74. Boehlich, *The Letters of Sigmund Freud to Eduard Silberstein*, p. 149.

75. Bernfeld, "Freud's Scientific Beginnings," p. 167.

76. Boehlich, *The Letters of Sigmund Freud to Eduard Silberstein*, p. 151.

77. The German reads "*Von dem Ausflug muß ich Dir mehr erzahlen, denn es hat mich manches besonders beruhrt*" (Schröter, op. cit., p. 175). Boehlich translated this as "I must tell you more about that excursion because I was strangely affected by several things" (*The Letters of Sigmund Freud to Eduard Silberstein*, pp. 151–152). "Deeply impressed or especially touched" seems more faithful.

78. Ibid., p. 153.

79. Ibid.

80. Ibid., p. 155.

81. Ibid., p. 156 n. 1, p. 157.

82. See ibid., letter of August 15, 1877, p. 165.

83. Ibid., p. 166.

84. Ibid., p. 167.

85. Ibid., p. 166.

## Chapter Five

1. Siegfried Bernfeld, "Freud's Scientific Beginnings," p. 171.

2. Ibid., p. 175.

3. Ibid., p. 170.

4. McGrath, *Freud's Discovery of Psychoanalysis,* p. 137.

5. Jones, op. cit., vol. 1, p. 44.

6. S. Freud. *The Interpretation of Dreams, SE*, vol. 5, p. 422.

7. Gay, op. cit., p. 47.

8. When his son died in 1873, Brücke had his pictures removed, forbade his family to mention his son's name, and redoubled his dedication to science. Whether this evidences an absence or a superfluity of feeling is a matter of interpretation. That the latter might have been the case is suggested by the enduring loyalty of his students.

9. Gay, op. cit., p. 34.

10. S. Freud, *An Autobiographical Study, SE*, vol. 20, pp. 9–10.

11. Jones, op. cit., vol. 1, p. 40.

12. Anna wrote that when Freud returned from visiting his half brothers in Manchester with the intention of becoming a practicing physician, Jacob demurred on the grounds that his son's sensibility was too tender for clinical work. Freud himself at one point jocularly announced to Silberstein that he has decided to cut up animals instead of people in what may have been a first step toward deciding to study tissue slides instead of cutting up anything alive (or recently so). In regard to Freud's sensitivity, Emma Eckstein's bloody operation comes to mind, an operation during which Freud had to leave to room to keep from fainting. See Chapter Four n. 61, this book, and Clark, op. cit., p. 42.

13. Joan Riviere, "A Character Trait of Freud's," p. 355.

14. Boehlich, *The Letters of Sigmund Freud to Eduard Silberstein*, p. 169.

15. Bernfeld, "Freud's Scientific Beginnings."

16. Fleischl-Marxow was born in 1846. Ten years older than Freud, he would have been about 30 when Sigmund Freud joined the laboratory.

17. When several years later Freud showed him his new method for preparing brain slides. Fleischl-Marxow fairly danced with joy and conjured up a scheme whereby he could support Freud while Freud exploited his new discovery.

18. Boehlich, *The Letters of Sigmund Freud to Eduard Silberstein*, pp. 171–172.

19. Masson, op. cit., p. 71 n. 1.

20. Ibid., p. 70.

21. E. Freud, *The Letters of Sigmund Freud*, p. 11.

22. Bernfeld, *Sigmund Freud, M.D., 1882–1885*, p. 206.

23. Masson, op. cit., p. 75 n. 2.

24. See Erik H. Erikson's *Childhood and Society* and his *Gandhi's Truth*. See also my "Samuel Johnson's Breakdown and Recovery in Middle Age."

25. Boehlich, *The Letters of Sigmund Freud to Eduard Silberstein*, pp. 171–172.

26. Bernfeld, "Freud's Scientific Beginnings," pp. 176–177.

27. Boehlich, *The Letters of Sigmund Freud to Eduard Silberstein*, p. 169.

28. See Frank Sulloway, *Freud: Biologist of the Mind*, p. 536. Freud's five scientific papers are as follows: "Über den Ursprung der hinteren Nervenwurzeln im Rückenmark von Ammocoetes (Petromyzon Planeri) [On the

Origin of the Posterior Nerve Roots in the Spinal Cord of the Ammocoetes]"
(1877); "Beobachtungen über Gestaltung und feineren Bau der als Hoden
beschriebenen Lappenorgane des Aals [Observations on the Formation and
the Fine Structure of the Lobes Described as the Testicles of the Eel]" (1877);
"Über Spinalganglien und Rückenmark des Petromyzon [About the Spinal
Ganglia and Spinal Cord of the Petromyzon]" (1878); "Notiz über eine
Methode zur anatomischen Präparation des Nervensystems [Comments About
a Method for the Anatomical Preparation of the Nervous System]" (1879);
"Über den Bau der Nervenfasern und Nervenzellen beim Flusskrebs [About
the Structure of Nerve Tracts and Neurons in the Crayfish]" (1882).

29. Bernfeld, "Freud's Scientific Beginnings," pp. 167–168, 177.

30. Wilhelm Knöpfmacher. See E. Freud, *The Letters of Sigmund Freud*,
p. 6.

31. Boehlich, *The Letters of Sigmund Freud to Eduard Silberstein*, p.
172.

32. Boehlich, "Sigmund Freud, M.D., 1882–1885," p. 215.

33. Bernfeld, "Freud's Scientific Beginnings," p. 179 n. 23.

34. Ibid., p. 182.

35. Bernfeld, "Sigmund Freud, M.D., 1882–1885," p. 214.

36. Bernfeld, "Freud's Scientific Beginnings," p. 178 n. 2.

37. Bernfeld, "Sigmund Freud, M.D., 1882–1885," p. 206.

38. Ernst Freud and Lucie Freud, op. cit., pp. 15–16.

39. Ibid., pp. 16–17.

40. Boehlich, *The Letters of Sigmund Freud to Eduard Silberstein*, p.
178.

41. He had been ready in January, but the requisite examiners could not
be gathered.

42. Bernfeld, "Sigmund Freud, M.D., 1882–1885," p. 206.

43. Jones, op. cit., vol. 1, pp. 99, 113.

44. Gay, op. cit., p. 41.

45. Sigmund Freud, " 'Civilized' Sexual Morality," *SE*, vol. 9, pp.
194–196.

46. Gay, op. cit., p. 37.

47. Jones, op. cit., vol. 1, pp. 103–104.

48. Rosa was born March 21, 1860, Martha Bernays on July 26, 1861.

49. Jones, op. cit., vol. 1, pp. 103–104.

50. E. Freud, *The Letters of Sigmund Freud*, p. 8.

51. Toward the end of their engagement, Freud imagined that he had
taken the initiative and that Martha had been reticent. See E. Freud, *The Letters of Sigmund Freud*, p. 153.

52. At least in photographs, Freud became handsome as he matured,
with his good looks reaching their fullest expression in his 50s.

53. E. Freud, *The Letters of Sigmund Freud*, p. 213 and n. 3.

54. Jones, op. cit., vol. 1, p. 110.

55. E. Freud, *The Letters of Sigmund Freud*, pp. 117–118.

56. Jones, op. cit., vol. 1, 114.

57. E. Freud, *The Letters of Sigmund Freud*, p. 86.

58. Ibid., p. 25; E. Freud and L. Freud, op. cit., p. 35.
59. E. Freud, *The Letters of Sigmund Freud*, p. 27. Although Freud liked Dickens, he criticized the mannerisms of his later work, including his portrayal of "flawless girls, selfless and good, so good that they are quite colorless." Jones, op. cit., vol. 1, p. 174.
60. E. Freud, *The Letters of Sigmund Freud*, pp. 29–30.
61. Ibid., p. 161.
62. Ibid., p. 197.
63. Jones, op. cit., vol. 1, p. 146.
64. E. Freud, *The Letters of Sigmund Freud*, p. 162.
65. Ibid., p. 197.
66. Jones, op. cit., vol. 1, p. 109.
67. Ibid., p. 111.
68. Ibid., p. 112.
69. Ibid., pp. 114–115.
70. Ibid., p. 115.
71. E. Freud, *The Letters of Sigmund Freud*, p. 23.
72. Jones, op. cit., vol. 1, p. 116.
73. Ibid.
74. Ibid., p. 117.
75. Ibid., p. 119. When Eli and Anna married in October 1883, Freud did not attend the ceremony. Ten years later, Eli and Anna Bernays emigrated to the United States, the enmity between the two men by then largely outgrown. The long-standing tension between Freud and his next (surviving) sibling, Anna, having been deepened, lingered until the end.
76. In his recent study of women, Levinson (*The Seasons of a Woman's Life*) has found that shifts in the priority of life structure components occur so commonly that he has come to call it "the age-26 shift"; personal communication.
77. Jones, op. cit., vol. 1, p. 59.
78. S. Freud, *An Autobiographical Study, SE*, vol. 20, p. 10.
79. Gay, op. cit., pp. 41–42.
80. Jones, op. cit., vol. 1, p. 64. As noted earlier, Jones thought the inhibition had to do with sadism. Freud, by contrast, thought that his sadism had been too weak to require the defense of reversing it into an interest in clinical care.
81. McGrath, *Freud's Discovery of Psychoanalysis*, p. 149.
82. Bernfeld, *Sigmund Freud, M.D., 1882–1885*, p. 209.
83. Clinics were teaching units consisting of a professor and the assistants he chose to help him. The terminology is the reverse of that used in American medical schools, where a department is a teaching unit and a clinic is a clinical unit.
84. Later that fall, Freud proposed to Martha that they make plans to immigrate to America. Jones, op. cit., vol. 1, pp. 179–180.
85. E. Freud, *The Letters of Sigmund Freud*, pp. 30–34.
86. Ibid., pp. 40–41.
87. Jones, op. cit., vol. 1, p. 224.

88. Though Breuer abandoned the case, his correspondence with a series of her doctors over the next several years makes it clear that his concern for her health continued. See Albrecht Hirschmuller, *The Life and Work of Josef Breuer*.

89. E. Freud, *The Letters of Sigmund Freud*, pp. 47–49.

90. Ibid., p. 56.

91. Ibid., pp. 67–68.

92. Professor Kufer was a professor of anatomy at the University of Vienna (ibid., p. 98 n. 1).

93. Ibid., pp. 98–99.

94. Sigmund Freud, "Die Struktur der Elemente des Nervensystems [The Structure of the Elements of the Nervous System]."

95. E. Freud, *The Letters of Sigmund Freud*, p. 107.

96. Sigmund Freud, "Ein Fall von Hirnblutung mit indirekten basalen Herdsymptomen bei Skorbut [A Case of Cerebral Hemorrhage with Indirect Basal Foci in Scurvy]." E. Freud, *The Letters of Sigmund Freud*, p. 91 n. 4.

97. E. Freud, *The Letters of Sigmund Freud*, p. 92.

98. Ibid., p. 94.

99. Ibid., p. 97.

100. Ibid., p. 98.

101. Bernfeld, *Sigmund Freud, M.D., 1882–1885*, pp. 214–215.

102. E. Freud, *The Letters of Sigmund Freud*, p. 111.

103. Ibid., pp. 101–103.

104. Ibid., p. 124 and n. 1.

105. Ibid., p. 118.

106. Jones, op. cit., vol. 1, p. 69.

107. E. Freud, *The Letters of Sigmund Freud*, pp. 121, 124, 132.

108. Ibid., p. 120.

109. Ibid., p. 107.

110. F. Sulloway, op. cit., p. 35.

111. Sigmund Freud, "Über Coca," and "Ein Fall von Muskelatrophie mit ausgebreiteten Sensibilitätsstörungen (Syringomyuelie) [A Case of Muscular Atrophy with Widespread Disturbances of Sensation]." Freud published a second paper on cocaine the following year: "Über die Allgemeinwirkung des Cocains [On the General Effect of Cocaine]." E. Freud, *The Letters of Sigmund Freud*, p. 138 n. 1.

112. Jones, op. cit., vol. 1, p. 79.

113. Sigmund Freud, "Bemerkungen über Cocainsucht und Cocainfurcht [Comments on Cocaine Addiction and Cocaine Fear]." See Jones, op. cit., vol. 1, pp. 94–96.

114. S. Freud, *An Autobiographical Study, SE,* vol. 20, pp. 14–15.

115. Jones, op. cit., vol. 1, p. 81.

116. Ibid., p. 91.

117. E. Freud, *The Letters of Sigmund Freud,* pp. 126–127. Also, see p. 135.

118. Ibid., p. 133.

119. S. Freud, *An Autobiographical Study, SE,* vol. 20, pp. 10–11.
120. E. Freud, *The Letters of Sigmund Freud,* p. 74.
121. Ibid., p. 89.
122. Ibid., p. 105.
123. Ibid., pp. 134–135.
124. Gay, op. cit., p. 36.
125. See S. Freud, *An Autobiographical Study, SE,* vol. 20, and Bernfeld, *Sigmund Freud, M.D., 1882–1885.*
126. E. Freud, *The Letters of Sigmund Freud,* p. 139.
127. Ibid., p. 140.
128. Ibid.


## Chapter Six

1. Bernfeld, *Sigmund Freud, M.D., 1882–1885,* pp. 212–213.
2. E. Freud, *The Letters of Sigmund Freud,* p. 144. See Jones, op. cit., vol. 1, p. 60.
3. See Sulloway, op. cit., and McGrath, *Freud's Discovery of Psychoanalysis.*
4. S. Freud, *An Autobiographical Study, SE,* vol. 20, p. 11.
5. Ibid., p. 12.
6. July 18 and September 5, 1885, respectively.
7. E. Freud, *The Letters of Sigmund Freud,* p. 139.
8. Ibid., p. 147.
9. Ibid., p. 154.
10. Ibid., p. 158.
11. Sigmund Freud, "Charcot," *SE,* vol. 3, p. 19.
12. Charcot's notion of a purely psychological mechanism was taken up by his pupil Janet and later by Breuer in Vienna. Ibid., pp. 22–23.
13. Gay, op. cit., p. 47.
14. E. Freud, *The Letters of Sigmund Freud,* p. 172.
15. Pierre Marie was only three years older than Freud. He would later become Charcot's successor at the Salpêtrière. E. Freud, *The Letters of Sigmund Freud,* p. 175.
16. Ibid., pp. 175–176.
17. Ibid., p. 175.
18. Ibid., p. 176.
19. E. Freud, *The Letters of Sigmund Freud,* p. 185.
20. E. Freud, *The Letters of Sigmund Freud,* pp. 184–185.
21. E. Freud and L. Freud, op. cit., p. 228.
22. S. Freud, "Charcot," *SE,* vol. 3, pp. 17–18.
23. Ibid., p. 13.
24. E. Freud, *The Letters of Sigmund Freud,* p. 185.
25. Ibid., p. 183; Gay, op. cit., p. 48. Freud did manage to publish a paper on brain anatomy with Darkschewitsch, an old Russian friend from Vienna whom he found working at Charcot's hospital, but these were data that

had been in his possession for some time and in which he no longer had great interest. A major part of the motivation for publishing the paper now was the competitive pleasure of beating a rival into print. The two old friends put their paper together in a matter of days. See E. Freud, *The Letters of Sigmund Freud*, pp. 191–192.

26. E. Freud, *The Letters of Sigmund Freud*, p. 185.

27. S. Freud, *An Autobiographical Study, SE*, vol. 20, pp. 20–21.

28. See Stephen Hobbs, *Male Mentor Relationships*, on how such relationships typically begin with a period of courting inaugurated by a gift from the aspiring protégé.

29. E. Freud, *The Letters of Sigmund Freud*, p. 190.

30. Ibid., p. 194.

31. Ibid.

32. Ibid., pp. 195–196.

33. Ibid., p. 196.

34. Ibid., p. 199.

35. Ibid., p. 201.

36. Ibid., pp. 202–203.

37. Ibid., p. 203.

38. Ibid.

39. Ibid.

40. Ibid., p. 206. If this great success required cocaine, as had the previous failure, Freud made no mention of it to Martha.

41. Ibid., p. 208.

42. Ibid., p. 209.

43. E. Freud and L. Freud, op. cit., p. 217.

44. E. Freud, *The Letters of Sigmund Freud*, p. 212.

45. Ibid., p. 213.

46. Ibid., p. 214.

47. Gay, op. cit., p. 53.

48. E. Freud, *The Letters of Sigmund Freud*, pp. 215–216.

49. S. Freud, *An Autobiographical Study, SE*, vol. 20, p. 20.

50. Ibid., p. 21.

51. E. Freud, *The Letters of Sigmund Freud*, pp. 412–413.

52. J. Breuer and S. Freud, *Studies on Hysteria, SE*, vol. 2, p. 40, pp. 40–41 n. 1. Hirschmüller, op. cit., p. 130.

53. Consider the modern preoccupation with object relations and the development of the self in infancy.

54. E. Freud, *The Letters of Sigmund Freud*, p. 218.

55. The italics are in Jones, op. cit., vol. 1, pp. 147–148. Presumably, these were words that Emmeline Bernays had underlined in her letter.

56. Clark, op. cit., p. 89.

57. Although it is English to believe in the possibility of a seamless domestic tranquility and to overlook the fact that this hardly ever occurs, this is also an example of the remarkable manner in which a psychological attitude can suddenly disappear when it comes to writing about the master psychologist himself. Jones, op. cit., vol. 1, p. 151.

58. E. Freud and L. Freud, op. cit., p. 228.

59. Ibid.

60. S. Freud, "Preface to the Translation of Bernheim's *Suggestion*," *SE*, vol. 1, p. 75.

61. Hirschmüller has shown that Breuer did not leave the field of nervous disorders entirely after 1882. He remained active as a consultant, diagnostician, and practioner of the more conventional therapies. What he did abandon was the cathartic method, inevitably pervaded by transference and countertransference, that had evolved empirically between himself and Anna O. Put simply, he ceased trying to plumb the depths. See Hirschmüller, op. cit., pp. 136–145.

62. Sigmund Freud, "Observation of a Severe Case of Hemi-Anaesthesia in a Hysterical Male," *SE*, vol. 1.

63. S. Freud, *An Autobiographical Study, SE*, pp. 15–16.

64. E. Freud and L. Freud, op. cit., p. 230.

65. Ibid., pp. 224–226.

66. E. Freud, *The Letters of Sigmund Freud*, p. 224.

67. Masson, op. cit., pp. 16–17.

68. Ibid, pp. 21–22.

69. Ibid., p. 22, and pp. 22–23 n. 3. The article appears as "Some Points for a Comparative Study of Organic and Hysterical Motor Paralyses" in *SE*, vol. 1.

70. Freud had reviewed Forel's book on hypnotism in 1889: Sigmund Freud, "Review of August Forel's *Hypnotism*," *SE*, vol. 1.

71. Peter Swales discovered "Cäcilie M's" identity, and most of the following biographical details are drawn from his research. See P. Swales, "Freud, His Teacher, and the Birth of Psychoanalysis." Breuer and Freud considered von Lieben a hysteric like Anna O., whereas a contemporary clinician would see both women, as does Swales, as having borderline psychotic personalities.

72. With von Lieben and Frau Emmy von N. (Fanny Moser), the widow of a great industrialist, Freud had two of the wealthiest women in Europe in treatment by 1889.

73. J. Breuer and S. Freud, *Studies in Hysteria, SE*, vol. 2, p. 178.

74. Ibid., p. 181 n. 1.

75. Ibid., pp. 179–180.

76. Swales, op. cit., p. 42.

77. S. Freud, *Studies on Hysteria, SE*, vol. 2, p. 48. Frau Emmy von N.'s treatment occurred discontinuously over a period of two years, and although a cure was not achieved, the treatment was more successful than von Lieben's; see ibid., p. 48 n. 1 and p. 84.

78. Schröter, op. cit., p. 243. See Swales, op. cit., p. 12.

79. S. Freud, "On the Psychical Mechanism of Hysterical Phenomena," *SE*, vol. 2. See Swales, op. cit., pp. 12–13, p. 59.

80. Ibid., pp. 19–20, p. 59 n. 2.

81. S. Freud, *An Autobiographical Study, SE*, vol. 20, p. 17.

82. Masson, op. cit., p. 61, p. 62 n. 7.

83. Swales, op. cit., p. 38.

84. S. Freud, *An Autobiographical Study, SE*, vol. 20, p. 21.

85. Ibid.

86. J. Breuer and S. Freud, *Studies on Hysteria, SE*, vol. 2, p. 48.

87. It is remarkable how many of the critical elements of analytic treatment Freud already had in hand by his early to mid-30s, some 10 years before his first great psychoanalytical work, *The Interpretation of Dreams:* (1) the idea that the necessary thoughts are those that come unbidden by the patient—they are *Einfalle*—when the analyst asks the patient to speak without censoring; (2) the notion that the relevant thoughts must always come in this way, that a blank mind is an impossibility; (3) the belief that the patient's critical faculty—or resistance—intervenes to dismiss the unbidden thought or image as incredible, irrelevant, or insignificant; and (4) the insight about resistance—expressed 20 years later in "Remembering, Repeating, and Working-Through"—namely, that having recovered a pathogenic memory, patients often dismiss it as something they have always known. See J. Breuer and S. Freud, *Studies on Hysteria, SE*, vol. 2, pp. 110–111 and S. Freud, "Remembering, Repeating, and Working-Through," *SE*, vol. 12, p. 148.

88. J. Breuer and S. Freud, *Studies on Hysteria, SE*, vol. 2, p. 110.

89. Freud had met Breuer at least as early as 1877 (and posssibly the year before that), but it was not until Freud left Brücke's physiology laboratory for clinical work at Vienna General Hospital in 1882 that the relationship became close. See Hirschmüller, op. cit., p. 133.

90. Ibid., p. 130.

## Chapter Seven

1. Masson, op. cit., p. 27.

2. Ibid.

3. Ibid.

4. Sigmund Freud, *Project for a Scientific Psychology, SE*, vol. 1., pp. 283–387.

5. We have found this to be a regularly occurring phase in the late 30s. Levinson calls it Becoming One's Own Man or Becoming One's Own Woman. The developmental task is to bring to fruition the culminating era of early adulthood by realizing one's youthful dream and establishing the basis for a claim to membership in the leadership group of the tribe. During this phase the individual's attempts to realize the dream take place under the lengthening shadow of the mid-life transition; thus the connotation of explosive velocity—one must hurry, time is running out.

6. It is interesting that Jones believed that Freud underwent a personality change at 37, despite the fact that there was no place in psychoanalytic theory for such a change—except in the instance of personality decompensation, and he was certainly not suggesting the latter. According to Jones, this personality change was one of several in Freud's adult life. Jones, op. cit., vol. 1, p. 242.

7. S. Freud, "Charcot," *SE,* vol. 3.

8. It was exceeded at 43, when the compendious *Interpretation of Dreams* was published, and at 49. See George F. Mahl, "Freud, Father and Mother: Quantitative Aspects," pp. 101–102.

9. Obscurities in the correspondence make it impossible to arrive at a precise number of visits between Freud and Fliess. It appears *certain* from the letters that the two men met in Salzberg during the summer of 1890 (see Masson, op. cit., letter from Freud to Fliess—abbreviated in the rest of this paragraph as "F/F"—of 8/11/90; Jones, op. cit., vol. 1, p. 305; Clark, op. cit., p. 96); in June of 1892 (F/F, 5/25/92 and 6/28/92); in the spring of 1893 (F/F, p. 46 n.1); in Munich in August of 1894 (F/F, 8/7/94 and 8/23/94); in February of 1895 (F/F, 1/24/95 and 3/4/95); in Berlin in the late summer of 1895 (F/F, 8/28/95 and 9/15/95), in Dresden in April of 1896 (F/F, 4/2/96 and 5/30/96); in August of 1896 (F/F, 8/17/96 and 8/29/96); in Nuremberg in April of 1897 (F/F, 4/6/97, 5/2/97, and 6/18/97); in Berlin in September of 1897 (F/F, 9/21/97 and 9/27/97); in Breslau in December of 1897 (F/F, 12/22/97 and 12/29/97); in July of 1898 (F/F, 7/30/98 and Jones, op. cit., p. 301); in Vienna at the end of December 1898 or the very beginning of January 1889 (F/F, 12/20/98 and 1/3/99); in Innsbruck in April of 1899 (F/F, 3/27/99 and Jones, op. cit., vol. 1, p. 301); in Vienna in late November or early December 1899 (F/F, 12/9/99); and in Achensee, near Innsbruck, in August 1900 for the last time (F/F, 7/10/00 and 9/14/00).

In addition, it seems probable that the friends also met in Vienna in September of 1891 (F/F, 9/11/91) and in late December 1894 or early January 1895 (F/F, 12/17/94 and 1/24/95).

There is some reason to believe that Freud and Fliess also met in August of 1892 (F/F, 7/12/92); in September of 1893 (F/F, 8/20/93); in late May or early June of 1898 (F/F, 5/18/98 and 5/24/98); in September of 1898 (F/F, 9/22/98 and 12/20/98); and a few other times as well.

10. A wiser Freud abandoned the attempt entirely at age 49, although he continued to argue for the necessity of an integrated psychophysiological conception of the mind.

11. Martin Gardner has shown that the formula Fleiss employed for juggling the numbers 23 and 28 is capable of producing any positive integer; see his article "Freud's Friend Wilhelm Fliess and His Theory of Male and Female Life Cycles."

12. Masson, op. cit., p. 394.

13. Fliess thought this obtained even on the level of the individual cell.

14. Our studies suggest that one loses the capacity to be a protégé by the end of early adulthood, at about 45. See Levinson et al., *The Season's of a Man's Life.*

15. Masson, op. cit., p. 28.

16. E. Freud, *The Letters of Sigmund Freud,* p. 229.

17. Masson, op. cit., p. 31.

18. Sigmund Freud, *On Aphasia.* See E. Stengel, "A Re-Evaluation of Freud's Book On Aphasia: Its Significance for Psycho-Analysis."

19.  Simund Freud, "A Case of Successful Treatment by Hypnotism," *SE*, vol. 1. See Jones, op. cit., vol. 1, p. 240.

20.  As early as 1891 Freud had written of a widening gap between himself and Breuer, a gap he was trying unsuccessfully to bridge. E. Freud, *The Letters of Sigmund Freud*, p. 229.

21.  Jones, op. cit., vol. 1, p. 250.

22.  Swales, op. cit., p. 9.

23.  Masson, op. cit., p. 32.

24.  Ibid., p. 36.

25.  Hirschmüller, op. cit., pp. 164–169.

26.  Freud wrote Fliess announcing the collaboration with Breuer on June 28, 1892. Freud sent Fliess the first of what would be an extended series of theoretical drafts on neurosis, "Draft A," on December 18, 1892. The first publication of *Studies on Hysteria* occurred in 1895. See Masson, op. cit., p. 64 and n. 2.

27.  The last reference to the *Studies on Hysteria* concerned the galley proofs on April 20, 1895. The book was published soon after, but Freud made no mention of it to Fliess again that year.

28.  Masson, op. cit., p. 171 and nn. 1 and 2; p. 184 and n. 1. Very brief and preliminary accounts appeared the previous year. See Masson, op. cit., p. 64 n. 2.

29.  The Marlborough song was a 17th-century hunting ballad later mistakenly used to elegize the still-living General Marlborough. See Masson, op. cit., pp. 53–55, p. 55 n. 4.

30.  In Freud's account in the *Studies on Hysteria*, the identity of the girl's seducer is disguised. After the death of her parents Freud wrote that it had actually been the father. See Swales, "Freud, Katharina, and the First 'Wild Analysis.' "

31.  J. Breuer and S. Freud, *Studies on Hysteria, SE,* vol. 2, p. 131.

32.  Masson, op. cit., p. 56.

33.  Ibid., p. 59.

34.  Ibid., p. 67.

35.  Ibid., p. 65 and n. 1.

36.  Ibid., p. 69.

37.  Ibid., p. 74. Appended to this letter was a draft of Freud's "Etiology and Theory of the Major Neuroses" and apparently (the dating of this document is difficult) a draft of his theory of the sexual origin of anxiety, that is, that anxiety results from the various forms of abstinence since each of these leads to an accumulation of physical, sexual tension.

38.  Ibid., p. 85.

39.  Ibid., p. 86.

40.  Ibid., p. 84.

41.  Ibid., p. 86.

42.  Eckstein is the main subject of the "Irma" dream, which Freud reported and analyzed in *The Interpretation of Dreams*.

43.  Masson, op. cit., p. 107.

44.  Schur, op. cit., p. 80.

45. Hirschmüller, op. cit., p. 144.
46. Masson, op. cit., p. 114.
47. Ibid., p. 127.
48. Jones, op. cit., vol. 1, p. 242.
49. Masson, op. cit., p. 129.
50. Sigmund Freud, "Sexuality in the Aetiology of the Neuroses," *SE*, vol. 3, pp. 263–285.
51. His name appears without consequence in the letters of July 13 and August 16, 1895.
52. See my "Freud's Mid-Life Crisis." Enlightenment imagery of light and darkness is also common, I have not noticed meaningful fluctuations in this imagery, but there may be some.
53. Freud also wrote that he has "feeling I to IIa. I need a lot of cocaine." Though the emphasis in this letter and elsewhere is on Freud's dependence on cigar smoking for a sense of well-being and creative endurance, the elliptical reference to cocaine raises the question of the relationship between Freud's recurrent expansiveness during these years and his cocaine use. This is tricky for us to evaluate. The anti-drug campaign in the United States is so extensive and is carried out with such religious zeal that it is hard to separate out realistic dangers and solutions from hysteria and propaganda. (For an early example of the latter, applied to Freud, see Thornton's *The Freudian Fallacy*.) Correlatively, we are in a period of panbiologism, which leads us to assume that causality always runs from soma to psyche, to assume, for example, that Freud was feeling expansive not because he was becoming his own man but because he was using cocaine. My own view is that concrete behaviors neither cause nor are caused by developmental periods, but rather that the meaning of behavior and events is strongly shaped by the developmental period in which they occur. The 29-year-old Freud had needed cocaine to give himself confidence in order to attend his first soirée at Charcot's home; now he used it to help fuel his flight to the heavens. Cocaine may have been jet fuel, but Freud was flying anyway. There is no evidence of cocaine use or withdrawal after Freud's "becoming his own man" phase ended. During the years between 36 and 45, Freud was telling Fliess virtually everything of personal significance about himself; if he had been using cocaine habitually, we would know that from the letters. After all, Fliess prescribed it as part of his nasal treatments.
54. Masson, op. cit., p. 133.
55. S. Freud, *The Interpretation of Dreams, SE*, vol. 4, p. 107.
56. Schur, op. cit., p. 87.
57. Ibid.
58. Masson, op. cit., pp. 134–135.
59. Ibid., p. 136.
60. Ibid., p. 144.
61. Ibid., p. 145.
62. Ibid., pp. 146–147.
63. Ibid., pp. 147–148.
64. Ibid., p. 149.

65. Schröter, op. cit., p. 154. Masson introduces a neck into the sentence, which is not in the German and which would constitute a pun or parapraxis. See Masson, op. cit., p. 150.

66. Masson, op. cit., pp. 150–151.

67. Ibid., p. 151.

68. Ibid., p. 159.

69. Note that the familial role of the seducer is not identified and has not yet been hypnothesized by Freud to be parental. See Mahl, "Explosion of Discoveries and Concepts: The Freud–Fliess Letters," p. 27.

70. Masson, op. cit., p. 171 n. 2.

71. Ibid., p. 172.

72. Ibid., p. 175.

73. Ibid., p. 180.

74. Ibid., pp. 183–184.

75. Ibid., p. 185.

## Chapter Eight

1. Sigmund Freud, "Zur Ätiologie der Hysterie," p. 430.

2. Sigmund Freud, "The Aetiology of Hysteria," SE, vol. 3, p. 193.

3. Ibid., p. 199.

4. S. Freud, "Zur Ätiologie der Hysterie," p. 439.

5. Masson, op. cit., p. 184.

6. Ibid., p. 190. See S. Freud, "The Aetiology of Hysteria," SE, vol. 3, pp. 189–221. The seduction theory had also appeared in print two weeks earlier in an article written for the Neurologisches Zentralblatt entitled "Further Remarks on the Neuro-Psychoses of Defence." Here for the first time in German the word psycho-analysis appeared. A French version had appeared at the end of March.

7. Gay, op. cit., p. 93.

8. Sigmund Freud, History of the Psycho-Analytic Movement, SE., vol. 14, p. 22.

9. Jeffrey Masson, The Assault on Truth, p. 110.

10. S. Freud, "The Aetiology of Hysteria," SE, vol. 3, pp. 192–193.

11. Sigmund Freud, "Futher Remarks on the Neuro-psychoses of Defence," SE, vol. 3, p. 164.

12. Masson, The Complete Letters of Sigmund Freud to Wilhelm Fliess (thereafter cited as Freud–Fliess), p. 164. Reembracing the theory after having abandoned it two months earlier, Freud wrote Fliess on November 14, 1897: "A release of sexuality (as you know, I have in mind a secretion which is rightly felt as the internal state of the libido) comes about, then . . . not only (1) through a peripheral stimulus upon the sexual organs, or (2) through the internal excitations arising from those organs, but also (3) from ideas — that is, from memory traces — therefore also by the path of deferred action. (You are already familiar with this line of thought. If a child's genitals have been irritated by someone, years afterward the memory of this will produce

by deferred action a release of sexuality far stronger at the time, because the decisive apparatus and the quota of secretion have increased in the meantime.)"

13. Ibid., p. 169.

14. Ibid., p. 171 n. 4.

15. In German, *Gesellschaft deutscher Naturforscher und Arzte.*

16. Ibid., pp. 186–187, p. 187 n. 1.

17. Mahl, in "Explosion of Discoveries and Concepts: The Freud–Fliess Letters," states his belief that Freud carried out his self-analysis throughout his life. He did so systematically during the period from August 1897 to February 1899, that is, from age 41¼ to 42¾.

18. Schröter, op. cit., p. 205. The German is "*Sonst nichts Neues und dringendes Bedurfnis nach Einleitung eines befruchtenden Stromes von andersher.*" Masson mistranslated "*befruchtenden Stromes*" as "stimulating current," inadvertently making the imagery electrical rather than procreative. Cf. Masson, *Freud–Fliess,* p. 195.

19. Masson, *Freud–Fliess,* pp. 195, 197.

20. Ibid., pp. 198, 199.

21. Ibid., p. 201.

22. When three years later Freud came to publish this dream in *The Interpretation of Dreams,* it had undergone several changes: Its occurrence had been moved backward to the night *before* the funeral (hence, there could not have been any reference to actually having been late for the event); the sign was changed to read:

the<br>"You are requested to close     eye(s)."<br>an

and, conformance with Jacob's preferences was given as the justification for the modest funeral arrangements (*SE,* vol. 4, pp. 317–318).

23. In German, *Die Beziehungen zwischen Nase und weiblichen Geschlechtsorganen: In ihrer biologischen Bedeutung dargestellt.*

24. Masson, *Freud–Fliess,* pp. 207–215, especially pp. 210–211.

25. The world *period* is represented by the symbol *p.*

26. Masson, *Freud–Fliess,* p. 215.

27. Ibid., 228.

28. The earliest unmistakable reference to Herr E. occured in Freud's letter to Fliess of January 24, 1897. Mahl believes that an earlier one may have appeared in Freud's letter to his friend on October 31, 1895. See his "Explosion of Discoveries and Concepts: The Freud–Fliess Letters," pp. 46–47. Two unnamed patients were mentioned in that letter, and Schröter (op. cit., p. 152) thinks that the other one may have been E.

29. Mass, *Freud–Fliess,* p. 228.

30. Ibid., pp. 231–232 n. 3.

31. Ibid., p. 236.

32. Ibid., p. 232.

33. Ibid., p. 465.

34. Ibid., p. 243. See also Schröter, op. cit., p. 258. In ordinary usage, a *Schub* is a push or thrust. As we have noted, Freud's method of doing creative work, and the imagery he used to characterize the process, was becoming increasingly feminine. During these next couple of years of intense intellectual invention, he would frequently use the word *Schub* for the products of his unconscious creative activity and to describe the growth of his ideas in pregnancy and germination imagery.

35. Schröter, op. cit., p. 258 n. 4. There may have been an earlier one. In his letter to Fliess of March 7, 1896, Freud includes a list of things he is planning to bring to their next congress. Fifth, and first among the intellectual items, was "The dream analysis [*Die Traumanalyse*]." His first announcement in print concerning the dream book occurred in his paper "Sexuality in the Aetiology of the Neuroses," *SE*, vol. 3, p. 281, written in the winter of 1897–1898.

36. Masson, *Freud–Fliess*, p. 243.

37. Ibid., pp. 250–252.

38. Schröter, op. cit., p. 271. The German reads "*Ich habe übrigens irgendetwas Neurotisches durchgemacht, komische Zustände, die dem Bewußtsein nicht faßbar sind. Dämmergedanken, Schleierzweifel, kaum hie und da ein Lichtstrahl.*" See Masson, *Freud–Fliess*, p. 254.

39. Masson, *Freud–Fliess*, p. 255.

40. Schröter, op. cit., p. 275. The German reads "(*17. Juli weibliche Menstruation in höchster Ausbildung, mit blutiger Nasensekretion ganz vereinzelt vor und nach*)."

41. Ibid., 281. The German reads, "*Meine kleine, aber durch die Arbeit sehr gehobene Hysterie hat sich ein Stück weiter gelöst.*"

42. Masson, *Freud–Fliess*, p. 261.

43. Freud's railroad phobia may have begun during his engagement to Martha or, more likely, in the first years of their marriage. It was either cured or placed in remission apparently as part of the several gains resulting from Freud's developmental work during his mid-life transition. See Masson, op. cit., p. 392.

## Chapter Nine

1. See Chapter Seven, this book.

2. Masson, *Freud–Fliess*, pp. 285, 290.

3. Ibid., p. 266. Freud's estimation, at least initially, proved correct.

4. Masson, *Freud–Fliess*, pp. 266–267 n. 3.

5. The German reads "*Der Traum steht ganz sicher da. . . .* " Schröter, op. cit., p. 286.

6. Freud's self-analysis had also produced an insight about resistance: "My insight that the difficulties in treatment are due to the fact that in the end one is laying bare the patient's evil inclinations, his will to remain ill, is becoming stronger and clearer" (Masson, *Freud–Fliess*, p. 269). It is insufficiently understood that this early antipathy toward resistance *remained* charac-

teristic of Freud's attitude. By interpreting resistance in psychoanalysis, Freud meant unmasking for the patient the resistance that underlay some apparently innocuous behavior. Apprised of the truth, patients were then to summon the moral courage to redouble their analytic effort and overcome it. See my "A Social System Approach to the Psychoanalytic Treatment of Personality Disorders" and my "Free Association and the Division of Labor in Psychoanalytic Treatment," as well as Lohser and Newton's *Freud's Therapeutic Technique Revisted*.

7. Mahl points out that Freud first discovered it in one or more patients and that the patient E. was probably one such source. See his "Explosions of Discoveries and Concepts: The Freud–Fliess Letters," p. 46.

8. Masson, *Freud–Fliess*, p. 274.

9. The German verbs are "*zurückwirbelt*" and "*packt und zerrt*" (Schröter, op. cit., p. 295).

10. See n. 6, this chapter. Note again Freud's approach to resistance. It was his job to expose it, the patient's to overcome it.

11. Masson, *Freud–Fliess*, p. 277; see also pp. 275–278.

12. The German reads "*Ich werde mich zwingen, den Traum zu schreiben, und herauszukommen*" (Schröter, op. cit., p. 300).

13. Masson, *Freud–Fliess*, p. 284.

14. The German is "*Die neueste Ausgeburt meiner Denkarbeit*" (The newest evil birth of my mental labor) (Schröter, op. cit., p. 311).

15. Masson, *Freud–Fliess*, p. 273.

16. S. Freud, *The Interpretation of Dreams, SE*, vol. 5, p. 454.

17. The German is "*Bi–Bi tönt mir in den Ohren*" (Schröter, op. cit., p. 316).

18. Masson, *Freud–Fliess*, p. 290.

19. Ibid., pp. 291–292.

20. Ibid., p. 294.

21. Ibid., p. 299.

22. Ibid., p. 300.

23. Ibid., p. 302.

24. Ibid., p. 303. Here, Freud refers to his work as the "*Traumarbeit*" (Schröter, op. cit., p. 331). A few lines later he uses the term "*Traummaterial*"

25. Masson, *Freud–Fliess*, p. 305. Freud here refers to his work as a "*Traummanuskript*" (Schröter, op. cit., p. 332).

26. Masson, *Freud–Fliess*, pp. 306–307.

27. Schröter, op. cit., pp. 335, 340.

28. Ibid., pp. 308–309.

29. Masson, *Freud–Fliess*, p. 337. Apparently, there was an intervening congress in the summer, for in his December 20, 1998, letter Freud refers to three months of separation. While no clear mention of that congress is made in the letters, it might have occurred in July or in September. See Masson, *Freud–Fliess*, pp. 320–321, 326–327.

30. Ibid., p. 312. The German is "*ich bin ganz im Traum und darin ganz blöde*" (Schroter, op. cit., 341). As noted, Freud had now stopped referring to it as a book.

31. Masson, *Freud–Fliess*, p. 314.

32. Ibid., p. 316.

33. The July 30, 1898, letter in Schröter is written from Aussee and does not carry the additional Berggasse, Vienna, address as Masson's translation has it. See Schröter, op. cit., p. 350, and Masson, *Freud–Fliess*, p. 320.

34. Masson, *Freud–Fliess*, p. 324.

35. Ibid., p. 325.

36. He complained either in person or by letter; see n. 29, this chapter.

37. Masson, *Freud–Fliess*, p. 328.

38. Ibid., p. 330.

39. Ibid., p. 332 n. 1.

40. Ibid., p. 333.

41. Ibid., p. 335.

42. Ibid.

43. Ibid., p. 336.

44. Much of this analysis of the "Screen Memories" paper comes from the careful work of Mahl; see his "Explosion of Discoveries and Concepts: The Freud–Fliess Letters," especially pp. 50–53.

45. Masson, *Freud–Fliess*, p. 265.

46. See his Draft N appendix to the May 31, 1897, letter, ibid., p. 251.

47. Ibid., p. 340.

48. Ibid., p. 342.

49. Ibid., p. 344; see pp. 342–344.

50. Ibid., p. 345.

51. See Masson, *Freud–Fliess*, p. 348 n. 3, for an opposite explantion of what Freud meant by "fantasies."

52. Ibid., p. 347.

53. Ibid., p. 352.

54. Ibid., p. 353.

55. Ibid., p. 354.

56. Ibid., p. 358.

57. Ibid., p. 360.

58. Ibid.

59. Ibid., p. 361.

60. Schröter, op. cit., p. 399.

61. Masson, *Freud–Fliess*, p. 367.

62. Ibid., p. 373.

63. The German is "*Traumschrift*" (Schröter, op. cit., p. 410).

64. Instead of *Non vivit*. Thus, Freud had said, "He did not live," when he had intended to say, "He is not alive."

65. S. Freud, *The Interpretation of Dreams, SE*, vol. 5, p. 421.

66. S. Freud, *The Interpretation of Dreams, SE*, vol. 5, p. 422.

67. Ibid.

68. Masson, *Freud–Fliess*; see pp. 375, 376, 377.

## Chapter Ten

1. Gay, op. cit., pp. 3–4. Freud told Fliess on January 17, 1902, that he had found only two reviews of his book in professional journals and both has been negative (Masson, *Freud–Fliess*, p. 454).

2. S. Freud, *Three Essays on a Theory of Sexuality, SE*, vol. 7.

3. Masson, *Freud–Fliess*, p. 73.

4. Though neither provides a source for the date, both Clark and Gay give 1895 as the year Minna moved in to stay.

5. See Lisa Appignanesi and John Forester, *Freud's Women*.

6. Ibid., p. 457.

7. Ibid., p. 381.

8. Ibid., p. 382.

9. Ibid., p. 383.

10. Ibid., p. 389.

11. Masson, *Freud–Fliess*, p. 397. In translating this letter from the German, Masson mistakenly rendered the patient E.'s initial as F (see Masson, op. cit., p. 397). The German reads "*Bei E. ist wieder eine Verzögerung und dunklere Region, das Frühere bleibt aufrecht*" (Schröter, op. cit., p. 436).

12. The German reads "*so würdest Du für meine neurotischen Eigen-schwankungen wahrscheinlich viel Nachsicht haben, besonders wenn Du an die Lebenssorgen dabei nicht vergissest*" (Schröter, op. cit., p. 439). See Masson, *Freud–Fliess*, p. 399.

13. The German is "*Mein zweites Eisen im Feuer ist ja die Arbeit, die Aussicht irgendwo zu Ende zu kommen, viele Zweifel zu erledigen und dann zu wissen, was ich von der therapeutischen Chance zu halten habe*" (Schröter, op. cit., p. 442). Beginning the sentence with "For," as Masson does, obscures the fact that Freud is turning from his disappointment in science to the disappointment of his clinical ambitions.

14. The German is "*Ich fand auch bald, daß es unmöglich ist, die wirklich schwere Arbeit unter Verstimmung und lauernden Zweifeln fortzusetzen*" (Schröter, op. cit., p. 442).

15. The patient hanged herself in her hotel room on April 20. See Masson, *Freud–Fliess*, p. 411, p. 412 n. 6.

16. Ibid., p. 410.

17. Ibid., p. 415.

18. The German is "*Ich hab es endlich bezwungen*" (Schröter, op. cit., p. 455).

19. Masson, *Freud–Fliess*, p. 418. See also the letter of June 18, 1900, p. 418.

20. S. Freud, *The Psychopathology of Everyday Life, SE*, vol. 6, p. 146. A similar diagnostic error is reported on p. 165, though the date of the error is unclear.

21. Masson, *Freud–Fliess*, p. 424.

22. Ibid., p. 427. Freud refers to the promised essay in his letter to Fliess of February 1, 1900.

23. Ibid., p. 428.

24. Ibid., p. 430.

25. Ibid., p. 427. This is a metaphor that later critics of the case—
ignoring Freud's use of it to describe male and female patients in his correspondence with Fliess—have found sinister. See Decker, op. cit., p. 119.

26. Sigmund Freud, "Fragment of an Analysis of a Case of Hysteria,"
*SE*, vol. 7, p. 23.

27. Ibid., p. 118.

28. Ibid., p. 119.

29. Decker's otherwise fine historical work is perhaps the most recent
victimological study of Dora's failed treatment.

30. See Decker, op. cit., pp. 101–102.

31. Ibid., pp. 121–122.

32. Ibid., p. 122.

33. Masson, *Freud–Fliess*, p. 432.

34. Ibid., p. 433.

35. Ibid., p. 435.

36. Ibid., pp. 436–437.

37. The German reads "*Es ist alles in einer gewissen Dumpfheit geschrieb-
en*" (Schröter, op. cit., p. 480).

38. Masson, *Freud–Fliess*, p. 439. *The Psychopathology of Everyday
Life* was published in two parts in the July and August issues of *Monatsschrift
für Psychiatrie und Neurologie* in the year 1901.

39. Ibid., pp. 443–444.

40. Ibid., pp. 446–448. Freud said this to Marie Bonaparte as she
prevailed upon him to allow the letters to be saved. See Masson, ibid., p.
448 n. 1, and Gay, op. cit., p. 668.

41. Masson makes reference to an updated and unpublished paper in
which Fliess quotes a letter of his own to Freud wherein he dismissed Freud's
psychotherapeutic efforts as irrelevant. See Masson, *Freud–Fliess*, p. 459.


## Chapter Eleven

1. In German, *Der Ablauf des Lebens*.

2. Masson, *Freud–Fliess*, p. 450; see also p. 447.

3. Ibid., p. 453.

4. Ibid., p. 454.

5. Ibid., p. 455.

6. Ibid., p. 456.

7. Ibid., p. 457.

8. Ibid.

9. Ibid.

10. Ibid., p. 460.

11. Ibid., p. 461.

12. Ibid., p. 462.

13. This indicates that there had been correspondence from Freud in 1903, but this was subsequently lost or destroyed.

14. Masson, *Freud–Fliess*, p. 463.

15. Ibid., pp. 465–466.

16. S. Freud, *The Psychopathology of Everyday Life, SE*, vol. 6, pp. 143–144, p. 144 n. 1.

17. Jones, op. cit., pp. 7–10.

18. By 1908 the early happy atmosphere of inspired co-religionists had already given way to acrimony and bad-tempered careerist self-assertion. In 1908 Freud, at 52, commented ruefully to the Swiss psychiatrist Binswanger after a meeting of the Vienna Society during which his Viennese followers had failed to distinguish themselves in any way other than by their rivalrous asininity, "So, now you've seen the gang." Increasingly, Freud entrusted his hopes for the future of his ideas with foreigners, such as Binswanger, Abraham, and Jung.

19. Adapted from Mahl's "The Chronology of Freud's Writing His Psychological Works." Following Mahl, the ages given in this paragraph are the ages at which Freud completed the works, not necessarily when they were published.

20. Didier Anzieu, *Freud's Self-Analysis*, p. 117.

21. Ernst Freud and Lucie Freud, op. cit., p. 353.

# References

Acsádi, G., and J. Nemeskéri. *History of Human Life Span and Mortality.* Budapest: Akademiai, 1970.

Anzieu, Didier. *Freud's Self-Analysis.* Madison: International Universities Press, 1986.

Appignanesi, Lisa, and John Forester. *Freud's Women.* New York: Basic Books, 1992.

Ariès, Philippe. *Centuries of Childhood.* New York: Vintage Books, 1962.

Baldwin, James. Review of Elia Kazan's *The Arrangement. New York Review of Books,* 23 March 1967.

Barclay, James R. "Franz Brentano and Sigmund Freud." *Journal of Existentialism* (1964) 5: 1–36.

Blatt, David. "The Development of the Hero: Sigmund Freud and the Reformation of the Jewish Tradition." *Psychoanalysis and Contemporary Thought* (1989) 4: 639–703.

Bernays, Anna Freud. "My Brother, Sigmund Freud," in *Freud as We Knew Him,* ed. Hendrik Ruitenbeek. Detroit: Wayne State University Press, 1973.

Bernfeld, Siegfried. "An Unknown Autobiographical Fragment by Freud," *American Imago* (1946) 6: 3–19.

_____. "Freud's Scientific Beginnings," *American Imago* (1949) 6: 163–196.

_____. "Sigmund Freud, M.D., 1882–1885." *International Journal of Psycho-Analysis* (1951) 32: 204–217.

Boehlich, Walter. *Sigmund Freud Jugendbriefe an Eduard Silberstein 1871–1881.* Frankfurt am Main: S. Fischer, 1989.

_____. *The Letters of Sigmund Freud to Eduard Silberstein,* trans. Arnold J. Pomerans. Cambridge, MA: Harvard University Press, 1990.

Brentano, Franz. *Psychology from an Empirical Standpoint* (1873), trans. A. Rancurello, D. Terrell, and L. McAllister. New York: Humanities Press, 1973.

Breuer, Josef, and Sigmund Freud. *Studies on Hysteria* (1895), in *The Standard Edition of the Complete Psychological Works of Sigmund Freud,* vol. 2, ed. James Strachey. London: Hogarth Press, 1955.

Brill, A. *Fundamental Conceptions of Psychoanalysis.* New York: Harcourt Brace, 1921.

Bury, J. B. *The Idea of Progress.* London: Macmillan, 1921.

Capote, Truman. *Other Voices, Other Rooms.* New York: Random House, 1949.

Case, Laurie. *H. D. and Her Poetry: An Adult Developmental Study.* Unpublished doctoral dissertation, The Wright Institute, Berkeley, CA, 1989.

Clark, Ronald. *Freud: The Man and His Cause.* New York: Random House, 1980.

Darwin, Charles. *The Origin of Species* (1859). New York: Mentor Books, 1958.

Decker, Hannah. *Freud, Dora, and Vienna 1900.* New York: Free Press, 1991.

Diller, Jerry. *Freud's Jewish Identity.* Teaneck, NJ: Fairleigh Dickinson University Press, 1991.

Eissler, Kurt R. "Creativity and Adolescence: The Effect of Trauma on Freud's Adolescence." *Psychoanalytic Study of the Child* (1978) 33: 461–517.

Ellenberger, Henri. *The Discovery of the Unconscious.* New York: Basic Books, 1970.

Erikson, Erik H. *Childhood and Society.* New York: Norton, 1950.

_____. *Young Man Luther: A Study in Psychoanalysis and History.* New York: Norton, 1958.

_____. "The First Psychoanalyst," in *Insight and Responsibility.* New York: Norton, 1964.

_____. *Gandhi's Truth.* New York: Norton, 1969.

Fliess, Wilhelm. *Die Beziehungen zwischen Nase und weiblichen Geschlechtsorganen: In ihrer biologischen Bedeutung dargestellt.* Leipzig and Vienna: Franz Deuticke, 1897.

_____. *Der Ablauf des Lebens: Grundlegung zur exakten Biologie,* 2nd ed. Leipzig and Vienna: Franz Deuticke, 1923.

Forel, August. *Der Hypnotismus, seine Bedeutung und seine Handhabung, in kurzgefasster Darstellung.* Stuttgart: Ferdinand Enke, 1889.

Freud, Ernst (ed.). *The Letters of Sigmund Freud,* trans. Tania Stern and James Stern. New York: Basic Books, 1960.

_____. "Some Early Unpublished Letters of Freud," *International Journal of Psycho-Analysis* (1969) 50: 419–427.

_____. "Jugendbriefe Sigmund Freuds." *Psyche* (1970), 24: 768–784.

_____, and Lucie Freud (eds.). *Sigmund Freud: Briefe 1873–1939.* Frankfurt am Main: S. Fischer, 1968.

_____, Lucie Freud, and Ilse Grubrich-Simitis (eds.). *Sigmund Freud: His Life in Pictures and Words.* New York: Harcourt Brace Jovanovich, 1978.

Freud, Martin. "Who Was Freud?," *The Jews of Austria,* ed. Josef Fraenkel. London: Vallentine & Mitchell, 1967.

_____. *Sigmund Freud: Man and Father.* New York: Jason Aronson, 1983.

Freud, Sigmund. "Über den Ursprung der hinteren Nervenwurzeln im Rückenmark von Ammocoetes (Petromyzon Planeri)." *Sitzungsberichte der kaiserlichen Akademie der Wissenschaften [Wien]* (1877) Mathematisch-Naturwissenschaftliche Klasse, 75, III. Abtheilung: 15–27.

_____. "Beobachtungen über Gestaltung und feineren Bau der als Hoden beschriebenen Lappenorgane des Aals." *Sitzungsberichte der kaiserlichen Akademie der Wissenschaften [Wien]* (1877) Mathematisch-Naturwissenschaftliche Klasse, 75, I. Abtheilung: 419–430.

_____. "Über Spinalganglien und Rückenmark des Petromyzon." *Sitzungsberichte der kaiserlichen Akademie der Wissenschaften [Wien]* (1878) Mathematisch-Naturwissenschaftliche Klasse, 78, III. Abtheilung: 81–167.

_____. "Notiz über eine Methode zur anatomischen Präparation des Nervensystems." *Zentralblatt für die medizinischen Wissenschaften* (1879) 17: 468–469.

_____. "Über den Bau der Nervenfasern und Nervenzellen beim Flusskrebs." *Sitzungsberichte der kaiserlichen Akademie der Wissenschaften [Wien]* (1882) Mathematisch-Naturwissenschaftliche Klasse, 85, III. Abtheilung: 9–46.

_____. "Ein Fall von Hirnblutung mit indirekten basalen Herdsymptomen bei Skorbut." *Wiener medizinische Wochenschrift* (1884) 34: 244–246, 276–279.

_____. "Über Coca." *Zentralblatt für die gesamte Therapie* (1884) 2: 289.

_____. "Die Struktur der Elemente des Nervensystems." *Jahrbucher für Psychiatrie* (1884) 5: 221.

_____. "Ein Fall von Muskelatrophie mit ausgebreiteten Sensibilitätsstörungen (Syringomyuelie)." *Wiener medizinische Wochenschrift* (1885) 35: 13–14, 389–392, 425–429.

_____. "Über die Allgemeinwirkung des Cocains." *Medizinisch-chirurgisches Zentralblatt* (1885) 20(32): 374.

_____. "Observation of a Severe Case of Hemi-Anaesthesia in a Hysterical Male" (1886), in *The Standard Edition of the Complete Psychological Works of Sigmund Freud,* vol. 1, ed. James Strachey. London: Hogarth Press, 1966.

_____. "Bermerkungen über Cocainsucht und Cocainfurcht." *Wiener medizinische Wochenschrift* (1887) 37: 929–932.

_____. "Review of August Forel's *Hypnotism*" (1889), *SE,* vol. 1, 1966.

_____. *On Aphasia* (1891), trans. E. Stengel. London: Imago Publishing, 1953.

_____. "A Case of Successful Treatment by Hypnotism" (1892–1893), *SE,* vol. 1, 1966.

_____. "On the Psychical Mechanism of Hysterical Phenomena" (1893), *SE,* vol. 2, 1955.

_____. "Some Points for a Comparative Study of Organic and Hysterical Motor Paralyses" (1893), *SE,* vol. 1, 1966.

_____. "The Neuro-Psychoses of Defence" (1894), *SE,* vol. 3, 1962.

_____. *Project for a Scientific Psychology* (1895), *SE,* vol. 1, 1966.

_____. "Further Remarks on the Neuro-Psychoses of Defence" (1896), *SE,* vol. 3, 1962.

_____. "Zur Ätiologie der Hysterie" (1896), in *Sigm. Freud: Gesammelte Werke*, vol. 1, eds. A. Freud, E. Bibring, W. Hoffer, E. Kris, and O. Isakower. London: Imago Publishing, 1952.

_____, "The Aetiology of Hysteria" (1896), *SE*, vol. 3, 1962.

_____. "Sexuality in the Aetiology of the Neuroses" (1898), *SE*, vol. 3, 1962.

_____. "The Psychical Mechanism of Forgetfulness" (1898), *SE*, vol. 3, 1962.

_____. "Screen Memories" (1899), *SE*, vol. 3, 1962.

_____. *The Interpretation of Dreams* (1900), *SE*, vols. 4, 5, 1953.

_____. *The Psychopathology of Everyday Life* (1901), *SE*, vol. 6, 1960.

_____. *Three Essays on the Theory of Sexuality* (1905), *SE*, vol. 7, 1953.

_____. "Fragment of an Analysis of a Case of Hysteria" (1905), *SE*, vol. 7, 1953.

_____. " 'Civilized' Sexual Morality" (1908), *SE*, vol. 9, 1959.

_____. *Notes upon a Case of Obsessional Neurosis* (1909), *SE*, vol. 10, 1955.

_____. *Leonardo Da Vinci and a Memory of His Childhood* (1910), *SE*, vol. 11, 1957.

_____. "Remembering, Repeating, and Working-Through" (1913), *SE*, vol. 12, 1957.

_____. *An Autobiographical Study* (1925), *SE*, vol. 20, 1959.

_____. "The Question of Lay Analysis" (1926), *SE*, vol. 20, 1959.

_____. "Postscript to the Question of Lay Analysis" (1927), *SE*, vol. 20, 1959.

Furth, Darby. *Melanie Klein: A Levinsonian Study of the Emergence of Creativity in the Mid-Life Transition.* Unpublished doctoral dissertation, The California School of Professional Psychology, Berkeley, 1991.

Gardiner, Muriel (ed.). *The Wolf-Man.* New York: Basic Books, 1971.

Gardner, Martin. "Freud's Friend Wilhelm Fliess and His Theory of Male and Female Life Cycles." *Scientific American* (1966) 215: 108–112.

Gay, Peter. *Freud: A Life for Our Time.* New York: Norton, 1988.

Gicklhorn, Renée. "The Freiberg Period of the Freud Family." *Journal of the History of Medicine* (1969) 24: 37–43.

Gould, Roger. *Transformations.* New York: Simon & Schuster, 1978.

Grinstein, Alexander. *On Sigmund Freud's Dreams.* Detroit: Wayne State University Press, 1968.

_____. *Freud at the Crossroads.* Madison, CT: International Universities Press, 1990.

Gutmann, David. "The Cross-Cultural Perspective: Notes toward a Comparative Psychology of Aging," in *Lifespan Developmental Psychology: Normative Life Crises,* eds. James E. Birren and K. Warner Schaie. New York: Academic Press, 1977.

Harris, Nancy. *Zelda Fitzgerald: A Levinsonian Study of Mental Illness in the Age-Thirty Transition.* Unpublished doctoral dissertation, The Wright Institute, Berkeley, CA, 1990.

Heller, Judith Bernays. "Freud's Mother and Father: A Memoir." *Commentary* (1956) 21: 418–421.

Heshel, Rabbi J. "The History of Hassidism in Austria," in *The Jews of Austria,* ed. Josef Fraenkel. London: Vallentine & Mitchell, 1967.

Hirschmüller, Albrecht. *The Life and Work of Josef Breuer*. New York: New York University Press, 1989.

Hobbs, Stephen. *Male Mentor Relationships*. Unpublished doctoral dissertation, The California School of Professional Psychology, Berkeley, 1982.

Homer. *Odyssey*, trans. Walter Shewring. Oxford: Oxford University Press, 1987.

Jaques, Elliott. "Death and the Mid-Life Crisis." *International Journal of Psycho-Analysis* (1965) 46: 502–514.

Jones, Ernest. *The Life and Work of Sigmund Freud*, 3 vols. New York: Basic Books, 1957.

Krüll, Marianne. *Freud and His Father*, trans. Arnold Pomerans. London: Hutchinson, 1990.

Lehman, Harvey. *Age and Achievement*. Princeton, NJ: Princeton University Press, 1953.

Levinson, Daniel J., with Charlotte N. Darrow, Edward B. Klein, Maria H. Levinson, and Braxton McKee. *The Seasons of a Man's Life*. New York: Alfred Knopf, 1978.

———, with Judy Levinson. *The Seasons of a Woman's Life*. New York: Knopf, 1994, in press.

Loewald, Hans. "On the Therapeutic Action of Psycho-Analysis." *International Journal of Psycho-Analysis*, (1960) 41: 16–33.

Lohser, Beate, and Peter M. Newton. *Freud's Therapeutic Technique Revisited*. New York: Guilford Press, 1995, in press.

Mahl, George F. "Father–Son Themes in Freud's Self-Analysis," in *Father and Child: Developmental and Clinical Perspectives*, eds. Stanley Cath, Alan Gurwitt, and John Ross. Boston: Little, Brown, 1982.

———. *The Chronology of Freud's Writing His Psychological Works*, Unpublished manuscript, Yale University, 1985.

———. "Freud, Father and Mother: Quantitative Aspects." *Psychoanalytic Psychology* (1985) 2: 99–113.

———. "Explosion of Discoveries and Concepts: The Freud–Fliess Correspondence," in *A First Course in Freud*. Westport, CT: Praeger, in press.

Maslow, Abraham. *Toward a Psychology of Being*. New York: Van Nostrand, 1962.

Masson, Jeffrey. *The Assault on Truth*. New York: Penguin Books, 1985.

——— (ed. and trans.). *The Complete Letters of Sigmund Freud to Wilhelm Fliess, 1887–1904*. Cambridge, MA: Harvard University Press, 1985.

McGrath, William J. *Freud's Discovery of Psychoanalysis*. Ithaca, NY: Cornell University Press, 1986.

———. "How Jewish Was Freud?" *The New York Review of Books*, 5 December 1991.

Mills, C. Wright. *The Sociological Imagination*. New York: Oxford University Press, 1959.

Morgan, Roger. "Avant-Garde Intimations." *London Times Literary Supplement* (1990, March): 9–15.

Morton, Frederic. *A Nervous Splendor: Vienna 1888/1889.* New York: Penguin, 1979.

Nemiroff, Robert A., and Calvin Colarusso. *The Race against Time.* New York: Plenum Press, 1985.

Neugarten, Bernice. *Personality in Middle and Late Life.* New York: Atherton Press, 1964.

_____, "A Developmental View of Adult Personality," in *Relations of Development and Aging,* ed. James E. Birren. Springfield, IL: Charles C. Thomas, 1965.

Newton, Peter M. "The Accursed Correspondence: The Freud/Jung Letters." *University Publishing* (1979, Spring): 24.

_____. "Samuel Johnson's Breakdown and Recovery in Middle Age: A Life-Span Developmental Approach to Mental Illness and Its Cure." *International Review of Psycho-Analysis* (1984) 11: 93–118.

_____. "Free Association and the Division of Labor in Psychoanalytic Treatment." *Psychoanalytic Psychology* (1989) 6: 31–46.

_____. "A Social System Approach to the Psychoanalytic Treatment of Personality Disorders," *Psychiatry* (1992) 55: 66–78.

_____. "Freud's Mid-Life Crisis." *Psychoanalytic Psychology* (1992) 9: 447–475.

Ornston, Darius (ed.). *Translating Freud.* New Haven, CT: Yale University Press, 1992.

Peskin, Harvey. "Uses of the Past in the Adult Lifespan," in *Aging: The Universal Human Experience,* eds. George Maddox and Ewald Busse. New York: Springer, 1987.

Pulzer, P. G. J. "The Development of Political Antisemitism in Austria," in *The Jews of Austria,* ed. Josef Fraenkel. London: Vallentine & Mitchell, 1967.

Riviere, Joan. "A Character Trait of Freud's," in *Freud as We Knew Him,* ed. Hendrik Ruitenbeek. Detroit: Wayne State University Press, 1973.

Roazen, Paul. *Freud and His Followers.* New York: Knopf, 1975.

Roberts, Priscilla, and Peter M. Newton. "Levinsonian Studies of Women's Adult Development." *Psychology and Aging* (1987) 2: 154–163.

Robertson, Priscilla. *Revolutions of 1848.* New York: Harper, 1952.

Schnitzler, Arthur. *My Youth in Vienna.* New York: Holt, Rinehart & Winston, 1970.

Schorske, Carl. *Fin de Siècle Vienna: Politics and Culture.* New York: Knopf, 1980.

Schröter, Michael (ed.). *Sigmund Freud: Briefe an Wilhelm Fliess, 1887–1904.* Frankfurt am Rhein: S. Fischer, 1986.

Schur, Max. *Freud: Living and Dying.* New York: International Universities Press, 1972.

Simonton, Dean. *Genius, Creativity, and Leadership.* Cambridge, MA: Harvard University Press, 1984.

Stanescu, Heinz. "Young Freud's Letters to His Rumanian Friend, Silberstein." *Israel Annals of Psychiatry and Related Disciplines* (1971) 9: 195–207.

Stengel, E. "A Re-Evaluation of Freud's Book 'On Aphasia': Its Significance for Psycho-Analysis." *International Journal of Psycho-Analysis* (1954) 35: 85–89.

Sulloway, Frank. *Freud: Biologist of the Mind.* New York: Basic Books, 1979.

Swales, Peter. "Freud, His Teacher, and the Birth of Psychoanalysis," in *Freud: Appraisals and Reappraisals: Contributions to Freud Studies,* vol. 1, ed. Paul Stepansky. Hillsdale, NJ: The Analytic Press, 1986.

———. "Freud, Katharina, and the First 'Wild Analysis,' " in *Freud: Appraisals and Reappraisals: Contributions to Freud Studies,* vol. 3, ed. Paul Stepansky. Hillsdale, NJ: The Analytic Press, 1988.

Thornton, E. M. *The Freudian Fallacy.* New York: Dial Press, 1984.

Vaillant, George. *Adaptation to Life.* New York: Little, Brown, 1977.

Wittels, Fritz. *Sigmund Freud: His Personality, His Teaching, and His School.* New York: Dodd, Mead, 1924.

———. *Freud and His Time.* New York: Grosset & Dunlap, 1931.

Wollheim, Richard. *Sigmund Freud.* New York: Cambridge University Press, 1990.

Zaretsky, Eli. *Psychoanalysis: From the Psychology of Authority to the Politics of Identity.* Unpublished manuscript, Department of History, University of Missouri, 1994.

# Index